TEACHER'S BOOK

English 4
Explorer

David A. Hill

NATIONAL
GEOGRAPHIC
LEARNING
|

CENGAGE
Learning·

Australia • Brazil • Japan • Korea • Mexico • Singapore • Spain • United Kingdom • United States

Contents

Introduction   3

Grammar Revision worksheets and key   8

Student's Book contents pages   20

Teaching notes   22

Working with words answer key   118

Video worksheet notes, tapescripts and answer keys   122

Grammar Explorer   138

Photocopiable communicative activities   150

Photocopiable tests   158

Test answer keys   176

Workbook answer key   179

Workbook tapescript   187

English Explorer and National Geographic

The *English Explorer* series incorporates original *National Geographic* material in two ways. Firstly, it is integrated into the core Student's Book and Workbook lessons, and secondly, it is used in other components (the class DVD and the MultiROM). The integration of *National Geographic* material brings the real world into your classroom in a natural and uncontrived way. The content has been selected and adapted to ensure that the topics will engage and motivate your students, and that they relate to the students' own world. They have also been selected as appropriate and natural contexts for the grammar and vocabulary syllabi.

English Explorer 4 includes original *National Geographic* material at several points in each unit, and in the video section. The teaching notes give background information on the topics and suggestions for procedure.

Unit openers

These pages set out the language aims for the unit. These aims are reviewed in the *Review* pages and in the tests. Students can use them as a checklist for revision at the end of each unit, as well as for end-of-term and end-of-year revision. The photographs (taken from *National Geographic* magazines), the listening activities and discussion tasks are intended to activate students' previous knowledge of both the topic and key language.

Skills lessons

National Geographic content included in the main lesson is fully integrated as part of the presentation and practice of the target language. The exercises are typical language practice tasks and no special background knowledge or treatment is needed.

Culture lessons

The *Culture* sections in each unit cover UK, European and World culture, with content drawn from *National Geographic*. In each unit, the topic is an extension of the main topics covered in the unit.

True stories

The *True story* sections tell the stories of real-life explorers around the world. The material includes comprehension tasks to ensure students' understanding and also offers questions for stimulating class discussions.

Project pages

Project pages at the end of each second unit focus on an aspect of cultural interest reinforcing the target language covered in previous units. Students are required to complete a selection of project/portfolio material based on the content of these pages.

Video worksheets

The Video worksheets are designed to maximise students' learning while they watch *National Geographic* videos. Each video is supported by a worksheet at the back of the Student's Book which students can work with in class. Background information and procedural suggestions are given in the teaching notes. The activities help students prepare for watching and listening by activating their existing knowledge *in the before you watch* sections.

MultiROM

Original *National Geographic* videos are included on the students' MultiROM together with additional practice activities.

Additional material
Grammar Revision

The worksheets on pages 8–18 are intended for students to complete individually, and are designed to re-activate the grammar students learnt in the previous levels. Each worksheet is followed by a game to be played in groups, creating an opportunity for the grammar points to be practised in a fun and interactive way.

Consolidation pages

These sections give practice in areas that are of particular difficulty to students. Each language area is presented clearly and concisely, with associated practice exercises. They are intended for classroom use, and give the teacher an opportunity to evaluate the students' competence and assign additional or remedial work as necessary.

Review pages

These pages review and reinforce the language covered. At the end of every two units, students complete discrete item tasks individually.

Working with words

The *Working with words* pages are both a vocabulary reference and a set of exercises that can be used in class at any time within the unit.

Grammar Explorer

The *Grammar Explorer* is a self-study grammar reference section for students, with explanations written in a clear, informal style. It presents all the grammatical points mentioned in the main units, and addresses the questions most commonly asked by students. The explanations are intended for the students to read at home whenever a new grammar point has been introduced in class.

Supplementary material
Workbook

As well as providing support for the Student's Book, the Workbook contains a full-colour reading skills section, entitled *Reading Explorer*, which is adapted from *National Geographic* magazines.

DVD

Original *National Geographic* video material with specially written commentaries supplements each unit. The topics are thematically linked to the units and can be used in class after students have completed the corresponding unit in the Student's Book.

Main lesson types – A

Presentation and practice of vocabulary and grammar

The **presentation text** has a variety of formats, each being the most appropriate context for the target grammar and vocabulary.

Clear **photos** support the language content of the page: use them to pre-teach vocabulary, as comprehension checks or to set the scene before reading and listening.

The **Speaking** section focuses on fluency through open-ended pair work and personalised task-types, whilst still practising the target language of the lesson.

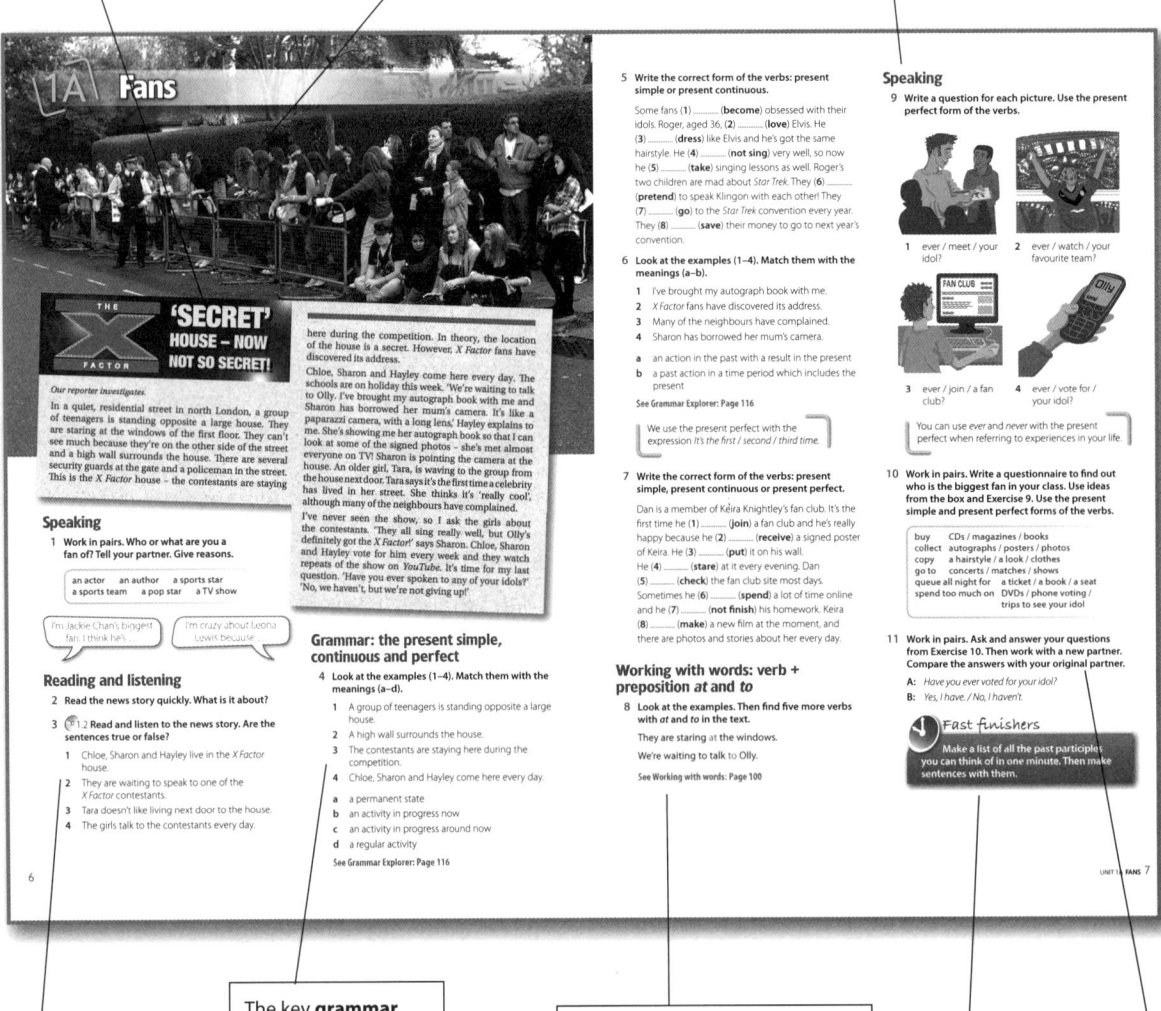

Comprehension tasks are clear and simple. They focus on content and so do not pre-empt your presentation of the grammar.

The key **grammar** is presented in clear tables that students complete by referring back to the text. You can support this with the full explanations of form and use in the *Grammar Explorer*.

The **Working with words** section introduces additional target language items, which have been presented in the main text, and gives sentence-level contextualised practice.

Practice moves from controlled to personalised exercises. Pair activities are fully guided and supported.

Fast finishers activities can be used in class or for homework. They practise the language in a fun way without needing teacher support. Additional extension activities are provided in the teaching notes.

Main lesson types – B

Skills work and presentation and practice of additional grammar

The **texts** (reading and listening) are about real people and the real world. They consolidate the main grammar from the first section, and present new grammar in context.

Use the **photographs/illustrations** to arouse students' interest in the new topic, to activate pre-knowledge and to pre-teach vocabulary.

Grammar practice tasks are extended in the Workbook.

Grammar sections are cross-referenced to the *Grammar Explorer* section at the back of the Student's Book, which gives further explanations and examples.

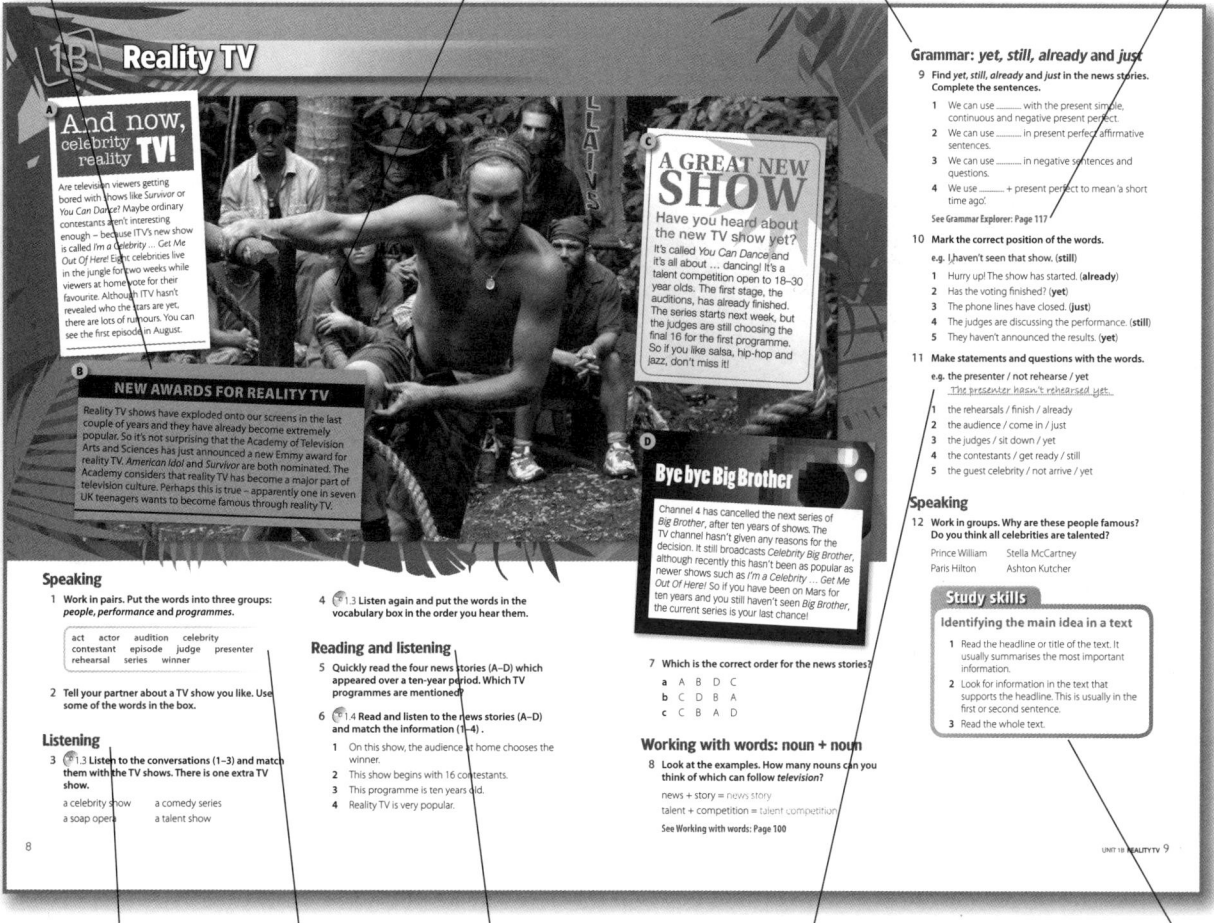

A **listening** text with carefully graded tasks. The **Listening** text is thematically related to the reading text, thus providing additional pre-listening support.

Reading and listening tasks give explicit practice in **study skills**.

Sentence-level writing practises key language and prepares students for the main writing task later in the unit.

Study skills boxes summarise the skills and techniques for independent learning which are integrated into the comprehension tasks.

Vocabulary tasks focus on the second of two main lexical areas for the unit. They are clear and simple and they provide interactive practice, inviting student input and personalisation.

Main lesson types – C

Practice in productive language use (speaking and writing) with pronunciation

You can use the **photographs** to pre-teach vocabulary, as comprehension checks, or to set the scene before reading and listening.

The **useful expressions** from the dialogue, needed for the students' speaking practice, are collected into an easy reference box.

The **pronunciation** tasks in this section practise individual sounds as well as stress, rhythm and intonation.

The **speaking** activity is simple to manage in the classroom and gives support so that the students can perform the task successfully. Extension activities are provided in the teaching notes.

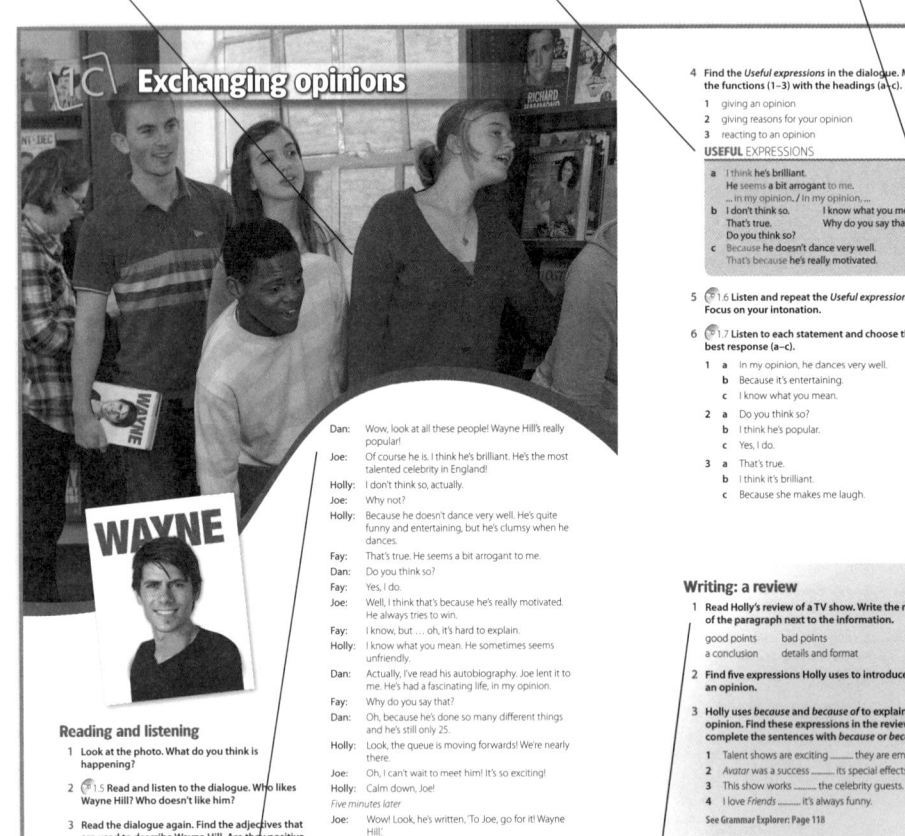

The main characters are featured in student-centred **situations** to present functional language in a clear context. The **dialogue** also recycles the main grammar points previously taught in the unit.

Students produce a real-world product in the **writing** activity, guided by a model (with exercises) and the language practice they have done in the unit. The activity can be done in class and is easy to assess – extension activities for homework and different abilities are suggested in the unit notes. The writing activities are for individual work. Group or collaborative writing is part of short projects within the units.

Main lesson types – D

Study school subjects through English, in lessons filled with cultural content

The **Culture** lessons give you an opportunity to show your students how their knowledge of English helps them to find out about the real world and things that interest them, and they invite your students to bring their own knowledge and experience into the English language classroom.

Every topic chosen for this lesson is an extension of one of the main topics covered in the unit. Authentic texts from *National Geographic* magazines have been specially selected to suit the purposes of English Language Teaching. These texts have been adapted to consolidate the target language covered in each unit.

Each lesson is heavily influenced by **Content and Language Integrated Learning (CLIL)**, whereby students are encouraged to use English as a means of studying a range of other school subjects such as maths, science and geography. With *National Geographic* content as a focus, this integration allows for the involvement of students whose English is weak, but who may be strong in other school subjects or outside interests. This provides yet another way of engaging and motivating students.

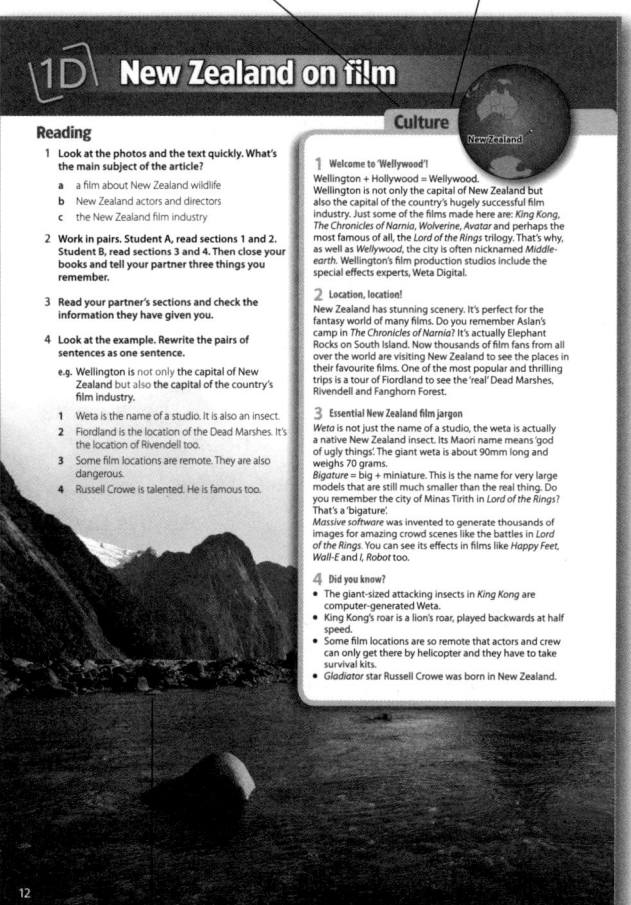

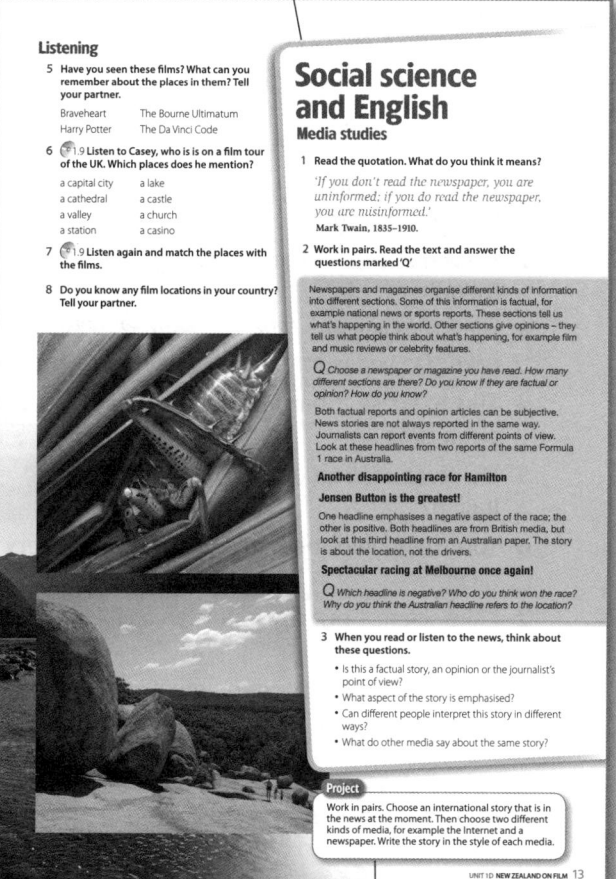

Large photographs and authentic texts give colourful background information about a range of different cultures around the world.

The **project** is an autonomous piece of work that students can begin in class and finish for homework, or it can be done wholly out of class. The task consolidates the target language while also giving opportunity for student input.

The present simple and the present continuous; verbs without a continuous form; positive and negative adjectives; greetings and introductions

1 Read each sentence and write *a* (a regular habit), *b* (a permanent state) or *c* (a feeling or thought).

  1 We live in a small flat in London.   .....

  2 British children often eat pizza for lunch.   .....

  3 I want a new desk for my bedroom.   .....

  4 Our house has a large garden and a garage.   .....

  5 I know everybody in my street.   .....

  6 I like my new school – everybody's very friendly.   .....

  7 My geography teacher gives us homework every Friday.   .....

  8 I prefer Italian food to French food.   .....

2 Choose the correct option.

  1 I *love / 'm loving* my bedroom. It's my favourite room.

  2 *Do you know / Are you knowing* that boy over there?

  3 'What *do you eat / are you eating*?' 'Chocolate cake. *Do you want / Are you wanting* a piece?'

  4 This exercise is hard to do. I *need / 'm needing* extra time.

  5 *Do you understand / Are you understanding* Italian?

  6 Your new neighbour *seems / is seeming* very nice.

  7 I like science but my friend *prefers / is preferring* art.

  8 My sister *hates / is hating* meat. She never *eats / is eating* it.

3 Complete the email with the correct present form of the verbs in brackets.

Hi Lee,

How are you? I (1) _____ (type) this with my left hand because I (2) _____ (have) a broken wrist! (A rugby injury!) It (3) _____ (hurt) every time I (4) _____ (move) it! I'm off school for two weeks. That's OK, because I (5) _____ (not / like) my new school very much. But I can't play rugby, and my team (6) _____ (play) in the school final today!

Anyway, what (7) _____ (you / do) at the moment? Is there any exciting news from my old school? (8) _____ (they / have) a talent competition again this year?

Write soon!

Matt

4 Complete the sentences with the correct form of the adjectives in the box. Add *un-* or *im-* where necessary.

comfortable	happy	healthy	kind
lucky	patient	polite	tidy

  1 I never win anything. I'm very _____.

  2 My bedroom is really _____. It's a disaster area.

  3 I'm always in a hurry. I'm quite _____.

  4 I hate junk food. I only eat _____ food.

  5 My dad is a _____ and helpful person.

  6 My friend is _____ because he doesn't like his new school.

  7 I can't sit on this chair. It's too _____.

  8 Don't be _____. Always say 'thank you'.

5 Put the words in the correct order to make greetings and introductions. Then write F (formal) or I (informal).

  1 are / Matt. / Hi, / you? / How

  _____

  2 meet / Pleased / you, / Mrs Wilson. / to

  _____

  3 sister, / is / This / Rachel. / my

  _____

  4 you / How / Mr Jackson? / do, / do

  _____

  5 you, / Nice / Lynne. / meet / to

  _____

  6 you? / fine. / I'm / And

  _____

  7 introduce / Let / Mrs Wilson. / my / me / neighbour,

  _____

Revision Game 1

Make a sentence

What	are you	doing	in geography	at the moment?
Do you	prefer	big cities	or	small towns?
My friend	doesn't	know	how to	type.
My school team	is	playing	chess	in a national competition.
How much	homework	do you	get	every day?
My group	usually	makes	too much noise	in the English class.
How many	books	do you	read	each month?

there was / there were; the past simple and the past continuous; *during, when* and *while*; the present perfect; comparing; asking for information

1 Complete the sentences with the correct form of *there was* or *there were*.

1 _____ a lot of people at the concert last night.

2 _____ any empty seats in the theatre?

3 _____ any tickets left for the show.

4 _____ any time to find your seat.

5 _____ a fantastic violinist in the orchestra.

6 _____ an interval during the performance?

2 Complete the text with the past simple or past continuous form of the verbs.

The UK punk movement (1) _____ (start) in London. Punk (2) _____ (be) a mixture of music and fashion. Two people, Malcolm McLaren and Vivienne Westwood, (3) _____ (have) a big influence on punk. McLaren (4) _____ (promote) young punk bands and Westwood (5) _____ (design) punk fashion. Once, while one punk band (6) _____ (play) on a TV programme, the guitarist (7) _____ (shock) the country when he swore. It (8) _____ (be) a popular programme and lots of young people (9) _____ (watch) it at the time. After this, the band (10) _____ (become) big stars.

3 Complete the sentences with *during, when* or *while*.

1 Bono made a surprise appearance _____ the concert.

2 I was listening to the radio _____ my favourite song came on.

3 What did you do _____ you left the theatre?

4 Did you take any photos _____ the show?

5 My guitar string broke _____ I was playing.

6 What were you doing _____ we were waiting for you?

4 Write the past participle of the verbs.

1 become _____

2 come _____

3 do _____

4 eat _____

5 go _____

6 have _____

7 hear _____

8 make _____

9 see _____

10 sing _____

11 take _____

12 write _____

5 Complete the text with the present perfect forms of the verbs in the box.

be	live	play
record	tour	win

Nigel Kennedy is a violinist. He (1) _____ classical, jazz and fusion CDs. He (2) _____ the world, giving concerts in many countries. He (3) _____ several awards, including one for his Outstanding Contribution to British Music. He (4) _____ with a Polish jazz band, and with British rock bands. He (5) _____ married twice and he (6) _____ in Poland for several years.

6 Choose the correct option.

1 London is different *as / from / than* my town.

2 My town isn't as big *as / from / than* London.

3 There are more people in London *as / from / than* in my town.

4 In my town, there aren't as many buildings *as / from / than* in London.

7 Match the questions (1–5) with the responses (a–e).

1 Can I help you?

2 Which show do you want to see?

3 Are there any tickets left?

4 What time does the performance start?

5 How much are the tickets?

a The prices range from £25 to £40.

b Well, is *Sister Act* still on?

c Yes, there are a few left.

d Yes, I'd like some information about the show tonight.

e There's an afternoon performance at 4 o'clock. The evening show is at 9 p.m.

Photocopies: one per group of six students, cut up into six cards.

Activity notes: Each student has one card. They have information about a show they have seen and need to find out information about a show they want to see. To do this they should mingle with the rest of the class and ask and answer questions. When they have the information they should return to their group. The group must then agree on one show to go and see.

Going out

The New Sherlock Holmes

place _____

dates _____

days / times _____

tickets _____

Legally Blonde

Savoy Theatre

Until February next year

Wednesday to Saturday, and Monday 19.30

Thursday and Sunday 15.00

£25 – £60

Mamma Mia!

place _____

dates _____

days / times _____

tickets _____

The New Sherlock Holmes

Royal Theatre

Nov 15th – Jan 10th

Tuesday to Saturday

8 p.m.

£15 – £35

Legally Blonde

place _____

dates _____

days / times _____

tickets _____

Summer Classics Festival

Central Park

July and August

Every evening at 9 p.m.

Free

Halloween Film Festival

place _____

dates _____

days / times _____

tickets _____

Mamma Mia!

The Victoria Theatre

Until the end of November

Every day 7.30 p.m.

Sunday 3.30 p.m.

£20 – £50

Summer Classics Festival

place _____

dates _____

days / times _____

tickets _____

Billy Elliot

Apollo Theatre

Until the end of this month

Every day except Tuesday 7 p.m.

£22.50 – £40

Billy Elliot

place _____

dates _____

days / times _____

tickets _____

Halloween Film Festival

ABC Cinema

October 20th – November 10th

Midnight, daily

£8.00

The present simple and past simple passive with *by*; quantifiers + nouns; giving examples, giving and checking information

1 Choose the correct option.

1 Three people *struck* / *were struck* by lightning at the weekend.

2 These jackets *make* / *are made* from recycled plastic.

3 Often, avalanches *cause* / *are caused* by warm temperatures.

4 A volcano in Iceland *erupted* / *was erupted* several times in 2010.

5 Every year, many homes *destroy* / *are destroyed* as a result of earthquakes.

6 Most of the forest in England *cut down* / *was cut down* years ago.

2 Look at the prompts (1–6) and write questions. Then match the answers (a–e) and write full sentences.

1 When / plastic / invent? ....

_____

2 What / plastic / make / from? ....

_____

3 What / Pompeii / destroy / by? ....

_____

4 When / the Canary Islands / create? ....

_____

5 What / climate change / cause / by? ....

_____

6 Where / plastic bags / ban / in 2007? ....

_____

    a 1855. _____

    b Greenhouse gases. _____

    c Millions of years ago. _____

    d Oil. _____

    e San Francisco. _____

    f The volcano, Mount Vesuvius. _____

3 Circle the bigger quantity or write = if they are the same.

1 a lot of people / some people ....

2 many towns / a lot of towns ....

3 a few trees / all trees ....

4 no time / little time ....

5 lots of pollution / a lot of pollution ....

6 most of the animals / some of the animals ....

4 Complete the text with expressions from the box. More than one answer is sometimes possible.

also	for example	including	such as	too

There are many ways of caring for the environment – (1) _____ , recycling things (2) _____ plastic and glass. Paper is easy to recycle, (3) _____. We can (4) _____ reduce the amount of greenhouse gases we produce, by burning less oil. We have a limited supply of natural resources, (5) _____ oil, so we should try to use less.

5 Choose the correct option to respond to the statements and questions.

1 Do you know how much a solar panel costs?
   a Is that possible?
   b I don't think so.
   c I have no idea.

2 I can tell you a lot about endangered species.
   a Really?
   b I don't think so.
   c Yes, I'm sure.

3 There are no wild wolves in Europe.
   a I have no idea.
   b Yes, I'm sure.
   c Are you sure?

4 Pandas only live in China.
   a I have no idea.
   b Is that possible?
   c I don't know much about it.

5 What do you know about recycling?
   a I don't know much about it.
   b I don't think so.
   c Are you sure?

Photocopies: one per student, one for the teacher cut up into individual questions.

Activity notes: Explain that each team of students will work together to answer the quiz questions, then compete against the other teams to win the quiz. Organise the class into teams of four to six students and give a list of questions to each student. Depending on the class, you can give out the optional answers or not. (All of the information appeared in English Explorer 3.) Students can choose team names – this makes later scoring on the board easier to follow.

When the teams are ready or after ten minutes, write 1–10 and the team names in a grid on the board. Take questions slips at random and ask each question. Each team should answer before you give the correct answer and keep score on the board.

Quiz night

1 Which is the only place in the world where both lions and tigers are found?	a Africa	b China	c India
2 Where did the Dodo live?	a Madagascar	b the Maldives	c Mauritius
3 Which animal is sacred in India?	a cow	b elephant	c rhinoceros
4 Where was paper invented?	a America	b China	c India
5 What's the name of the molten rock produced by volcanoes?	a ash	b lava	c smoke
6 What natural phenomenon is sometimes caused by undersea earthquakes?	a drought	b mudslide	c tsunami
7 What is produced when things like oil and petrol are burnt?	a hurricanes	b greenhouse gases	c rain
8 What is malaria caused by?	a dirty water	b human contact	c a parasite in a mosquito
9 What type of illness is treated with antibiotics?	a bacterial	b tropical	c viral
10 Who was penicillin discovered by?	a Alexander Fleming	b Alexander Graham Bell	c David de Rothschild

Permission and obligation; relative pronouns and relative clauses; reflexive pronouns; phrasal verbs; talking about problems

1 Rewrite the sentences with the words in brackets.

1 I can stay out late at weekends. (allowed)

_____

2 I can't have tattoos. (my parents / not let)

_____

3 I must get up early on weekdays. (my dad / make)

_____

4 I can't borrow my brother's motorbike. (not allowed)

_____

5 I can dye my hair. (my parents / let)

_____

6 I must tidy my room once a week. (have to)

_____

2 Cross out any options which are not correct.

1 The man *who* / *that* lives next door is a teacher.

2 The room *where* / *which* my family spends most time is the kitchen.

3 The time *when* / *which* I feel most anxious is before an exam.

4 Politeness and punctuality are the two things *that* / *which* are important to my parents.

5 A person *which* / *who* eats lots of chocolate is a chocoholic.

6 A map is a diagram *that* / *which* shows roads and towns.

3 Complete the sentences with the words in the box.

each other	each other	himself	myself
themselves	yourself		

1 My cousin and I don't see _____ very often.

2 I didn't enjoy _____ at school today.

3 My brother likes to look at _____ in the mirror.

4 My friends talk to _____ on Skype all the time.

5 Babies are too young to look after _____.

6 Be careful with the knife. Don't cut _____.

4 Complete the sentences with the words in the box. You can use some words more than once.

after	on	out	up

1 Rosie and Jack argued a lot, so they broke _____ .

2 Are you going _____ with anyone at the moment?

3 When my mum is travelling, my gran looks _____ us.

4 Do you take _____ anybody in your family?

5 Do you get _____ with your brothers and sisters?

6 I try not to fall _____ with my friends.

7 If I argue with friends, I try to make _____ with them as soon as possible.

8 Jack looks _____ to his older brother. He often asks him for advice.

5 Match the sentences (a–d) to the spaces (1–4) to complete the dialogue about a problem.

a Cheer up.

b Hey! What's wrong?

c I can't believe that!

d Tell me all about it.

Andy: (1) _____

Ron: Oh, I've fallen out with Beth again.

Andy: Not again! What happened this time? (2) _____

Ron: Well, she says I'm selfish.

Andy: (3) _____ You're the opposite! You always think about other people, especially Beth!

Ron: I don't know, maybe she's right.

Andy: (4) _____ You know Beth. She'll be fine tomorrow.

Ron: Hmm. Maybe.

Photocopies: one for each student or pair of students.

Activity notes: The crossword reviews relative clauses and vocabulary. Explain that some answers are compound adjectives and the hyphen is shown in the grid.

ACROSS

2 A kind of picture which is drawn on your skin. You can't wash it off, however!

4 A word to describe people who are tolerant and relaxed.

7 A type of paint which you can put on your fingers or toes is called ..... varnish.

8 Somebody who doesn't have brown, green, grey or black eyes!

12 A kind of hairstyle which is popular among reggae musicians.

13 This kind of person believes in their own abilities.

14 She's in your family and you have the same parents.

15 You can sometimes feel like this when you are on your own.

16 Somebody who is generally happy and optimistic.

17 An adjective to describe somebody who has an attractive face.

DOWN

1 Objects, often made of silver or gold, that you wear as decoration on different parts of your body.

3 This kind of person prefers things and ideas from the past.

5 Your mum or dad's mum and dad.

6 These are decorative things to wear in your ears. Very popular with pirates!

9 Somebody who gets angry a lot of the time.

10 A person or a situation that makes you feel uncomfortable.

11 The child of your aunt or your uncle is your ..... .

The first conditional; predictions with *will/won't, may* and *might*; *going to* for plans and intentions; prepositions; offering, requesting and accepting help

1 Mark the correct position of 'if' in the sentences.

   1 I'll be ready for my exam I revise this weekend.

   2 we use Skype, we'll be able to talk to each other.

   3 my phone won't work I don't charge the battery.

   4 you use your GPS, you won't get lost.

   5 I'll change your photo on the computer you don't like it.

   6 You give me your camera I'll take your photo.

2 Complete the sentences with the correct form of the verbs in brackets.

   1 If you _____ (look) through this telescope, you _____ (can) see the stars.

   2 If digital books _____ (become) popular, _____ you _____ (buy) one?

   3 I _____ (upload) your photos if you _____ (give) me your camera.

   4 How _____ you _____ (contact) me if you _____ (not got) my phone number?

   5 If I _____ (send) you the document, _____ you _____ (print) it for me?

   6 If the space craft _____ (reach) Mars, it _____ (can) tell us a lot about the solar system.

3 Complete the sentences with the words in the box and the correct form of the verbs in brackets. ✓ means you are 100% sure, ? means you are not 100% sure.

might / may	will	won't

   1 We _____ (find) life on Mars.   ✓

   2 Human beings _____ (not live) on another planet.   ✓

   3 We _____ (can) live in space cities.   ?

   4 We _____ (have) robots in our homes.   ✓

   5 Human beings _____ (operate) computers with our thoughts.   ?

   6 There _____ (be) water on Mars.   ?

4 Look at Lauren's holiday plans. Write sentences using *going to* or *might*.

Summer holiday plans	yes	no	maybe
go to the beach	✓		
get a part time job			✓
spend time with friends	✓		
think about school work		✓	
get a suntan			✓

   1 She _____.

   2 She _____.

   3 She _____.

   4 She _____.

   5 She _____.

5 Choose the correct option.

   1 Could you explain *me / to me* what this word means?

   2 I'll pick you *down / up* at 5 p.m. Don't be late.

   3 I never stay out late *at / on* night.

   4 Don't forget to switch *off / out* the TV when you go to bed.

   5 I can't hear the radio – can you turn it *over / up*?

   6 The Spider-man comic was made *in / into* a film.

6 Choose the correct option to complete the shopping expressions.

   1 How can I _____ you?

     a help

     b look at

     c show

   2 _____ you explain how it works, please?

     a Will

     b Could

     c Shall

   3 _____ to look at some cameras, please.

     a I'll

     b I'd like

     c Can I

   4 It's great. I _____ take it!

     a 'll

     b 'd like

     c could

Photocopies: one for each group of students, cut up into cards.

Activity notes: Students work in groups of two, three or four. Place the cards spread out, face down, in front of the students. The first student turns over two cards at random. If they can connect them, using the first conditional or *may/ might*, they keep the cards. If not, the cards are turned face down again and the next student chooses two cards. The winner is the student with the most cards.

Circulate to make sure students are making accurate and logical sentences. For example:

travel to other planets   find alien life

If we travel to other planets, we might find alien life.

Predictions – matching game

install Skype	save money on phone bills	send a text	cost less
phone you	give me your number	send a message	add to contacts
pass my exams	be really pleased	work harder	get better marks
reach Mars	find alien life	develop new spacecraft	travel to other planets
cure all diseases	live for ever	sit in the sun	skin go red
use sun cream	not get burned	not charge the battery	MP3 not work
go to the beach	see a shark	get a part time job	have more money

Reporting verbs; reported requests and orders; indirect questions; words that are easy to confuse; giving and taking messages

1 Complete the sentences with the past simple of the verbs in the box.

ask	invite	order	remind	warn

1 My little brother _____ me to help him with his homework.

2 My friend _____ me to stay at his house this weekend.

3 My dad _____ my sister to recharge her phone before she went out.

4 The police officer _____ the crowd to stay behind the line.

5 The zoo keeper _____ people not to touch the snakes.

2 Report the teacher's words to his students. Use the verbs in brackets.

1 Don't cheat in this exam. (warn)

_____

2 Find a space and sit down. (tell)

_____

3 Wait a moment, please. (ask)

_____

4 Don't talk! (order)

_____

5 Can you listen to me? (want)

_____

3 Write the actual words each person said.

1 The policeman ordered the driver to stop his car.

_____

2 The teacher told the class to be quiet.

_____

3 The boy wanted his mum to give him some money.

_____

4 The customer asked the shop assistant to show her the jacket.

_____

5 The man warned his children not to fight with each other.

_____

4 Look at the prompts and the answers. Complete the indirect questions.

1 The festival dates are 10–13 September.
Can anyone tell _____?

2 Yes, the tickets are on sale now.
Do you know _____?

3 The cheapest tickets are about £15.00.
Could you tell _____?

4 No, there aren't any discounts for students.
Could you tell _____?

5 You can buy tickets online.
Does anyone know _____?

5 Choose the correct option.

1 Can I *borrow / lend* your pen, please?

2 Somebody *robbed / stole* my bike last night.

3 Please *bring / take* some DVDs when you come to my house tonight.

4 We went on a great *travel / trip* this summer.

5 My mum *said / told* me to be home early tonight.

6 Choose the correct option to complete the expressions for giving and taking messages.

1 Could you _____ him a message, please?
  a ask
  b give
  c tell

2 Can you _____ him to phone me back?
  a ask
  b give
  c want

3 Yes, I _____ tell her when she comes in.
  a 'd
  b 'm going to
  c 'll

4 Jenny _____ she wants to borrow your laptop.
  a asks
  b reminds
  c says

Worksheet 1

1 1 b 2 a 3 c 4 b 5 c 6 c 7 a 8 c

2 1 love 2 Do you know 3 are you eating, Do you want 4 need 5 Do you understand 6 seems 7 prefers 8 hates, eats

3 1 'm typing 2 have 3 hurts 4 move 5 don't like 6 is playing 7 are you doing 8 Are they having

4 1 unlucky 2 untidy 3 impatient 4 healthy 5 kind 6 unhappy 7 uncomfortable 8 impolite

5 1 Hi, Matt. How are you? I   2 Pleased to meet you, Mrs Wilson. F   3 This is my sister, Rachel. I   4 How do you do, Mr Jackson? F   5 Nice to meet you, Lynne. I   6 I'm fine. And you? I   7 Let me introduce my neighbour, Mrs Wilson. F

Worksheet 2

1 1 There were 2 Were there 3 There weren't 4 There wasn't 5 There was 6 Was there

2 1 started 2 was 3 had 4 promoted 5 designed 6 was playing 7 shocked 8 was 9 were watching 10 became

3 1 during 2 when 3 when 4 during 5 while 6 while

4 1 become 2 come 3 done 4 eaten 5 gone 6 had 7 heard 8 made 9 seen 10 sung 11 taken 12 written

5 1 has recorded 2 has toured 3 has won 4 has played 5 has been 6 has lived

6 1 from 2 as 3 than 4 as

7 1 d 2 b 3 c 4 e 5 a

Worksheet 3

1 1 were struck 2 are made 3 are caused 4 erupted 5 are destroyed 6 was cut down

2 1 When was plastic invented? **a** Plastic was invented in 1855.
2 What is plastic made from? **d** Plastic is made from oil.
3 What was Pompeii destroyed by? **f** Pompeii was destroyed by the volcano, Mount Vesuvius.
4 When were the Canary Islands created? **c** The Canary Islands were created millions of years ago.
5 What is climate change caused by? **b** Climate change is caused by greenhouse gases.
6 Where were plastic bags banned in 2007? **e** Plastic bags were banned in 2007 in San Francisco.

3 1 a lot of people 2 = 3 all trees 4 little time 5 = 6 most of the animals

4 1 for example 2 such as 3 too 4 also 5 including / such as

5 1 c 2 a 3 c 4 b 5 a

Revision Game 3: Quiz

1 c 2 c 3 a 4 b 5 b 6 c 7 b 8 c 9 a 10 a

Worksheet 4

1 1 I'm allowed to stay out late at weekends.   2 My parents don't / won't let me have tattoos.   3 My dad makes me get up early on weekdays.   4 I'm not allowed to borrow my brother's motorbike.   5 My parents let me dye my hair.   6 I have to tidy my room once a week.

2 2 ~~which~~ 3 ~~which~~ 5 ~~which~~

3 1 each other 2 myself 3 himself 4 each other 5 themselves 6 yourself

4 1 up 2 out 3 after 4 after 5 on 6 out 7 up 8 up

5 1 b 2 d 3 c 4 a

Revision Game 4: Crossword

Across

2 tattoo
4 easy-going
7 nail
8 blue-eyed
12 dreadlocks
13 confident
14 sister
15 lonely
16 cheerful
17 good-looking

Down

1 jewellery
3 old-fashioned
5 grandparents
6 earrings
9 bad-tempered
10 embarrassing
11 cousin

Worksheet 5

1 1 … if I revise …   2 If we use Skype …   3 … if I don't charge the battery.   4 If you use …   5 … if you don't like it.   6 If you give me your camera …

2 1 look, will be able to 2 become, will … buy 3 'll upload, give 4 will … contact, haven't got 5 send, will … print 6 reaches, will be able to

3 1 will find 2 won't live 3 might / may be able to live 4 will have 5 might / may operate 6 might / may be

4 1 She's going to go to the beach.   2 She might get a part time job.   3 She's going to spend time with friends.   4 She isn't going to think about school work.   5 She might get a suntan.

5 1 to me 2 up 3 at 4 off 5 up 6 into

6 1 a 2 b 3 b 4 a

Worksheet 6

1 1 asked 2 invited 3 reminded 4 ordered 5 warned

2 1 The teacher / He warned the students not to cheat in this / the exam.   2 The teacher / He told the students to find a space and sit down.   3 The teacher / He asked the students to wait a moment.   4 The teacher / He ordered the students not to talk.   5 The teacher / He wanted the students to listen to him.

3 1 'Stop the / your car!'   2 'Be quiet!'   3 'Could you give me some money, please?'   4 'Could you show me the jacket, please?'   5 'Don't fight (with each other)!'

4 1 … me what the festival dates are?   2 … when the tickets are on sale? / if the tickets are on sale yet?   3 … me how much the (cheapest) tickets are / cost?   4 … me if there are any discounts for students?   5 … how / where you can buy tickets?

5 1 borrow 2 stole 3 bring 4 trip 5 told

6 1 b 2 a 3 c 4 c

Contents

	Grammar	Vocabulary	Skills: Reading & Writing
Starter page 4			
Unit 1 **Fame** page 5	The present simple, present continuous and present perfect simple *yet, still, already* and *just*	Mass media TV shows	**Reading:** The *X Factor* secret house – now not so secret; Reality TV True story: Music explorer **Writing:** A review
Unit 2 **The mind** page 15	The present perfect continuous Relative clauses Question tags	The mind Adjectives to describe personality	**Reading:** Meet the cleverest animals known to science; Hypnosis – controlling the mind **Writing:** A description of people
Consolidation Units 1 and 2 page 25		**Review Units 1 and 2** page 26	
Project page 28			
Unit 3 **In the past** page 29	The past perfect *used to*	Time Archaeology Cooking	**Reading:** Ice Baby Remembering the past True story: Mike Parker Pearson **Writing:** A recommendation
Unit 4 **Careers** page 39	*will* *going to* Present continuous for the future Future continuous	Jobs Sports people and places Clothes	**Reading:** Sports careers Designing the future **Writing:** An email about arrangements
Consolidation Units 3 and 4 page 49		**Review Units 3 and 4** page 50	
Project page 52			
Unit 5 **Special things** page 53	The present simple, past simple, present continuous, past continuous, present perfect passive The passive with modal verbs: *can, must, will*	Materials Adjectives to describe size and shape	**Reading:** Win a Wonderful Holiday for Two! Gold True story: Searching for gold **Writing:** A description of a person
Unit 6 **Mysteries** page 63	Modal verbs for speculation (*can't be, must be, could be*) The second conditional	Art and books	**Reading:** A literary mystery Crop circles – alien art? **Writing:** An apology
Consolidation Units 5 and 6 page 73		**Review Units 5 and 6** page 74	
Project page 76			
Unit 7 **Moments in history** page 77	The third conditional *could/should have done*	Science and technology Politics	**Reading:** The Enigma story and the DNA story; Nelson Mandela's Long Walk to Freedom True story: John Glenn **Writing:** A story
Unit 8 **Shopping** page 87	Reported statements Reported questions	Shops and services Money	**Reading:** Advertising Spending money **Writing:** A formal letter
Consolidation Units 7 and 8 page 97		**Review Units 7 and 8** page 98	
Working with words pages 100–107		**Video worksheets** pages 108–115	

Skills: Listening & Speaking	Working with words Study skills Pronunciation	Culture & CLIL
Listening: Conversations about TV shows **Speaking:** Exchanging opinions	**Working with words:** verb + preposition *at*, *to*; noun + noun **Study skills:** identifying the main idea in a text **Pronunciation:** words ending in *-ght* and *-ghed*	**Reading:** New Zealand on film **Listening:** A conversation about film locations **CLIL:** Social science and English Media studies
Listening: A podcast about phobias **Speaking:** Checking information	**Working with words:** abstract nouns; verb + *-ing* **Study skills:** making notes **Pronunciation:** intonation in question tags	**Reading:** Irish traditions **Listening:** A survey about beliefs **CLIL:** Biology and English Animals and people
Listening: Recipe instructions **Speaking:** Talking about quantity, time, distance, etc.	**Working with words:** verb + *to* + infinitive; American English **Study skills:** listening for key words **Pronunciation:** words containing *ui*	**Reading:** American food **Listening:** Meal-time conversations **CLIL:** Maths and English The history of numbers
Listening: A conversation about clothes **Speaking:** Talking about preferences	**Working with words:** adjective + *to* + infinitive; verb + noun combinations **Study skills:** mind maps **Pronunciation:** words with /s/ and /z/ sounds	**Reading:** Sport in Australia **Listening:** Sports news **CLIL:** Physics and English Newton's law of motion
Listening: A story from Greek mythology **Speaking:** Expressing purpose and giving reasons	**Working with words:** adjective order; verb + preposition **Study skills:** scanning and skimming **Pronunciation:** the letter 'o' and the vowel sounds /əʊ/ and /ʌ/	**Reading:** Boom-town Canada **Listening:** Statistics about Canada **CLIL:** Chemistry and English Elements
Listening: A radio programme about an art forgery **Speaking:** Making and responding to requests	**Working with words:** phrasal verbs; noun + preposition combinations **Study skills:** answering questions **Pronunciation:** words containing *au*	**Reading:** British best-sellers **Listening:** A radio programme about women authors **CLIL:** Art and English Leonardo da Vinci
Listening: Comments about four famous people **Speaking:** Talking about regrets and making criticisms	**Working with words:** prefixes; suffixes **Study skills:** dictionary skills **Pronunciation:** silent letters	**Reading:** South African life **Listening:** A tour of Cape Town **CLIL:** History and English The human journey
Listening: A shopping questionnaire **Speaking:** Returning things to shops	**Working with words:** reporting verbs; word combinations with *money* **Study skills:** listening and checking **Pronunciation:** syllable stress	**Reading:** Shopping online in the UK **Listening:** A telephone conversation following an online purchase **CLIL:** Maths and English Statistics

Page aims

To introduce students to the characters used in the book.

To revise the past simple, present perfect and *going to*

KEY

1 1 c 2 b 3 d 4 a

2 1 Dan 2 Joe 3 Holly 4 Fay

3 acting: Fay
animals: Holly
clothes: Dan
photography: Joe

1 Personal descriptions

Students read the descriptions and match them with the characters in the photo.

2 Reading for detail

 **S1 CD 1 track 02**

Students read and listen to the dialogue and complete the sentences which say what the four characters have been doing, and what their intentions are for the new school year. Note that these facts will not necessarily be explicitly stated in the dialogue, so students will have to infer the information from clues.

3 Hobbies and interests

Students now match the four characters with the interests. Again, students will have to infer the information from clues.

4 Writing practice

Following the examples in the dialogue, students write their own sentences using past simple, present perfect and *going to*.

Starter

1 **Match the descriptions (1–4) with the people in the photo (a–d).**

1 Fay has got long dark hair. She's wearing a red jacket.
2 Dan has got short black hair. His top is white and red.
3 Holly has got fair hair in a ponytail. She's wearing a white top and jeans.
4 Joe is tall and he's got short dark hair. He's wearing jeans and white trainers.

2 **S.1 Read and listen to the dialogue. Complete each sentence with the correct name.**

1 .... has just been to the shops.
2 .... has changed his/her appearance.
3 .... went camping in Scotland.
4 .... is going to study at lunchtime.

3 **Read the dialogue again. Who is interested in each of these things?**

> acting animals clothes photography

4 **Write sentences about these things. They can be true or false. Exchange your sentences with a partner. Find your partner's false sentences.**

- places you've been to recently
- things you did in the summer holidays
- things you're going to do this term

4

Dan:	Hi, Fay! Hi, Holly!
Holly:	Hi, Dan! Are you ready for tomorrow?
Dan:	Oh, don't remind me. I hate the first day back at school. But I've bought some great new trainers – what do you think?
Holly:	Cool!
Fay:	Hey, Dan, have you heard from Joe? Is he back from Australia?
Dan:	Yes, he is. In fact, look! Here he comes.
Fay:	Oh, yes … he looks different. Is he thinner?
Holly:	No, I think he's changed his hairstyle.
Joe:	Hi, everyone!
Fay:	Hi, Joe! What was Australia like?
Joe:	It was cold – it's winter there now, you know! But it was brilliant. I took thousands of photos. What about you? Have you had a good summer?
Fay:	Yeah, it's been OK.
Holly:	I went camping on the west coast of Scotland.
Dan:	Oh, I've been there. It's nice but a bit boring.
Holly:	Well, OK, there aren't a lot of clothes shops, Dan, but I joined this wildlife group – they were doing a survey on dolphins. I was thinking about …
Joe:	Don't tell me! You're going to start a new wildlife club at school this year.
Holly:	Well, why not? What are you going to do?
Joe:	Hmm, I'm not going to miss any deadlines, that's for sure! Last year was a disaster.
Fay:	I know! I'm going to do all my homework at lunchtime – I need to be free after school for the drama group.
Holly:	Anyway, Joe. You look …
Joe:	Taller? I've grown eight centimetres this summer! I'm as tall as my dad now.
Fay:	No way!

Fame

> ## Grammar
Review the present simple, present continuous, and the present perfect simple.
Review *yet, still, already* and *just*.

> ## Vocabulary
Learn words connected with mass media and TV shows.
Work with verb + preposition *at* and *to* combinations, and noun + noun combinations.

> ## Skills
Read about a reality show's secret house, Cheryl Cole's career, and New Zealand on film.
Listen to conversations about TV shows, and a conversation about film locations.
Write a review.

> ## Communicate
Exchange opinions.

1 What do you think is happening in the photo?

2 Work in pairs. Connect the words in the vocabulary box to these words. How many connections can you make?

TV   newspapers and magazines
radio   the Internet

article	audience	channel	front page
headline	journalist	listener	podcast
programme	reader	reporter	station
video-sharing	viewer	website	

3 Ask and answer questions about the media.
1 How many hours a week do you watch TV?
2 Which radio programmes do you like?
3 What is the best way to follow the news?
4 Which magazines do you read?

4 🎧 1.1 Listen to a survey about the media. What answers does the person give?

5

1 Warm-up

2 Vocabulary: mass media

Read through the words in the vocabulary box. Elicit or explain the meaning of each item, and elicit which one or more of the media the item is connected to.

3 Speaking

Ask students to role-play a survey by asking and answering the list of questions.

4 Listening for information

 *1.1 CD 1 track 03*

Explain that students will hear Holly being asked the questions in

Exercise 3, and that they should note Holly's answers in brief form – that is, using no more than three words.

Tapescript

(I = interviewer; H = Holly)

I: Hi. Can I ask you some questions?

H: Yes, sure.

I: OK, thanks. Do you watch a lot of television? How many hours a week do you usually watch TV, do you think?

H: Oh, I'm not sure. I don't really like TV, actually. There are so many channels, I find it very confusing. I watch the news every evening, just to see the headlines really. And sometimes I watch a documentary. So, in a week, I only watch a few hours, I suppose.

Fame

Unit aims

Grammar: present simple, present continuous, present perfect simple; *yet, still, already* and *just*

Vocabulary: media and TV; verb + preposition; noun + noun

Functions: exchanging opinions

Reading about: a reality show's secret house; reality TV shows; New Zealand on film

Listening to: conversations about TV shows; film locations

Writing a review

KEY

4 1 a few hours   2 (pop) music programmes   3 reading newspapers online   4 games magazines

I: And what kind of radio programmes do you like?

H: Well, I listen to the radio a lot, especially Radio 1. That's all pop music, really.

I: Right, that's great. And you say you're interested in the news, so in your opinion what's the best way to follow the news? Do you buy a newspaper?

H: Well, actually I read the newspapers online. Most newspapers have a good website these days, with podcasts and news videos too. I don't like the TV news because it's very sensationalist. But I like to read different newspapers on the Internet because I get more information that way.

I: OK. And my last question is, what kind of magazines do you usually read?

H: Well, I sometimes look at fashion magazines, but they're a bit boring to be honest. The articles are always the same. I'm into computer games, so really I prefer games magazines. They usually come with a disc so you can see new games, which is brilliant. I like reading about them on the Internet as well.

I: OK, thanks very much.

23

1A Fans

Spread aims

Grammar: present simple, continuous and perfect

Vocabulary: verb + preposition

Functions: talking about personal experiences related to famous people

Reading about a reality show's secret house

KEY

2 It's about fans discovering the *X Factor* house

3 1 F 2 T 3 F 4 F

4 1 b 2 a 3 c 4 d

1 Warm-up

Students tell their partner about their favourite people, teams, shows etc. using the ideas in the box and the language in the speech balloons. Elicit some responses from the class.

2 Reading for gist

Students skim the article to find out what it is about.

3 Reading and listening for detail

 *1.2 CD 1 track 04*

Ask students to read the four sentences first, then to read and listen to the article to check the information.

Stronger students cover the text and just listen.

Weaker students follow the article while they listen.

4 Grammar: present simple, continuous and perfect

First ask students for examples of the three tenses and some ideas about when we use them. Then ask them to match the sentences with the uses. If necessary, refer students to the *Grammar Explorer*, page 116, for a more detailed explanation.

Give **weaker students** a thematically linked phrase (e.g. *make a film*) and elicit examples around that (e.g. *John makes a new film every year; Susan and Lucy are making a film about school at*

the moment; Anne has just made her first documentary film for TV).

Extension: ask students to find other examples of the three tenses in the text.

5 Grammar: present simple and continuous verb forms

Students complete the text as required; they can then check with a partner. Elicit the correct verb forms from the whole class.

Weaker students suggest that students first read the text and decide which tense is required for each gap (present simple 1, 2, 3, 4, 6, 7; present continuous 5, 8), then write in the correct forms.

6 Grammar: present perfect

Read the questions with the class, then ask them to look at the sentences and answer. Check the answers with the whole class. If necessary, refer students to *Grammar Explorer*, pages 116–117.

7 Grammar: present simple, continuous and perfect

Present the explanation in the grammar box before students complete the task; they can then check their answers with a partner. Elicit the correct verb forms from the class.

1A Fans

THE X FACTOR 'SECRET' HOUSE – NOW NOT SO SECRET!

Our reporter investigates.

In a quiet, residential street in north London, a group of teenagers is standing opposite a large house. They are staring at the windows of the first floor. They can't see much because they're on the other side of the street and a high wall surrounds the house. There are several security guards at the gate and a policeman in the street. This is the *X Factor* house – the contestants are staying

here during the competition. In theory, the location of the house is a secret. However, *X Factor* fans have discovered its address.

Chloe, Sharon and Hayley come here every day. The schools are on holiday this week. 'We're waiting to talk to Olly. I've brought my autograph book with me and Sharon has borrowed her mum's camera. It's like a paparazzi camera, with a long lens,' Hayley explains to me. She's showing me her autograph book so that I can look at some of the signed photos – she's met almost everyone on TV! Sharon is pointing the camera at the house. An older girl, Tara, is waving to the group from the house next door. Tara says it's the first time a celebrity has lived in her street. She thinks it's 'really cool', although many of the neighbours have complained.

I've never seen the show, so I ask the girls about the contestants. 'They all sing really well, but Olly's definitely got the *X Factor*!' says Sharon. Chloe, Sharon and Hayley vote for him every week and they watch repeats of the show on *YouTube*. It's time for my last question. 'Have you ever spoken to any of your idols?' 'No, we haven't, but we're not giving up!'

Speaking

1 Work in pairs. Who or what are you a fan of? Tell your partner. Give reasons.

an actor   an author   a sports star
a sports team   a pop star   a TV show

I'm Jackie Chan's biggest fan. I think he's …

I'm crazy about Leona Lewis because …

Reading and listening

2 Read the news story quickly. What is it about?

3 *1.2* Read and listen to the news story. Are the sentences true or false?

1 Chloe, Sharon and Hayley live in the *X Factor* house.

2 They are waiting to speak to one of the *X Factor* contestants.

3 Tara doesn't like living next door to the house.

4 The girls talk to the contestants every day.

Grammar: the present simple, continuous and perfect

4 Look at the examples (1–4). Match them with the meanings (a–d).

1 A group of teenagers is standing opposite a large house.

2 A high wall surrounds the house.

3 The contestants are staying here during the competition.

4 Chloe, Sharon and Hayley come here every day.

a a permanent state

b an activity in progress now

c an activity in progress around now

d a regular activity

See Grammar Explorer: Page 116

6

---

5 Write the correct form of the verbs: present simple or present continuous.

Some fans (**1**) .... (**become**) obsessed with their idols. Roger, aged 36, (**2**) .... (**love**) Elvis. He (**3**) .... (**dress**) like Elvis and he's got the same hairstyle. He (**4**) .... (**not sing**) very well, so now he (**5**) .... (**take**) singing lessons as well. Roger's two children are mad about *Star Trek*. They (**6**) .... (**pretend**) to speak Klingon with each other! They (**7**) .... (**go**) to the *Star Trek* convention every year. They (**8**) .... (**save**) their money to go to next year's convention.

6 Look at the examples (1–4). Match them with the meanings (a–b).

1 I've brought my autograph book with me.
2 *X Factor* fans have discovered its address.
3 Many of the neighbours have complained.
4 Sharon has borrowed her mum's camera.

a an action in the past with a result in the present
b a past action in a time period which includes the present

See Grammar Explorer: Page 116

We use the present perfect with the expression *It's the first / second / third time.*

7 Write the correct form of the verbs: present simple, present continuous or present perfect.

Dan is a member of Keira Knightley's fan club. It's the first time he (**1**) .... (**join**) a fan club and he's really happy because he (**2**) .... (**receive**) a signed poster of Keira. He (**3**) .... (**put**) it on his wall. He (**4**) .... (**stare**) at it every evening. Dan (**5**) .... (**check**) the fan club site most days. Sometimes he (**6**) .... (**spend**) a lot of time online and he (**7**) .... (**not finish**) his homework. Keira (**8**) .... (**make**) a new film at the moment, and there are photos and stories about her every day.

Working with words: verb + preposition *at* and *to*

8 Look at the examples. Then find five more verbs with *at* and *to* in the text.

They are staring at the windows.

We're waiting to talk to Olly.

See Working with words: Page 100

Speaking

9 Write a question for each picture. Use the present perfect form of the verbs.

1 ever / meet / your idol?

2 ever / watch / your favourite team?

3 ever / join / a fan club?

4 ever / vote for / your idol?

You can use *ever* and *never* with the present perfect when referring to experiences in your life.

10 Work in pairs. Write a questionnaire to find out who is the biggest fan in your class. Use ideas from the box and Exercise 9. Use the present simple and present perfect forms of the verbs.

buy	CDs / magazines / books
collect	autographs / posters / photos
copy	a hairstyle / a look / clothes
go to	concerts / matches / shows
queue all night for	a ticket / a book / a seat
spend too much on	DVDs / phone voting / trips to see your idol

11 Work in pairs. Ask and answer your questions from Exercise 10. Then work with a new partner. Compare the answers with your original partner.

A: *Have you ever voted for your idol?*
B: *Yes, I have. / No, I haven't.*

Fast finishers

Make a list of all the past participles you can think of in one minute. Then make sentences with them.

Grammar

KEY

5 1 become   2 loves
3 dresses   4 doesn't sing
5 's (is) taking   6 pretend
7 go   8 're saving

6 1 a   2 b   3 b   4 a

7 1 has joined   2 has received
3 has put   4 stares   5 checks
6 spends   7 doesn't finish
8 is making

8 explains to, look at, pointing the camera at, waving to, spoken to

9 1 Have you ever met your idol?   2 Have you ever watched your favourite team?
3 Have you ever joined a fan club?   4 Have you ever voted for your idol?

They can either write them in pairs, or exchange work afterwards to check each other's questions.

11 Speaking: asking and answering questions

Ideally, you should do this activity as a 'mingle' activity, with everyone on their feet exchanging questions and answers with a whole range of different people, especially those they don't usually talk to. At the end you can take feedback from the whole class to find out who is the biggest fan.

Fast finishers

Students check their knowledge of past participles.

Weaker students: suggest that students decide which tense is needed for each gap (present perfect: 1, 2, 3; present simple: 4, 5, 6, 7; present continuous: 8), then write in the correct verb forms.

8 Working with words: verb + preposition *at, to*

There are two *Working with words* activities in every unit; they are not linked into the other activities and can be completed at any point (usually once the reading activity has been completed).

Read through the examples with students before they look for the other verb + *at / to* combinations in the text. Refer also to *Working with words*, page 100.

9 Writing: present perfect questions

Present the grammar box explanation about *ever* and *never*. Students then use the cues and the picture clues to produce questions with *ever* in the present perfect tense. Point out the example with *never* in paragraph 3 in the text.

10 Writing a questionnaire

Present the rubric and the prompts in the box. Elicit some examples, using both tenses, to make sure that students understand the task and the grammar needed. Students then use the prompts from the box and the language from the unit so far to write questions for a questionnaire.

1B Reality TV

Spread aims

Grammar: present perfect with *yet, still, already, just*

Vocabulary: performances; TV shows

Reading news about TV shows

Listening to people talking about TV shows

KEY

1 people: actor / celebrity / contestant / judge / presenter / winner
performance: act / audition / rehearsal
programme: episode / series

3 1 a comedy series 2 a talent show 3 a celebrity show

4 1 episode 2 series
3 actor 4 audition 5 act(s)
6 rehearsal 7 judge
8 contestant 9 winner
10 presenter 11 celebrities

5 *Survivor, You Can Dance, I'm a Celebrity … Get Me Out Of Here! American Idol, Big Brother* and *Celebrity Big Brother*

6 1 A 2 C 3 D 4 B

7 c

8 Possible answers: programme, presenter, show, series, viewers

9 1 still 2 just 3 yet 4 already

---

1 Warm-up

Read out the words in the box and ask the class to repeat. Point out the words with stress on the second syllable (au**di**tion, ce**leb**rity, con**test**ant, pre**sent**er, re**hear**sal). Elicit the answers and list them on the board.

2 Speaking: vocabulary activation

Students use the vocabulary from Exercise 1 to tell their partner about their preferences.

3 Listening for gist

 1.3 CD 1 track 05

Check students know what the four types of show in the box are by eliciting examples for each category.

1B Reality TV

A

And now, celebrity reality TV!

Are television viewers getting bored with shows like *Survivor* or *You Can Dance*? Maybe ordinary contestants aren't interesting enough – because ITV's new show is called *I'm a Celebrity … Get Me Out Of Here!* Eight celebrities live in the jungle for two weeks while viewers at home vote for their favourite. Although ITV hasn't revealed who the stars are yet, there are lots of rumours. You can see the first episode in August.

B

NEW AWARDS FOR REALITY TV

Reality TV shows have exploded onto our screens in the last couple of years and they have already become extremely popular. So it's not surprising that the Academy of Television Arts and Sciences has just announced a new Emmy award for reality TV. *American Idol* and *Survivor* are both nominated. The Academy considers that reality TV has become a major part of television culture. Perhaps this is true – apparently one in seven UK teenagers wants to become famous through reality TV.

Speaking

1 Work in pairs. Put the words into three groups: *people, performance* and *programmes.*

| act actor audition celebrity |
| contestant episode judge presenter |
| rehearsal series winner |

2 Tell your partner about a TV show you like. Use some of the words in the box.

Listening

3 *1.3* **Listen to the conversations (1–3) and match them with the TV shows. There is one extra TV show.**

a celebrity show a comedy series
a soap opera a talent show

4 *1.3* **Listen again and put the words in the vocabulary box in the order you hear them.**

Reading and listening

5 Quickly read the four news stories (A–D) which appeared over a ten-year period. Which TV programmes are mentioned?

6 *1.4* **Read and listen to the news stories (A–D) and match the information (1–4).**

1 On this show, the audience at home chooses the winner.

2 This show begins with 16 contestants.

3 This programme is ten years old.

4 Reality TV is very popular.

8

Tapescript

1 (D = Dan; H = Holly)

D: *What are you laughing at?*

H: *Oh, it's an old* <u>episode</u> *of Friends.*

D: *Are they still making that?*

H: *No, this is a repeat from the first* <u>series</u>*. It's on every night at six o'clock. I always watch it.*

D: *But haven't you seen it before?*

H: *Yes, I've seen all of these episodes before.*

D: *Really? So, why are you watching it again?*

H: *Because it's still funny. It makes me laugh every time I watch it.*

D: *I like the* <u>actor</u> *who plays Chandler.*

H: *Me too. He's the funniest character in the whole show.*

2 (F = Fay; J = Joe)

F: *What's on TV tonight?*

J: *The* <u>auditions</u> *for Britain's Got Talent are on at seven o'clock.*

F: *Oh yes! That's usually entertaining. Some of the* <u>acts</u> *are terrible!*

J: *I know. Do you think they have a* <u>rehearsal</u> *before they go on stage?*

F: *I don't know! Because some of the people are really confident …*

J: *… and they're still terrible!*

F: *I know. But there are some amazing* <u>acts</u>*, even in the auditions.*

J: *Yeah. So why do the* <u>judges</u> *make horrible comments?*

F: *I don't know. Anyway, I think there are different judges this year. Let's watch later and find out.*

A GREAT NEW SHOW

Have you heard about the new TV show yet?

It's called *You Can Dance* and it's all about … dancing! It's a talent competition open to 18–30 year olds. The first stage, the auditions, has already finished. The series starts next week, but the judges are still choosing the final 16 for the first programme. So if you like salsa, hip-hop and jazz, don't miss it!

Bye bye Big Brother

Channel 4 has cancelled the next series of *Big Brother*, after ten years of shows. The TV channel hasn't given any reasons for the decision. It still broadcasts *Celebrity Big Brother*, although recently this hasn't been as popular as newer shows such as *I'm a Celebrity … Get Me Out Of Here!* So if you have been on Mars for ten years and you still haven't seen *Big Brother*, the current series is your last chance!

7 **Which is the correct order for the news stories?**

- a A B D C
- b C D B A
- c C B A D

Working with words: noun + noun

8 **Look at the examples. How many nouns can you think of which can follow *television*?**

news + story = news story

talent + competition = talent competition

See Working with words: Page 100

Grammar: *yet, still, already* and *just*

9 **Find *yet, still, already* and *just* in the news stories. Complete the sentences.**

1 We can use .... with the present simple, continuous and negative present perfect.

2 We can use .... in present perfect affirmative sentences.

3 We can use .... in negative sentences and questions.

4 We use .... + present perfect to mean 'a short time ago'.

See Grammar Explorer: Page 117

10 **Mark the correct position of the words.**

e.g. I haven't seen that show. (**still**)

1 Hurry up! The show has started. (**already**)

2 Has the voting finished? (**yet**)

3 The phone lines have closed. (**just**)

4 The judges are discussing the performance. (**still**)

5 They haven't announced the results. (**yet**)

11 **Make statements and questions with the words.**

e.g. the presenter / not rehearse / yet

The presenter hasn't rehearsed yet.

1 the rehearsals / finish / already

2 the audience / come in / just

3 the judges / sit down / yet

4 the contestants / get ready / still

5 the guest celebrity / not arrive / yet

Speaking

12 **Work in groups. Why are these people famous? Do you think all celebrities are talented?**

Prince William   Stella McCartney

Paris Hilton   Ashton Kutcher

Study skills

Identifying the main idea in a text

1 Read the headline or title of the text. It usually summarises the most important information.

2 Look for information in the text that supports the headline. This is usually in the first or second sentence.

3 Read the whole text.

Grammar and skills

KEY

10 1 has already started
2 finished yet?   3 have just closed   4 are still discussing
5 results yet.

11 1 The rehearsals have already finished.   2 The audience has just come in.   3 Have the judges sat down yet?   4 The contestants are still getting ready.   5 The guest celebrity hasn't arrived yet.

7 Reading for detail

Students choose the correct chronological order for the news stories using clues from the texts.

8 Working with words: noun + noun

Ask the students to work in pairs to find other nouns like the examples. See *Working with words*, page 100, for further examples and practice.

9 *Yet, still, already, just*

Ask the students to complete the sentences individually, then check with a partner. If necessary, refer students to *Grammar Explorer*, page 117–118.

10 Grammar: word order

Students decide where the words go in each sentence. Check answers with the whole class.

11 Grammar: controlled writing practice

The students use the prompts to write sentences. Check students' answers around the class.

12 Speaking: talented people

Make sure the students know who the four celebrities are.

Study skills: identifying the main idea in a text

Present the information and guide students as they practise the suggestions with the texts on this spread.

---

3 (H = Holly; M = Holly's mum)

M: *I've never seen this programme before. What's it about?*

H: *It's a dancing competition.*

M: *What do you mean?*

H: *Well, the <u>contestants</u> dance and the viewers choose the <u>winner</u> – they vote for their favourites. It's on every week. Millions of people watch it.*

M: *Oh, yes, I think I've read about it. Oh, I recognise the <u>presenter</u>!*

H: *Yeah, he's quite famous.*

M: *And I recognise some of the dancers too. She reads the news on the BBC. And he's a singer.*

H: *Yes, all the dancers are <u>celebrities.</u> They learn to dance for the show.*

M: *What a good idea!*

4 Listening for detail

 1.3 CD 1 track 05

Ask students to read through the words again before listening.

5 Reading: scanning for information

Students scan the newspaper stories to find the titles of six TV programmes. Check answers with the whole class.

6 Reading and listening for detail

 1.4 CD 1 track 06

Students read and listen to the stories to find the matching information.

1C Exchanging opinions

Spread aims

Vocabulary: TV and entertainment
Functions: exchanging opinions
Skills: reading and listening for gist
Pronunciation: words ending in *-ght* and *-ghed*
Writing a review

KEY

2 Joe and Dan like Wayne Hill; Holly and Fay didn't like him at first.

3 positive: popular, brilliant, talented, funny, entertaining, motivated, fascinating, nice
negative: clumsy, arrogant, unfriendly

4 1 a   2 c   3 b

---

1 Warm-up

Students discuss their ideas in pairs and report back to the class.

2 Reading and listening for gist

 1.5 CD 1 track 07

Students listen to identify the opinions of the four speakers.

Stronger students cover the text and listen and answer.

Weaker students follow the text as they listen.

3 Vocabulary: positive and negative adjectives

Check that students remember what an adjective is (a word which describes a noun) before they do the exercise. Elicit the adjectives from the dialogue and list them in positive / negative columns on the board.

Extension: have the students repeat the adjectives chorally and individually for pronunciation practise.

4 Identifying functions

Ask the students to match each of the three sets of phrases with one of the linguistic functions (1–3).

1C Exchanging opinions

WAYNE

Reading and listening

1 **Look at the photo. What do you think is happening?**

2 *1.5* **Read and listen to the dialogue. Who likes Wayne Hill? Who doesn't like him?**

3 **Read the dialogue again. Find the adjectives that are used to describe Wayne Hill. Are they positive or negative?**

10

Dan: Wow, look at all these people! Wayne Hill's really popular!

Joe: Of course he is. I think he's brilliant. He's the most talented celebrity in England!

Holly: I don't think so, actually.

Joe: Why not?

Holly: Because he doesn't dance very well. He's quite funny and entertaining, but he's clumsy when he dances.

Fay: That's true. He seems a bit arrogant to me.

Dan: Do you think so?

Fay: Yes, I do.

Joe: Well, I think that's because he's really motivated. He always tries to win.

Fay: I know, but … oh, it's hard to explain.

Holly: I know what you mean. He sometimes seems unfriendly.

Dan: Actually, I've read his autobiography. Joe lent it to me. He's had a fascinating life, in my opinion.

Fay: Why do you say that?

Dan: Oh, because he's done so many different things and he's still only 25.

Holly: Look, the queue is moving forwards! We're nearly there.

Joe: Oh, I can't wait to meet him! It's so exciting!

Holly: Calm down, Joe!

Five minutes later

Joe: Wow! Look, he's written, 'To Joe, go for it! Wayne Hill.'

Holly: Yeah … and I've changed my mind, Joe. Wayne Hill isn't unfriendly at all. I think he's really nice!

5 Useful expressions: intonation

 1.6 CD 1 track 08

Play the recording through a couple of times while the students just listen and follow. Then pause it after each phrase for them to repeat chorally and individually. Point out that 'in my opinion' can be used at the beginning of a sentence or at the end.

6 Listening for detail

 1.7 CD 1 track 09

Ask the students to read through each set of responses (a–c), and imagine what the statement might be. Then listen and choose the correct response.

Tapescript

1 *I think this magazine's a bit boring.*

2 *Well, he's popular because he's talented.*

3 *Why do you say she's funny?*

Student Book Page (facsimile)

4 Find the *Useful expressions* in the dialogue. Match the functions (1–3) with the headings (a–c).

1 giving an opinion
2 giving reasons for your opinion
3 reacting to an opinion

USEFUL EXPRESSIONS

a I think he's brilliant.
He seems a bit arrogant to me.
... in my opinion. / In my opinion, ...
b I don't think so.   I know what you mean.
That's true.   Why do you say that?
Do you think so?
c Because he doesn't dance very well.
That's because he's really motivated.

5 🎧 1.6 **Listen and repeat the *Useful expressions*. Focus on your intonation.**

6 🎧 1.7 **Listen to each statement and choose the best response (a–c).**

1 a In my opinion, he dances very well.
   b Because it's entertaining.
   c I know what you mean.

2 a Do you think so?
   b I think he's popular.
   c Yes, I do.

3 a That's true.
   b I think it's brilliant.
   c Because she makes me laugh.

Writing: a review

1 Read Holly's review of a TV show. Write the number of the paragraph next to the information.

good points   bad points
a conclusion   details and format

2 Find five expressions Holly uses to introduce an opinion.

3 Holly uses *because* and *because of* to explain her opinion. Find these expressions in the review. Then complete the sentences with *because* or *because of*.

1 Talent shows are exciting .... they are emotional.
2 *Avatar* was a success .... its special effects.
3 This show works .... the celebrity guests.
4 I love *Friends* .... it's always funny.

See Grammar Explorer: Page 118

Speaking

7 Work in pairs. Put the sentences in order. Then practise the dialogue.

a I think *TV Star* magazine is fascinating!
b Oh, because it's full of celebrity gossip.
c That's true. But it seems a bit repetitive to me.
d Well, I don't think so.
e Why do you say that?

8 Work in pairs. Read the statements below and think about your opinions. Then work in groups and discuss each statement. Use the *Useful expressions* to help you.

1 Reality TV is rubbish!
2 U2 – the best band of all time!
3 Too much TV makes people stupid.
4 Everybody wants to be famous these days.

Pronunciation: *-ght* and *-ghed*

9 🎧 1.8 Listen and repeat the past participles. Which two are different to the others?

bought	brought	caught	coughed
fought	laughed	taught	thought

10 Write sentences with four of the past participles. Give them to your partner to read aloud. Who has the best pronunciation?

1 *Young Tycoon* is a new reality TV show. Students aged 13–21 compete to make the most money. They have to try out a different business idea every week. There are three judges who set the tasks.

2 On the one hand, it's an entertaining show. I think this is because of the contestants. They're really ambitious and motivated. They're fascinating to watch because they get totally involved with the tasks.

3 On the other hand, the business ideas seem dull to me. In my opinion, washing cars (the idea in Episode 1) is not especially exciting television! In my view, reality TV shows work best when viewers can vote for the contestants, and *Young Tycoon* isn't interactive like that.

4 In conclusion, I'd watch *Young Tycoon* once a week, but not every night.

4 Write a review of a TV show you have seen. Use Holly's review to help you.

UNIT 1C **EXCHANGING OPINIONS** 11

Communicate

2 Reading for detail

Tell **weaker students** they will find all the expressions in paragraphs 2 and 3, at the start of sentences.

3 *Because / because of*

Ask the students to find the phrases in the text and complete the sentences correctly. Elicit complete sentences from the class, and make sure students understand the grammar of *because* + subject + verb and *because of* + noun or noun phrase. If necessary, refer students to *Grammar Explorer*, page 118, for further examples.

4 Personalised writing practice

This can be done for homework, using Holly's review as a model.

Give **weaker students** a handout based on Holly's review, but with the specific information deleted, so that they just have to complete the text with details of their TV programme.

---

7 Speaking: practising a dialogue

8 Speaking: exchanging opinions

Students exchange opinions about the statements provided, using phrases for agreeing and disagreeing from the *Useful expressions*.

Extension: pairs perform a dialogue for the class.

9 Pronunciation: words ending in *-ght* and *-ghed*

 *1.8 CD 1 track 10*

Ask the students to listen to the recording a couple of times before they answer the question, then have them repeat chorally and individually.

10 Pronunciation practice

Once students have written the sentences and practised with one partner, ask them to change partners and practise with another set of sentences.

Writing: a review

1 Reading for gist

Ask the students to read and match the paragraphs with the descriptions in the box. Elicit answers from the class.

Tell **weaker students** that 'details and format' is the first paragraph.

1D New Zealand on film

Spread aims

Vocabulary: New Zealand films

Skills: reading and listening for gist and detail

Culture: New Zealand

CLIL: Social sciences and English: media studies

KEY

 c

---

1 Reading: skimming for gist

Ask students to read the three options first, then scan the texts to find the answer. Set a short time limit to encourage students to skim the text.

2 Reading for information: jigsaw reading

Students read part of the text and then pass the information they have found on to their partner.

Allow **weaker students** to take notes as they read.

3 Reading for information

Students read the other sections to check what their partner said, and also to make sure they got all of the information.

4 Writing: *not only … but also*

Read the example with the class before they do the exercise and check that they understand the meaning.

5 Speaking: film locations

First check that the students are familiar with the films. Then get students to discuss the most interesting places they remember from the films. Elicit answers from the class.

6 Listening for detail

 1.9 CD 1 track 11

Read through the places in the list with the class before they listen.

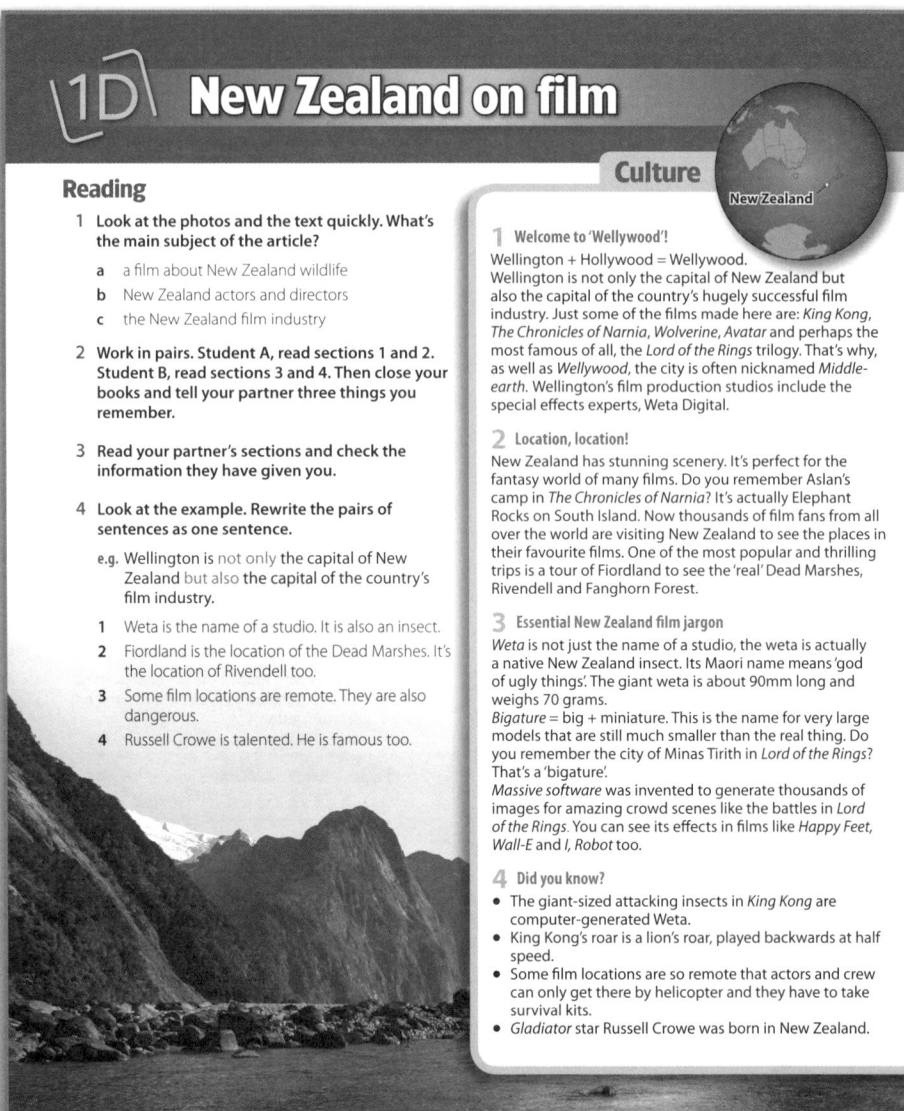

Culture New Zealand

Reading

1 Look at the photos and the text quickly. What's the main subject of the article?

a a film about New Zealand wildlife

b New Zealand actors and directors

c the New Zealand film industry

2 Work in pairs. Student A, read sections 1 and 2. Student B, read sections 3 and 4. Then close your books and tell your partner three things you remember.

3 Read your partner's sections and check the information they have given you.

4 Look at the example. Rewrite the pairs of sentences as one sentence.

e.g. Wellington is not only the capital of New Zealand but also the capital of the country's film industry.

1 Weta is the name of a studio. It is also an insect.

2 Fiordland is the location of the Dead Marshes. It's the location of Rivendell too.

3 Some film locations are remote. They are also dangerous.

4 Russell Crowe is talented. He is famous too.

1 Welcome to 'Wellywood'!

Wellington + Hollywood = Wellywood. Wellington is not only the capital of New Zealand but also the capital of the country's hugely successful film industry. Just some of the films made here are: *King Kong*, *The Chronicles of Narnia*, *Wolverine*, *Avatar* and perhaps the most famous of all, the *Lord of the Rings* trilogy. That's why, as well as *Wellywood*, the city is often nicknamed *Middle-earth*. Wellington's film production studios include the special effects experts, Weta Digital.

2 Location, location!

New Zealand has stunning scenery. It's perfect for the fantasy world of many films. Do you remember Aslan's camp in *The Chronicles of Narnia*? It's actually Elephant Rocks on South Island. Now thousands of film fans from all over the world are visiting New Zealand to see the places in their favourite films. One of the most popular and thrilling trips is a tour of Fiordland to see the 'real' Dead Marshes, Rivendell and Fanghorn Forest.

3 Essential New Zealand film jargon

Weta is not just the name of a studio, the weta is actually a native New Zealand insect. Its Maori name means 'god of ugly things'. The giant weta is about 90mm long and weighs 70 grams.

Bigature = big + miniature. This is the name for very large models that are still much smaller than the real thing. Do you remember the city of Minas Tirith in *Lord of the Rings*? That's a 'bigature'.

Massive software was invented to generate thousands of images for amazing crowd scenes like the battles in *Lord of the Rings*. You can see its effects in films like *Happy Feet*, *Wall-E* and *I, Robot* too.

4 Did you know?

- The giant-sized attacking insects in *King Kong* are computer-generated Weta.
- King Kong's roar is a lion's roar, played backwards at half speed.
- Some film locations are so remote that actors and crew can only get there by helicopter and they have to take survival kits.
- *Gladiator* star Russell Crowe was born in New Zealand.

12

Tapescript

Casey: Hi, Mom, it's me.

Mom: Hi, Casey. Where are you calling from?

Casey: We've just got back to the hotel in Edinburgh.

Mom: That's in Scotland, right?

Casey: Yes, Mom, it's the capital of Scotland!

Mom: OK, honey. So are you having a good trip?

Casey: It's awesome! We've been to lots of different places in the north of England. We've already visited two of the places from the Harry Potter films – Durham Cathedral – that's the inside of Hogwarts School in the films – and Alnwick Castle – that's the outside of Hogwarts where they

play Quidditch. They're really, really old and beautiful buildings. I love the cathedral at Durham especially. You can climb up to the top of the tower!

Mom: And what about Braveheart? Have you seen where they filmed that?

Casey: No, not yet. That's here in Scotland. Just a moment, I'm looking at my tour map. Here it is … it's in a wild place called Glen Nevis: it says Glen is the word for valley in Scotland. I guess it's the valley next to the highest mountain here. I think we're going there on Tuesday.

Mom: So have you seen anything else interesting?

Casey: Oh yeah, we've been to a lovely little church that's in The Da Vinci Code. It's here in Edinburgh, not far from our hotel, actually. Oh, I forgot

Listening

5 Have you seen these films? What can you remember about the places in them? Tell your partner.

Braveheart   The Bourne Ultimatum
Harry Potter   The Da Vinci Code

6 🔊1.9 Listen to Casey, who is is on a film tour of the UK. Which places does he mention?

a capital city   a lake
a cathedral   a castle
a valley   a church
a station   a casino

7 🔊1.9 Listen again and match the places with the films.

8 Do you know any film locations in your country? Tell your partner.

Social science and English
Media studies

1 Read the quotation. What do you think it means?

'If you don't read the newspaper, you are uninformed; if you do read the newspaper, you are misinformed.'
Mark Twain, 1835–1910.

2 Work in pairs. Read the text and answer the questions marked 'Q'

Newspapers and magazines organise different kinds of information into different sections. Some of this information is factual, for example national news or sports reports. These sections tell us what's happening in the world. Other sections give opinions – they tell us what people think about what's happening, for example film and music reviews or celebrity features.

Q *Choose a newspaper or magazine you have read. How many different sections are there? Do you know if they are factual or opinion? How do you know?*

Both factual reports and opinion articles can be subjective. News stories are not always reported in the same way. Journalists can report events from different points of view. Look at these headlines from two reports of the same Formula 1 race in Australia.

Another disappointing race for Hamilton

Jensen Button is the greatest!

One headline emphasises a negative aspect of the race; the other is positive. Both headlines are from British media, but look at this third headline from an Australian paper. The story is about the location, not the drivers.

Spectacular racing at Melbourne once again!

Q *Which headline is negative? Who do you think won the race? Why do you think the Australian headline refers to the location?*

3 When you read or listen to the news, think about these questions.

- Is this a factual story, an opinion or the journalist's point of view?
- What aspect of the story is emphasised?
- Can different people interpret this story in different ways?
- What do other media say about the same story?

Project
Work in pairs. Choose an international story that is in the news at the moment. Then choose two different kinds of media, for example the Internet and a newspaper. Write the story in the style of each media.

UNIT 1D NEW ZEALAND ON FILM **13**

Culture

Social Sciences and English

1 Warm-up

Ask the class for suggestions about the meaning and discuss whether they agree with the quotation.

2 Reading for detail

Ask students to bring in newspapers or magazines to do the first Q task with.

to tell you! I've got some fantastic photos of Waterloo Station in London – it's just like in The Bourne Ultimatum! *You kind of expect Matt Damon to get off one of the trains!*

Mom: Oh, that's such a good film!

Casey: I know. OK, I have to go – our tour leader is waiting for us.

Mom: OK, have fun.

Casey: Yeah. I'll call you again in a couple of days.

7 Listening for detail

 1.9 CD 1 track 11

Suggest that students write the film titles on paper, so they can write the name of the place next to them.

8 Speaking: film locations

Follow up brief pairwork with a whole-class discussion (e.g. the backgrounds for *Narnia* were shot in the Tatra Mountains and the Dunajec River).

Project

Ask students to bring in recent newspapers and magazines, and discuss what international stories have been in the news. Suggest they look on the Internet, too. Ask them to write up their chosen story as indicated, then bring their stories to class, and share them in groups of four.

True story: Music explorer

Page aim

Reading for interest on the topic of the unit

Warm-up

Ask students what they understand by the term *world music*, and ask them to discuss and exemplify it – if possible with actual examples of music played in class (they may have some on their MP3 players), and talking about particular performers from around the world.

1 Reading for detail

Students read the text about Charlie Gillett and answer the questions individually, then check with a partner. Check the answers with the whole class.

Background information

For further information about Charlie Gillett, these web-sites are suggested:

http://charliegillett.com
http://en.wikipedia.org/wiki/
  Charlie_Gillett

2 Vocabulary

Ask students to match the words and meanings individually, then check with a partner; suggest they use the context of the reading passage to help their understanding. Then elicit answers from the whole class.

3 Discussion

Ask students to form groups of three or four to discuss the three questions. They should appoint a secretary, who keeps notes, and reports back to the whole class in a feedback session. Encourage students to bring into class music and pictures related to the performers they discuss.

Background information

Some well-known world music performers are:

Youssou N'Dour (Senegal); Ali Farka Toure (Mali); Toumani Diabaté (Mali); Márta Sebestyén/Muzsikás (Hungary); Cesaria Evora (Cape Verde); The Imagined Village (UK); Ravi Shankar (India)

Music explorer

Charlie Gillett was an explorer and a pioneer who travelled the world in search of what mattered to him most. But Charlie wasn't looking for hidden treasure or lost tribes; Charlie was motivated by music. His explorations led him to discover hugely talented musicians from around the world. He then introduced these new sounds to thousands of other people through his entertaining and informative radio shows.

In 1970 Charlie wrote a book about the history of rock and roll. Then it was while working as a music journalist that Charlie began his career as a radio broadcaster. What made him so fascinating to listen to was his knowledge of the music and his genuine enthusiasm for new bands and performers. He turned down the chance to present a popular TV programme because, as he said, he would have found it difficult to introduce bands who he didn't find exciting.

It was on the radio that Charlie felt most comfortable and he eventually turned his attention to playing music from outside of Britain and the US. Charlie was partly responsible for the phrase *world music*, which is how we now refer to this type of music. Later, he often travelled abroad, keen to meet local musicians and to bring home recordings of music which he could play to his growing audience in Britain.

Each year from 2000 to 2009, Charlie helped create a series of CDs highlighting the best talents of world music. By the time of his death in 2010, Charlie had become one of the most respected figures in broadcasting. Thanks to his hard work, many of his discoveries became hugely successful performing artists.

1 Read the information and choose the correct endings (a or b) for the sentences.

1 Charlie explored different countries to look for
   a hidden treasure and lost tribes.
   b talented musicians.
2 Audiences liked Charlie because he
   a knew a lot about the music he presented.
   b played songs that people knew well.
3 Charlie was
   a keen to break into television broadcasting.
   b happiest presenting radio programmes.
4 Later in his career, Charlie
   a became more interested in world music.
   b focused on music from Britain and the US.
5 Many performers benefited from Charlie's
   a expert knowledge of music.
   b enthusiasm for different sounds.
6 Charlie helped produce CDs of
   a music he had made himself.
   b important world music performers.

2 Match these words to their meanings.

1	pioneer (1)	a	important
2	tribes (1)	b	refused
3	influential (2)	c	appreciated
4	turned down (2)	d	the first person to do something
5	respected (3)	e	groups of people

3 Talk about one or more of the following questions with a partner.

• Can you name any popular performers from outside Britain and the US?
• How easy is it to discover new music from different countries?
• Which performers from your country do you think deserve a wider audience? Why?

14

The mind

> **Grammar**

Learn about the present perfect continuous, relative clauses, and question tags.

> **Vocabulary**

Learn words connected with the mind, and adjectives to describe personality.

Work with abstract nouns, and verb + *-ing*.

> **Skills**

Read about the cleverest animals known to science, hypnosis, and Irish traditions.

Listen to a podcast about phobias, and a survey about beliefs.

Write a description of people.

> **Communicate**

Check information.

1 Work in pairs. What do you think the orangutan is thinking about?

2 Complete the questions with words from the vocabulary box. How many questions can you make?

Can animals … ?   Have you got a good … ?
When do you feel … ?

afraid	happy	remember
angry	imagination	sad
creative	imagine	think
feel	intelligent	understand
forget	memory	

3 2.1 Listen to part of a documentary. Which of your questions do you hear?

4 Work in groups. Choose three of your questions from Exercise 2 and discuss your answers.

15

The mind

Unit aims

Grammar: present perfect continuous; relative clauses; question tags

Vocabulary: the mind, adjectives for personality; abstract nouns; verb + *-ing*

Functions: checking information

Reading about: the cleverest animals; hypnosis; Irish traditions

Listening to: a podcast about phobias; results of a survey about beliefs

Writing a description of people

KEY

2 (possible answers)
1 Can animals feel / forget / imagine / remember / think / understand? 2 Have you got a good imagination / memory? 3 When do you feel afraid / angry / creative / happy / sad?

but I'm sure Dr Smith can answer you, Laura. Robbie from Liverpool wants to know why he can remember the names of England World Cup footballers, but he forgets everything when he has an exam at school. Poor Robbie – it's not fair, is it? Have you got a good memory for some things, like Robbie?

OK, we've got our first track in a moment, the fantastic Chasing cars *by Snow Patrol. What a great song! For me, they are one of the most original and creative bands around. After the track, we'll talk about creativity and imagination with our guest, psychologist Dr Alex Smith. When do **you** feel creative? When you're listening to music? When you're in the art class at school? When you're on the bus? Think about it while you listen to this.*

1 Warm-up

Ask the students to form pairs and discuss what the orangutan is thinking.

2 Vocabulary: making questions

Read through the words in the vocabulary box, and have the students repeat them chorally and individually. Practise second syllable stress in three-syllable words with: creative, remember, imagine; take care with the changing syllable stress in: imagine and imagination. Students then make as many sentences as they can. Elicit and list the questions on the board.

3 Listening for detail

💿 *2.1 CD 1 track 12*

Ask students to raise their hands when they hear one of the questions on the board.

Tapescript

Hello and welcome to today's show. We've got music from Snow Patrol, Eminem and Lily Allen, and later on our studio guest is the psychologist Dr Alex Smith. Dr Smith is here to tell us all about how the mind works. You can email or text your questions for Dr Smith on the usual number and some listeners have already sent questions to the website. Laura, from Manchester, asks 'Can animals think?' Now that's an interesting idea! I'm not sure about that

4 Speaking: the mind

Ask students to form groups of three or four. The groups can choose three questions from the list on the board to discuss. Elicit their ideas and extend it into a whole-class discussion.

2A Animal minds

Spread aims

Grammar: present perfect continuous
Vocabulary: the mind
Functions: talking about recently completed past actions
Reading animal minds

KEY

2 1 remember 2 think
3 understand

4 1 Memory 2 Creativity
3 Communication

1 Warm-up

Students discuss the three animals' intelligence in pairs; remind them of the *Useful expressions* from the previous unit. Elicit ideas for a whole-class discussion of the question.

2 Vocabulary: choosing the correct verb

Elicit the correct sentences from the whole class and ask for their opinions on the content.

3 Reading for gist

Students read the text to check their answers to Exercise 2.

4 Reading and listening for gist

 *2.2 CD 1 track 13*

Ask students to read the headings before they listen and read. Ask them to think about what the words mean and try to predict what the text might say in the sections relating to these headings. They then match each paragraph to one of the heading words.

Stronger students cover the text and listen and answer.

Weaker students follow the text as they listen.

5 Working with words: abstract nouns

Make sure students understand the concept of 'abstract' nouns before they search the text. This activity can be done at any appropriate point in this spread. Refer also to *Working with words*, page 101, for further examples and practice.

2A Animal minds

MEET THE cleverest animals KNOWN TO SCIENCE ...

There are some skills which are key signs of intelligence in humans. They include memory, creativity and communication. Recently, scientists have been investigating these skills in animals too. They've found out some surprising things!

1 ....
Biologist Keith Kendrick has been testing the memory of sheep like Edward for several years. He's proved that sheep can remember faces for about two years. They recognise both other sheep and humans, and they prefer faces that show happiness to anger or fear!

2 ....
In the wild, orangutans make leaves into rain hats, pillows and even gloves. Orangutans are expert tool users. An orangutan called Fu Manchu has escaped from a zoo three times, using a piece of wire to unlock his cage. Scientists have been studying how animals use tools since 1960, when Jane Goodall first reported it. They've discovered that in addition to primates, elephants, many birds and even octopuses use tools.

3 ....
Kanzi is a bonobo. Bonobos are a type of chimpanzee which only live in the Congo, but Kanzi has always lived in captivity. He's been 'talking' to humans since he was a baby. He's learned to use more than 360 keyboard symbols and he understands thousands of spoken words. He's been playing the piano for us this morning. He's pretty good at it – he's even played with Paul McCartney! And finally, meet Betsy, who has been busy today too. She's been running around, collecting objects for researchers. Betsy is so clever that she understands pictures as well as spoken words. So, when you show her a photo of a ball, she brings you a ball. Do you think she'll recognise herself in this photo?

Edward

Kanzi

Betsy

Reading and listening

1 Look at the photos. Which of the three animals do you think is the most intelligent? Explain your opinion to your partner.

2 Choose the correct verb. Then decide if you think the sentences are true or false.

  1 Sheep can **imagine / remember** faces.
  2 Primates can **think / forget** about answers to problems.
  3 Some dogs **feel / understand** pictures of objects.

3 Read the text quickly. Check your answers to Exercise 2.

4 🔊 2.2 Read and listen to the text. Complete the gaps (1–3) with the headings. There is one extra heading.

Communication   Creativity
Fear   Memory

16

6 Grammar: present perfect continuous

Read the question and examples to the whole class and elicit the answer. Reinforce the structure if the students are unsure (*have / has + been + -ing* form of main verb).

7 Grammar: present perfect continuous

Students do the gap-fill individually, then check with a partner.

Read through the information box about the use of the present perfect continuous with the class. Refer also to *Grammar Explorer*, pages 118–119.

8 Grammar: present perfect continuous and present perfect simple

Students do the matching individually, then check with a partner.

Help **weaker students** to match by eliciting the pronoun which will replace the subject of each sentence (i.e. *Keith Kendrick = He, Scientists = They* and *Betsy = She*).

9 Grammar practice

Students complete the sentences individually using the present perfect continuous, following the patterns in Exercise 7, then check with a partner.

Working with words: abstract nouns

5 Look at the examples. Find five more abstract nouns in the text.

intelligence
memory

See Working with words: Page 101

Grammar: present perfect continuous

6 Look at the examples. Which verbs do we use to make the present perfect continuous?

e.g. Scientists have been investigating these skills in animals.
Keith Kendrick has been testing the memory of sheep like Edward for several years.

7 Complete the table with the words in the box.

've been   has   hasn't been   have
haven't been

Affirmative
He's been testing his memory. We (1) .... studying sheep.
Negative
She (2) .... practising the piano. They (3) .... paying attention.
Questions
(4) .... you been running? (5) .... he been playing the piano?

We use the present perfect continuous to talk about recent or unfinished activities. We use the present perfect simple to talk about the results of recent activities.

See Grammar Explorer: Page 118

8 Match the activities (1–4) with the results (a–d).

1 Keith Kendrick has been testing the memory of sheep.
2 Scientists have been investigating intelligence in animals.
3 Researchers have been showing Betsy photos.
4 I've been thinking about the problem.

a I've decided to ask my teacher.
b He's proved that they can remember faces.
c She's brought them lots of objects.
d They've found out some surprising things!

9 Complete the sentences with the present perfect continuous form of the verbs in the box.

look for   not practise   think about   wait for
watch

1 Look at the time! We .... you since four o'clock.
2 There it is! My mum .... that book for days!
3 'You're brilliant at this!' 'Really? I ....'
4 I'm exhausted! I .... this maths problem for hours.
5 Switch off that TV. You .... it all day!

Speaking

10 Work in pairs. Ask and answer questions about the pictures. Use the verbs in the box.

A: *What has the boy been doing?*
B: *I think he's been eating chocolate.*

dig   drink   eat   hide   play   read   run
study

Verbs like *be, know, believe, like*, etc. do not usually have a continuous form.

11 Complete the questions using the present perfect continuous or simple. Then work in pairs. Ask and answer the questions. Use *for* or *since* in your answers.

1 How long .... (**learn**) English?
2 How long .... (**know**) your best friend?
3 How long .... (**be**) in this class?
4 How long .... (**do**) this exercise?
5 How long .... (**have**) your school bag?

Fast finishers

Write an A–Z of animals. How many letters can you use?

Grammar

10 Speaking practice: present perfect continuous

Look at the instructions and the example with the whole class.
Ask them to work in pairs to write short dialogues giving alternative suggestions for the situations in the pictures. Ask pairs of students to perform the dialogues in a whole-class setting.

11 Verbs not used in continuous forms

Present the grammar box before the students do this exercise; they then decide which form is appropriate.

They then work in pairs to ask and answer the questions, using *for* or *since* in the answers. Revise the use of these first if necessary (*for* + period of time, *since* + point in time).

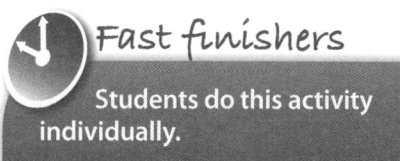

Fast finishers

Students do this activity individually.

35

2B Mind control

Spread aims

Grammar: relative clauses
Vocabulary: personality
Reading and listening for details about phobias

KEY

3 sharks, clowns

4 aren't dangerous; spiders, small spaces, flying; feeling sick; clowns, having a shower, flowers

5 snakes

6 1 He hypnotises people.
2 Because it's interesting to see people change their behaviour.
3 It can change behaviour that causes people problems.

7 a hypnotist; hypnosis; swinging a watch, counting backwards, repeating phrases; phobias e.g. (fear of) flying, snakes

1 Warm-up

Ask the students to look at the three pictures and tell a partner what they feel about them. Then elicit reactions for a whole-class discussion.

2 Pre-listening

Write the word *phobia* on the board and ask students what it means (fear of something). Ask students to discuss their fears in pairs. Elicit comments and encourage students to talk about how fear makes them feel (e.g. sweating, wanting to run away).

3 Listening for gist

 2.3 CD 1 track 14

Students listen and tick the pictures of things which are mentioned.

Tapescript

Hello, and welcome to the best of 'In your mind' series podcasts. Thanks for downloading it and we hope you enjoy it!

What are you afraid of? Sharks? Spiders? And how do you react when you are afraid? Do you want to run away and hide? Well, psychologists, who understand fear and our reactions to it,

say that some fears are quite normal. For example, sharks are large, frightening, dangerous animals which sometimes attack swimmers, so fear is a normal reaction. But some people experience fear, or phobia, of things or situations that aren't dangerous. Most spiders, in Europe anyway, aren't dangerous and can't hurt you. But arachnophobia, which is the name for 'fear of spiders', is a very common phobia. You've probably heard of lots of the more common phobias: as well as fear of spiders there's fear of small spaces – claustrophobia – or fear of flying. Pyschologists say that because small spaces or flying aren't really dangerous, the fear we feel is in our minds. On the other hand, the reactions we show are definitely physical. People who suffer from phobias show the typical physical signs of fear, such as sweating or feeling sick. But can

you imagine feeling sick with fear when the sun shines? That's one of the more unusual phobias. In fact people can be frightened of very unusual things – clowns, having a shower, flowers – the list is very, very long! The good news is that you can train your mind not to be afraid of things, with the help of various therapies.

4 Listening for detail

 2.3 CD 1 track 14

Read through the notes with the whole class so that they know what to listen for.

Weaker students after the second listening give students a copy of the tapescript.

HYPNOSIS
– controlling the mind

It's Friday evening and the Tennant family are at home in front of the TV. The programme is fascinating – they haven't moved for an hour. In fact, they seem to be stuck to the sofa, unable to move! They've been watching Derren Brown. He's the hypnotist whose weekly TV show attracts millions of viewers. In the programme, which is live, Brown has tried to hypnotise the audience so that they can't stand up. It's a huge experiment in mind control.

Hypnotising people through the TV is very unusual, although we've probably all seen hypnosis acts on TV. The hypnotist uses methods like swinging a watch, counting backwards or repeating phrases to make people 'sleep'. Then the hypnotist makes the people, who are usually volunteers, do silly things. People who are shy become sociable. Introverts become extroverts. People imagine they are animals, and so on. These changes in people's behaviour, which are funny and entertaining for the audience, are temporary. The volunteers don't become creative or clever if they weren't like that before. And after the show, they can't remember what they've been doing.

However, lots of people believe that hypnosis can change behaviour and habits which cause them problems. Many people have stopped smoking after hypnosis or have cured phobias, such as the fear of flying or snakes. One man, whose life was changed by hypnosis, even gave up his job and trained as a hypnotist so that he could help other people!

But let's go back to the Tennant family. At the end of Brown's programme, he sends a secret message that 'frees' the viewers who are stuck (or believe they're stuck!) and life in the Tennant home can go back to normal!

Speaking

1 Look at the photos.
Do you think these things are frightening?

2 Work in pairs. What are you afraid of? How do you react when you are afraid? Tell your partner.

Listening

3  2.3 Listen to a podcast about phobias. Tick the photos you hear about.

4  2.3 **STUDY SKILLS** Listen again and make notes on the phobias.

Phobia = fear of things that ....
Common phobias: fear of .... , ... , ...
Physical signs: sweating and ....
Unusual phobias: .... , ...

18

Reading and listening

5 Look at the photos in Exercise 1 again. Then read the text quickly. Are any of the things mentioned in the text?

6  2.4 Read and listen to the text. Answer the questions.

  1 What does Derren Brown do in his TV show?
  2 Why do people find hypnosis acts entertaining?
  3 How can hypnosis help people?

7 **STUDY SKILLS** Read the text and complete the notes. Compare with your partner.

  Derren Brown: a ....
  Derren Brown's TV show: ....
  Methods of hypnosis: .... , ... , ...
  Hypnosis can cure: .... , ... , ...

Working with words: verb + -*ing*

8 Look at the examples. Find five more activities with this form in the text.

  control ➝ controlling
  smoke ➝ smoking

  See Working with words: Page 101

Grammar: relative clauses

9 Look at the examples. Find the relative clause in each sentence. Which relative clause can be omitted from the sentence because it gives extra information?

  1 People who are shy become sociable.
  2 The people, who are usually volunteers, do silly things.

  See Grammar Explorer: Page 119

---

10 Find six more sentences with relative clauses in the text. Find the relative clauses which give extra information.

> We use the relative pronouns *who, which,* and *whose,* and the relative adverbs *when* and *where* in both types of sentence. We only use *that* in sentences which don't give extra information.

11 Look at the example. Then rewrite each pair of sentences, putting the second sentence inside the first. Use the relative pronoun or adverb. Be careful with the position of the commas.

The programme is very popular. It lasts one hour. (which)

e.g. The programme, which lasts one hour, is very popular.

  1 Derren Brown is a hypnotist. He's from London. (who)
  2 Brown's show is fascinating. It's on TV. (which)
  3 Friday night is the best night of the week. We watch Brown's show. (when)
  4 This hypnotist is American. His act is great. (whose)
  5 Los Angeles is a centre for hypnosis therapies. This hypnotist lives in Los Angeles. (where)

12 Work in pairs. Do you agree with the definition? Write more definitions for the words in the box.

People who are creative have a good imagination and can make original things.

clever	creative	extrovert	funny
imaginative	introvert	logical	moody
organised	practical	shy	sociable

Speaking

13 Work in groups. Discuss the questions.

  1 Do you believe hypnosis works?
  2 Have you ever seen a hypnotist?
  3 Would you like to be hypnotised?

Study skills

Making notes

  1 Listen or read for the main points.
  2 Note down key words and additional information.
  3 Use abbreviations, such as: =, &, etc.

Grammar and skills

KEY

8 hypnotising, swinging, counting, repeating, flying

9 who are shy; who are usually volunteers; the clause can be omitted in 2

10 ... hypnotist whose weekly show attracts ...; ... programme, <u>which is live</u>, Brown ... ; ... behaviour, <u>which are funny and entertaining; for the audience,</u> are ... habits which cause them problems; One man, <u>whose life was changed by hypnosis,</u> even ... ; ... viewers, who are stuck (or believe they're stuck!) and ...

11 1 Derren Brown, who is from London, is a hypnotist.
  2 Brown's show, which is on TV, is fascinating.
  3 Friday night, when we watch Brown's show, is the best night of the week.
  4 This hypnotist, whose act is great, is American.
  5 Los Angeles, where this hypnotist lives, is a centre for hypnosis therapies.

10 Identifying relative clauses

Elicit the sentences and write them on the board, then elicit which of the relative clauses give extra information, and underline these. Present the grammar box and elicit which of the sentences on the board could use that ("habits that cause them problems", "viewers that are stuck").

11 Writing relative clauses

Read the instructions and example with the class. Note that in 3 and 5, the subject of the clause is different to that in the main clause, so it needs to be included.

12 Vocabulary: personality

Read the definition, then present words in the box and ask students to write a definition for each one.

13 Discussion: hypnotism

Ask students to discuss the topic in groups, then open to a class discussion.

Study skills: making notes

Present the suggestions in the box.

---

5 Reading for gist

Students now scan the *Hypnosis* text and decide which things are mentioned.

6 Reading and listening for detail

🔘 *2.4 CD 1 track 15*

Read through the three questions with the class so they focus on the information they need.

7 Reading for detail

Check students understand the distinction between the words *hypnotist* (the person), *hypnosis* (the state), *hypnotise* (the verb) before they do this activity.

8 Working with words: verb + -*ing*

Discuss the form with the class and look at *Working with words,* page 101. Check students' answers and note that *fascinating* is an adjective and *they've been watching* is a verb phrase.

Ask **weaker students** to list all the words with an -*ing* ending, and then decide if the word describes an activity, as in the examples.

9 Grammar: relative clauses

Do this exercise with the whole class. Explain that the difference highlighted here is a key difference between the two types of sentence, and point out that commas are used in 2 but not in 1. See also *Grammar Explorer,* pages 119–120.

2C Checking information

Spread aims

Skills: Reading and listening for gist and detail

Functions: checking information

Pronunciation: question tags

Writing a description of people

KEY

1 the script and the slideshow

2 a haven't b hasn't c doesn't want

3 he's surprised.

Don't you want to do it? (she's surprised) Can't I do the slideshow instead? (he expects the listener to agree)

4 We've still got two weeks, haven't we?
Oh, Joe, you haven't forgotten it again, have you?
You're joking, aren't you?
You don't mind, do you?

1 Reading and listening for gist

 2.5 CD 1 track 16

Present the question and encourage students to focus on listening for the two things.

Stronger students cover the text and listen and answer.

Weaker students follow the text as they listen.

2 Reading for detail

Students read the text and find the information to complete the sentences.

Extension: the students read through the dialogue in groups of four, each taking one role; they then change roles and do it again.

3 Grammar: negative questions

Discuss Dan's question with the class and complete the statement. Compare with the usual question form *Is the presentation …?* Students then find two more similar examples in the text. Discuss with the class what Dan's feelings are in this dialogue, and how these feelings are reflected in the questions.

4 Grammar: question tags

Students search the text for other examples. Elicit answers from the class and write them on the board for students to see the language pattern. See also *Grammar Explorer,* page 120. Check that students understand what the speaker means with each question (e.g. *You haven't forgotten it again, have you?* – Fay thinks that Joe <u>has</u> forgotten it and she is right!).

5 Useful expressions: intonation

 2.6 CD 1 track 17

Students listen and repeat chorally and individually. Draw particular attention to the rise and fall on the question tags.

6 Grammar: question tags

 2.7 CD 1 track 18

Students complete the sentences, then check by listening to the recording.

7 Pronunciation: intonation in question tags

 2.7 CD 1 track 18

Students listen and repeat chorally and individually.

8 Speaking: question tags

Ask the students to complete the sentences with the correct question tags. They should then work in pairs and take it in turns to ask the questions, which their partner

---

2C Checking information

Reading and listening

1 *2.5* **Dan, Fay and Joe are at Holly's house. Read and listen to the dialogue. What two things do they need for their presentation?**

2 **Read the dialogue again. Choose the correct option.**

1 They **have / haven't** got two weeks to prepare.

2 Joe **has / hasn't** brought the script.

3 Dan **wants / doesn't want** to do the introduction.

3 **Choose the correct option. Then find two more questions with this form. Match each question with one of the options.**

Dan asks 'Isn't the presentation on the 18th?' because **he's surprised / he expects the listener to agree**.

4 **We also use tags to check information. Look at the example and find four similar questions in the dialogue.**

He's lovely, isn't he?

See Grammar Explorer: Page 120

5 *2.6* **Listen and repeat the *Useful expressions*. Focus on your intonation.**

USEFUL EXPRESSIONS

He's lovely, isn't he?
We've still got two weeks, haven't we?
You haven't forgotten it again, have you?
You're joking, aren't you?
You don't mind, do you?

20

Holly:	Sorry I'm late. Have you been waiting long?
Fay:	That's OK. We've been playing with your dog. He's really smart!
Holly:	I know. He's lovely, isn't he?
Fay:	Yes, he is. OK, shall we start? We haven't got much time.
Dan:	We've still got two weeks, haven't we?
Fay:	No, we haven't.
Dan:	Isn't the presentation on the 18th?
Fay:	No, it's on the eighth. And today's the second! Joe, have you brought the script?
Joe:	Oh … erm …
Fay:	Oh, Joe, you haven't forgotten it again, have you?
Joe:	Sorry, I've got a really bad memory.
Holly:	It's OK, I've got a copy on my memory stick. And I've got the slideshow on there too. Here you are.
Joe:	Oh, Holly, you're very organised, as usual!
Holly:	Well, my mum reminded me! Have you been practising the introduction, Dan?
Dan:	Oh dear, not really, no.
Holly:	Don't you want to do it?
Dan:	I'm not sure. I think I've got a public speaking phobia!
Joe:	You're joking, aren't you? You're not usually shy!
Dan:	Can't I do the slideshow instead? You don't mind, do you?
Joe:	Hey, no problem! I'll do the introduction.

6 🔊 2.7 **Read and complete Holly's questions on the day of the presentation. Choose the correct option (a–b). Then listen and check your answers.**

1 You've got your memory stick, ... ?
   a have you   b haven't you
2 The slide show is ready, ... ?
   a is it   b isn't it
3 You know what to say, ... ?
   a do you   b don't you
4 Dan's here, ... ?
   a is he   b isn't he
5 You're not nervous, ... ?
   a are you   b aren't you

Pronunciation: question tag intonation

7 🔊 2.7 **Listen again to the questions from Exercise 6. Which question tag does not have falling intonation? Repeat the questions.**

1 You've got your memory stick, haven't you?

> We use a falling intonation when we expect the person to agree.

Writing: a description of people

1 **Read Dan's description of his family. Find the adjectives he uses to describe them.**

2 **Read the extra information. Match the relative clauses (a–e) with the places in the text (1–5).**
   a when we are all at home
   b where she spends all her time
   c which we aren't allowed to see
   d who lives with us
   e whose name is Anna

3 **Complete the sentences with the correct relative pronoun.**
   1 My mum, ... is scared of cats, wants to get a dog.
   2 My best friend, ... desk is next to mine, is called Ali.
   3 On Fridays, ... we all meet, we go to the cinema.
   4 My room, ... I do my homework, is quite messy.
   5 My friend's jokes, ... I've heard before, aren't funny.

Speaking

8 **Look at the example. Complete the questions. Then ask and answer the questions with your partner. Give true answers.**
   e.g. It's Sunday today, _isn't it_?
   A: *It's Sunday today, isn't it?*
   B: *No, it isn't.*

   1 It isn't cold today, ... ?
   2 You're not fifteen, ... ?
   3 We haven't got maths today, ... ?
   4 You're good at English, ... ?
   5 You don't speak Italian, ... ?

9 **How well do you know your partner? Choose one of the options and complete each question. Then ask and answer the questions.**
   1 You **like / don't like** football, ... you?
   2 You**'ve got / haven't got** relatives in the USA, ... you?
   3 You **can / can't** swim 500 metres, ... you?
   4 You**'re / aren't** scared of snakes, ... you?
   5 You**'ve been / haven't been** to London, ... you?

4 **Choose a group of people you know well. Make notes about each person. Then write a short text describing the people.**

Name	Personality	Example	Extra information
my grandma	really bossy	likes giving orders	lives with us

My family

Everybody in my family has a strong personality, but we all get on well together. My grandma (1) , ... , is really bossy. She likes giving us all orders.
My parents are quite similar to each other. They're both practical and good at fixing things. And they both think they are always right!
My sister (2) , ... , can be a bit moody. Communication is not her strong point! She likes painting and her bedroom (3) , ... , is full of her work. She's been working on her latest picture (4) , ... , for about a week. My brother loves jokes and funny stories. In the evenings (5) , ... , he talks all the time. He likes telling jokes that he gets off the Internet. He's a lot more entertaining than the TV!
All in all, we're a happy family – most of the time!

Communicate

2 Relative clauses

Students match the clauses to the gaps.

Remind **weaker students** that the relative pronoun or relative adverb in each clause gives a useful clue: *who* refers to a person, *where* to a place, *when* to a time, *which* to a thing, *whose* to something belonging to a person.

3 Relative pronouns and relative adverbs

Students complete the sentences.

4 Personalised writing

Read through the instructions and the table with the class. You could exemplify the task by talking about a character everyone knows on TV or in a film, and completing a table on the board together. Students can also use the adjectives in the vocabulary box in Exercise 12, page 19.

Weaker students could concentrate on just one or two people they know well.

should answer truthfully. They can then ask / answer the questions with a different partner. Emphasise the importance of the correct intonation.

Extension: students rewrite the sentences, replacing positive verbs with negative and vice versa. Discuss the difference in meaning between the two sentences in each pair.

9 Personalised speaking practice

Read the instructions with the class and make sure that they understand that they should phrase the question according to the answer they expect their partner to give. Remind them that a negative question should have a positive tag, and a positive question should have a negative tag.

Weaker students can write down the questions and the answers.

Writing: a description of people

1 Identifying adjectives

Ask for some examples of adjectives from students before they do this exercise. When students have underlined the adjectives, elicit answers from the class and write a full list on the board. Check students understand the meanings.

Follow-up: ask students to list the quantifiers (*really* etc.) used with the adjectives, then review these with the whole class.

2D Irish traditions

Spread aims

Vocabulary: folklore-related words

Skills: reading and listening for detail

Culture: Irish traditions

CLIL: Biology and English: animals and people

KEY

1   a a lament   b nocturnal
    c –   d folklore   e a fairy

2   1 black cats, opening umbrellas indoors, putting shoes on the table
    2 a horseshoe on the front door, a rabbit's foot, a four-leaf shamrock
    3 they live all over Ireland, you shouldn't offend them, they're invisible
    3 leprechaun, banshee, merrow, pooka

3   1 leprechaun   2 banshee
    3 pooka

4   they: many people   one: a four-leaf shamrock
    them: fairies   us: humans
    him: a leprechaun   Both: the merrow and the banshee
    This: that it can appear in different forms   there: Ireland

1 Vocabulary: defining words

Students should first find the words the text and try to guess the meaning from the context. If they find it difficult, they could use a dictionary.

Tell weaker students that *c* is the extra definition.

Follow-up: ask them to find a word for which *c* is the definition (*invisible*); then ask them to choose three other words in the text and write definitions of them for others to match.

2 Reading and listening for detail

 *2.8 CD 1 track 19*

Read through the groups of things they have to find and ensure that they understand what they are.

Stronger students cover the text and listen and answer.

Weaker students follow the text as they listen.

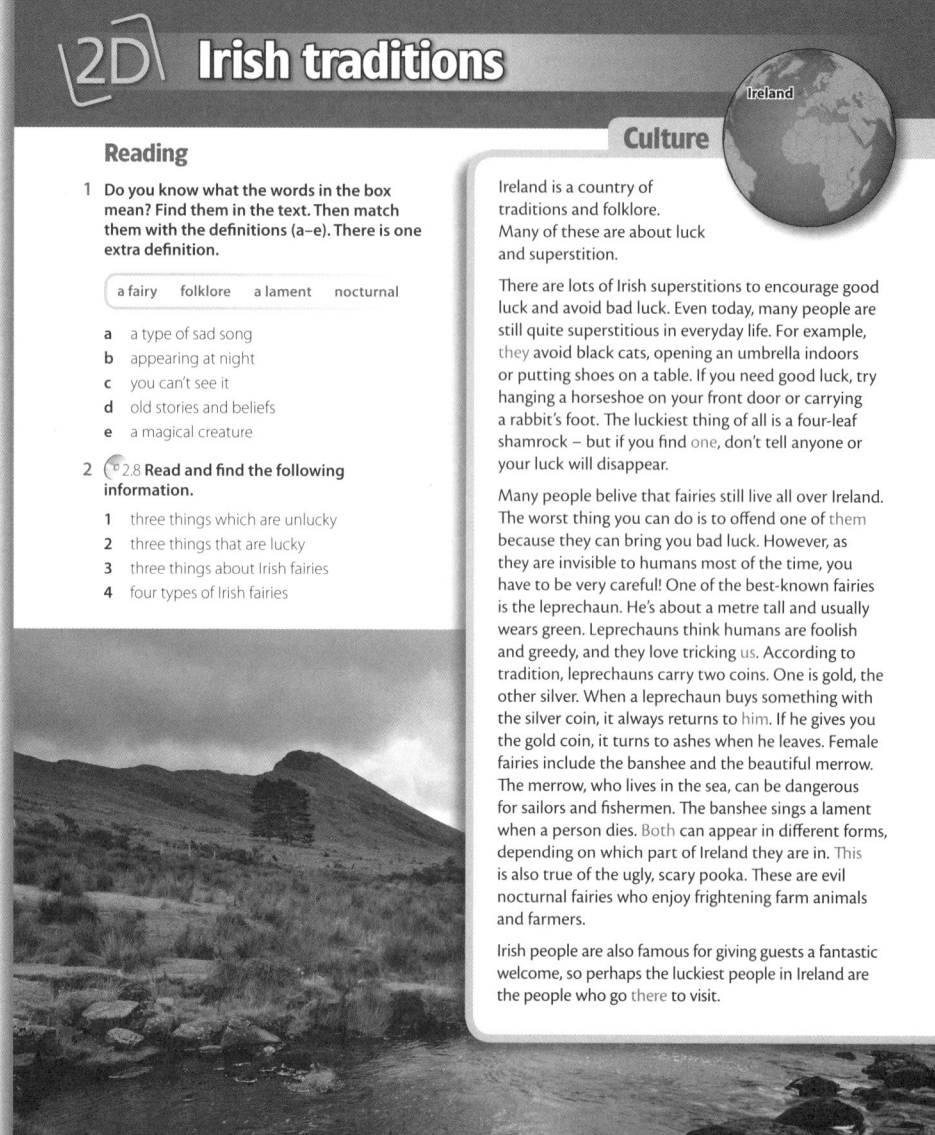

2D Irish traditions

Reading

1 **Do you know what the words in the box mean? Find them in the text. Then match them with the definitions (a–e). There is one extra definition.**

> a fairy   folklore   a lament   nocturnal

   a   a type of sad song
   b   appearing at night
   c   you can't see it
   d   old stories and beliefs
   e   a magical creature

2 *2.8* **Read and find the following information.**

   1   three things which are unlucky
   2   three things that are lucky
   3   three things about Irish fairies
   4   four types of Irish fairies

Culture

Ireland is a country of traditions and folklore. Many of these are about luck and superstition.

There are lots of Irish superstitions to encourage good luck and avoid bad luck. Even today, many people are still quite superstitious in everyday life. For example, they avoid black cats, opening an umbrella indoors or putting shoes on a table. If you need good luck, try hanging a horseshoe on your front door or carrying a rabbit's foot. The luckiest thing of all is a four-leaf shamrock – but if you find one, don't tell anyone or your luck will disappear.

Many people belive that fairies still live all over Ireland. The worst thing you can do is to offend one of them because they can bring you bad luck. However, as they are invisible to humans most of the time, you have to be very careful! One of the best-known fairies is the leprechaun. He's about a metre tall and usually wears green. Leprechauns think humans are foolish and greedy, and they love tricking us. According to tradition, leprechauns carry two coins. One is gold, the other silver. When a leprechaun buys something with the silver coin, it always returns to him. If he gives you the gold coin, it turns to ashes when he leaves. Female fairies include the banshee and the beautiful merrow. The merrow, who lives in the sea, can be dangerous for sailors and fishermen. The banshee sings a lament when a person dies. Both can appear in different forms, depending on which part of Ireland they are in. This is also true of the ugly, scary pooka. These are evil nocturnal fairies who enjoy frightening farm animals and farmers.

Irish people are also famous for giving guests a fantastic welcome, so perhaps the luckiest people in Ireland are the people who go there to visit.

Suggest **weaker students** first find and underline the information in the text, then write the answers.

3 Reading for information

Present the statements and make sure students realise that this information is not given in the text, so they will need to find other clues to match the statements to the fairies.

Tell **weaker students** the information is in paragraph 3.

4 Pronouns

As a practical example, look at the word *these* in the second sentence of the first paragraph. Ask students what it refers to (*traditions and folklore*). Ask

students to do the same thing with the words in red.

5 Speaking: beliefs and legends

Elicit one or two examples from the whole class before setting the students in pairs to think of their own lists. Elicit suggestions and note these on the board for further whole-class discussion.

6 Speaking: personal beliefs

Make sure the students know what all the items listed are before they discuss them; stress that they should give reasons. Elicit ideas and start a whole-class discussion.

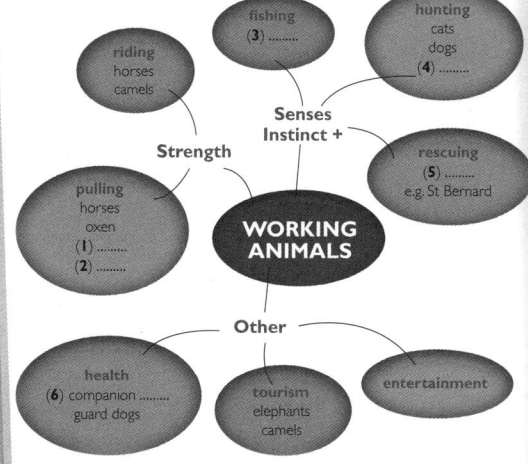

3 Read the statements (1–3) and match each one with a type of fairy mentioned in the text.

1 They are always male, never female.

2 Their song can be beautiful or like an animal noise.

3 They stop hens from laying eggs.

4 Look at the words in red in the text. What or who do they refer to?

5 Work in pairs. Are there any similar beliefs and legends in your country? Tell your partner.

Listening

6 Work in pairs. Do you believe in these things? Or are you not sure? Explain your answers.

1 ghosts and haunted houses
2 witches
3 UFOs
4 astrology
5 predicting the future
6 spiritual healing

7 2.9 A survey asked American people about the things in Exercise 6. Listen and write the numbers (per cent) of people who believe in each thing.

1 ....
2 ....
3 ....
4 ....
5 ....
6 ....

8 2.9 Listen again. Is the number of people who aren't sure about each thing bigger or smaller?

1 ....
2 ....
3 ....
4 ....
5 ....
6 ....

Project

Work in groups. Research a story on one of the topics in Exercise 6. Prepare a presentation for the class.

Biology and English
Animals and people

1 Look at the mind map. What information do you think goes in the gaps?

- riding — horses, camels
- fishing (3) ....
- hunting — cats, dogs (4) ....
- Senses — Instinct +
- Strength
- rescuing (5) .... e.g. St Bernard
- pulling — horses, oxen (1) .... (2) ....
- **WORKING ANIMALS**
- Other
- health (6) companion .... guard dogs
- tourism — elephants, camels
- entertainment

2 Read the text and complete the mind map.

Throughout history, humans have had close associations with certain animals. The ancient Egyptians even believed that cats were gods. People have used animals to help them with work, using their strength and their highly developed senses for different purposes. Horses and oxen can pull heavy farm machinery, for example, while huskies and reindeer can pull sleds across snowy ground.

Some animals have instincts that humans can exploit for hunting other animals and food. In China birds called cormorants catch fish for their human owners, and pigs are very good at finding truffles (a special kind of mushroom) in the ground. Dogs have a fantastic sense of smell and they are better than machines at finding people who are trapped under avalanches or by earthquakes. They are just as good at sniffing out drugs and finding criminals too.

Sometimes animals can work for us as well as with us. Doctors say that our stress levels go down and that we become happier and healthier when we have a pet for company. Companion dogs are dogs which visit elderly people, patients in hospital and even people in prison. We also enjoy animals as entertainment, as the success of movies like *Free Willy* and *Babe* show!

3 Work in pairs. Add at least three more animals to the mind map in Exercise 1.

Culture

spiritual healing. More than half – 56% of people – think that religious belief can cure physical illnesses. And quarter of those who were interviewed aren't sure what they think. This number hasn't changed over the last ten years.

8 Listening for detail

 2.9 CD 1 track 20

Students note the figures and compare with those for Exercise 7. Discuss which figures students find surprising.

Project: beliefs and legends

Ask students to work in pairs or threes. They should choose one of the topics in Exercise 6 and use the Internet and books to research just one story, which they should be able to present to the class, either as a poster, a Powerpoint presentation, or as a talk. Encourage them to use illustrations, where possible.

All students in the group should take part in the presentation.

Biology and English: animals and people

1 Reading for gist

Ask the whole class to look and try to predict what the answers might be.

2 Reading for detail

Students read the text and complete the mind map.

3 Writing: adding details

Students discuss what animals they could add to the mind map.

7 Listening for detail

 2.9 CD 1 track 20

Students write the percentage of people who believe in each numbered item from Exercise 6.

Tapescript

Researchers at an American university have been investigating fairies, ghosts, witches and other similar things. Actually, they've been asking people if they believe in these things or not. Over the last few years there have been several surveys on this topic and the results have been quite consistent. It seems that people don't change their minds very much about these things, in the United States at least.

The recent survey found that 39% of Americans believe in ghosts and haunted houses, and about 29% are not sure.

That's about the same as the number who believe in witches, although there is no specific information about good witches or bad witches. Another question was about UFOs – unidentified flying objects – and aliens. You may be surprised to find out that 17% of people think aliens have already visited Earth at some time in the past and 34% are not sure. Staying with the subject of space and the stars, the same number of people also believe in astrology – about 17%, and again about 30% say they aren't sure. Now, there are two aspects to astrology. The first is about your personality and how it is affected by the date of your birth. The second is about the future, and if it's possible to predict your future using astrology. Interestingly, more people – about 24% – believe that it's possible to predict the future, with about 33% saying they're not sure. The most widely-held belief of all was in

2E Consolidation Units 1 and 2

Spread aims

Reading and **listening:** practising receptive skills

Grammar: consolidating understanding of the key grammar points from Units 1 and 2

KEY

Reading

1 1 good, bad, some kinds, common, typical
2 interpretations, mean, meanings

2 1 c   2 b

3 1 b   2 c

Listening

3 C

Reading

1 Identifying key words

Present the reading strategies and discuss them with the class. Ask students to underline the words which express the main ideas in the two paragraphs.

2 Matching

Students read and match individually, then check with a partner.

Suggest **weaker students** underline the key words in the headings that help to identify the difference in meaning.

3 Reading for gist

Students use the same strategy to complete the task.

Listening

1 Predicting key words

Present the listening strategies and discuss them with the class. Students list vocabulary individually for each of the three pictures. Suggest they do it in three columns.

2 Predicting key words

Students can do this activity in pairs, first sharing their words from the previous exercise. Make a table of

three columns on the board, eliciting the three animals' names for the headings (a Tiger, b Leopard, c Cat). Then elicit words which are the same for each picture (e.g. *food, eating, cat/ big cat*) and then words which help to separate them (e.g. picture a: *zoo, cage, keeper/hand, meat*; picture b: *wild, carrying, dead, animal*; picture c: *bowl, cat food, inside*).

3 Listening for information

 2.10 CD 1 track 21

Students listen and answer the question. Play the recording at least twice.

Reading

Identifying the main ideas of sections of a text
• Read the whole text quickly before you look at the headings and identify the main idea in each section.
• If the headings are questions, predict the kind of information that answers the question. Then look for this information in the text.
• **Important!** If there is an extra heading, make sure it doesn't match any of the sections.

1 Find the words that help you decide on the main idea of these sections of a text.

> 1 There are both 'good' dreams and 'bad' dreams (nightmares). Some kinds of dream are quite common. Typical dreams can be about flying, water or trees. Some are in colour and others are in black and white.
>
> 2 There are different interpretations of dreams. A bad dream can mean something good – that you will be lucky or happy. Some people don't believe that dreams have meanings.

2 Match the correct heading (a–c) with each section (1–2) in Exercise 1. There is one extra heading.

a my dreams   c types of dream
b the meaning of dreams

3 Read part of a text about 'memory' and match the correct heading (a–c) with each section (1–2).

> 1 Yes. Eating 'brain food' which has lots of vitamins is one way. Protein is also good for your memory. But the best way is to use your brain more.
>
> 2 This is our ability to remember things that happened very recently, for example a few minutes ago. The brain stores this new information in a special way.

a Why have I got a bad memory?
b Can I improve my memory?
c What is short-term memory?

24

Listening

Identifying detailed information
• Read the task and the options before listening.
• For text options, think about the pronunciation of each option.
• For picture options, think about what distinguishes each option.
• **Important!** Don't try to understand everything. Listen only for the answers to the questions.

1 Look at the pictures below and write as many words as you can for each one.

2 Choose the words in your list that show the differences between the pictures. Add more words which show the differences to your list.

3 2.10 **Listen to the conversation. Which animal are they talking about?**

Tapescript

Holly: It's amazing, watching them eat, isn't it?

Fay: I know. And they are such good hunters. They are really intelligent animals.

Holly: Did you know that lions only eat about once a week in the wild?

Fay: Ha! I have to feed Fluffy every day. She's always hungry.

Holly: What kind of food does she like best?

Fay: Fish, of course, especially salmon. That's what she's eating now. Have you finished, Fluffy?

Holly: Do you talk to your cat a lot?

Fay: Yes, of course I do. Everyone talks to their pets, don't they?

Adverbs of frequency

> Adverbs of frequency go before the main verb, except when the verb is *be*.
> She always wears black.
> She's never worn brown.
> Her clothes are never colourful.

1 Mark the correct position of the adverbs.

1 I don't do my homework with my friends. (usually)
2 I'm shy when I meet new people. (sometimes)
3 We watch TV in the morning. (never)
4 My dad is funny at parties. (always)

both, all

> *All* and *both* go before the main verb, except when the verb is *be*. They can also go before the subject of the verb.

2 Mark the two possible positions of *all* and *both*.

1 My parents are vegetarians. (both)
2 My brother and I can play the piano. (both)
3 My friends like sport. (all)
4 This summer my cousins and I are going camping. (all)

Adverbs of place and time

> Adverbs of time usually go after adverbs of place.
> I'm going to bed early.

3 Complete the sentences with the information in the box. Use two pieces of information in each sentence. How many sentences can you make?

before lunchtime   for ages   home
last summer   late   to school
to Scotland   to the cinema

1 Did you go .... ?
2 I don't want to get ....
3 We haven't been ....
4 Please be ....

enough

> *Enough* goes after adjectives and before nouns.

4 Mark the correct position of *enough*.

1 You aren't strong to lift that box.
2 My class is good to win the competition.
3 Are there people to play football?
4 We don't have time to prepare well.

Phrasal verbs

> Some phrasal verbs have an object. We can put the object in two positions when it is a noun. The object pronoun only has one possible position.
> She tried on the shoes.
> She tried the shoes on.
> She tried them on.

5 For each sentence, write two more sentences with the same meaning. Use a pronoun in one of the sentences.

1 I switched on the TV.
2 I found out the answers.
3 I picked the bags up.
4 I turned the computer off.

Questions

> Be careful with word order in negative questions, indirect questions and questions with prepositions.

Why isn't everyone here?   Do you know where they are?
What are you looking at?

6 Look at the examples above and do the tasks.

1 Your friend doesn't want to come to a party. Ask him why not.
2 Rewrite the question: When does the film start? Do you know .... ?
3 Write a question for this answer. I'm thinking about my lunch.

CONSOLIDATION **UNITS 1 AND 2** 25

KEY

Grammar

1
1 don't usually do
2 I'm sometimes shy
3 We never watch
4 is always funny

2
1 Both my / are both   2 Both my / can both   3 All my friends / My friends all
4 summer all my / are all going

3
(possible answers)
1 home before lunchtime / to Scotland last summer?
2 home late / to the cinema late / to school late.
3 to Scotland for ages / home for ages / late for ages / to the cinema for ages.
4 home before lunchtime.

4
1 strong enough   2 good enough   3 enough people
4 enough time

5
1 I switched the TV on. / I switched it on.
2 I found the answers out. / I found them out.
3 I picked up the bags. / I picked them up
4 I turned off the computer. / I turned it off.

6
1 Why don't you want to come to the party?
2 ... when the film starts?
3 What are you thinking about?

Grammar

1 Adverbs of frequency

Present the grammar summary, and then ask students to mark where the adverb of frequency should go.

2 *Both, all*

Present the grammar summary, and then ask students to mark the possible positions of the word in brackets.

3 Adverbs of place and time

Present the grammar summary, and then ask students to complete the question in number one. Elicit as many options as students can think of and write them on the board. Students then do the same with 2–4.

4 *Enough*

Present the grammar summary, and then ask students to mark where *enough* should go.

Tell **weaker students** to look carefully at each sentence and decide whether the missing 'enough' relates to an adjective (1, 2 and 4) or a noun (3 and 5). They then mark the position after the adjective or before the noun.

5 Phrasal verbs

Present the grammar summary, and then ask students to rewrite each sentence in the exercise in two different ways, as in the examples in the grammar summary.

6 Questions

Present the grammar summary, and then ask students to write the questions.

Review Units 1 and 2

Spread aims

Reviewing vocabulary, grammar and functions from Units 1 and 2; giving students the opportunity to assess their own progress

KEY

1
1 channels 2 journalist
3 article 4 headline
5 audience

2
1 actor / actress 2 rehearsal
3 presenter 4 episode
5 judge

3
1 shy 2 funny 3 creative
4 intelligent / imaginative
5 clever

4
1 feel 2 understand 3 think
4 remember 5 imagine

5
1 at 2 to 3 club 4 truth
5 telling

6
1 is doing 2 is trying
3 smokes 4 goes 5 takes

7
1 wants 2 said / has said
3 is filming 4 have been
5 haven't done

8
1 book yet? 2 I'm still
reading 3 it yet 4 have
already started 5 I still
haven't

9
1 have been working
2 Have you been eating
3 hasn't been feeling
4 have you been waiting
5 haven't been watching

10
1 whose 2 which 3 who
4 when 5 where

Introduction

There is a review section after every two units of this course, designed to assess student progress and check understanding of what they learnt in the preceding units.

Total marks add up to 100 so student achievement can easily be measured. Students can also be graded, if you wish, so they can compare their achievements with the rest of the class.

Review Units 1 and 2

Vocabulary

1 Complete the sentences.

1 There are lots of c............ on satellite TV.
2 My mum's a j............ with the local paper.
3 I've read an a............ about hypnosis.
4 The h............ gives us the most important news.
5 *X Factor* got the biggest a............ last night.

1 mark per item: …/5 marks

2 Write the words.

1 He/She appears in films.   a............
2 A practice performance.   r............
3 He/She introduces TV shows.   p............
4 One programme in a series.   e............
5 He/She chooses the winner.   j............

1 mark per item: …/5 marks

3 Complete the sentences with adjectives.

1 I don't like meeting people. I'm s............ .
2 He makes me laugh. He's f............ .
3 She makes beautiful things. She's c............ .
4 She writes amazing stories. She's i............ .
5 He always passes exams. He's c............ .

1 mark per item: …/5 marks

4 Complete the sentences with verbs.

1 Can fish f............ pain?
2 Do you u............ Chinese?
3 Can animals t............ about the future?
4 Can you r............ being a baby?
5 I can't i............ how big space is.

1 mark per item: …/5 marks

5 Complete the sentences.

1 Why are you staring............ me?
2 Come and talk............ us.
3 Are you a member of *Take That*'s fan............ ?
4 Don't lie. Tell me the............ .
5 My dad's good at............ jokes.

1 mark per item: …/5 marks

Grammar

6 Complete the paragraph with the present simple or present continuous.

My dad (1)............ (**do**) a course of hypnosis. He (2)............ (**try**) to give up smoking because he (3)............ (**smoke**) too much. He (4)............ (**go**) to the hypnotist every day. Each session (5)............ (**take**) half an hour.

1 mark per item: …/5 marks

7 Complete the paragraph with the present simple, present continuous or present perfect.

A TV station (1)............ (**want**) to film our school and the head teacher (2)............ (**say**) 'yes'! The cameraman (3)............ (**film**) now. It's the first time we (4)............ (**be**) in front of a camera. We (5)............ (**not / do**) any lessons for days!

1 mark per item: …/5 marks

8 Mark the correct position of the words.

1 Have you finished that book? (**yet**)
2 No, I'm reading it. (**still**)
3 I haven't finished it. (**yet**)
4 The judges have started voting. (**already**)
5 I haven't seen Matt Damon's latest film. (**still**)

1 mark per item: …/5 marks

9 Write the present perfect continuous.

1 I'm tired. I............ all day. (**work**)
2 .... you............ my cake? (**eat**)
3 My dad............ well. (**not / feel**)
4 How long............ you............ ? (**wait**)
5 I............ TV very much recently. (**not / watch**)

1 mark per item: …/5 marks

10 Complete the sentences with *when, where, which, who* or *whose*.

1 The hypnotist,............ new show is great, is world-famous.
2 *Invictus*,............ stars Morgan Freeman, is about South Africa.
3 Matt Damon,............ is American, is in the film.
4 February,............ the Oscars are announced, is an exciting month.
5 Los Angeles,............ the ceremony is held, is in California.

1 mark per item: …/5 marks

26

Communicate

11 Match the statements and questions (1–5) with the responses (a–e).

1 What do you think of Dale Smith?
2 Do you like *Take That*?
3 Leona Lewis is amazing.
4 Why do you say that?
5 It's hard to explain what I think about hypnosis.

a Because they write good songs.
b He seems a bit arrogant to me.
c I know what you mean.
d Do you think so?
e Yes, I think they're great.

2 marks per item: .../10 marks

12 Complete the questions with question tags.

1 You can speak French, ... ?

2 It's not a holiday today, ... ?

3 We've got an exam tomorrow, ... ?

4 You like maths, ... ?

5 You're sixteen, ... ?

2 marks per item: .../10 marks

13 Do the words sound the same (S) as or different (D) from *bought*?

1 thought ....
2 laughed ....
3 caught ....
4 taught ....
5 coughed ....

2 marks per item: .../10 marks

14 Complete the sentences with *because* or *because of*.

1 I enjoy reality TV .... the people.
2 Kanzi was famous .... his skills.
3 I get this magazine .... I like animals.
4 Derren Brown is popular .... his TV shows.
5 I sometimes watch TV .... I'm bored.

2 marks per item: .../10 marks

15 Complete the review with these words.

a	at	for	have	on	the
their	to	which	who		

Magic Animals is a new TV series. It's
(1) .... Channel Six on Wednesdays
(2) .... 7 p.m. **(3)** .... first episode,
(4) .... was on last night, was about dolphins.
Apparently, dolphins can talk **(5)** .... each other
in their own language. Scientists **(6)** .... been
trying to understand this language **(7)** ....
years. They explained **(8)** .... findings on this
programme. In my view, this is **(9)** .... great
series for anyone **(10)** .... likes animals.

1 mark per item: .../10 marks

Total: .../100

I can...

I can give my opinion and explain it.
I can react to someone else's opinion.
I can use question tags to check information..

KEY

11 1 b   2 e   3 d   4 a   5 c

12 1 can't you   2 is it   3 haven't we   4 don't you   5 aren't you

13 1 S   2 D   3 S   4 S   5 D

14 1 because of   2 because of   3 because   4 because of   5 because

15 1 on   2 at   3 The   4 which   5 to   6 have   7 for   8 their   9 a   10 who

Project: Personality test

Page aim

Reading for detail **Writing** a personality test

Warm-up

With books shut, ask students what they know about human personality; elicit some personality traits (e.g. friendly, shy, aggressive) and list them on the board. Ask students to tell their partner what kind of personality they think they themselves have and why; the partner should see if they agree. Elicit some ideas from individuals who don't mind discussing their personality in front of the whole class.

1 Reading for detail

Students read the text and answer the questions individually; then they can check with a partner. Elicit the answers from the whole class.

Extension: practise saying the five OCEAN words, taking care with the syllable stress (**o**penness, consci**en**tiousness, extro**ver**sion, a**gree**ableness, neur**ot**icism). Then make sure students are familiar with the meanings.

2 Reading and answering

Students read the five sentences individually and keep a record of their *yes/no* answers.

Personality test

1 Read the information and answer the questions.

1 Why do people take a personality test?
2 How do you take a test?
3 What do you have to remember when taking a test?
4 Why is this type of testing called OCEAN?

There are many different reasons for using personality tests. These can include helping people with problems, finding out whether people are suitable for a job, or choosing the right kind of education for a child. Many researchers today use testing based on what they call the *Big Five*, also known as the *Five Factor Model* (FFM) or *OCEAN* (see box). By asking a series of questions, testers believe that they can identify what kind of person you are. For the person taking the test, however, it is important to understand that you must be honest when you answer the questions. There are no right or wrong answers, so do not choose an answer because you imagine it is the best thing to say. Depending on your answers, the tester can tell certain things about you, like whether you are more introverted or extroverted, or whether you are a logical and practical person.

The letters in the word OCEAN refer to the following characteristics:

Openness – describing people who are creative, adventurous and have a lot of imagination, and who like art and are open to new ideas and adventure

Conscientiousness – describing people who are organized and like to plan and achieve things

Extroversion – describing people who have a lot of energy and positive emotions, and enjoy the company of other people

Agreeableness – describing people who are friendly and work well with others

Neuroticism – describing people who easily feel sad or afraid, or have negative emotions such as anger

2 Now try a test for yourself. Answer *Yes* or *No* to each question. Remember to be honest with your answers.

1 You have been planning a day out. Is it likely to be somewhere you've never been before?
2 You have been working on a project all day. You're tired but you want to get it finished.
3 There is a new boy or girl at school. Are you probably the first person to speak to him or her?
4 Do you like working on exercises and projects with your classmates?
5 You have been waiting for five minutes and your friend hasn't arrived. Are you angry?

3 What do you think your answers say about you? Look at the list below and choose the correct word or phrase.

If you answered:
No to question 1, you are probably **adventurous / not very adventurous**.
Yes to question 2, you **are probably / are probably not** very conscientious.
No to question 3, being friendly **is / is not** very important to you.
Yes to question 4, you are probably quite **agreeable / difficult**.
No to question 5, you probably **show / don't show** negative emotions.

Project

Write your own personality test and ask your friends to do it

- Choose questions similar to those above.
- You can ask about anything you like but try to keep the questions related to the characteristics in the OCEAN list.
- Ask your questions (you can do this by telephone or email if the person lives far away).
- Decide what you think the answers say about that person. You could say whether the answers suggest that the person is shy or sociable, organised, practical, imaginative, etc.
- Ask the other person if he or she agrees with you and discuss how well the test worked.

---

3 Reading for detail

Students first work out which word/phrase is the correct answer for each sentence. Elicit the answers from the whole class, and make sure everybody has them. Then ask students to check their own answers to the personality test against the sentences.

Discussion: students tell a partner what they found out about themselves, and discuss whether they agree or not.

Project

Present the instructions in the Project box and make sure all students know

what to do. Decide if you want them to do it individually or in pairs, or let them choose how they work. When students have written their tests, allow them time to 'test' their classmates in class, and/or encourage them to ask friends, family etc. outside the class. Once they have the results, they can discuss them with the individuals concerned. It would be interesting to compare their results for an individual with (a) the test in Exercise 2, and (b) with the results of somebody else's test – were they the same? why/why not?

In the past

> **Grammar**

Learn about the past perfect, and *used to.*

> **Vocabulary**

Learn words connected with time and archaeology, and for cooking. Work with verb + *to* + infinitive, and American English.

> **Skills**

Read about an amazing find, memories of the past, and American food.

Listen to recipe instructions and two meal-time conversations.

Write a recommendation.

> **Communicate**

Talk about quantity, time, distance, etc.

1 ◎ 3.1 **Listen to the information about Stonehenge and make notes. Then compare your notes with your partner.**

Location?   Age?   Purpose?

2 **Put the words in the vocabulary box in order, from the shortest (1) to the longest (11) period of time.**

century	fortnight	minute	week
day	hour	month	year
decade	millennium	second	

3 **Find words in the vocabulary box for these periods of time.**

four weeks   sixty seconds
a thousand years   fourteen days

4 **Work in pairs. How many things can you remember that you did or that happened at these times?**

an hour ago   in the last decade
last weekend   during the Roman Empire
a year ago   before the last Ice Age

In the past

Unit aims

Grammar: past perfect; *used to*

Vocabulary: time, archaeology, cooking; verb + *to* + infinitive; American English

Functions: talking about quantity, time, distance

Reading about: an amazing find; memories of the past; American food

Listening to: recipe instructions; meal-time conversations

Writing a recommendation

KEY

1 Location: near the River Avon in southwest England
Age: 4,500/5,000 years   Purpose: unknown, possibly a cemetery or temple

2 second, minute, hour, day, week, fortnight, month, year, decade, century, millennium

3 four weeks – month
sixty seconds – minute
a thousand years – millennium
fourteen days – fortnight

only guess. Archaeologists recently started a new study of the stones...

2 Vocabulary: time words

Students read through the words in the list and order them.

Tell **weaker students** that second is first and millennium is last.

3 Vocabulary: matching time words

Students match the words with the periods of time in the list in Exercise 2.

Extension: students think of more time periods to match with words in the list in Exercise 2.

4 Speaking: talking about the past

Students discuss the question in pairs. Elicit answers from the whole class.

Warm-up

Ask the students to look at the picture and say what they know, e.g. what the place is called, where it is, what it is and what it was for. Elicit ideas and list them on the board for comparison after the listening activity.

1 Listening for detail

 3.1 CD 1 track 22

Check that students understand the three headings given. Play the recording and ask students to make notes under the headings, and then to check with a partner. You might play the recording again for them to check, correct and complete.

Tapescript

Stonehenge is possibly the most amazing and mysterious place in Britain. The giant circle of stones, near the River Avon in southwest England, seems to make a huge impression on everybody who visits it. Archaeologists think that these ancient stones have stood in this circle for about 4,500 years. There were different stages in the building of Stonehenge. It probably began about 5,000 years ago, with a wooden structure. The stone circle followed this. But although we can be more or less sure about the age of Stonehenge, we still don't really understand its purpose. Why did the ancient people of Britain build this huge stone circle? Was it a cemetery to bury people when they died? Was it a religious temple? We simply don't know – we can

3A Digging up the past

Spread aims

Grammar: past perfect; verb + *to* + infinitive

Vocabulary: archaeology

Functions: talking about the past

Reading about archaeological finds

KEY

1 archaeologist, palaeontologist; ruins, site

2 fossil, remains, artefacts, pottery, jewellery, fragments, palaeontologist

3 c

4 A 2, 1, 3   B 3, 1, 2   C 2, 3, 1

1 Vocabulary: studying the past

This activity is best done as a dictionary activity. When students have found the words, elicit an explanation of the two professions (an *archaeologist* studies human sites and artefacts, and a *palaeontologist* studies fossils and prehistoric life).

2 Scanning for words

Students scan the texts to find the words – you might suggest that they underline them. Set a time limit to encourage students to scan rather than read the text.

3 Reading and listening for gist

 3.2 CD 1 track 23

Stronger students cover the text and listen and answer.

Weaker students follow the text as they listen.

4 Ordering events

Students read the text and order the events given within each group. Emphasise that students have to think about the order in which the events happened, not the order they are mentioned in the text.

5 Grammar: past perfect

Elicit the verbs from the text and refer to *Grammar Explorer,* pages 120–121.

6 Grammar: the order of past events

Read the sentence with the students and ask them to underline the first event. Check the answer and present the grammar note.

7 Past simple and past perfect

Read the example with the class.

Check **weaker students** understand that all the verbs with '1' in brackets will be in the past perfect because it is the first event.

8 Gapfill: past simple or past perfect

Suggest **weaker students** first note which tense should be used in each gap, then write the correct verb form.

9 Working with words: verb + *to* + infinitive

Present the example and ensure they understand how the structure works before they read the text. Refer also to *Working with words,* page 102.

Ice Baby

A few years ago, a Nenet herder called Yuri Khudi was working with his reindeer in northern Siberia. In front of him, on the river bank, there was an unbelievable sight – a frozen baby mammoth. Mammoths lived about 40,000 years ago. They were hunted for food and their fossil remains tell us a lot about Stone Age life. It is very difficult to find artefacts, such as pottery or jewellery, from those times. Mammoth remains help us to understand how Stone Age people hunted.

Yuri had seen mammoth tusks and fragments of animals before, but he'd never seen a whole animal. He wasn't a palaeontologist so he wasn't sure what to do. He decided to ask a friend for advice. Together, they went to the local museum and spoke to the director. When they all got back to the river, Yuri was horrified – the baby mammoth had disappeared! Yuri got on his snowmobile and drove to the nearest town. Fortunately, it didn't take long to find the mammoth. Some local people had taken it from the river bank and sold it to a shop keeper! Yuri managed to get the mammoth back and it was taken to a museum. The museum officials wanted to thank Yuri, so they decided to call the baby mammoth Lyuba, in honour of Yuri's wife.

Palaeontologists from all over the world wanted to examine Lyuba. Their studies showed that the mammoth hadn't lived long – only one month. It had probably died after getting trapped in mud, and because of that it was so well preserved.

Reading and listening

1 Work in pairs. Look at the words in the box. Find two words for professions and two words for places where these people can work.

> archaeologist   artefact   fossil   fragment
> jewellery   palaeontologist   pottery
> remains   ruins   site   treasure

2 Look at the story quickly. How many words from the vocabulary box can you find?

3 🔊3.2 **Read and listen to the story. What is it about? Choose the correct option (a–c).**

a   Ancient treasure found by an archaeologist.

b   An amazing find on an archaeological site.

c   An accidental discovery of ancient remains.

4 Read the story again. Put each group of events in the order they actually took place.

A 1   Yuri found a baby mammoth.
    2   Yuri saw mammoth tusks.
    3   Yuri talked to a museum director.

B 1   Yuri returned to the river bank.
    2   Yuri went to a local shop.
    3   Some people took the mammoth.

C 1   Palaentologists studied the mammoth.
    2   The mammoth lived for one month.
    3   The mammoth was taken to a museum.

30

Grammar: past perfect

5 Look at the example. Find five more past perfect verbs in the story.

Yuri had seen mammoth tusks before.

See Grammar Explorer: Page 120

6 Read the following sentence about an event in the story and choose the action that happened first.

When Yuri got back to the river, the mammoth had disappeared.

> We use the past perfect to show that an event took place before other events we have mentioned.

7 Complete the sentences with the correct forms of the verbs: past simple or past perfect. The numbers give the order in which the events happened.

e.g. When the museum director (**arrive** – 2), the men (**leave** – 1).
When the museum director arrived, the men had left.

1 When Yuri (**talk** – 1) to the shop keeper, he (**give back** – 2) the mammoth.

2 When they (**find** – 2) the mammoth, it (**start** – 1) to thaw.

3 Yuri (**go** – 2) to the museum when he (**speak** – 1) to his friend.

4 Tests (**show** – 2) that the mammoth (**fall** – 1) into mud.

5 Palaeontologists (**can** – 2) learn a lot because the mammoth (**remain** – 1) frozen.

8 Write the correct form of the verbs: past simple or past perfect.

Modern archaeology (**1**) ..*began*.. (**begin**) in the 19th century. Before then, although people (**2**) .... (**dig up**) ruins, they (**3**) .... (**not use**) their discoveries in systematic studies. In the 19th century, archaeological sites in Italy, Greece and Egypt (**4**) .... (**become**) very popular. In Europe, lots of information (**5**) .... (**come**) from ancient rubbish tips where people (**6**) .... (**throw away**) their broken, unwanted objects. However, in Egypt archaeologists (**7**) .... (**hope**) to find valuable treasure. Often, tomb robbers (**8**) .... (**get**) there before them.

Working with words: verb + *to* + infinitive

9 Look at the example. Find two similar patterns in the text on page 30.

He decided to ask a friend for advice.

See Working with words: Page 102

Speaking

10 Work in pairs. Look at the pictures. Complete the sentences with the correct form of the verbs: past simple or past perfect.

At lunchtime I (**1**) .... (**open**) my lunchbox and I (**2**) .... (**realise**) that I (**3**) .... (**leave**) my lunch at home.

I (**4**) .... (**try**) to buy a sandwich, but I (**5**) .... (**not / can**) because I (**6**) .... (**not bring**) any money to school.

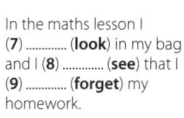

In the maths lesson I (**7**) .... (**look**) in my bag and I (**8**) .... (**see**) that I (**9**) .... (**forget**) my homework.

After school I (**10**) .... (**go**) to borrow a library book, but someone (**11**) .... (**already borrow**) it.

11 Ask and answer questions using the ideas in Exercise 10.

A: *What happened when you opened your lunchbox?*

B: *I realised I'd left my lunch at home.*

 Fast finishers

There are two 'false friends' on this page and the opposite page. Can you find them?

Grammar

KEY

5 he'd never seen, had disappeared, had taken / sold, hadn't lived, had probably died

6 the mammoth disappeared

7 1 had talked, gave back
2 found, had started   3 went, had spoken   4 showed, had fallen   5 could, had remained

8 2 had dug up   3 hadn't used
4 became   5 came   6 had thrown away   7 hoped
8 had got

9 it didn't take long to find
Yuri managed to get
officials wanted to thank
they decided to call
wanted to examine

10 1 opened   2 realised   3 had left   4 tried   5 couldn't
6 hadn't brought   7 looked
8 saw   9 had forgotten
10 went   11 had already borrowed

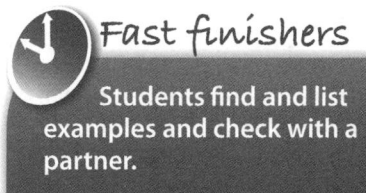 false friends: bank, examine

10 Speaking: past simple or past perfect

Elicit the fact that each of the pictures shows the boy's reaction to an event or omission which had already taken place, some time before.

Fast finishers

Students find and list examples and check with a partner.

11 Speaking: further practice

Ask the students to get into pairs and take it in turns to take the 'I' role in the four situations in Exercise 10. Present the example so that they understand what to do.

49

3B Remembering the past

Spread aims

Grammar: *used to*
Vocabulary: cooking
Functions: talking about the past
Listening to recipe instructions

KEY

2 preparation: chopping, peeling, slicing
cooking: baking, boiling, frying, grilling, heating up, roasting

3 b

4 1 sugar 2 butter 3 eggs
4 flour 5 baking soda
6 chocolate

5 d, e, b, a, f, g, c

6 1 d 2 a 3 b 4 c 5 –

7 1 baking, heating up, grilling, frying, roasting
2 bake – cakes / biscuits heat up – TV dinners / baked beans grill – sausages fry – eggs roast – chicken
3 regular activities

---

1 Speaking: favourite meals

Ask students to ask and answer the questions about their favourite meal. Elicit some answers from students around the class.

2 Vocabulary: cooking words

Ask students to list the words in two columns. They should use a dictionary for unknown words.

3 Reading for gist

Make sure that the students know what the three dishes listed are, and the ingredients – either elicit the information from them, tell them, or ask them to use a dictionary.

4 Listening for information

 *3.3 CD 1 track 24*

Play the recording a couple of times for the students to complete this task.

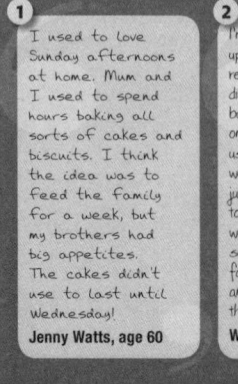
Speaking

1 Work in pairs. What's your favourite meal? Have you always liked it – or have your tastes changed? Tell your partner.

2 Put the words in the box into two groups: *preparation* and *methods of cooking*. Use your dictionary. Which methods are used in your favourite meal?

baking	boiling	chopping	frying
grilling	heating up	peeling	roasting
slicing			

Listening

3 Look at the ingredients. What is the recipe for? Choose one of the options (a–c).

a apple pie
b chocolate chip cookies
c chicken curry

250g butter

150g sugar

baking soda

300g flour

2 eggs

175g chocolate

4 3.3 Listen and number the ingredients in the order you hear them.

5 **STUDY SKILLS** 3.3 Listen again and put the instructions in the correct order.

a Add the chocolate.
b Add the flour and baking soda.
c Bake for 15 to 20 minutes.
d Heat the oven.
e Mix the sugar, butter and eggs.
f Put spoonfuls of the mixture on a baking tray.
g Put the tray into the oven.

32

Reading and listening

6 Look at the photos (a–d) and read the texts (1–5) quickly. Which texts do the photos illustrate? There is one extra text.

7 3.4 Read and listen to people talking about memories of the past. Answer the questions.

1 Which cooking methods are mentioned?
2 Find examples of food you can cook by each method.
3 Are the memories about regular activities or single events?

1 I used to love Sunday afternoons at home. Mum and I used to spend hours baking all sorts of cakes and biscuits. I think the idea was to feed the family for a week, but my brothers had big appetites. The cakes didn't use to last until Wednesday!
Jenny Watts, age 60

2 I'm American, so I grew up in the States. I remember the first TV dinners. My mom used to buy them at the store on a Saturday. She didn't use to cook them – they were already cooked. She just put them in the oven to heat up. Everything was in a separate section. I remember my favorite was roast beef and vegetables. Actually, they tasted awful!
Wayne Bridges, age 65

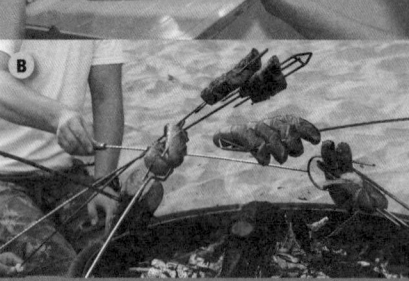

Tapescript

For this recipe you need 150 g of sugar, 250 g of butter, 2 eggs, 300 g of flour, 3 teaspoons of baking soda and 175 g of chocolate, which you need to chop into small pieces. You can use M&Ms instead of the chocolate.

First, heat the oven to 180ºC. Then mix the sugar, butter and eggs in a large bowl. Next, carefully add the flour and baking soda and mix everything together well. You can do this by hand or use a food processor. Now add the pieces of chocolate, or M&Ms if you are using them. Put spoonfuls of the mixture onto a baking tray, with quite a lot of space between each spoonful. Put the tray into the hot oven and bake the cookies for about 15 to 20 minutes. This recipe makes about 18 cookies.

5 Listening for detail

3.3 CD 1 track 24

Ask the students to write the numbers next to the instructions in their book.

Give **weaker students** a copy of the transcript to follow on the second listening. On the final listening, pause the recording after each instruction so that students have time to find the item in the list.

6 Reading: skimming for gist

Ask the class to say what they can see in each picture before they skim the texts to match them with the pictures.

Grammar: *used to*

8 Look at the text and complete the table.

Used to
I (**1**) .... love Sunday afternoons at home.
Negative
She (**2**) .... cook them.
Questions
What (**3**) .... do before we had microwaves?

See Grammar Explorer: Page 121

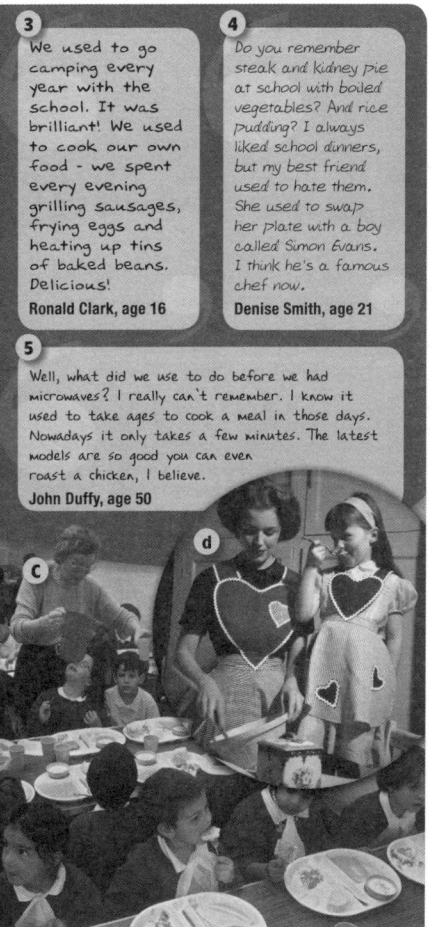

3

We used to go camping every year with the school. It was brilliant! We used to cook our own food – we spent every evening grilling sausages, frying eggs and heating up tins of baked beans. Delicious!

Ronald Clark, age 16

4

Do you remember steak and kidney pie at school with boiled vegetables? And rice pudding? I always liked school dinners, but my best friend used to hate them. She used to swap her plate with a boy called Simon Evans. I think he's a famous chef now.

Denise Smith, age 21

5

Well, what did we use to do before we had microwaves? I really can't remember. I know it used to take ages to cook a meal in those days. Nowadays it only takes a few minutes. The latest models are so good you can even roast a chicken, I believe.

John Duffy, age 50

9 Complete the text with the verbs in the box. Use the past simple or *used to*.

> ask   be   buy   come   go   meet
> not answer   put   sell   swim

When I was little, we (**1**) .....used to go... swimming on Friday evenings. We (**2**) .... fish and chips afterwards. They (**3**) .... them wrapped in newspaper and (**4**) .... lots of salt on them. My sister only (**5**) .... with us once because she (**6**) .... scared of water. But she (**7**) .... us at the chip shop. The man in the shop always (**8**) .... us, 'How many lengths (**9**) .... you .... tonight?' But my sister (**10**) .... !

10 Write five true or false sentences about your childhood. Then work in pairs and exchange your sentences. Find your partner's false sentences. Use ideas from the box and ideas of your own.

e.g. ...I didn't use to live in this town...

> comics   food   friends   hobbies   music
> pets   school   sports   town   TV

11 Work in pairs. Ask and answer questions about your childhood.

A: *Which comics did you use to read?*
B: *I used to read the* Beano.

Working with words: American English

12 Look at the examples. How many American English words can you think of?

> **cookie** *n, US* a sweet biscuit, e.g. chocolate chip cookies

> **store** *n, US* a shop, e.g. a shoe store

See Working with words: Page 102

Study skills

Listening for key words

1 Different kinds of texts can have different types of key words: verbs in instructions, past tenses in stories, adjectives in descriptions, etc.

2 Decide what kind of key words you need to listen for.

3 Focus on those words the first time you listen. Then listen for additional information.

Grammar and skills

10 Grammar: *used to*

Suggest that the students write three true sentences and two false ones, using the prompts in the box. They then guess their partner's false sentences.

11 Speaking: asking and answering about the past

Students ask and answer questions in pairs about what they used to and didn't use to do.

12 Working with words: American English

Read the examples with the whole class, then elicit some other examples of American English that they know, e.g. by asking: *What do Americans call the pavement / trousers / the boot of the car…?* etc. For further examples and practice, see *Working with words,* page 102.

Study skills

Present the suggestions in the box and discuss them with the class.

Weaker students could note key words relating to the pictures, then look for related words in the texts (e.g. *school dinners, camping, sausages*, etc.).

7 Reading and listening for information

 *3.4 CD 1 track 25*

Read through the questions with the class to help them focus on the information they need. Check their answers and use question 3 to lead into Exercise 8.

Stronger students cover the text and listen and answer.

Weaker students follow the text as they listen.

Extension: students can add other foods to the lists.

8 Grammar: *used to*

Discuss the grammar and meaning of *used to* with the class; emphasise that it is used for regular activities. If necessary, refer students to *Grammar Explorer*, page 121.

Tell **weaker students** they will find the examples in texts 1, 2 and 5.

9 Grammar: *used to*

Tell **weaker students** which verb to use for each gap, leaving them to put the verbs in the correct form.

3C Talking about quantity

Spread aims

Vocabulary: quantity, time, distance

Functions: talking about quantity, time, distance

Skills: reading and listening for gist and detail

Pronunciation: words containing *ui*

Writing a recommendation

KEY

1 He didn't make it – he used packet food (Holly sees the packets in the bin).

2 1 delicious 2 amazing 3 absolutely disgusting 4 too bad

3 1 How long...? 2 How many...? 3 How much...? 4 When...? 5 How far...? 6 What time...?

---

1 Reading and listening for gist

 *3.5 CD 1 track 26*

Students listen to the recording and answer the question. Elicit answers and ask students to explain their views.

Stronger students cover the text and listen and answer.

Weaker students follow the text as they listen.

2 Reading for detail

Students read the dialogue and find and underline the phrases.

3 Vocabulary: questions

Read through the *Useful expressions* in the box with the class, and ask them to find them in the dialogue. They then match the questions to the type of information.

4 Useful expressions: intonation

 *3.6 CD 1 track 27*

Play the recording while the students listen and follow. Then play it again, pausing after each phrase for the students to repeat chorally and individually; they should pay attention to the rise-and-fall intonation of the questions.

Talking about quantity

Reading and listening

1 *3.5* **Read and listen to the dialogue. Do you think Dan made the curry himself? Why? / Why not?**

2 **Read the dialogue again. Find the words that follow these phrases.**

  1 That smells   3 it tasted
  2 it looks   4 That doesn't sound

3 **Find the *Useful expressions* in the dialogue. How do you ask about these things?**

  1 a period of time
  2 a quantity of a countable thing
  3 a quantity of an uncountable thing or of weight/volume
  4 a date
  5 a distance
  6 a time

Fay:	Wow, Dan! That smells delicious!
Holly:	Yeah, and it looks amazing too.
Fay:	How long did it take you to make all this?
Dan:	Oh, not long. About half an hour.
Holly:	Really? How much did you make? There's enough food for ten people here!
Dan:	No, there isn't!
Holly:	So, Dan, when did you learn to make curry?
Dan:	Oh, ages ago. My gran used to make it a lot.
Holly:	I'm terrible at cooking. I once made a steak pie and it tasted absolutely disgusting. I'd put too much salt in it.
Fay:	That doesn't sound too bad! I quite like salty food.
Holly:	Well, the recipe said 10 grams and I put in 100 grams! Honestly, it was revolting!
Fay:	What time are we eating, Dan?
Dan:	At six, I hope. Joe phoned earlier. He's on his way, but he might be late. He's been to Stonehenge today.
Fay:	How far is that? Isn't it quite a long way?
Holly:	No, I think it's about 60 miles.
Fay:	OK, then. Let's set the table. How many people are coming?
Dan:	Just the four of us.
Holly:	Fay, don't look now, but what are those packets in the bin?

34

5 Completing quantity questions

Students complete the questions, referring to the question forms in the *Useful expressions* box. They then ask and answer them in pairs before checking their answers against the key at the bottom of page 37.

6 Pronunciation: words containing *ui*

 *3.7 CD 1 track 28*

Students read through the list and decide how to say the words, then compare their ideas with a partner before listening to the recording. Ask students to repeat chorally and individually.

Writing: a recommendation

1 Identifying adjectives

Students read the text and find the adjectives from the box.

2 *So / such a ... that*

Students complete the sentences with words from the text. Refer to *Grammar Explorer,* page 121, for further examples and an explanation of this construction.

3 Combining sentences with *so / such a ... that*

Students write compound sentences like those in Exercise 2, using the information in the *Grammar Explorer.*

4 🔊3.6 **Listen and repeat the *Useful expressions*. Focus on your intonation.**

Speaking

5 **Work in pairs. Complete the questions. Use the *Useful expressions* to help you. Then ask and answer the questions. Check your answers at the bottom of page 37.**

1 .... boil an egg?
  a 1 minute **b** 10 minutes
  c 30 minutes

2 .... kilometres are in a mile?
  a 1.6 km **b** 5 km **c** 8.3 km

Writing: a recommendation

1 **Read Fay's comments about the Jorvik Viking Centre. Which adjectives does she use?**

boring busy expensive
frightening good interesting
poor realistic

2 **Complete these sentences from the text.**

1 It was so busy ....
2 The street scenes were so realistic ....
3 We had such a good time ....

See Grammar Explorer: Page 121

3 **Rewrite the pairs of sentences using the words in brackets.**

1 The queue was long. We left. (**so**)
2 It was a realistic display. I was scared. (**such**)
3 It was a great place. I wanted to stay. (**such**)
4 It was a hot day. I needed a drink. (**such**)
5 I was hungry. I ate three sandwiches. (**so**)

4 **Choose a place you have visited – a tourist attraction, a town, a museum, etc. Make notes about its good and bad points, and what you did there. Then write a paragraph for a website to recommend (or not) the place.**

3 .... from London to New York?
  a 1,385km **b** 5,585km
  c 8,573km

4 .... Stone Age man live?
  a 4,000 years ago **b** 40,000 years ago
  c 400,000 years ago

5 .... a litre of water weigh?
  a 375 grams **b** 1,000 grams
  c 1,200 grams

Pronunciation: words containing *ui*

6 🔊3.7 **How do you pronounce these words? Compare with your partner. Then listen and repeat.**

biscuit building cruise fruit
guide juice liquid quick
quiet quite quiz ruins

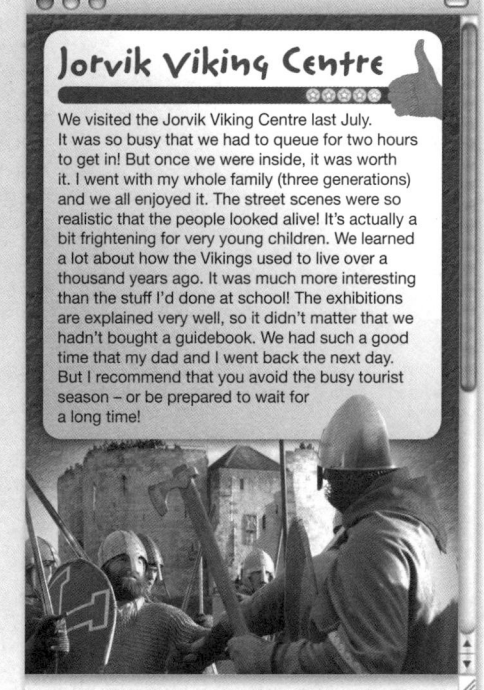

Jorvik Viking Centre

We visited the Jorvik Viking Centre last July. It was so busy that we had to queue for two hours to get in! But once we were inside, it was worth it. I went with my whole family (three generations) and we all enjoyed it. The street scenes were so realistic that the people looked alive! It's actually a bit frightening for very young children. We learned a lot about how the Vikings used to live over a thousand years ago. It was much more interesting than the stuff I'd done at school! The exhibitions are explained very well, so it didn't matter that we hadn't bought a guidebook. We had such a good time that my dad and I went back the next day. But I recommend that you avoid the busy tourist season – or be prepared to wait for a long time!

Communicate

KEY

5 1 How long does it take to (b) 2 How many (a)
3 How far is it (b) 4 When did (b) 5 How much does (b)

Writing

1 busy, frightening, good, interesting, realistic

2 1 that we had to queue for two hours
2 that the people looked alive
3 that my dad and I went back the next day

3 1 The queue was so long that we left.
2 It was such a realistic display that I was scared.
3 It was such a great place that I wanted to stay.
4 It was such a hot day that I needed a drink.
5 I was so hungry that I ate three sandwiches.

Suggest **weaker students** first mark where *so / such* and *that* should go in each sentence, following the information they have been given, then write each compound sentence in full.

can, if they choose, write a negative description and recommend that people do not visit the place. When they have written their text, they should exchange it with a partner for comment.

4 Personalised writing

Students use the Jorvik text as a model to write about a place they have visited. Suggest that students

3D American food

Spread aims

Vocabulary: food; maths

Skills: reading and listening for gist and detail

Listening to people talking about meals

Culture: American food; Thanksgiving

CLIL: Maths and English: the history of numbers

KEY

2 1 400 years ago   2 Their survival and the harvest 3 just over 100 years old

3 corn, squash, turkey, sweet potatoes, pumpkin, tomatoes, potatoes, chocolate

4 1 feast   2 crops   3 harvest 4 bitter

---

1 Warm-up

Encourage students to match any food items in the photo to those in the box, and look up any they can't guess in the dictionary. Ask them to discuss each one with a partner. Elicit some answers from the class and discuss what additional foods they can see in the photo.

2 Reading and listening for gist

 3.8 CD 1 track 29

Ask students to read the questions and look at the picture to focus their attention before they listen and read. Check the answers as a whole class.

Stronger students cover the text and listen and answer.

3 Reading for detail

Students read the text to find the native American foods. Elicit answers from the class and list them on the board.

4 Vocabulary: matching words with definitions

Students find the words in the text.

5 Grammar: verb forms

Students find the verbs in the text, and use the context to infer the meaning, then complete the sentences with the correct form.

 **American food**

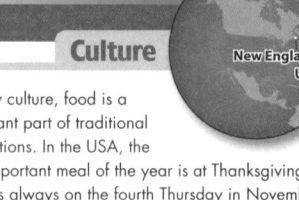

Reading

1 Have you ever eaten these foods? Are they used a lot in dishes in your country?

> cornbread   pumpkin pie   squash
> mashed sweet potatoes   roast turkey

2   3.8 **Read the text and answer the questions.**

1 When was the first 'thanksgiving' meal?

2 What did the first 'thanksgiving' meal celebrate?

3 How old is the tradition of Thanksgiving?

3 Read the text again. **How many foods can you find that are native to the Americas?**

4 **Find words in the text which match the definitions.**

1 a special meal with lots of different dishes

2 plants that provide food

3 the collection of food from plants

4 the opposite to a sweet taste

Culture
New England, USA

In every culture, food is a significant part of traditional celebrations. In the USA, the most important meal of the year is at Thanksgiving, which is always on the fourth Thursday in November. Thanksgiving celebrates a time in American history when the 'New World' and the 'Old World' began to mix. Almost 400 years ago, a group of English families arrived on the northeast coast of America – in an area which they called New England. During their first winter, they nearly ran out of the food they had brought with them. The local people, called the Wampanoag, showed them how to grow crops like corn and squash. The English had never seen these plants before as they were native to the New World. At the first harvest, the Wampanoag and the English (the Pilgrims) shared a feast that lasted for three days. This was the first 'thanksgiving' meal. However, the modern tradition only became popular at the end of the 19th century. These days, Thanksgiving is a day when families spend time together. It takes such a long time to make all the food that the whole family has to help. Then everyone sits down to enjoy the meal. Turkey, cornbread, sweet potatoes and pumpkin pie are always on the menu.

Many foods that we now think of as European originally came from the New World. Can you imagine Italian cooking without tomatoes? Or traditional English fish and chips without potatoes? Or life without chocolate? The Maya and Aztec peoples of Central and South America ate all of these things. They used to mix cacao with chilli to make a strong, bitter drink – that's a little different to a chocolate milkshake!

36

---

6 Listening for gist

 3.9 CD 1 track 30

Students read the options before they listen.

Tapescript

1

Fay's dad: This is lovely, isn't it?

Fay's mum: Yes, it is.

Fay's dad: It's almost as delicious as your cooking!

Fay's mum: Don't be silly, it's much better than anything I can make.

Fay's dad: What have you got, Fay?

Fay: Strawberry cheesecake with vanilla sauce. It's fantastic. What's your tiramisu like?

Fay's dad: Oh, I'm really enjoying it.

Fay: Haven't you ordered dessert, Mum?

Fay's mum: Yes, but they haven't brought it yet. Excuse me! Waiter!

Fay's dad: He's coming.

Fay's mum: Aha! My fruit salad. Thank you very much. And could you bring us some more water, please.

Fay: This is such a nice meal that I think we should come here every week.

Fay's mum: Ha! Well I'm happy that you've enjoyed it. It is your birthday! But I think we should only come on special occasions.

Fay: OK, we'll come here for every birthday meal. What do you think?

Fay's dad: That's not a bad idea.

5 Complete the sentences with the correct form of these verbs from the text.

run out	last	spend	take

1 The festival usually .... for two days – from Saturday morning to Sunday night.
2 How do you like to .... your free time?
3 I can't finish the exam – I'm going to .... of time!
4 I hope you like your cake – it .... me hours to make it!

Listening

6 ⏺3.9 **Listen to two conversations. Where are the people? Write 1 or 2 next to the correct option (a–c).**

a at home
b in a restaurant
c in a school dining room

7 ⏺3.9 **Listen again and choose the correct answers (a–c).**

1 What are they eating?
  a packed lunches
  b a take-away
  c dessert
2 What dishes are mentioned?
  a cheesecake, fruit salad and tiramisu
  b cheesecake, ice cream and yogurt
  c chicken sandwiches, tuna salad and burgers
3 What's the occasion?
  a the last day of term
  b someone's birthday
  c passing an exam

Project

Choose a popular local or national celebration which has special food associated with it. Prepare a brochure for English visitors. Write a menu in English. Write a paragraph explaining the different dishes, their ingredients and how they are cooked.

KEY 1b 2a 3b 4b 5b

Maths and English
The history of numbers

1 **Read the text. What is the difference between numbers and numerals?**

2 **Read the text again and work in pairs to answer the questions marked Q.**

This is the Ishango bone, which is about 20,000 years old. It was found in Africa, near where the River Nile begins. Scientists think that the marks on it are evidence that 20,000 years ago people used a counting system. Each mark equals 'one' – so two marks equal 'two', and so on. In Europe today, we use different symbols, or numerals, for different numbers. We use ten numerals, and we combine them to make other numbers.

These numerals came to Europe from the Arabic culture of North Africa, but they were originally invented in India in around 500 B.C. They are called Hindu-Arabic numerals. After their introduction to Europe around 1,000 A.D., it took several hundred years for the system to become commonly used. Until then, Europeans had used Roman numerals.

Q How do you write the current year in Roman numerals?

Both the Hindu-Arabic and the Roman systems are based on counting in groups of ten. The ancient Egyptians also had a system based on ten. Here are the hieroglyphics for 10, 100, 1,000 and 1,000,000.

Not all cultures counted in groups of ten. The Maya system used a combination of groups of four and five – together they made a group of twenty. These are the Maya symbols for 4, 5 and 6.

Q Can you work out what these Maya numbers are?

3 **Work in pairs. Why do you think different cultures counted in groups of four, five and ten?**

UNIT 3D AMERICAN FOOD 37

Project: a local celebration

Read the instructions with the whole class. Ask them to work in pairs or threes to do this project. Allow them time at home to research and write it up. In class have a 'show-and-tell' session, where students talk to other pairs / groups about their work and read each other's projects. Try to encourage them to present their work attractively, with pictures if possible.

Maths and English: the history of numbers

1 Reading for detail

Students scan the text to find the information.

2 Using numeral systems

Students read and answer the questions in red in the text.

3 Discussion

Students discuss the question; elicit ideas from the whole class and open up the discussion.

2

Joe: What have you got?

Holly: Cheese.

Joe: I've got chicken. I hate chicken. Do you want to swap?

Holly: No thanks, I don't like chicken either.

Dan: I'll swap with you. You can have my tuna salad.

Joe: Oh, thanks. Here you are. I don't know why my mum always makes me chicken sandwiches.

Dan: Your mum makes your packed lunch?

Joe: Yeah. It's always the same – pasta salad, chicken sandwiches and a yogurt.

Holly: Why don't you make it yourself? Honestly, boys!

Joe: Well, tomorrow I'm going to get a burger from the new place on the High Street. What's it called?

Dan: The American Diner.

Joe: Yeah, the burgers are so good I think I'll go there every day of the holidays.

Holly: Oh, the holidays! How long have we got? Two whole weeks?

Dan: Two weeks and one day.

Joe: Brilliant!

7 Listening for detail

 3.9 CD 1 track 30

Ask the students to read through the options first. They should answer the questions twice – once for conversation 1 and then again for conversation 2.

55

True story: Mike Parker Pearson

Page aim

Reading for interest on the topic of the unit

Warm-up

Print out a picture of Stonehenge and/or an important archaeological site in your students' country. Show it/them to the students and ask them what they know about it. Open a discussion about prehistoric life and the value of archaeology.

1 Reading for detail

Ask students to read the text and answer the questions individually, then check with a partner. Elicit answers from the whole class.

Background information

You can find out more about Mike Parker Pearson and his work at and around Stonehenge on the following websites:

En.wikipedia.org/wiki/Mike_Parker_
    Pearson
heritage-key.com/mike-parker-
    pearson
www.stonehengenews.co.uk/tag/
    mike-parker-pearsons

And there is a great video to watch here:

News.nationalgeographic.com/
    676130-stonehenge-video.html

Mike Parker Pearson

1 Read the article and choose the correct answers, a, b or c.

1 Mike's interest in archaeology began
  a because his grandfather taught him about it.
  b around the age of 14.
  c after a discovery in his own garden.

2 Mike has been working at Stonehenge
  a since he was 14.
  b for four years.
  c since 2003.

3 Bluestonehenge was
  a another name for Stonehenge.
  b like Stonehenge.
  c the name of the village.

4 The village that Mike uncovered
  a was very big.
  b was small.
  c is now used for homes for workers.

5 The remains found in the village tell us about
  a farming methods.
  b cooking methods.
  c farming and cooking methods.

6 As a result of Mike's work, we now believe that the original stone circle
  a was not the only building.
  b had a road through it.
  c had people living in it.

Mike Parker Pearson is a professor of archaeology at Sheffield University, and his most recent explorations have been on the Stonehenge Riverside Project.

When Mike was four years old, some workers left a few stones in his garden. They contained lots of fossils, which sparked an interest in the young boy. By the time he was 14, Mike had been on his first archaeological dig, and a lifelong interest had begun. After he left Southampton University, Mike studied at Cambridge and took part in archaeological digs in Britain and many other countries.

Since 2003 Mike has directed projects at Stonehenge, where a major important discovery was the remains of Bluestonehenge – another stone circle similar to the one we know. They have also found a village with many small, square houses at a place nearby called Durrington Walls. This discovery was the largest Neolithic village that had ever been found in Britain. Mike's theory is that the village was where the workers lived when they were building Stonehenge 4,500 years ago. Bones and pottery fragments suggest that the workers were among the very first farming communities in Britain. They used to cook their meat over an open fire in the centre of the house and the people living in the village also had regular feasts.

Thanks to the findings of Mike's team, we now know much more about prehistoric life. The research continues to give us regular new evidence of what life was like in the distant past, why people went to such great trouble to build Stonehenge and what it was used for. A road and river route from the stone circles to a similar wooden construction at Durrington suggests that the Stonehenge monument was part of a much larger complex of buildings where people lived and worked, and not a single, separate building. We are now closer than ever before to solving the puzzle of this mysterious site.

Mike Parker Pearson has written or co-written 14 books, including *The Archaeology of Death and Burial* and *The English Heritage Book of Bronze Age Britain*. He is a regular and popular guest on many television programmes.

2 Choose the correct meanings as they are used in the text.

1	sparked (2)	started / made a small fire
2	dig (2)	prepare the earth for growing food / a project
3	took part (2)	helped / directed
4	communities (3)	groups of people / groups of animals
5	feasts (3)	daily meals / large celebrations
6	findings (4)	ideas / discoveries
7	evidence (4)	what helps us learn / what the police look for
8	the distant past (4)	not long ago / a long time ago
9	construction (4)	building / road
10	solving (4)	finding the answer to / asking questions about

3 Talk about one or more of the following questions with a partner.

- What do you know about the people who lived in your country thousands of years ago?
- Which archaeological sites do you know about? What are they famous for?
- Have you ever thought about becoming an archaeologist? What would be good or bad about the job?
- How helpful is it for us to understand the past?

---

2 Vocabulary

Students decide which of the two meanings on the right match the word or phrase on the left, in the context of the article they have read; the number in brackets indicates the paragraph in which the word or phrase occurs. Students should work individually, and then check with a partner; finally, elicit answers from the whole class.

3 Discussion

Ask students to work in groups of three or four to discuss the four points. They should appoint a person to keep notes on what is said, and present the group's ideas in a whole-class discussion.

Careers

> ## Grammar
Learn about *will*, two uses of *going to*, the present continuous for the future, and the future continuous.

> ## Vocabulary
Learn words for jobs, sports people and places, and clothes.

Work with adjective + *to* + infinitive combinations, and verb + noun combinations.

> ## Skills
Read about sports champions, careers in design, and sport in Australia.

Listen to a conversation about clothes, and the sports news.

Write about arrangements.

> ## Communicate
Talk about preferences.

---

1 Look at the photo and choose the best caption.

a The paramedics are discussing a patient.
b The engineers are checking the measurements.
c The mechanics are fixing the engine.

2 Find jobs in the vocabulary box where people:

- wear a uniform
- work outdoors
- work indoors
- use machines

accountant	electrician	paramedic
actor	engineer	postal worker
architect	lawyer	secretary
chef	manager	soldier
designer	mechanic	

3 4.1 Listen to three people talking about their jobs. Write the numbers (1–3) next to the jobs in the vocabulary box.

4 Tell your partner two jobs that you'd like to do and two you wouldn't like to do. Explain your reasons.

A: *I'd like to be a chef. I like cooking.*
B: *I'd like to be a secretary. I like organising things.*

---

1 Warm-up

Read through the captions with the students and ask them to work in pairs to match one of them with the picture. Elicit suggestions and ask students to give reasons for their choices.

2 Vocabulary: jobs

Read through the words in the jobs box and have students repeat. Take care with the syllable stress (second syllable: a**coun**tant, de**sign**er, me**chan**ic; third syllable: elec**tri**cian, engi**neer**, para**med**ic). Make sure they understand what the jobs are. People may sometimes work indoors and sometimes outdoors; ask students to justify and explain their choices.

3 Listening for gist

 4.1 CD 1 track 31

Play the recording twice, then ask students to check their answers with a partner. If necessary, play the recording a third time. Check the answers with the whole class.

Give **weaker students** a copy of the tapescript to follow on the second listening.

Tapescript

1 I start work early in the morning and I sort all the letters. Most days my bag is quite heavy. I walk a lot every day. I do the same route, so I know the streets and the people who live there quite well. I don't collect the post – someone else does that.

Careers

Unit aims

Grammar: the future with *will, going to*, present continuous and future continuous

Vocabulary: jobs, sports people and places, clothes; adjective + *to* + infinitive; verb + noun combinations

Functions: talking about preferences

Reading about: sports champions; careers in design; sport in Australia

Listening to: a conversation about clothes; the sports news

Writing about arrangements

KEY

1 b

2 (possible answers) wear a uniform: chef, paramedic, postal worker, soldier
work indoors: accountant, actor, chef, clerk, designer, lawyer, manager, secretary
work outdoors: paramedic, postal worker, soldier
use machines: chef, electrician, engineer, mechanic

3 1 postal worker 2 mechanic 3 accountant

2 I work in a garage. There are four of us, including the boss. He's the owner of the garage. I like working on old cars best. New cars aren't as interesting because they usually have computers that tell you what to do and when to do it. My job's a bit dirty, but I don't mind. I've always enjoyed fixing things.

3 I work for several small companies. I look after each company's money and finances. I work out how much money they get from selling things and how much money they spend. I like maths and I'm good at it, so it's a perfect job for me.

4 Speaking: talking about preferences

Read the model dialogue with the class, and point out the constructions to be used: *I'd like to be a …* and *I like ___-ing.*

4A Sporting success

Spread aims

Grammar: the future

Vocabulary: sports people and places

Functions: talking about advantages and disadvantages

Reading about the life of a sports person

KEY

1 Robert Korzeniowski – athletics   Serena Williams – tennis   Lionel Messi – football   Justyna Kowalczykç – skiing

2 people: coach, manager, physiotherapist, player, referee, sponsor, trainer, umpire
places (and sports): court (badminton, volleyball, tennis, squash, basketball), pitch (football, rugby, hockey, cricket), pool (swimming, water polo), ring (boxing), stadium (football, baseball), track (athletics, Formula 1, cycling)

3 1 physiotherapist   2 manager   3 sponsor   4 coach, trainer   5 referee, umpire

4 motor racing, gymnastics

5 1 F   2 NI   3 T   4 NI

6 it's easy to forget; it's hard to imagine

7 1 c   2 b   3 a

8 going to, going to

4A Sporting success

Chris: Now, who can forget the Brazilian grand prix last season – it was so exciting to watch, wasn't it? Let's see those last few minutes again.

Commentator: They're nearly at the finish line. Webber is in the lead and he's going to win the race ... yes! It's Webber first, with Kubica second. But here's Button. Button only needs a few more points to win the championship. Can he do it? He's going to finish in fifth place ... there he goes across the line. Yes! It's Hamilton third, Button fifth and so he wins the championship! What a day for British racing!

Chris: Fantastic! But what's next for millionaire racing driver Jenson Button? Will he stay with Brawn or will he go to McLaren? What do you think, Alan?

Alan: Well, he's said that money isn't the key factor and I don't think he'll change his mind. He also earns a lot from advertising, of course. On the other hand, a contract with McLaren is worth £6 million a year. So it's difficult to say what he'll do.

Chris: OK, we'll come back to the glamorous world of Formula One later this afternoon, but first let's look at the career of another world champion, Beth Tweddle. Now, gymnastics doesn't make as many headlines as motor racing, so it's easy to forget that Tweddle became champion on the same day as Button.

Alan: And that gymnastics is a tough sport. Beth has had six ankle operations and she's having another operation next week. She's competing in the European Championships next year, but it's hard to imagine she'll win another medal there.

Chris: I'm not sure I agree. She trains six days a week and injuries don't stop her! She's 24 now, which is quite old for a gymnast, but she's going to carry on for as long as she can and she's definitely not going to retire until after the next Olympics.

Vocabulary: sports people and places

1 Which sports do you associate with these people? Add four more names and test your partner.

Robert Korzeniowski   Serena Williams
Lionel Messi   Justyna Kowalczykç

2 Work in pairs. Put the words into two groups: *people* and *places*. What sports are played in each place?

> coach   court   manager   physiotherapist
> pitch   player   pool   referee   ring
> sponsor   stadium   track   trainer
> umpire

3 Complete the sentences with words from the box in Exercise 2.

1 A .... treats sports injuries.
2 A football .... chooses the team and plans its activities.
3 A .... gives money to teams and sports people.
4 A .... or a .... makes sure athletes are fit.
5 A .... or an .... keeps the score during a sports event.

Reading and listening

4 4.2 Read and listen to a commentary from a TV sports programme. Which sports are mentioned?

> athletics   boxing   football   gymnastics
> motor racing   tennis

40

---

1 Warm-up

Ask the students to do the first part of the activity individually, then check their answers and do the second part of the activity with a partner.

2 Sport vocabulary

Ask students to do this individually, then check with a partner. Elicit answers from the class and list them on the board.

Give **weaker students** a list of sports and ask them to match them with the places.

3 Vocabulary: sports jobs

Students complete the sentences with the people in Exercise 2

Follow-up: ask students to think of sports to match the people in Exercise 2 (e.g. *umpire – tennis, referee – football*).

4 Reading and listening for gist

💿 *4.2 CD 1 track 32*

Stronger students cover the text and just listen.

5 Reading for detail

Read through the sentences with the class first to help students focus on the information they need.

5 Read the text again. Are the sentences true or false – or is there not enough information to decide?

1 Lewis Hamilton won the grand prix race.
2 Jenson Button wants to change teams.
3 Beth Tweddle is a gymnast.
4 Beth Tweddle can't train at the moment.

Working with words: adjective + *to* + infinitive

6 Look at the examples. Find two more similar patterns in the text.

It was so exciting to watch.
It's difficult to say what he'll do.

See Working with words: Page 103

Grammar: the future

7 Look at the examples (1–3). Match them with the meanings (a–c).

1 I don't think he'll change his mind.
2 She's having another operation next week.
3 She's going to carry on for as long as she can.

a a plan or intention
b an arrangement at a specified time in the future
c a prediction

See Grammar Explorer: Page 121

8 Complete this sentence from the text. Then choose the correct option.

He's .... win the race.
We use *going to* / *will* to make predictions based on the situation now.

9 Look at the pictures. Write sentences about what's going to happen. Use verbs from the box.

beat	crash	fall off	save	score	win

10 Choose the correct option.

1 Arsenal **will play** / **are playing** against Manchester United tomorrow.
2 Look! The referee **will give** / **is going to give** him a red card!
3 Murray **will win** / **is winning** the next game.
4 After the match, the winners **are celebrating** / **are going to celebrate**.
5 I think Bolt **will break** / **is breaking** the record again.

11 Read an interview with an athlete and choose the correct options.

Q: Is it true that you (**1**) .... your manager?
A: No, it isn't. I've got no intention of doing that!
Q: And (**2**) .... in the next Olympics?
A: Of course. In fact, I (**3**) .... my training programme next month.
Q: Do you think you (**4**) .... a medal?
A: Well, I hope so. I (**5**) .... my best.

1	a	are going to change	b	will change
2	a	are you going to compete	b	will you compete
3	a	am starting	b	will start
4	a	are winning	b	will win
5	a	am doing	b	am going to do

Speaking

12 Work in groups. What are the good things or bad things about being a sports professional?

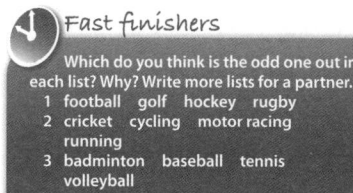

training routine   travel   personal life
money   injury   fame

Fast finishers

Which do you think is the odd one out in each list? Why? Write more lists for a partner.
1 football golf hockey rugby
2 cricket cycling motor racing running
3 badminton baseball tennis volleyball
4 boxing fencing judo skiing

Grammar

KEY

9 1 The British athlete is going to win. She's going to beat the other athletes.
2 The gymnast is going to fall off (the beam).
3 The cyclist is going to crash into the dog.
4 He's going to score a goal. The goalkeeper isn't going to save it.

10 1 are playing 2 is going to give 3 will win 4 are going to celebrate 5 will break

11 1 a 2 a 3 a 4 b 5 b

10 Grammar: choosing future forms

Students choose the correct option.

11 Future forms multiple choice

Students choose the correct option.

Follow-up: students can practise the dialogue in pairs.

12 Speaking: being a sports professional

Make sure the students know all the words in the box. Ask them to work in groups of three or four. Suggest one of them is secretary and records their ideas in two columns. Elicit ideas in a whole-class discussion.

Fast finishers

There are many possible ways of answering these questions – the students need to justify their answers (e.g. *Golf is the odd one out because one person plays against another, while the other three are team games*).

6 Working with words: adjective + *to* + infinitive

Read through the examples and ensure that students understand the construction. Check their answers. For further practice refer to *Working with words*, page 103.

7 Use of future forms

See *Grammar Explorer*, page 121, for further examples and a more detailed explanation.

Weaker students: make sure the students understand the metalanguage of this exercise first (*intention, arrangement, prediction*).

8 Grammar: *going to* / *will*

Students find the sentence in the text and fill in the gap, then choose the correct option to complete the explanation.

9 Describing future events

Make sure the students know the meaning of the six verbs in the box. Also check the necessary vocabulary from the pictures (e.g. *athlete/runner, gymnast, beam, cyclist, goalkeeper*). Ask them to write the sentences individually, then check with a partner. Elicit answers from the class and check they are using the correct construction.

4B Designing the future

Spread aims

Grammar: future continuous
Vocabulary: clothes; verb + noun
Functions: talking about your future
Reading about careers advice
Listening to people talking about clothes

KEY

1 styles: flared, hooded, long-sleeved, loose, round-neck, short-sleeved, tight, V-neck
garments: dress, jacket, trousers
patterns: flowered, spotted
fabrics: cotton, denim
colours: bright, pastel

2 c

3 1 b   2 a

1 Vocabulary: clothes

Students classify the words in the box under the five headings. Make sure they understand the metalanguage (*styles, garments, fabrics*) first. This could be done as a dictionary exercise. Elicit answers from the whole class and complete the mind map on the board.

Extension: add other words to the mind map.

2 Listening for gist

 4.3 CD 1 track 33

Read through the options with the class before they listen.

Give **weaker students** a copy of the script to follow on second listening.

Tapescript

Presenter: We've been to Fashion Week and I have to say, it's been surprising to see the different styles there. A lot of the designs will influence the clothes that will be in the shops later in the year. So, what will be popular this summer, Susie?

Susie: Well, it's hard to say! Elizabeth Morris used to have a lot of punk influences in her designs and her collections are always interesting. But this year, I don't think her designs will be popular for summer. The

colours are pale – mostly beige and brown – which is a bit dull for June and July. Also, the fabrics are plain with no patterns at all.

Presenter: But I think the fabrics – cotton and denim – will be great for summer.

Susie: Well, I'm not sure. Brown denim?

Presenter: Janice Spencer's collection was more bright and colourful.

Susie: Yes. I think lots of people will be looking for Spencer's style in the shops. She's got lots of short-sleeved and sleeveless tops in silk and cotton. And some great loose trousers which will be perfect if we get a hot summer!

Presenter: I agree. A lot of her clothes will be good for summer parties too. They're not too formal and they'll be easy to wear.

Susie: What about Paul Smith's collection? What did you think of that?

3 Listening for detail

 4.3 CD 1 track 33

Read through the options with the class before the students listen again.

Extension: give out copies of the tapescript for pairs to practise the dialogue in preparation for the speaking activities which follow.

4 Speaking: describing clothes

In pairs, students describe the appearance and clothes of the people in the photos.

4B Designing the future

Vocabulary: clothes

1 **STUDY SKILLS** Add the words from the vocabulary box to the mind map.

> bright   cotton   denim   dress   flared
> flowered   hooded   jacket   long-sleeved
> loose   pastel   round-neck   short-sleeved
> spotted   tight   trousers   V-neck

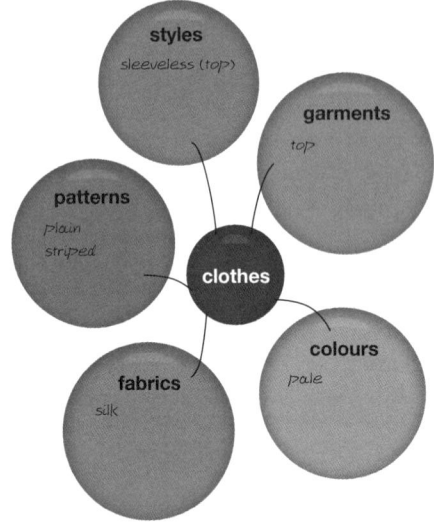

Listening

2 *4.3* Listen to two people talking about clothes. Choose the correct option (a–c).

a   They are buying clothes in a shop.
b   They are choosing clothes for a party.
c   They are discussing summer clothes.

3 *4.3* Listen again and choose the correct answers (a–c).

1   Elizabeth Morris's collection
  a   is brightly-coloured and patterned.
  b   is plain cotton and denim.
  c   has long-sleeved shirts and T-shirts.
2   Janice Spencer's collection
  a   has sleeveless tops and loose trousers.
  b   is in pale colours.
  c   has striped and checked jackets.

42

Speaking

4 Work in pairs. Describe the people in the photos using words from the vocabulary box in Exercise 1.

5 Choose someone in the class and describe their clothes. Can your partner identify the person? Take turns.

Reading and listening

6 Read the webpage quickly. What is its purpose? Choose the correct option (a–c).

a   to give advice to high-school students
b   to help unemployed people to get a job
c   to give information about different universities

7 *4.4* Read and listen to the webpage. Answer the questions.

1   What kind of jobs do designers do?
2   What is CAD?
3   What do you need to get a job as a designer?

Working with words: verb + noun

8 Look at the examples. Think of two more expressions with *get* or *have*.

Get help from our careers files.

Perhaps you have a future as a designer.

See Working with words: Page 103

Grammar: future continuous

9 Complete these sentences from the webpage. Which verbs do we use to make the future continuous?

We .... new sections every week.

.... you .... or studying?

> We make the negative form with *won't*:
> *I won't be living at home five years from now.*.

See Grammar Explorer: Page 122

Careers
advice service

Welcome to this new service! We'll be adding new sections every week, so come back often.

Where will you be five years from now? Will you be working or studying? Will you be living with your parents or travelling the world? Decisions that you make now can affect your career choices later. Get help from our careers files. Click on the jobs to find out more.

Careers in *Design*

What will life in the future look like? What will the latest mobile phone be like? What will we be wearing? What kind of cars will we be driving? If these questions interest you, perhaps you have a future as a designer. Designers work in a range of fields. Most people are familiar with fashion design. Graphic designers can work in advertising, publishing, and so on. Web design is a new and popular field. Many product designers use computer programs (CAD) in their jobs.

What do I need?
You need to be good at art, of course. Designers also need to be able to express ideas visually. For example, choosing the best image for the book cover of a detective story – a picture of flowers, an abstract design, a gun? Each image will send a different message to the reader. You'll also need to get a qualification from a college or art school and build up a good portfolio. Click here for a list of courses.

10 Complete the sentences with the future continuous form of the verbs in the box. There is one extra verb.

e.g. This summer, everyone ..will be wearing.. pale colours.

| do | drive | go | live |
| play | wear | work | |

1 By the time I'm 25, I .... in my dream job.
2 Ten years from now, we .... electric cars.
3 This time on Sunday, I .... football.
4 What .... you .... this time tomorrow?
5 In a few months' time, we .... on holiday.

Speaking

11 Work in groups. Write sentences about your future. Don't write your name. Mix up the sentences and read them to the group. Can you guess who wrote them?

e.g. ..In two / five / ten years' time,......

Study skills

Mind maps

1 Mind maps are a good way to help you learn new words. Look at the maps on the opposite page and on page 23. Then organise vocabulary on these topics: *animals, sport, mass media.* Choose your own sub-categories.

2 Mind maps are useful to help you plan essays. Make a mind map before you do the writing task on page 45.

UNIT 4B DESIGNING THE FUTURE 43

Grammar and skills

10 **Grammar practice**

Students complete the sentences using the verbs in the box.

11 **Speaking practice**

Provide the students with paper – A4 sheets folded and cut into eight parts is ideal. Give each student three pieces and ask them to write three sentences about themselves; nobody else must see what they write. Groups of four or five students then sit around one table, and mix the papers up in the centre. They take it in turns to pick a paper and read it out. The others then try to decide whose sentence it is and why (e.g. *I think Marcin will be working as a chef in five years time, because he really likes cooking now*).

Weaker students write as many sentences as they can manage, even if it's only one.

Study skills: mind maps

Present the suggestions in the box and discuss how to work in this way.

---

5 **Speaking: guessing game**

Students describe a classmate's clothes for their partner to guess.

6 **Reading: skimming for gist**

Students read the text quickly to find the answer.

7 **Reading for detail**

 *4.4 CD 1 track 34*

Read through the questions with the class and ask them to find the answers individually, then to check with a partner.

8 **Working with words: verb + noun**

Read the sentences with the whole class and elicit other examples from students; note them on the board. Refer also to *Working with words*, page 103.

9 **Formation of future continuous**

Ask students first to complete the sentences from the text, then discuss the question. If necessary, look at the *Grammar Explorer,* page 122. Present the information in the grammar note.

Tell **weaker students** where to look (top section) for the sentences.

4C Talking about preferences

Spread aims

Functions: talking about preferences
Skills: reading for gist and detail
Pronunciation: words with /s/ and /z/
Writing: making arrangements by email

KEY

1 Fay: actress   Joe: sportsman
Dan: fashion designer

2 1 Dan   2 Joe

3 1 Dan   2 Fay   3 Joe   4 Joe
5 Dan   6 Joe

1 Reading and listening for gist

 *4.5 CD 1 track 35*

Stronger students cover the text and just listen.

Weaker students follow the conversation while they listen.

2 Reading for detail

Students read the dialogue and decide which student matches each statement.

3 Reading for detail

Students write the name of the person who says each phrase on the dotted line.

4 Useful expressions: intonation

 *4.6 CD 1 track 36*

Play the recording two or three times while the students just listen. Then play it again, pausing after each phrase for them to practise chorally and individually.

Extension: students work in threes; they practise the whole dialogue, imitating the intonation on the recording and using as much expression as they can. They can do it three times, in a different role each time.

5 Pronunciation: /s/ and /z/

 *4.7 CD 1 track 37*

Ask students to look at the words in the box and say them to themselves

Reading and listening

1 *4.5 **Read and listen to the dialogue. What jobs do Fay, Joe and Dan want to do?***

2 Read the dialogue again and answer the questions.

1   Who wants to do media studies and art?
2   Who doesn't want to do media studies or French?

3 Find the *Useful expressions* in the dialogue. Who says each sentence?

USEFUL EXPRESSIONS

.... I'd like to drop French.
.... I want to do media studies.
.... I don't want to do French.
.... I prefer chemistry to media studies.
.... I'd rather do media studies.
.... I'd rather be in the gym than in a classroom.

4 *4.6 **Listen and repeat the *Useful expressions*. Focus on your intonation.***

44

Fay:	Oh, no. Another D for chemistry. I'm going to fail next week's test, I know.
Joe:	I'll help you revise, if you like.
Fay:	Thanks, but it doesn't really matter. I'm going to drop chemistry next year. I want to do media studies instead.
Joe:	Really? I prefer chemistry to media studies.
Dan:	Not me, I'd rather do media studies. Anyway, Fay, won't you need chemistry?
Fay:	No, I don't think I will – not if I'm going to be a famous actress!
Dan:	OK, so which other subjects are you going to take?
Fay:	I'm not sure. It's hard to decide. I'd like to do just music and drama all the time! What about you?
Dan:	I haven't got a clue. Well, I need art, obviously, to be a fashion designer. I'd like to drop French, though.
Joe:	I don't want to do French either. I'd rather be in the gym than in a classroom.
Fay:	And what will you do when you're an international sports star? You'll need to speak different languages, won't you?
Joe:	Ah well, I'll be rich enough to have a translator by then!

to see whether they think the letter 's' sounds like /s/ or /z/. They should write s or z in front of each word. They then listen to the recording and write what they hear, – s or z – after each word. They can compare the results.

6 Pronunciation practice: /s/ and /z/

 *4.7 CD 1 track 37*

Play the recording and pause after each word for the students to say it chorally and individually. They then work in pairs and practise the words, monitoring their partner's production.

Extension: students find twenty more words, ten of which contain the letter 's' with the /s/ sound and ten with the /z/ sound.

7 Speaking about preferences

Students complete the sentences in pairs. Check the answers as a whole class and make sure students correct their answers. They can then practise the dialogues in pairs.

8 Speaking about your preferences

The students use the table to talk about their real preferences, using the phrases from Exercise 7.

Pronunciation: words with /s/ and /z/ sounds

5 ◯ 4.7 **Listen to the words. Which words have an *s* sound and which have a *z* sound?**

> baseball   busy   design   disappear
> fossil   history   instead   museum
> pleased   presentation   sponsor
> thousand   used (*past simple*)   used to

6 ◯ 4.7 **Listen and repeat the words in Exercise 5.**

Writing: arrangements

1 **Read the emails and answer the questions.**

1 Where are Holly and Lisa going next week?
2 Why are they going there?
3 Which day are they going there?
4 How will they find each other?

2 **Complete these sentences from the emails. Which tenses are used?**

1 By the time you .... this, I .... probably ....
2 Can you let me know as soon as you .... out the day of your visit?
3 I'll wait until you .... there.
4 Text me when you .... home.

See Grammar Explorer: Page 122

3 **Complete the sentences with the expressions in the box. More than one answer is sometimes possible.**

> as soon as   by the time   when   until

1 Can you phone me .... your sister arrives?
2 I'll text you .... the match ends.
3 I'll probably be home .... my dad hears my message.
4 I can't go home .... the bell rings.
5 .... I finish this question, the exam will be over.

4 **Write a message to your partner arranging to meet. Reply to your partner's message and confirm the details. Use some of the expressions from Exercise 3. Use these ideas or ideas of your own.**

a sports event   a concert
a shopping trip   a day trip

Speaking

7 **Work in pairs. Choose the correct option (a–c). Then practise the dialogues.**

1 A: Do you like tennis? There's a game on TV.
   B: Oh, I (**1**) .... athletics, really.
   A: OK, I think there's athletics on another channel.
   B: Actually, I (**2**) .... read my book.

   1 a 'd like to   b 'd rather   c prefer
   2 a 'd rather   b prefer   c want

2 A: Do you prefer plain or patterned T-shirts?
   B: Plain – and with long sleeves.
   A: Oh, I (**1**) .... short sleeves.
   B: But I (**2**) .... wear a shirt than a T-shirt, anyway.

   1 a 'd like to   b 'd rather   c prefer
   2 a 'd like to   b 'd rather   c prefer

8 **Work in pairs. Compare your preferences. Use the dialogues in Exercise 7 to help you.**

basketball football tennis	boots shoes trainers	burger pasta pizza	maths English biology

---

Hi Lisa,
I've just seen the list of work experience placements and I see you're going to PC World next week – so am I! If we're going to be there on the same day, we can go together. I'm not sure which day it is yet, but by the time you get this, I'll probably know. Can you let me know as soon as you find out the day of your visit?
See you
Holly

Hi Holly,
I saw your name too – we're both going to PC World on Wednesday. We can meet outside the main entrance (PC World is quite close to my house actually). I'll wait until you get there. Or you can text me when you leave home on Wednesday morning if you like.
See you then!
Lisa

Communicate

KEY

5 /s/ baseball, disappear, fossil, history, instead, sponsor, used to
/z/ busy, design, museum, pleased, presentation, thousand, used

7 1 1 c   2 a   2 1 c   2 b

Writing

1 1 PC World   2 For a work experience placement
3 Wednesday   4 They'll meet outside the main entrance.

2 1 get ... 'll ... know
2 find   3 get   4 leave
The present simple and future simple are used.

3 1 as soon as / when
2 as soon as / when   3 by the time / when   4 until   5 By the time

Weaker students can follow Holly and Lisa's emails very closely, just changing the important details.

Extension: students can pass the same email to different partners and get different replies and answer other emails.

Writing: arrangements

1 Reading for detail

Students find the information in the emails to answer the questions.

Tell **weaker students** that 1 and 2 are in Holly's email, and 3 and 4 are in Lisa's.

2 Writing: sentence completion

Students complete the sentences from the emails with verbs and answer the question. If possible, elicit when each tense is used (i.e. the present simple is used after the time expression). Refer also to *Grammar Explorer,* page 122.

Tell **weaker students** that 1 and 2 are in Holly's email, and 3 and 4 are in Lisa's.

3 Writing: using time expressions

Ask students to find the expression that fits the sentence best, then include any other possible options.

4 Writing practice: email arrangements

Students write the first email individually, using the expressions in Exercise 3, and referring to Holly's email for help. They should choose a different topic from their partner – either from those in the box, or their own ideas. Once they have written their first email, they give it to their partner, and write a reply to what they have been given.

4D Sport in Australia

Spread aims

Vocabulary: sports and outdoor activities

Skills: Reading and listening for detail

Culture: Australian sports

CLIL: Physics and English: Newton's laws of motion

1 Warm-up

With books closed, students first make a list of sports associated with Australia (e.g. *surfing, tennis, swimming*); elicit suggestions from the whole class and list them on the board. Then ask them to open their books and scan the text to see if their sports are mentioned.

2 Reading for detail

 4.8 CD 1 track 38

Ask the students to write short answers to the questions.

Weaker students can underline the sentences which contain the answers and circle the words which are the answers.

3 Vocabulary: synonyms

Tell **weaker students** they will find the answer to question 1 in the introduction, to questions 2 and 3 in the *International Events* paragraph, and to question 4 in the *Did you know?* paragraph.

4 Vocabulary: verbs used with sports

Students find the phrases in the text and answer the question, then group the sports activities according to the verb we use them with.

Reading

1 What sports do you associate with Australia? Read the text quickly and see if they are mentioned.

2 4.8 Read the text again. Answer the questions.

1 What is 'Surfers Paradise'?
2 What is the 'Australian Open'?
3 Who is Ian Thorpe?
4 What is 'footy'?

3 Find words in the text that mean the same as the underlined words.

1 It's nice to eat <u>outside</u> in the summer.
2 There were 50,000 <u>people in the audience</u> at the tennis final.
3 There's a lot of <u>competition</u> between Arsenal and Chelsea.
4 The <u>best</u> athletes take part in the world championships.

Culture Australia

Australia has the perfect ingredients for life outdoors – warm, sunny weather and lots of open spaces. Australians are so passionate about sport that nine of the ten most popular TV shows are about sports. But taking part is equally important.

Beach sports

As an island continent, Australia has more than 34,000 kilometres of coastline – mostly sandy beaches and the warm water of the Pacific and Indian Oceans. Almost everyone in Australia learns to swim when they are young – either at primary school, in the pool at home or at a nearby beach. Kids who live near the ocean often go surfing after school. The big surfing fashion and clothing companies sponsor the best surfers, so some people have a professional career as surfers. There's even a town in the state of Queensland called Surfers Paradise!

International events

The Formula One grand prix at Melbourne is a huge spectator event. Spectators also fill every available seat at the 'Ashes series' cricket matches. This sports rivalry between England and Australia has a long history, going back to 1882. But you can also see people playing cricket in parks and on beaches all through the summer. The Australian Open is one of the four 'grand slam' tennis tournaments. It's also the first big event of the tennis year and all the top players compete there.

The Olympic Games

Australia has hosted the Summer Olympics twice – in Melbourne in 1956 and in Sydney in 2000 – and it's one of only a few countries that has taken part in all of the summer Olympics. Swimmer Ian Thorpe won a total of nine Olympic medals, including five golds, before he retired in 2006. Australia has won Olympic medals in sports such as canoeing, water polo and beach volleyball too.

Did you know?

Make sure you know the names of sports if you go to Australia. Football is called soccer there. And they play a game which looks like rugby, but it's called Aussie Rules football or footy!

46

Weaker students answer the first part of the question together and read out the sentences from the text about surfing and cricket. Students then group the words in the box.

5 Listening for detail

 4.9 CD 1 track 39

Read through the sentences with the whole class and make sure they understand them before they listen.

Give **weaker students** a copy of the tapescript to follow after the first or second listening.

Tapescript

Hi, this is Peter Barrymore with the latest sports update. You can get all the details on our website as usual, but here are the headlines.

Bad weather is continuing to disrupt sports events all over the country. There is no horse racing at all and several premier league football matches have been cancelled as there is so much snow on the pitches that it will be impossible to play.

Staying with football, Manchester United have more injury problems. Wes Brown has injured his foot and Wayne Rooney's suffering with a knee injury, but he will be able to play in the Champions League match against Milan next week. Rugby now, and France continue to dominate the Six Nations championship with an incredible win over Ireland. France will play their last match against England next month and are favourites to win the championship. Scotland are having their worst championship for several years.

In Glasgow, the athletics grand prix finishes tomorrow. The British team is

4 Which verbs do we use with *surfing* and *cricket*? Check in the text. Then put these sports into two groups.

> beach volleyball   canoeing
> football   rugby   swimming
> tennis   water polo

Listening

5 🎧 4.9 **Listen to the sports news. Are the sentences true or false?**

1 Snow has affected many sports events.
2 Wayne Rooney will be playing in the next Champions League match.
3 France has won the Six Nations rugby championship.
4 The British athletics team is top of the medals table in Glasgow.
5 Roger Federer is launching a new fashion collection.

6 🎧 4.9 **Listen again and choose the correct option (a–c).**

1 Wayne Rooney has a .... injury.
   a foot
   b head
   c knee
2 France beat .... in the last Six Nations game.
   a England
   b Ireland
   c Scotland
3 Venus Williams has her own .... label.
   a clothing
   b jewellery
   c perfume

Project

Write a short text about sport in your country. Find some photos in a magazine or on the Internet. Use the questions to help you.

• Do people prefer outdoor or indoor sports?
• What sports are popular after-school activities?
• What kind of international events are held?
• What are your national sports?

Physics and English
Newton's laws of motion

1 Read the text and answer the questions.

1 What's the scientific word that describes 'pushing' or 'pulling'?
2 What's another word for 'movement'?
3 What's the name of the force that pulls things to the Earth?

Sir Isaac Newton (1642–1727) was an English physicist. He described some of the basic laws of nature. These laws are known as 'Newton's laws of motion' and 'Newton's law of universal gravitation'.

We can see these laws in action when we watch sports. Imagine the world champion ski jumper, Lindsey Van, at the top of a ski jump. She is waiting to jump and she is standing still. She won't begin to move until she pushes herself forward. A push, or a pull, is called a 'force' in physics. Then, when Van pushes forward, she starts to move down the ski jump. She doesn't need to push now. This is Newton's first law of motion. It says that objects stay still if there is no force. It also says that objects keep moving in the same direction until they meet another force.

Van reaches the end of the ski jump and takes off into the air. But she doesn't continue in the same direction – flying through the air – forever, because she meets another force. The most important force in action here is gravity. Gravity pulls everything towards the centre of the Earth, and that means it pulls Van towards the ground. But she falls slowly, not instantly. Why? This is because while her body pushes down on the air, the air also pushes her up. It's Newton's third law of motion: forces act in pairs.

2 Read the text again and decide if these sentences about Newton's first law of motion are true or false.

1 An object won't move unless something pushes or pulls it.
2 A moving object won't stop if there is no force against it.

3 Can you think of other examples which demonstrate Newton's laws? Compare with your partner.

Culture

KEY

4 go: canoeing, swimming
play: beach volleyball, football, rugby, tennis, water polo

5 1 T   2 T   3 F   4 F   5 F

6 1 c   2 b   3 a

Physics and English

1 1 a force   2 motion
3 gravity

2 1 T   2 T

2 Reading for detail

Tell **weaker students** that they will find the answers to 1 and 2 after the sentence that says: *this is Newton's first law of motion.*

3 Speaking: Newton's laws

Ask students to think of other examples from sport – the movement of footballs or tennis balls, for example – or from other areas of life, such as transport. Once they have shared ideas with a partner, elicit some examples from the whole class and discuss them.

---

currently second in the medals table, behind the USA. Most of the athletes in the team will also be competing in the world indoor meeting next month.

And finally, will Roger Federer follow other tennis celebrities, like Venus Williams, into fashion design? His outfits on court are usually designed by Nike and feature his personal 'RF' logo. Venus Williams has been in the news this week with her latest collection for her clothing label, Eleven. Venus wore outfits from the label in her doubles match with her sister, Serena, at the Australian Open …

6 Listening for detail

 4.9 CD 1 track 39

Ask students to read through the options carefully before they listen again.

Project: sport

Present the instructions and question prompts in the box and perhaps elicit some answers from the students to get them thinking. They can do the writing for homework. Ask them to produce a poster, with writing and pictures. Organise a presentation session, perhaps in groups of five or six, where each student talks to the others about their work, and they read each other's posters.

Physics and English: Newton's laws of motion

1 Vocabulary: physics

Read through the questions with the whole class before they look for the answers.

4E Consolidation Units 3 and 4

Spread aims

Reading and **language response:**
developing subskills

Consolidating understanding of the key grammar points from Units 3 and 4

Reading

1 Identifying key words

Present the reading strategies and discuss the strategies given for finding the main idea in a text. Students underline the key vocabulary in the text in Exercise 1, then check their ideas with a partner. Elicit suggestions from the whole class, and discuss which words are most important. Elicit ideas for the main topic of the text.

2 Choosing the topic

Ask students to read the paragraph again and decide which of the three options fits best.

3 Reading for gist

Ask students to read the paragraph and decide which topic it is about; suggest that they mentally underline the key vocabulary as they read it through first.

Reading

Identifying the main idea
• Read the whole text quickly without worrying about words you don't understand.
• Decide what you think the main topic of the text is and look for this in the options in the task.
• Read the text again to confirm your choice and to make sure that the alternatives are not correct.
• **Important!** You need to read the whole text to find the main idea.

1 Read the text and find the key words. What do you think the topic of the text is?

> Not everybody has the talent to be a professional sportsperson, but there's a variety of jobs you can do – from being an instructor to being a professional referee. You need to be good at sports, of course, and for most jobs you'll need a qualification. You'll also need excellent 'people skills'.

2 Which option (a–c) matches your answer to Exercise 1?

a Sports celebrities
b Studying sport
c Careers in sport

3 Read the text and choose the correct option (a–c).

> I love fashion and I want to be a fashion designer. There's a course at my local college, so I'm going to apply for a place there. It's a three-year course and with that qualification, I'll be able to work in one of the big fashion companies. I'll probably move to London, which will be quite exciting, or even Paris! I know that it's a difficult career, but I'm going to work really hard to succeed. In 2020, someone will be wearing one of my designs to the Oscars!

The text is about the writer's … .

a designs
b experience
c plans

Grammar

Choosing the correct word form
• Read the whole text quickly.
• Look at the gapped sentences. What kind of words are missing?
• Look at the options given for each gap. Choose the option that matches the grammar and logic of the gapped sentence.
• **Important!** Try each option before you decide.

1 Look at the words in each group. Are they nouns, verbs, adjectives or pronouns?

1 amazed frightening brilliant
2 buy play go
3 that which who
4 do have will

2 What kind of word is missing from each gap?

1 We .... never seen such a brilliant athlete!
2 What time are you .... to the party?
3 It wasn't a very good match. It was a bit ....
4 This is the race .... is the most important.

3 Look at the options for each gap in Exercise 2. Choose the correct answers.

	a		b		c	
1	has		have		having	
2	going		go		went	
3	boring		bore		bored	
4	who		what		which	

4 Read the text and choose the correct option (a–c).

> Hi Dan,
> We've got tickets for the Cup Final next month! I'm so (1) .... ! Do you want to come with us? It's on Saturday 11th and (2) .... leaving at about 6 a.m. I know it's really early, but my dad thinks it (3) .... us about four hours to get there. I'd love you to come – and you don't have to pay for the ticket either!
> (4) .... call you later.
> Joe

	a		b		c	
1	excite		excited		exciting	
2	we'll		we're		we've	
3	takes		is taking		will take	
4	I'm		I'd		I'll	

Grammar

1 Identifying word classes

Present the bullet points and discuss the strategies given for completing gapped sentences from a multiple choice. Students look at Exercise 1 and decide which word class each group of three words belongs to.

2 Identifying the type of missing word

Students decide what kind of word (e.g. noun, verb etc.) is missing from each space.

3 Choosing gap-fill options

Students select the correct word from the multiple choices given.

4 Gapped text

Students select the correct word from the multiple choices given. Suggest they think about what class of word is necessary the first time they read it through, without looking at the actual options below. Elicit answers from the whole class.

Verb + -ing

We use verb + -ing after certain verbs such as *avoid, enjoy, finish, imagine, mind, recommend, suggest, stop.*

Jojo really enjoys eating bananas.

1 Complete the sentences with the correct form of the verbs in the box.

avoid	finish	imagine
mind	recommend	stop

1 Superstitious people .... opening umbrellas in the house.
2 Have you .... reading that book yet?
3 The show is very popular, so I .... buying tickets in advance.
4 I can't .... being hypnotised.
5 Please .... whistling! It's very annoying.
6 'Sorry, I'm not ready yet.' 'It's OK. I don't .... waiting.'

A verb which follows a preposition ends in *-ing*.

Mark's great at fixing things.

2 Match the beginnings of the sentences (1–5) with the endings (a–e).

1 English people are famous for
2 You can improve your English by
3 Are you afraid of
4 What did Jensen Button do after
5 I'm not really interested in

a flying?
b playing games or doing sports.
c practising every day.
d talking about the weather.
e winning the Formula One championship?

We use verb + -ing as the subject of a sentence.

Looking for UFOs is a waste of time.

3 Complete the sentences with the -ing form of the verbs. Make as many sentences as you can.

act	dance	meet
perform	see	sing

1 .... in a competition is terrifying.
2 .... in front of an audience feels amazing.
3 .... my idol was fantastic.

to + infinitive

We use *to* + infinitive after verbs such as *agree, decide, want* and after adjectives such as *easy, impossible, pleased.*

See Working with words: Page 102.

Begin, continue, hate, like, love, start can be followed by both *to* + infinitive and verb + -*ing*. The meaning is the same. The meaning is different with other verbs such as *try.*

4 How many verbs from the box can you use to complete each sentence?

begin	continue	hate	like
love	start		

1 I really .... eating chocolate cake.
2 OK, you can .... to fry the sausages now.
3 When did you .... learning English?
4 She says she'll .... to do lots of sport when she leaves school.

5 Write the verb in the correct form.

1 I'm quite excited about .... (**go**) on holiday.
2 I'm pleased .... (**meet**) you, Mr Jones.
3 The league has decided .... (**cancel**) the match.
4 Do you enjoy .... (**cook**)?
5 .... (**make**) dinner for ten people is hard work.

5 Gerund or infinitive

Students decide whether the gerund or infinitive form of the verbs in brackets is correct.

1 Verb + -*ing*

Read through the box with students before they attempt the gap-fill.

2 Matching parts of a sentence

Students match the halves of the sentences in a way that is logical as well as grammatically correct.

Extension: students could combine the halves in more unusual or funny ways.

3 Completing sentences with verb + -*ing*

Students complete the sentences with as many sensible options as they can.

Weaker students make one answer for each sentence.

4 Verbs + to / -*ing*

Students decide which verbs would make sense in each sentence.

Review Units 3 and 4

Spread aims

Reviewing vocabulary, grammar and functions from Units 3 and 4; giving students the opportunity to assess their own progress

KEY

1 1 a minute   2 a century
3 a fortnight   4 a decade
5 an hour

2 1 soldier   2 chef   3 postal worker   4 paramedic
5 mechanic

3 1 pool   2 track   3 pitch
4 ring   5 court

4 1 c   2 e   3 b   4 d   5 a

5 1 vacation   2 apartment
3 store   4 cookie   5 fries

6 1 had started   2 went
3 hadn't lived   4 hadn't written down   5 saw (had seen)

7 1 Which cartoons did you use to watch?
2 I used to love Bugs Bunny.
3 Did they use to read comics?
4 We didn't use to like cheese.
5 My brother used to cry a lot.

8 1 's going to score   2 'm going to work hard   3 is playing
4 are going to be   5 are we meeting

9 1 correct   2 correct
3 incorrect ('ll like)   4 correct
5 incorrect ('ll win)

10 1 taking   2 to lose
3 meeting   4 waiting
5 to speak

Review **Units 3 and 4**

Vocabulary

1 Write the words.

1 sixty seconds = ...
2 100 years = ...
3 two weeks = ...
4 ten years = ...
5 sixty minutes = ...

1 mark per item: .../5 marks

2 Write the jobs.

1 ....
2 ....
3 ....
4 ....
5 ....

1 mark per item: .../5 marks

3 Complete the sports places.

1 a swimming p............
2 a racing t............
3 a football p............
4 a boxing r............
5 a tennis c............

1 mark per item: .../5 marks

4 Match the words (1–5) with the categories (a–e).

1 cotton, silk   a patterns
2 bright, pastel   b garments
3 a skirt, a top   c fabrics
4 hooded, V-neck   d styles
5 striped, plain   e colours

1 mark per item: .../5 marks

5 Write the American English word that means the same as the British English word.

1 holiday = ...
2 flat = ...
3 shop = ...
4 biscuit = ...
5 chips = ...

1 mark per item: .../5 marks

Grammar

6 Complete the sentences with the past simple or past perfect form of the verbs.

1 I was late. The lesson .... (**start**).
2 After you left, I .... (**go**) home.
3 Tests showed that the animal .... (**not / live**) very long.
4 I couldn't call you because I .... (**not / write down**) your number.
5 The man .... (**see**) a robbery and called the police.

1 mark per item: .../5 marks

7 Make statements and questions with used to.

1 Which cartoons / you / watch?
2 I / love / Bugs Bunny.
3 they / read / comics?
4 We / not like / cheese.
5 My brother / cry / a lot.

1 mark per item: .../5 marks

8 Complete the sentences with the present continuous or going to form of the verb.

1 Look at Rooney! He .... (**score**)!
2 I've decided I .... (**work / hard**).
3 Chelsea .... (**play**) Milan tonight.
4 What a win! The fans .... (**be**) pleased.
5 What time .... we .... (**meet**) on Friday?

1 mark per item: .../5 marks

9 Is the future continuous correct in each sentence?

1 This summer, we'**ll be wearing** lots of red and blue.
2 This time next week, we'**ll be watching** the final.
3 Do you think you'**ll be liking** university?
4 In a month's time, I'**ll be doing** my final exams.
5 I think he'**ll be winning** the race.

1 mark per item: .../5 marks

10 Write the verb in the correct form.

1 I'm worried about .... (**take**) the test.
2 It's easy .... (**lose**) against that team.
3 Did you enjoy .... (**meet**) the Queen?
4 .... (**wait**) for the results of an exam is always horrible.
5 Did you learn .... (**speak**) French at school?

1 mark per item: .../5 marks

Communicate

11 Complete the questions.

1 .... does it take to fry an egg?
2 .... people live in your house?
3 .... is it from London to Manchester?
4 .... money have you got?
5 .... was the last Ice Age?

2 marks per item: …/10 marks

12 Complete the dialogue with the expressions.

> do you want   I don't want   I prefer   I'd like
> I'd rather

Dad: What (1) .... for lunch today?
Mum: Oh, I don't know.
Kate: (2) .... sausage and chips, please.
Dad: Oh, no. We had that the other day.
        (3) .... to have it again.
Mum: Well, (4) .... go out than eat at home.
Dad: No, we're not going out. You can have pasta
        or sandwiches.
Kate: Well (5) .... sandwiches to pasta.
Dad: OK, sandwiches.

2 marks per item: …/10 marks

13 Does the s in these words sound like /s/ or /z/?

1   busy   ....
2   design   ....
3   disappear   ....
4   fossil   ....
5   museum   ....
6   newspaper   ....
7   pleased   ....
8   roasting   ....
9   sausage   ....
10 thousand   ....

2 marks per item: …/10 marks

14 Rewrite the sentences with *that* and *so* or *such*.

1 I was tired. I had to sit down. (**so**)
2 It was a hard exam. I couldn't do it. (**such**)
3 The stadium was full. We couldn't get in. (**so**)
4 It was a boring game. I fell asleep. (**such**)
5 My friend was thirsty. He drank three cans of cola.
   (**so**)

2 marks per item: …/10 marks

15 Complete the email with these words.

> as   at   if   next   not   them   to
> until   when   will

Here are the arrangements for (1) .... Saturday.
Please read (2) .... carefully. I don't want anyone
(3) .... miss the trip!

Please give your name to me as soon (4) .... you
arrive and then get on the bus. (5) .... everyone
is on the bus, we (6) .... leave. However, if you
aren't there by eight o'clock, we will (7) .... wait.

After we set off, there will be no stops (8) .... we
arrive at the stadium. (9) .... there are any
questions, please email me immediately. See you all
(10) .... 8 a.m. on Saturday!

1 mark per item: …/10 marks

Total: …/100

I can...

I can talk about quantity, time and distance.
I can talk about preferences.

KEY

11 1 How long   2 How many
    3 How far   4 How much
    5 When

12 1 do you want   2 I'd like
    3 I don't want   4 I'd rather
    5 I prefer

13 1 /z/   2 /z/   3 /s/   4 /s/
    5 /z/   6 /z/   7 /z/   8 /s/
    9 /s/   10 /z/

14 1 I was so tired that I had to
    sit down.
    2 It was such a hard exam that
    I couldn't do it.
    3 The stadium was so full that
    we couldn't get in.
    4 It was such a boring game
    that I fell asleep.
    5 My friend was so thirsty that
    he drank three cans of cola.

15 1 next   2 them   3 to   4 as
    5 When   6 will   7 not
    8 until   9 If   10 at

Project: Talking about the future

Page aim

Reading for detail; writing predictions for the future

KEY

1 1 are going to; 2 will probably; 3 will need; 4 are coming; 5 are going to; 6 will finally see; 7 will be wearing; 8 will; 9 will all have to; 10 is going to; 11 will be; 12 will have to learn; 13 will be doing; 14 will always be; 15 are going to have to

Warm-up

With books closed, ask students for some simple predictions about the future: what will the weather be like at the weekend; who will win the football league in your country; what they'll do when they leave school.

1 Reading for detail

The object of this exercise is for students to collect, and thereby revise, ways of making predictions. Ask students to do it individually, then check with a partner, before eliciting the answers from the whole class as complete sentences. You may want to collect the different possible forms exemplified on the board.

2 Discussion

Ask students to discuss the six topics in pairs, using the phrases from Exercise 1. Suggest students give reasons for their predictions.

Extension: When they have finished, elicit ideas from the whole class and try to expand the discussion, having students express different predictions. (Pre-teach: *I'm sorry, but I don't agree...; I'm afraid I don't think that will happen...*as ways of introducing a new opinion after another student has spoken.)

3 Writing notes

Ask students to make notes about different aspects of their own future;

you could suggest they think about education, jobs, marriage, children, home-owning, hobbies, holidays etc. For follow-up, ask students to compare their future with a partner's.

Extension: ask pairs to tell the class about their similarities and differences (e.g. *We're both going to University after school; While he's going to get married and have a family, I'm going to get a job and stay single.*).

Project

Present the Project box and ask students to do the two parts of the Project (selecting one of the 3 topics, then also writing about themselves).

Suggest they write two paragraphs (50–75 words about the main topic, and 50–75 words about themselves). Encourage them to illustrate their predictions with pictures.

Presentation

Students bring their writing (and pictures) into class and share them in groups of four, reading and commenting on each others' work, comparing and contrasting their ideas. You might arrange it so that the groups are based on which of the 3 main topics they chose.

PROJECT — Talking about the future

1 Read the predictions from the article and complete the gaps.

1 I think Spain .... win the European Championships.
2 I think Uruguay .... do well.
3 Jenson Button and Lewis Hamilton .... beat Mark Webber.
4 The summer collections .... out in the next couple of months.
5 I think we .... see some major changes in clothes.
6 In five years' time, I think we .... the end of denim.
7 By 2020, I don't think we .... the same kind of clothes.
8 I think they .... invent new fabrics.
9 Fifty years from now, we .... wear loose clothing to stay cool.
10 The world .... change and it's difficult to say exactly how.
11 I don't think the jobs today .... available.
12 I'm sure we .... new skills.
13 Machines .... the work in the future.
14 There .... a demand for some jobs.
15 People .... keep up-to-date with the latest developments.

2 With a partner, discuss these questions.

- Who do you think is going to win the next Formula One Championship / tennis tournament / basketball championship, etc)?
- Which sports will become more/less popular?
- What will people be wearing this summer / in five years' time / 50 years from now?
- Do you think any of the things we wear today will disappear in the future?
- What kind of jobs and skills will/won't we need in the future?
- Do you think people will earn more or less money than today?

3 Make notes about *your* future. Use phrases like those below. Compare notes with a partner.

I will probably …   I'd like to …
I want to …   I'd rather …
I'm going to …

52

What's going to happen?
Angela Brown continues her series of predictions for the future.

Sport

I think Spain are going to win the European Championship. It's possible that one of the South American teams will win the next World Cup. I think Uruguay will probably do well again. In Formula One, Jenson Button and Lewis Hamilton will need to beat Mark Webber, who I think is going to be the next champion.

Clothes

The summer collections are coming out in the next couple of months, and everyone is excited. But, looking further ahead, I think we are going to see some major changes in the clothes we wear. In five years' time, I think we will finally see the end of denim. And, looking further ahead, by 2020, I don't think we will be wearing the same styles, and I think they will invent new fabrics. Fifty years from now, I think we will all have to wear loose clothing, with long-sleeved tops and perhaps flared trousers, to cover up from the sun and to stay cool.

Careers

The world is going to change, and it's difficult to say exactly how. I don't think the jobs that are out there today will be available in a few years and I'm sure we'll have to learn new skills as the job market changes. I think people will have to learn how to use new machines but, mostly, I think the machines will be doing the work in the future. We'll just be watching them to make sure they don't break down. But there will always be a demand for some jobs – we'll always need doctors, paramedics, mechanics and accountants, for example. But people are going to have to keep up-to-date with the latest developments because – and this is my last prediction – things are going to be changing fast!

Project

Write about your predictions for the future.
- Choose one of the headings: **Clothes / Sport / Careers**
- Write about what you think *will / is going to* happen
- Add one heading called **Me** and write about your future
- When you write about yourself, you can use *I'd like to, I want to* and *I'd rather* for the future
- You can also use the future continuous or the present continuous for the future
- Don't forget to use the vocabulary from Unit 4
- Try to find interesting pictures showing now or the future (or draw your own)

Special things

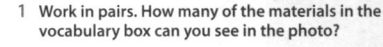

Special things

Unit aims

Grammar: the passive in various tenses and with modal verbs *can, must, will; have something done*

Vocabulary: materials; adjectives of size and shape; adjective order; verb + preposition combinations

Functions: expressing purpose and giving reasons

Reading about: the New Seven Wonders of the World; gold; natural resources in Canada

Listening to: a Greek myth; statistics about Canada

Writing a description of an object

> Grammar
Learn about the present simple, past simple, present continuous, past continuous, present perfect passive, and the passive with modal verbs: *can, must, will.*

> Vocabulary
Learn words for materials, and adjectives for size and shape.
Work with adjective order, and verb + preposition combinations.

> Skills
Read about the New Seven Wonders of the World, gold, and natural resources in Canada.
Listen to a story from Greek mythology, and some statistics about Canada.
Write a description of an object.

> Communicate
Express purpose and give reasons.

---

1 Work in pairs. How many of the materials in the vocabulary box can you see in the photo?

brick	glass	paper	stone
concrete	leather	plastic	wood
fabric	metal	rubber	wool

2 What are these things made of? Use words from the vocabulary box.

books	bottles	cars
clothes	computers	school desks
shoes	skyscrapers	toothbrushes

3 5.1 Listen to two conversations. Answer the questions. Can you identify the objects?
1 How big is it?
2 What's it made of?
3 What's it for?

4 Work in pairs. Choose four objects each. Ask and answer questions about your objects and discover your partner's objects.

53

KEY

2 books – paper, leather; bottles – glass, plastic; cars – glass, metal, plastic, rubber; clothes – fabric, leather, wool; computers – metal, plastic; school desks – metal, plastic, wood; shoes – fabric, leather, plastic, rubber; skyscrapers – brick, concrete, glass, metal; toothbrushes – plastic

3 1 very big; made of brick; for living in: house
2 quite small; made of paper; for making notes in: notebook

Joe: What's it made of?

Fay: It's made of paper.

Joe: When was it made?

Fay: I don't know … last year, perhaps?

Joe: Where was it made?

Fay: It was made in England.

Joe: Well, it's some kind of book isn't it? … What's it for?

Fay: To make notes in!

4 Speaking practice

Students choose four objects, then take turns asking and answering the questions from Exercise 3 and the recording.

---

1 Warm-up

Present the words in the box, and have the students repeat them. Students should find the materials they know in the picture, then look up the remaining words in the dictionary.

2 Identifying materials

Students work in pairs to discuss the materials used. Point out that most items are (or can be) made of at least two materials.

3 Listening for gist

 5.1 CD 2 track 01

Read the questions with the class before they listen and answer.

Tapescript

1

Holly: How big is it?

Dan: It's very big.

Holly: What's it made of?

Dan: It's made of brick, mainly.

Holly: When was it made?

Dan: I'm not sure. About thirty years ago, I think.

Holly: Where was it made?

Dan: Oh, it was made in the same place as it is now – in my street.

Holly: Oh, I know what it is… what's it for?

Dan: It's for living in!

2

Joe: How big is it?

Fay: It's quite small.

5A World wonders

Spread aims

Grammar: passive

Vocabulary: adjective order; size and shape

Functions: talking about size and shape

Reading the new Seven Wonders of the World

KEY

3 The Great Wall of China; China; brick; to keep out enemies

Petra; Jordan; pink (limestone) rock; as a market town

Colosseum; (Rome) Italy; — ; for entertainment

Chichén Itzá; Mexico; stone; to live in

Machu Picchu; Peru; granite stones; —

Christ the Redeemer; (Rio de Janeiro) Brazil; concrete and stone; to celebrate independence

5 largest human-made structure; magnificent pink-coloured rock city; wealthy, busy market city; important trade routes; enormous stone city; massive granite stones; huge concrete and stone statue

6 You put the verb *to be* into the same tense as the active verb would be, and then add the past participle of the main verb (e.g. *they chose the New 7 Wonders – the New 7 Wonders were chosen*)

7 1 is 2 was 3 are 4 being
5 was 6 being 7 has 8 been

8 1 was … abandoned
2 are … being eroded
3 was … constructed
4 have … been damaged

---

1 Warm-up

Ask the students to tell each other what they know (or can guess) about the two places. Emphasise that they shouldn't read the texts, since they will do this in the next exercise.

2 Reading and listening for gist

🔘 *5.2 CD 2 track 02*

Students listen and read and check their answers to Exercise 1.

Stronger students cover the text and listen and answer.

Weaker students follow the text as they listen.

3 Reading for detail

Ask students to copy the table and complete it with information about the places in the text. Elicit answers, using present or past simple passives (e.g. *it is made of / was built of marble*), and complete a master table on the board. Note that information is not given for all parts of the table.

4 Speaking: personal opinion

The students tell their partner which place they'd like to visit and why.

Extension: students discuss which continent each Wonder is in.

5 Working with words: adjective order

Read the two examples and ask students to find similar word groups. Elicit answers from the class and write them on the board. Refer to *Working with words*, page 104.

6 Grammar: passive construction

Read the example with the whole class, and elicit ideas until students can give a correct explanation. If necessary, refer students to *Grammar Explorer*, page 123.

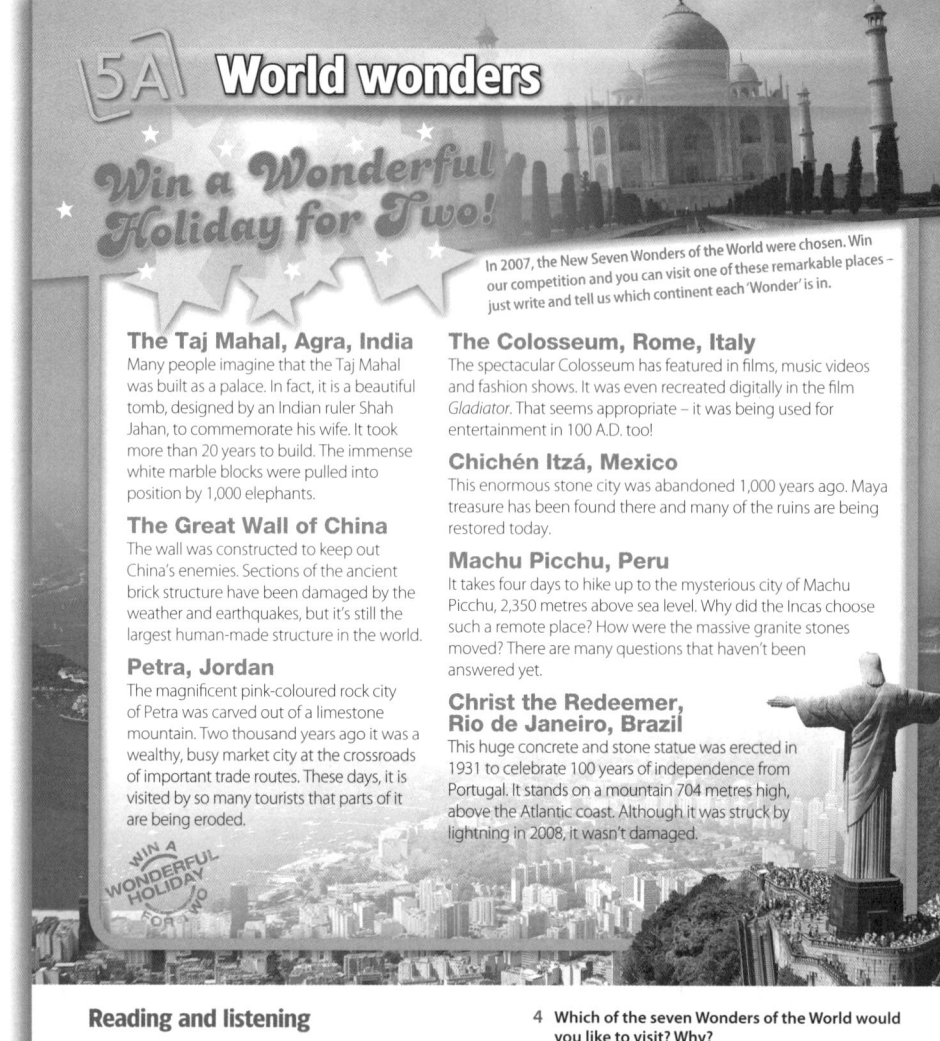

5A World wonders

Win a Wonderful Holiday for Two!

In 2007, the New Seven Wonders of the World were chosen. Win our competition and you can visit one of these remarkable places – just write and tell us which continent each 'Wonder' is in.

The Taj Mahal, Agra, India
Many people imagine that the Taj Mahal was built as a palace. In fact, it is a beautiful tomb, designed by an Indian ruler Shah Jahan, to commemorate his wife. It took more than 20 years to build. The immense white marble blocks were pulled into position by 1,000 elephants.

The Great Wall of China
The wall was constructed to keep out China's enemies. Sections of the ancient brick structure have been damaged by the weather and earthquakes, but it's still the largest human-made structure in the world.

Petra, Jordan
The magnificent pink-coloured rock city of Petra was carved out of a limestone mountain. Two thousand years ago it was a wealthy, busy market city at the crossroads of important trade routes. These days, it is visited by so many tourists that parts of it are being eroded.

The Colosseum, Rome, Italy
The spectacular Colosseum has featured in films, music videos and fashion shows. It was even recreated digitally in the film *Gladiator*. That seems appropriate – it was being used for entertainment in 100 A.D. too!

Chichén Itzá, Mexico
This enormous stone city was abandoned 1,000 years ago. Maya treasure has been found there and many of the ruins are being restored today.

Machu Picchu, Peru
It takes four days to hike up to the mysterious city of Machu Picchu, 2,350 metres above sea level. Why did the Incas choose such a remote place? How were the massive granite stones moved? There are many questions that haven't been answered yet.

Christ the Redeemer, Rio de Janeiro, Brazil
This huge concrete and stone statue was erected in 1931 to celebrate 100 years of independence from Portugal. It stands on a mountain 704 metres high, above the Atlantic coast. Although it was struck by lightning in 2008, it wasn't damaged.

Reading and listening

1 Work in pairs. Where are the two places in the photos? How much do you know about them?

2 🔘 5.2 Read and listen to the text. Check your answers to Exercise 1.

3 Read the text again. Copy and complete the table for the other six Wonders of the World. Some information isn't in the text.

Name	Location	Material	Reason
Taj Mahal	India	marble	to commemorate a ruler's wife

4 Which of the seven Wonders of the World would you like to visit? Why?

Working with words: adjective order

5 Look at the examples. Find similar adjective groups in the text.

immense white marble blocks
ancient brick structure

See Working with words: Page 104

54

Grammar: passive

6 Look at the example. How do we make the passive?

In 2007, the New Seven Wonders of the World were chosen.

See Grammar Explorer: Page 123

7 Complete the table with the words in the box.

are	been	being	being	has	is
was	was				

Simple tenses	
present	Petra (**1**) .... visited by too many tourists.
past	It (**2**) .... carved out of rock.
Continuous tenses	
present	Parts of it (**3**) .... (**4**) .... eroded.
past	It (**5**) .... (**6**) .... used for entertainment.
Present perfect	
Maya treasure (**7**) .... (**8**) .... found there.	

> We make the negative form by adding *n't* to *be* or *have: It wasn't damaged. The questions haven't been answered.*

8 Look at the example. Then complete the questions. Use the text to help you.

How were the massive granite stones moved?

1 'When .... Chichén Itzá .... ?''A thousand years ago.'
2 'Why .... parts of Petra .... ?''Because there are so many tourists these days.'
3 'Why .... the Great Wall of China .... ?''To keep out China's enemies.'
4 'How .... sections of the Great Wall of China .... ?'
   'By the weather and earthquakes.'

9 Rewrite each active sentence in the passive.

e.g. 20,000 workers built the Taj Mahal.
   The Taj Mahal was built by 20,000 workers.

1 They completed the Taj Mahal in the 1650s.
2 People have stolen bricks from the Great Wall of China.
3 They are stopping some visits to Petra.
4 The Romans were exploiting the gladiators.
5 They didn't accept the first plans for the statue.
6 Nobody has discovered all the Chichén Itzá treasure yet.

10 Look at your sentences for Exercise 9. Write questions as in the example.

e.g. Who? _Who was the Taj Mahal built by?_

1 When?   3 Where?   5 What?
2 What?   4 Who?   6 What?

11 Write the verbs in the correct active and passive forms.

United Kingdom of Great Britain
Pet Passport
Type P   Code of Issuing State GBR
Surname WONDER PUP
Given names WILLOW
Date of birth JANUARY 2005
Sex M   Place of birth BLACKPOOL

You'll need an up-to-date passport in order to travel to see your 'Wonder'. Passports (**1**) .... (**use**) for centuries, although only very important travellers (**2**) .... (**have**) them originally. In the past, passports (**3**) .... (**sign**) by a country's ruler! In the 1800s, travel for pleasure (**4**) .... (**become**) so popular in Europe that passports (**5**) .... (**abandon**) by several countries. These days, passports (**6**) .... (**change**). Data chips (**7**) .... (**introduce**) in some countries. And in the EU, passports for pets (**8**) .... (**need**) too!

Vocabulary: size and shape

12 Put the adjectives into two groups: *size* and *shape*. Divide the first group into *big* and *small*.

enormous	huge	immense	little
massive	microscopic	oval	rectangular
round	square	tiny	triangular

13 Choose the correct option.

1 Inca roads were made of **microscopic / rectangular** stones.
2 Bacteria are **immense / tiny** organisms.
3 The Colosseum is **huge / oval** in shape.
4 Pyramids usually have a **square / round** base.
5 Data chips contain **triangular / massive** amounts of information.

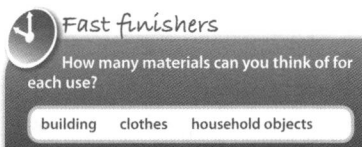

Fast finishers

How many materials can you think of for each use?

building   clothes   household objects

Grammar

9 1 The Taj Mahal was completed in the 1650s.
2 Bricks have been stolen from the Great Wall of China.
3 Some visits to Petra are being stopped.
4 The gladiators were being exploited (by the Romans).
5 The first plans for the statue were not accepted.
6 All the Chichén Itzá treasure has not been discovered yet.

10 1 When was the Taj Mahal completed?
2 What has been stolen from the Great Wall of China?
3 Where are some visits being stopped?
4 Who were / was being exploited by the Romans?
5 What was / were not accepted?
6 What has not yet been discovered (at Chichén Itzá)?

11 1 have been used   2 had
3 were signed   4 became
5 were abandoned   6 have changed   7 have been introduced   8 are needed

12 size (small): little, microscopic, tiny
size (big): enormous, huge, immense, massive
shape: oval, rectangular, round, square, triangular

13 1 rectangular   2 tiny   3 oval
4 square   5 massive

---

7 Grammar: passive simple and continous forms

Students complete the table with different tenses of the passive, then check with a partner.

8 Grammar: the passive

Present the grammar note about negative forms of the passive. Then look at the example question in Exercise 8 and discuss how passive questions are formed. Students find the information in the text and complete the questions using the same passive forms as those used in the text.

9 Grammar practice

The students transform the sentences from the active to the passive voice.

10 Grammar: passive questions

The students write questions for the sentences in Exercise 9.

11 Grammar: active and passive verbs

Suggest that **weaker students** first note whether each verb should be active or passive, then decide which tense to use and write the correct form. Do an example together first.

12 Vocabulary: size and shape

Ask students to make a table of three columns to list the words.

Help **weaker students** by drawing the table on the board as a model,

and doing the first word together as an example.

13 Vocabulary practice

Students choose the correct words to complete each sentence.

Extension: students can write sentences of their own using the incorrect word from each sentence.

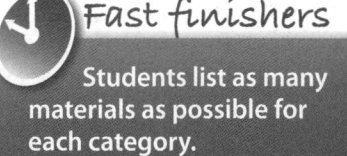

Fast finishers

Students list as many materials as possible for each category.

5B Gold fever

Spread aims

Grammar: passive with modal verbs
Vocabulary: gold
Functions: talking about myths
Reading about gold
Listening to a Greek myth

KEY

1 gold (The first three are made of gold; 50-year anniversaries are called 'golden'.)

3 1 enough to fill 3 Olympic-sized swimming pools
2 a solid piece of natural gold
3 dentistry, communications, computer and space technology, medicine

4 1 T   2 F   3 F

5 created from, discovered in, exchanged for, found in, mined from, separated from, turned into, used in

6 1 can be   2 must be
3 will be

7 Can it be made into fine threads?
It can't be made into fine threads.
Must it be separated from the rock?
It mustn't be separated from the rock.
Will a cancer treatment be developed this century?
A cancer treatment won't be developed this century.

5B Gold fever

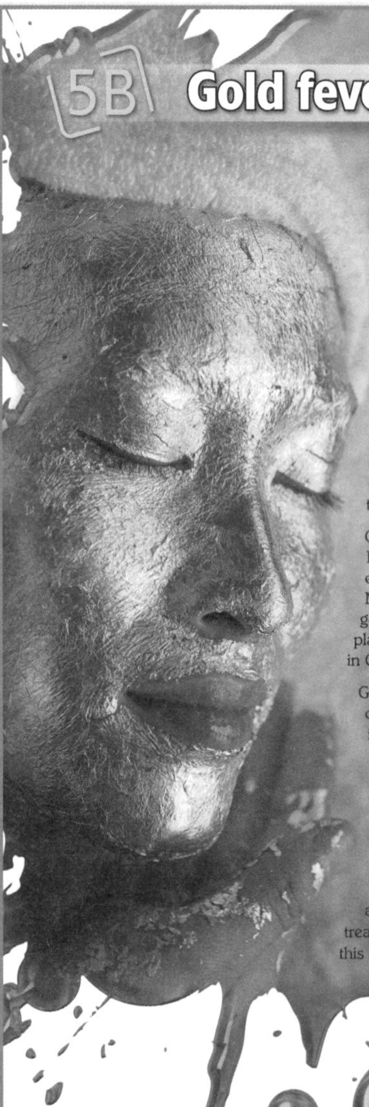

Gold

Gold is special in every culture in the world. But why has this shiny yellow metal always been valued as a fabulous treasure?

Firstly, it's soft and dense, so it's easy to shape. It can be made into fine threads, flat sheets or intricate shapes. A great variety of both decorative and functional things can be created from gold. Secondly, it never loses its shine. This means that beautiful gold objects from centuries ago will always be treasured. And thirdly, it's extremely rare. All the gold that has ever been mined would only fill two Olympic-sized swimming pools.

Gold has been discovered in different times and places in our history. Each time, the people who owned it became rich and powerful – for example, the Incas and the Aztecs in the Americas, or the Egyptian and Mali Empires in Africa. Their gold was exchanged for other valuable goods such as Arabic horses, luxurious silk and exotic spices from places as far away as China. In the 19th century, there were gold rushes in California, South Africa and southeast Australia.

Gold can be found in rivers or mined from the ground. Most of the time it must be separated from the rock before it can be used, but occasionally large solid pieces, called nuggets, are discovered. The biggest nugget ever found weighed 72 kilograms and measured 61 x 31 centimetres.

About 60 per cent of the world's gold is turned into jewellery, but it's also used in dentistry, communications, computer and space technology and medicine. Doctors think a cancer treatment, using gold, will be developed this century.

Speaking

1 Work in pairs. What connects these things? Explain your answer.

| a wedding ring | Olympic first-place medal |
| the Oscar statuette | 50-year anniversaries |

Reading and listening

2 Work in pairs. Can you guess the answers to these questions?
1 How much gold is there in the world?
2 What's a nugget?
3 Apart from jewellery, what other things is gold used for?

3 **STUDY SKILLS** Read the text quickly to find the answers to Exercise 2.

56

---

1 Warm-up

Write the four items on the board, and ask students to close their books and work in pairs to discuss the connection between the items. Elicit answers from the whole class.

2 Pre-reading: facts about gold

Ask students in pairs to share their ideas on the three questions, without looking at the text.

3 Reading for gist

Students scan the text to check their ideas.

4 Reading and listening for details

 *5.3 CD 2 track 03*

This information is not specifically given in the text, so students have to find evidence to support or contradict the statement. Do an example together first (e.g. *gold is a hard metal*). Ask students to predict information to support or contradict this (e.g. *gold is soft, difficult / easy to bend / break*), then find information in the text.

Background information: a strong alcoholic drink called 'Goldwasser' is produced in Gdansk, and contains small flakes of gold. The biggest nugget of gold was called the 'Welcome stranger', and was found in Australia in 1869.

5 Working with words: verb + preposition

Read through the examples with the class, and ask them to find the eight other verb + preposition combinations in the text. Refer also to *Working with words,* page 104.

Weaker students: elicit prepositions from students and write them up on the board to help students identify the examples in the text.

6 Grammar: passive with modal verbs

Students find the sentences in the text and complete the table with the correct forms. Refer to *Grammar Explorer,* page 123.

4 ◯5.3 **Read and listen to the text. Based on the information in the text, do you think these sentences are true or false?**

1 Gold is a useful metal.
2 Gold can be made artificially.
3 Gold is poisonous to humans.

Working with words: verb + preposition

5 Look at the examples. Find eight more verb + preposition combinations in the text.

But why has this shiny yellow metal always been valued as a fabulous treasure?

It can be made into fine threads.

See Working with words: Page 104

Grammar: passive with modal verbs

6 Look at the text and complete the sentences.

Modal verbs	
can	It (1) .... (2) .... made into fine threads.
must	It (3) .... (4) .... separated from the rock.
will	A cancer treatment (5) .... (6) .... developed this century.

See Grammar Explorer: Page 123

7 Look at the examples. Then write the question and negative forms of the sentences in Exercise 6.

Can gold be made artificially?
Gold can't be made artificially.

8 Rewrite the sentences in the passive. Begin with the underlined words.

e.g. It's possible to shape gold easily.
   Gold can be shaped easily.

1 It's possible to make jewellery from many materials.
2 It's necessary to clean this ring carefully.
3 It's not possible to repair these earrings.
4 They will announce the Oscar winners tonight.
5 It's necessary to keep the results secret.

Listening

9 ◯5.4 **Listen to a story from Greek mythology. Choose the correct option.**

1 Match the names (1–3) with their roles (a–c).
   1 Dionysus a a king
   2 Midas   b a servant
   3 Silenus   c a god

2 Midas asked for
   a payment in gold.
   b everything he touched to become gold.
   c Dionysis to make him a god.

3 Midas's daughter
   a ate some fruit and became ill.
   b hurt her hand.
   c turned into gold.

4 According to the myth, there is gold in the river Pactolus because
   a Midas bathed there.
   b Dionysus swam there.
   c the river is magic.

Speaking

10 Work in groups. Discuss the statements. Do you think they are true or are they myths?

1 The Great Wall of China can be seen from the moon.
2 The common cold can be cured with antibiotics.
3 Hyperactivity is caused by too much sugar.
4 Hiccups can be cured by standing on your head.
5 Vampires can't be killed.

Study skills

Scanning and skimming

1 You can improve your reading skills if you read with a purpose.
   • Looking through a text quickly to find specific information, e.g. the answers to questions, times, dates, specific words. This is called scanning.
   • Looking at a text to decide what it is about, if it interests you or if it is useful. This is called skimming.
2 Which technique did you use on the *Gold* text? Use the same technique when you read the text in Workbook Unit 5.

Grammar and skills

he wanted. Midas quickly asked for everything he touched to turn into gold. Dionysus looked at him for a few moments. Then he agreed.

Midas was extremely happy with his new power. He tried it out on a stone. The stone turned into gold. He hurried home and picked up a bowl of fruit. The wooden bowl and the fruit all turned into gold. At that moment, his young daughter came in. 'Quick, come here!' Midas said. He took his daughter's hand and pulled her into the room, but she didn't move. Midas looked at her. He was horrified. She, too, had turned into gold!

Immediately, Midas understood that he had been a fool. He begged Dionysus for help. Luckily, Dionysus agreed and told Midas to go and swim in the river Pactolus. The magic power was washed away by the river, and ever since that time, people have found gold in that river.

10 Discussing myths

Make sure that students understand the two slightly different uses of *myth*: firstly, meaning an old story with impossible events in it, and secondly, meaning ideas which people commonly believe to be true, though they probably aren't. Once the students have expressed their opinions in groups of four or five, elicit ideas from the whole class about each issue and open it up for general discussion.

Study skills: scanning and skimming

Present the contents of the Study skills box and discuss them with the class.

7 Grammar: *can / must / will*

Present the task and examples, then elicit the questions and negative sentences from students around the class.

8 Grammar practice

Present the example before students do the exercise.

9 Listening for detail

 5.4 CD 2 track 04

Ask the students to read through the questions very carefully before they listen, to help them to focus on the information they need.

Give **weaker students** a transcript of the text to follow on the second listening.

Tapescript

In Greek mythology, Midas was the king of an area called Phrygia, which corresponds to a part of modern-day Turkey.

One day, Midas found a servant called Silenus asleep in his garden. He knew that Silenus was a servant of the god Dionysus. Midas gave Silenus some food, drink and a bed, and generally looked after him very well for several days.

Dionysus found out about this and he was very pleased. In return for Midas's friendly behaviour and hospitality, Dionysus offered Midas a reward. He said he could have anything

5C Expressing purpose and reasons

Spread aims

Functions: expressing purpose and giving reasons

Skills: reading and listening for detail

Pronunciation: the letter 'o' and the vowel sounds /əʊ / and /ʌ /

Writing a description of an object

KEY

 1 c

 2 1 F   2 T   3 F   4 F

---

1 Reading and listening for gist

 5.5 CD 2 track 05

Read through the options with the whole class to help them focus on the information they need.

Stronger students cover the text and listen and answer.

Weaker students follow the text as they listen.

2 Reading for detail

Students find the information in the text and decide if the statements are true or false. Elicit answers and the sentences from the text, and write them on the board. Refer to *Grammar Explorer*, pages 123–124, for an explanation of this construction.

3 & 4 Useful expressions

 5.6 CD 2 track 06

Ask students to find the expressions in the text. Then have the students repeat them chorally and individually, taking care with intonation.

5 Grammar: paraphrasing expressions

Explain that the students should complete the sentences with the constructions used in the *Useful expressions*, to explain the reason why Joe needs a computer.

Help **weaker students** by writing the missing words in the wrong order, so they just have to put them into the correct sentence.

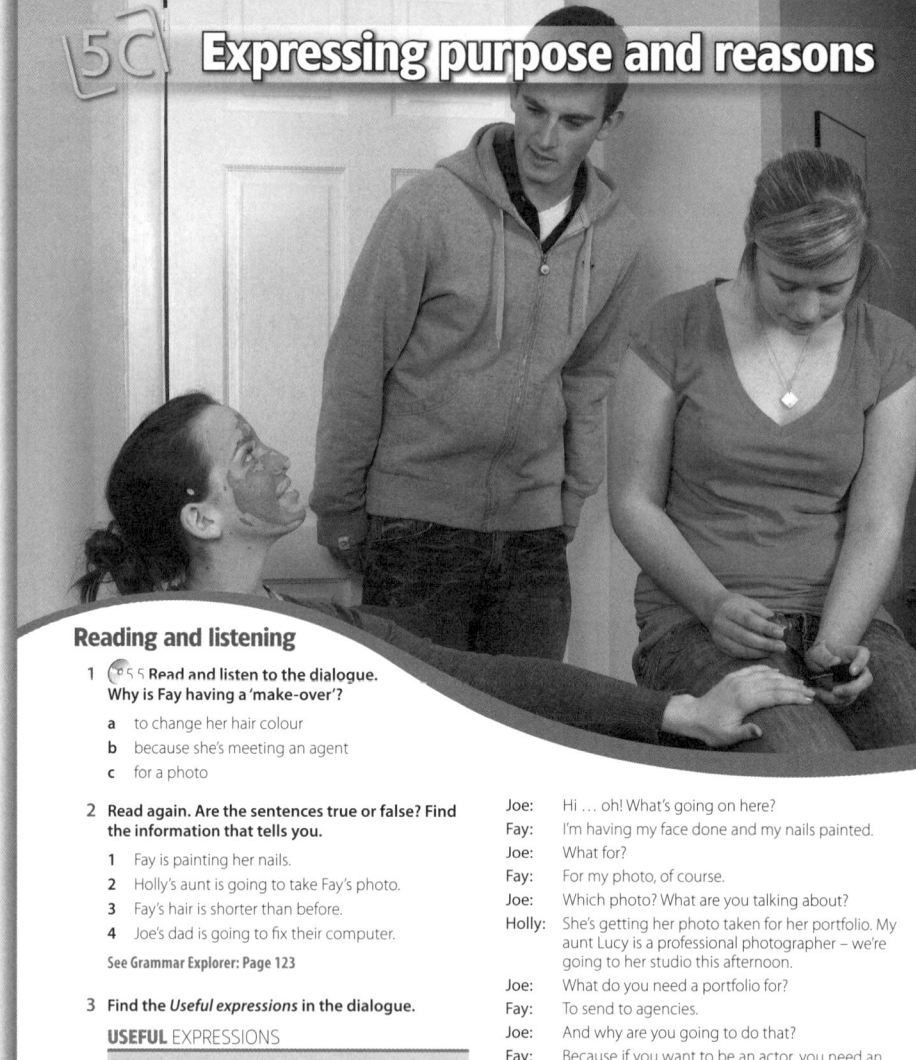

5C Expressing purpose and reasons

Reading and listening

1 *5.5* **Read and listen to the dialogue. Why is Fay having a 'make-over'?**

a   to change her hair colour
b   because she's meeting an agent
c   for a photo

2 **Read again. Are the sentences true or false? Find the information that tells you.**

1   Fay is painting her nails.
2   Holly's aunt is going to take Fay's photo.
3   Fay's hair is shorter than before.
4   Joe's dad is going to fix their computer.

See Grammar Explorer: Page 123

3 **Find the *Useful expressions* in the dialogue.**

USEFUL EXPRESSIONS

Asking about purpose and reason
What **for**?
What do you need a portfolio **for**?
Why are you going to do that?
Explaining purpose and reason
Because I need a favour.
For my photo.
So that they can promote you.
To send to agencies.

4 *5.6* **Listen and repeat the *Useful expressions*. Focus on your intonation.**

58

Joe:	Hi … oh! What's going on here?
Fay:	I'm having my face done and my nails painted.
Joe:	What for?
Fay:	For my photo, of course.
Joe:	Which photo? What are you talking about?
Holly:	She's getting her photo taken for her portfolio. My aunt Lucy is a professional photographer – we're going to her studio this afternoon.
Joe:	What do you need a portfolio for?
Fay:	To send to agencies.
Joe:	And why are you going to do that?
Fay:	Because if you want to be an actor, you need an agent to find work for you! And an agent needs to have your details so that they can promote you.
Joe:	Oh, I get it. Like models?
Fay:	Yes, a bit. Do you like my hair?
Joe:	Erm, what's different about it? Have you had it cut?
Fay:	No, I've had it dyed. It's a bit darker now. Honestly!
Holly:	What did you come round for, Joe, by the way?
Joe:	Oh, well, actually, because I need a favour. I'd like to use your computer, if that's OK. Ours isn't working. I'm waiting for dad to get it fixed.
Holly:	No problem. We're going to be busy all morning!

6 Listening for detail

 5.7 CD 2 track 07

Ask the students to read through the sentences so that they can focus on what they have to listen for.

Give **weaker students** a copy of the tapescript to follow on the second listening.

Tapescript

1 Hi, Fay, it's Holly. Listen, I want to ask you a favour. Can I borrow your gold earrings on Saturday? You know, the ones you got for your birthday? They go really well with my gold necklace, and I want to look good because I'm going to a party.

2 Hi Holly. It's Fay. Look, I can't see you and your aunt at the museum tomorrow. Guess what! I've got an interview in London! I can't believe it!

3 Hey Joe, it's Dan. I need a favour. Can you lend me your football boots? You're size 40, the same as me, aren't you? It's for the match on Saturday. Mine are so old I can't wear them.

7 Speaking preparation

Students make combinations with the *get/have* construction used in the text (e.g. *get your nails painted*). Ask students to make a list, and then elicit answers from the class and list them on the board.

5 Look at the *Useful expressions* and complete the sentence in four different ways.

Joe needs a computer ...
1 .... do his homework.
2 .... he can do his homework.
3 .... his homework.
4 .... he has to do his homework.

6 ⏺ 5.7 **Listen to the phone messages. First, complete the missing information. Then choose the correct option.**

1 Holly wants to borrow Fay's .... **because she's going out / to wear in a photo.**
2 Fay can't meet them at the .... She's going to London **for an interview / so she can meet her aunt.**
3 Dan wants borrow Joe's .... **for the match / because he's lost his.**

Writing: a description of an object

1 Read about Joe's favourite possession. Answer the questions.

1 What is it?
2 Where is it from?
3 What is it made of?
4 What is it like?

2 Look at the words in red. Which option (a–d) can be used instead of them?

a because
b for
c so that
d to

3 Rewrite the pairs of sentences with *as*, *because* and *since*.

1 My camera is digital. I don't need film.
2 My bike is easy to ride. It's got lots of gears.
3 My watch is waterproof. I can wear it when I go diving.
4 I don't wear earrings. I haven't had my ears pierced.

4 Write about your favourite possession. Use Joe's description to help you.

Speaking

7 Work in pairs. Match the words in group 1 and the verbs in group 2. How many combinations can you make?

	1	2
have/get (your)	bedroom	cut
	ears	dyed
	eyes	painted
	hair	pierced
	head	tested
	nose	shaved
	tongue	

8 Ask and answer questions using the expressions.

A: *Would you like to get your nose pierced?*
B: *No, I wouldn't. What about you?*

Pronunciation: the letter 'o' and the vowel sounds /əʊ/ and /ʌ/

9 ⏺ 5.8 **Does the 'o' in these words sound like the o in *gold* /əʊ/ or *some* /ʌ/? Listen and put them into two groups.**

above   chosen   clothes   come   done
erode   nose   other   oval   own
remote   show   stone   won   wonder

My most treasured possession is an old camera. It used to belong to my grandfather. He gave this object to me a few years ago because I'm interested in photography. It was made in the USA about 50 years ago and it's made of a kind of black plastic. It's a very simple, square-shaped camera and it used film. As they don't make the film now, I can't take photos with it. My grandfather used it to photograph all his friends and family. I've got some of the photos, but since he didn't write any names on them, we don't know who they are! Now I keep the camera in a cupboard so that it doesn't get damaged.

Communicate

KEY

5 1 to   2 so that   3 for
4 because

6 1 earrings / because she's going out
2 museum / for an interview
3 football boots / for the match

7 have / get:
your bedroom painted; your ears pierced; your eyes tested; your hair dyed / cut; your head shaved; your nose pierced; your tongue pierced

9 gold: chosen, clothes, erode, nose, oval, own, remote, show, stone
some: above, come, done, other, won, wonder

Writing

1 1 an old camera   2 the USA   3 black plastic   4 very simple and square-shaped

2 a

3 1 As / Because / Since my camera is digital, I don't need film.
2 My bike is easy to ride as / because / since it has lots of gears.
3 As / Because / Since my watch is waterproof, I can wear it when I go diving.
4 I don't wear earrings as / because / since I haven't had my ears pierced.

---

8 Speaking: *get something done*

Ask students to work in pairs and ask and answer the questions truthfully.

Extension: they can ask for and give a reason, using the phrases from Exercise 3.

9 Pronunciation: the letter 'o' and the vowel sounds /əʊ/ and /ʌ/

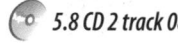 *5.8 CD 2 track 08*

Ask the students to read through the words and think about how they sound. Then play the recording for them to listen without answering. Then they should write them in two columns depending on the pronunciation of the 'o'.

Writing: a description of an object

1 Reading for detail

Ask the students to read the questions, then to read the text and answer.

2 Linking words

Students choose the word that can replace both red words in the text.

3 *As, because, since*

Tell students that there are different ways of combining each pair of sentences. They can choose any word to join each pair, but check all possibilities together in feedback.

4 Writing a description

Students choose something of theirs – preferably something interesting, old or unusual – and write a description of it, using the text about the camera as a model.

5D Boom-town Canada

Spread aims

Vocabulary: resources and materials
Skills: reading and listening for detail
Culture: Canada
CLIL: Chemistry and English: elements

KEY

1. oil
2. animals, fish, minerals (gold), trees, water
3. They brought people to Canada from all over the world
4. A town which is expanding rapidly (*booming*) and where there is a lot of work.
5. 1 get rich quickly 2 get away 3 get (well-paid) jobs

1 Warm-up

Present the task and the words in the box and check that students understand the vocabulary, including *industrial* and *natural resource*. Students then discuss what resource the photos might be about, from the suggestions in the box. Emphasise that they should not read the article!

2 Reading for gist

Students skim the text to check their answer and tick any other resources mentioned.

3 Reading and listening for detail

 *5.9 CD 2 track 09*

Students can find the sentences in the text that give the key information.

Stronger students students can use the information from the text to write a short paragraph.

Weaker students underline or write out the key sentences from the text that answer this question.

4 Reading for detail

Students find the expression in the text and use the context to infer the meaning.

5D Boom-town Canada

Reading

1 Work in pairs. Look at the photos of an industrial town in Canada. Which natural resource is being worked with?

| animals | coal | fish | land | minerals | oil |
| trees | water | | | | |

2 Read the text quickly and check your answer to Exercise 1. Tick the other natural resources that are mentioned.

3 *5.9* Read the text again. How have natural resources been important in Canadian life?

4 What do you think the expression 'boom town' means?

5 Find three expressions with *get* in the text that mean the same as the underlined words.
1 Lots of people want to <u>make a lot of money</u>.
2 We try to <u>escape</u> from city life at weekends.
3 The men went to London to <u>find work</u>.

Culture — Canada

Canada is the second largest country in the world, but it only has 0.5 per cent of the world's population. Canadian lakes and rivers contain one fifth of all the fresh water on Earth and there are vast areas of forest and open land. The fish, animals and trees from these areas have always been extremely important to Inuit communities across Canada.

These natural resources also brought many Europeans to Canada in the 17th and 18th centuries. Then, in 1896, gold was discovered in the Yukon. This changed the lives of thousands of people. Men from the USA, South Africa and Australia rushed to the area to seek their fortune. In two years, a fishing camp on the Klondike River turned into Dawson City, with a population of more than 40,000. The men were not only miners, but also doctors, teachers and other professionals. Many women also travelled there to get away from their traditional, restricted lives. Although they had to work in typical jobs like cooking and nursing, it was a new life of opportunity and adventure.

These days, Canada's boom towns are in Alberta, where oil has been found. It's easy to understand why oil is often called 'black gold'. Workers from over 70 countries have moved there to get well-paid jobs in the oil industry. Many of them live in tiny rooms in work camps. Just like in the Klondike gold rush, there are lots of opportunities. As you don't have to be physically strong to operate the 'high-tech' machinery used in the oil fields, the giant-sized vehicles are often driven by women. These trucks move more than a million tons of material every day. The women, like most of the oil workers in Alberta, hope to get rich quickly and then go home.

 60

---

5 Reading: phrases with *get*

Students look for phrases with *get* which mean the same as the underlined words.

6 Pre-listening: numbers

Elicit the numbers from the class and correct as necessary. Students then find the written figures in the text.

7 Listening for detail

5.10 CD 2 track 10

Present the information box below the questions and check students understand the meaning of the

different numbers. Then read the questions with the class and ensure they understand what they are being asked to listen for. Play the recording through once while they just listen and focus on the questions; then a second time for them to answer; then a third time for them to complete, check and correct.

Tapescript

In total, about 160,000 tons of gold have been found in all the sites in the world, so the amount of gold found in the Yukon was quite significant. About 390 tons of gold was mined from the area during its busiest time. Mining continues there today but on a much smaller scale. These days, the population

Listening

6 How do you say these numbers? How are they written in the text?

0.5%   ⅕
forty thousand   seventy
1,000,000

7 🔊 5.10 **Listen to the statistics about Canada's natural resources. Choose the correct option (a–c).**

1 The amount of mined gold in the world is .... tons.
   a 160
   b 16,000
   c 160,000

2 The amount of gold mined in the Yukon was .... tons.
   a 190
   b 390
   c 3,900

3 The population of the Yukon today is .... of Dawson City's gold-rush population.
   a ¾
   b ⅔
   c ¼

4 Alberta produces .... barrels of oil a day.
   a 12 million
   b 0.12 millon
   c 1.2 million

5 The USA gets .... of its oil from Canada.
   a 9 per cent
   b 19 per cent
   c 90 per cent

UK	Europe
1,000,000	1.000.000
1.5	1,5

Project

Work in groups. Choose at least twelve things you use or consume every day – clothes, objects, food, etc. Find or make a large map of the world and show where the things come from.

Chemistry and English
Elements

1 **Find out about elements. Read the text and answer the questions.**

1 What are elements made of?
2 What are some examples of elements?
3 What happens when elements are mixed together?

Gold is an element. Elements are pure materials. An element can't be separated into different materials. It is made of identical atoms. Atoms are so tiny that you can't see them.

Most elements are solid at room temperature. Examples of solid elements are gold, silver, carbon, copper and aluminium. A few elements are gases at room temperature, for example oxygen, hydrogen and nitrogen. Some elements can be mixed together to make 'compounds'. For example, hydrogen and oxygen together form a very common compound: water. Another common compound is made of the two elements sodium and chlorine: salt.

silver

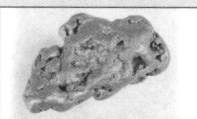
gold

copper

carbon

Elements can be divided into two groups, metals and non-metals. Most elements are metals. Metals are shiny and strong but can be bent quite easily. They also conduct electricity and heat. Gold is a typical metal. Non-metals include solid elements and gases. Solid non-metals are not shiny or strong and they break easily.

Each element is known by a chemical symbol, as well as its name. This is always written the same way and it's the same in every language of the world:

aluminium	**Al**	hydrogen	**H**
carbon	**C**	nitrogen	**N**
copper	**Cu**	oxygen	**O**
gold	**Au**	silver	**Ag**

2 **What are the two main groups of elements and what are their properties?**

3 **Why is it a good idea to use chemical symbols instead of names?**

Culture

KEY

6 0.5 per cent   one fifth
40,000   70   a million

7 1 c   2 b   3 a   4 c   5 b

Chemistry and English

1 1 identical atoms   2 gold, silver, carbon, copper, aluminium   3 some elements make a compound

2 metals – shiny, strong and easily bent
non-metals – solid elements which are not shiny or strong and break easily; gases

3 because they are written the same way in every language of the world

When they have finished, have a 'show-and-tell' time in class when they can walk round and talk about each other's posters.

Chemistry and English: elements

1 Reading for detail

Students read the text and answer the questions.

Tell **weaker students** that they will find the answers in the first 2 paragraphs above the pictures.

2 Reading for detail

Ask students to note the characteristics of the two groups of elements in two columns.

Tell **weaker students** to read the third paragraph immediately below the pictures to find the answers.

3 Reading for detail

Tell **weaker students** to read the final paragraph to find the answer.

---

of the whole territory is about three-quarters of the population of Dawson City at the time of the gold rush.

In the Alberta oil fields, oil production is currently about 1.2 million barrels a day. At the moment, most of the oil is exported to the United States and the rest is used in Canada. The USA gets about 19% of its oil needs from Canada. This amount will probably increase in the future.

Project: mapping where things come from

It might be a good idea to photocopy an A3 size world map for each group to use. This should be the centre of a poster, put onto a piece of flip-chart (A1) paper, so that there is room around the outside for students to write about the products, and then draw arrows to the correct places. Suggest that they each take one or two products and find all the materials used in it and their provenance (e.g. a pair of sandals: leather from … for the upper; rubber from … for the sole; metal from … for the buckle). They should list these first, then arrange the information clearly around the map with lines pointing to the relevant countries. Encourage them to do an illustration of each product, and also ensure that there is a good range of product type (i.e. not all food or clothes …). They will probably need to do Internet research and make some 'educated guesses' about where materials come from, as not everything is listed on the packets and labels.

True story: Searching for gold

Page aim

Reading for interest on the topic of the unit

KEY

2 1 came into the area quickly in large crowds   2 search   3 someone who went to California in 1849 to search for gold   4 the population increased enormously in 20 years   5 most of them found no gold and had to do other jobs

3 1 enthusiasts; 2 to go it alone; 3 genuinely; 4 generous; 5 tips; 6 hiking

---

Warm-up

Ask students if they own anything made of gold; also ask what gold objects there are at home. Ask why people think gold is so valuable.

1 Discussion

Ask students to do Exercise 1 with a partner, then elicit answers from the whole class, opening a discussion where possible.

2 Reading for detail

Ask students to read the first part of the text and answer the questions individually, then to check with a partner. Elicit the answers from the whole class.

3 Vocabulary

Ask students to find the words in the text that are synonyms for the phrases given; the number in brackets indicates which paragraph to look in.

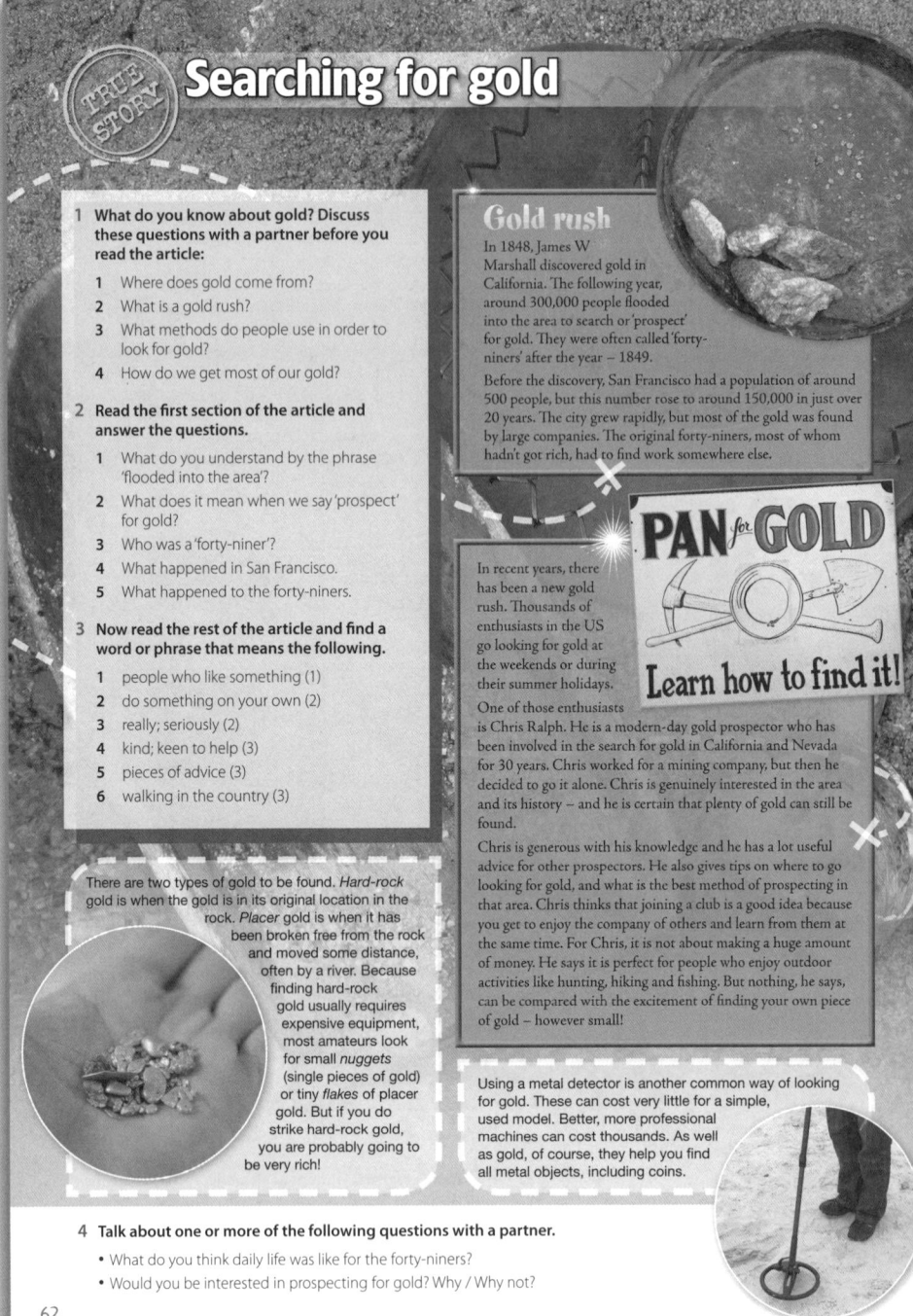

Extension

Ask students to read the two extra boxes of information and elicit answers to these questions:

a) What are the two kinds of gold, and which is more valuable and why?
b) What is a metal detector used for and how do you use one?

4 Discussion

Ask students to form groups of three or four and discuss one or both of the questions. They should appoint a secretary who keeps notes and reports back to the whole class when you open up the discussion to everyone.

NATIONAL GEOGRAPHIC

Mysteries

> Grammar
Learn about modal verbs for speculation, and the second conditional.

> Vocabulary
Learn words connected with art, and for types of book.

Work with phrasal verbs, and noun + preposition combinations.

> Skills
Read about Agatha Christie, crop circles, and British best-sellers.

Listen to a story of an art forgery, and a radio programme about women authors.

Write an apology.

> Communicate
Make and respond to requests.

---

1 Put the words from the vocabulary box into two groups: *art* and *books*.

abstract	novel	portrait
drawing	oil	sculpture
fiction	painting	still life
landscape	play	watercolour
non-fiction	poetry	

2 Look at the photo on this page. What do you think it is? Use words from the vocabulary box.

3 6.1 Listen to three people talking about art. Which one is talking about the photo?

4 Do you like this kind of art? Tell your partner why or why not. What kind of art do you like?

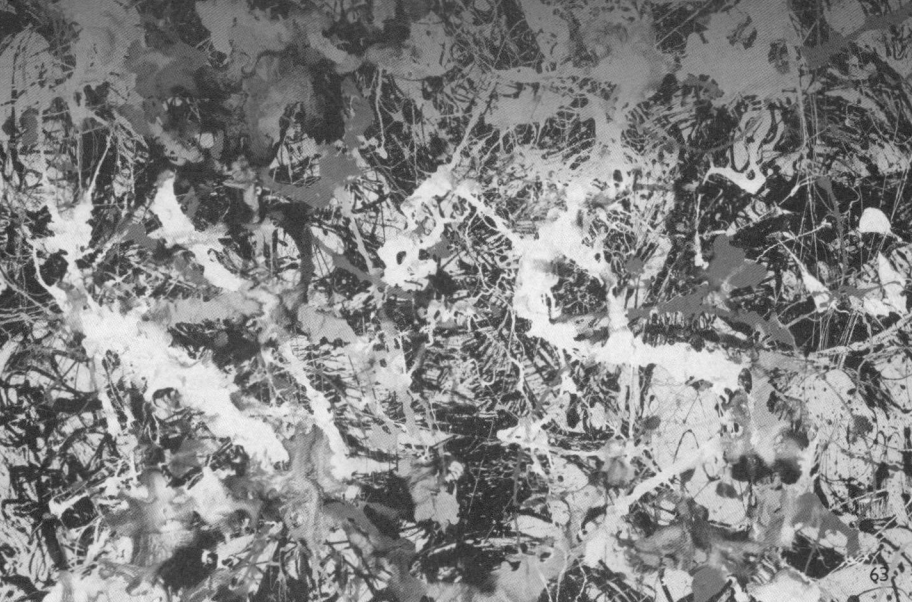

63

Mysteries

Unit aims

Grammar: modal verbs for speculation; the second conditional

Vocabulary: art and books; phrasal verbs; noun + preposition combinations

Functions: making and responding to requests

Reading about: Agatha Christie; crop circles; British best-sellers

Listening to: a story of an art forgery; a radio programme about women authors

Writing an apology

KEY

1 Art: abstract, drawing, landscape, oil, painting, portrait, sculpture, still life, watercolour
Books: fiction, non-fiction, novel, play, poetry

2 It's a section of an abstract painting.

3 2

Pollock and it really inspired me. I started to experiment with oil paints. The Pollock painting is great – lots of black and white with red and yellow. It has no straight lines or real shapes. It's impossible to say what it is.

3

I'm learning to paint using watercolours. It's more difficult than I expected. That's probably because I'm trying to copy Turner, who was one of the greatest English artists ever! I love this watercolour of his – of a castle next to the sea. I love the pale blue and brown colours – it's very dreamy.

4 Speaking about art

Elicit some phrases for giving opinions from the class (e.g. *I like / I don't like…, I prefer…, I'd rather have…, I agree/disagree*).

---

1 Vocabulary: classifying words

Present the vocabulary in the box, then students repeat the words chorally and individually. Point out that the words all have the stress on the first syllable. Elicit the meaning of each word, or perhaps make this into a dictionary activity. Elicit the correct category for each word and list them in columns on the board.

Extension: students add more words of their own to each of the two categories.

2 Speaking about a picture

Ask the students to discuss their ideas about the photo in pairs, then ask the whole class for suggestions.

3 Listening for gist

 6.1 CD 2 track 11

Tapescript

1

I don't like abstract art at all. I prefer paintings of real people or real things – portraits and landscapes. My favourite artist is Monet. I've got a print of one of his paintings in my living room. It's of two people walking through a field of poppies. I love the colour of the red flowers and the green grass. It makes me think of summer.

2

I'm quite good at art, actually. I didn't use to like drawing, but then I saw a painting by the abstract artist Jackson

---

6A A literary mystery

Spread aims

Grammar: modal verbs for speculation
Vocabulary: books; phrasal verbs
Functions: speculating about mysteries
Reading a conversation about Agatha Christie

KEY

2 fiction: classic, detective, historical, humour, mystery, romance, science fiction, thriller
non-fiction: autobiography, biography, cookery, humour, reference

3 1 F   2 NI   3 F   4 F

4 worked out = a   turned up = b
run away = a

1 Speaking: books

Students talk about the topics given. Elicit comments from the class and try to get some discussion going (e.g. if a student says she has read *Harry Potter and the Deathly Hallows*, ask if anyone else has read it, and get opinions and reasons for their feelings about it).

2 Vocabulary: types of books

Ask students for a definition of *fiction* (an invented story) and *non-fiction* (fact-based writing). Then read out the words in the box, having the class repeat them chorally and individually. Pay attention to the syllable stress in these words: autobi**o**graphy; bi**o**graphy; de**tec**tive; his**tor**ical. The categorisation activity can perhaps be a dictionary activity. Elicit answers and make a list in two columns on the board. Check students understand what each type of book is, and ask for examples of each category. If they do not have many ideas, suggest book titles that they are likely to know (in their own language), and ask them to categorise them.

3 Reading and listening for gist

 *6.2 CD 2 track 12*

Present the brief facts about Agatha Christie which accompany the conversation, and ask whether students have read any of her work;

then present the sentences and make sure students understand them; elicit or explain who Poirot is (a detective in many Agatha Christie stories) and what the *plot* is (the action of the story).

4 Working with words: phrasal verbs

Ask students to do this exercise individually, then check with a partner. They could perhaps use their dictionaries. Refer also to *Working with words*, page 105.

Background information: Agatha Christie's first story, *The Mysterious Affair at Styles*, was published in 1920, and introduced her Belgian detective Hercule Poirot. Her other

main detective, Miss Jane Marple, first appeared in the short story *The Tuesday Night Club* in 1927. Her novels are estimated to have sold four billion copies worldwide, which makes them, along with *The Bible* and Shakespeare's works, the most read books in history. Her play *The Mousetrap* was first performed in London on 25 November, 1952 and was still running in 2010 after 23,000 performances – the longest running play ever!

5 Grammar: modal verbs for speculation

Ask students to match the three sentences and the meanings individually, then check with a partner. Check the answers and

---

6A A literary mystery

Tom: Oh, you're reading *Murder on the Orient Express*! I've read that – it's great! Have you worked out who the murderer is?

Chloe: No, and don't tell me! It's really confusing. All I know is, it can't be Poirot because he's the detective! So it must be one of the other passengers on the train – but at this point it could be anybody!

Tom: That's true. It might be the train driver …

Chloe: No, let's not talk about it. You'll give me too many clues.

Tom: OK. Did you know that Agatha Christie herself once disappeared? The police were looking for her all over the country.

Chloe: No way!

Tom: Yes, it was just before Christmas in 1926. She was missing for eleven days and then she turned up in a hotel in the north of England under a false name.

Chloe: So what had happened to her?

Tom: Well, a local doctor thought she could have lost her memory. On the other hand, she might have run away from her husband. They'd had a big argument because he wanted a divorce.

Chloe: But didn't she explain anything?

Tom: No, she never said a word. So because of that, some people decided that it must have been a fake disappearance – to get publicity for her books.

Chloe: Well, that couldn't have been true because she was already a best-selling author. Why would she need any more publicity? So what was the real explanation in the end?

Tom: Nobody knows. It's a real-life mystery.

AGATHA CHRISTIE
Murder on the Orient Express
A HERCULE POIROT MYSTERY

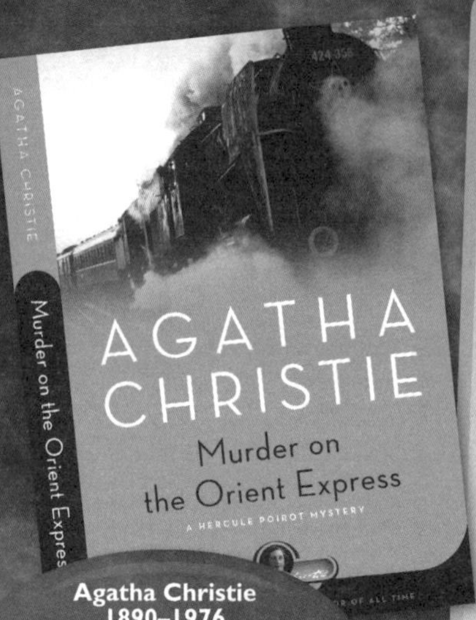

Agatha Christie
1890–1976
The 'Queen of Crime'
Novels, short stories and plays
The most translated author in the world
(more than 56 languages)
The best-selling writer of books
of all time

Speaking

1 Work in pairs. Tell your partner about two of these things.

> a book you're reading at the moment
> a book you've read recently
> your favourite book

2 Put the types of book into two groups: *fiction* and *non-fiction*. How many authors or book titles can you name for each type of book?

> autobiography   biography   classic
> cookery   detective   historical   humour
> mystery   reference   romance
> science fiction   thriller

Reading and listening

3 *6.2* **Read and listen to the conversation. Are the sentences true or false – or is there not enough information to decide?**

1 Chloe thinks Poirot is a murderer.
2 Agatha Christie was married to a doctor.
3 Tom explains the plot of *Murder on the Orient Express*.
4 Agatha Christie wrote a mystery story about herself.

64

Working with words: phrasal verbs

4 Choose the correct meaning for these phrasal verbs from the conversation.

Have you worked out who the murderer is? = **a** decided, **b** asked

She turned up in a hotel. = **a** worked, **b** was found

She might have run away from her husband. = **a** left, **b** raced

See Working with words: Page 105

Grammar: modal verbs for speculation

5 Read the sentences (1–3) from the text and match them with the correct meaning (a–c).

1 It can't be Poirot.
2 It must be one of the other passengers.
3 It could be anybody.

a I think it's possible.
b I think it's impossible.
c I think it's almost certain.

See Grammar Explorer: Page 124

6 Look at this sentence and find three similar verbs in the text.

A local doctor thought she could have lost her memory.

7 Complete the table with the correct modal verbs.

Speculation about the present		
possible	may / might / (1)	
impossible	(2)	be
certain	(3)	
Speculation about the past		
possible	may / (4) .... / (5)	have
impossible	can't / (6)	+ past
certain	(7)	participle

We don't normally use *can* to speculate.

8 Choose the correct options.

I love reading murder mystery stories. In my favourite murder mystery stories, there are often several suspects who (1) **might be / must be** the murderer. The first thing I do is write down the names of the people who are definitely innocent and (2) **have killed / couldn't have killed** the victim. As the story progresses and the evidence is revealed, sometimes I'm sure who the killer is (3) **may be / must be**. Then I find he has an alibi and so (4) **couldn't have done / might have done** it. I don't like stories where it's too obvious who (5) **must have killed / can't have killed** the victim. I prefer books where you keep guessing right to the end.

---

9 Complete the sentences with the correct modal form of the verbs. Sometimes more than one answer is possible.

1 All the doors are locked. The killer .... (**escape**) through the window.
2 Hercule Poirot always catches the criminal. He .... (**be**) very intelligent.
3 The girl had the opportunity to steal the diamonds. It .... (**be**) her.
4 The main suspect was in prison at the time of the robbery. He .... (**do**) it.
5 We don't know where the attacker is. He .... (**be**) somewhere in the building.

Speaking

10 Work in pairs. Ask and answer questions about the picture. Use the verbs in the box or your own ideas. Then write sentences about the picture.

be come in eat go out hear leave
open take out

A: *Why is the window open?*
B: *Someone must have come in that way.*
A: *Yes, or they might have gone out that way.*

11 Work in pairs. Imagine your English teacher hasn't come to class. Speculate on the reasons.

be sick sleep in have an accident forget
be on a course win the lottery

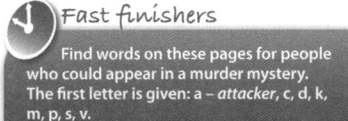

Fast finishers

Find words on these pages for people who could appear in a murder mystery. The first letter is given: a – *attacker*, c, d, k, m, p, s, v.

Grammar

KEY

5 1 b 2 c 3 a

6 she might have run away; it must have been a fake disappearance; that couldn't have been true

7 1 could 2 can't 3 must 4 might 5 could 6 couldn't 7 must

8 1 might be 2 couldn't have killed 3 must be 4 couldn't have done 5 must have killed

9 1 must have escaped 2 must be 3 may / might / could have been 4 can't / couldn't have done it 5 may / might / could be

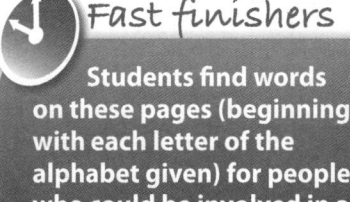 criminal, detective, killer, murderer, police, suspect, victim

---

do. Ask students to speculate on what happened using the correct modal verb with the verbs in the box. If necessary, elicit or provide suitable vocabulary (e.g. *drawer, paw prints, bookcase*).

11 Personalised speaking practice

Students use the verb phrases in the box to discuss the situation described.

Fast finishers

Students find words on these pages (beginning with each letter of the alphabet given) for people who could be involved in a murder mystery.

---

refer students to *Grammar Explorer,* page 124. Explain that talking in this way about possibilities is called *speculation*.

6 Grammar: identifying speculative sentences

Write the example sentence on the board and elicit or explain that it expresses speculation about the past rather than the present. Elicit the other three sentences which use this form and write them up underneath the example. Underline the main verbs to emphasise their construction.

7 Grammar: speculating verbs

Students complete the table using information from Exercises 6

and 7. Review the completed table and present the grammar note which follows it.

8 Grammar: choosing correct options

Students complete the text by selecting the correct modal verbs.

9 Grammar: sentence completion

Students complete the sentences using the correct modal verb construction.

10 Speaking practice: speculation

Present the task and example, and ensure that students know what to

6B Art mysteries

Spread aims

Grammar: second conditional
Vocabulary: the art world; noun + preposition
Functions: speculating
Reading about crop circles
Listening to a story about art forgery

KEY

1
1 They are found in fields of crops in southern England.
2 They are patterns made by flattening the crops.
3 They look like intricate patterns of circles.

2 strong winds, aliens, two local painters
The last one is correct.

3 1 Original   2 value
3 collector   4 forgery
5 expert

4 b

5 Eduardo de Valfierno organised the plan; he paid someone to steal the Mona Lisa and paid a forger to make six copies.
Vicenzo Perugia stole the painting; he tried to sell it and ended up in prison.
Yves Chaudron painted six copies of the painting.

6 (possible answers)
He must have changed his name, he might have gone to live in a foreign country.

7 damage to, area of, idea of, work of

8 1 wouldn't   2 could   3 would

9 the present and the future

10 1 c had / would come
2 e wasn't / wouldn't fool
3 a painted / would put
4 d exhibited / would be
5 b said / would believe

---

1 Reading for gist

Students look at the pictures and discuss what they see. Make sure they understand the word *crop* in this sense. Read the three sentences with the class to help them to focus on the information they need. If you wish, you could give them a time limit to complete the task.

2 Reading and listening for detail

 6.3 CD 2 track 13

Stronger students can cover the text and just listen

Weaker students can listen and follow the text.

3 Vocabulary: the art world

Present the words in the box and make sure that students understand them. Note that both *original* and *collector* have the stress on the second syllable.

Tell **weaker students** that *hoax*, *painter* and *sculptor* aren't used.

4 Listening for gist

 6.4 CD 2 track 14

Present the three sentences to focus students' attention before playing the recording.

Tapescript

Presenter: Next, we come to an astonishing story. It seems that even the best museums, like the Louvre in Paris, can sometimes be the victim of art criminals. Isn't that right, Nigel?

Nigel: Yes ... about a hundred years ago, Leonardo da Vinci's most famous painting, the Mona Lisa, disappeared from the Louvre Museum in Paris. It was missing for two years. For a short time the French police even suspected the famous poet

6B Art mysteries

crop circles
alien art?

When crop circles first appeared in southern England, nobody knew how to explain them. What could be the cause of such unusual patterns in fields of crops? Many newspapers speculated that a strong wind might have flattened the plants. But if wind was the cause, the circles wouldn't be so complex. Some of the circles were like huge works of art. They had detailed, intricate patterns and were up to 200 metres across.

Other observers had a different reaction to the circles and said that they were too big and complex for humans to make. They decided that aliens must have made them! However, if extra-terrestrials wanted to make contact with humans, would they make crop circles? It seems like a bizarre explanation. Nevertheless, every summer more crop circles appeared and more tourists came to look at them. While some farmers were unhappy about the damage to their crops, others were unhappy that they didn't have a crop circle on their land. Many said, 'If I had one, I could earn money from the tourists.'

Eventually, two local painters, Doug Bower and Dave Chorley, explained how the hoax had begun. One summer evening in 1978, they were looking at an area of wind-flattened wheat. Bower said, 'If we made something like that, people would think a flying saucer had landed,' and that gave them the idea of trying to fool people.

Now there's a group of sculptors and artists from London called the 'Circlemakers'. And companies like Pepsi, Sky and the BBC pay to have their own circles made. However, the most curious thing about this hoax is that some people still believe crop circles are the work of aliens.

Reading and listening

1 **Read the text quickly and answer the questions.**

  1 Where are crop circles found?
  2 What are crop circles?
  3 What do crop circles look like?

2 **6.4 Read and listen to the text. Find three explanations for the origin of crop circles. Which one is correct?**

Vocabulary: the art world

3 **Complete the sentences with words from the box.**

collector	expert	forgery	hoax
original	painter	sculptor	value

  1 .... works of art by famous artists are unique.
  2 Art often has a very high ....
  3 A work of art can be bought by a museum or a private ....
  4 A copy of an original work is called a fake or a ....
  5 An art .... can sometimes be fooled by clever fakes.

66

Listening

4 🔊6.3 **Listen to part of a radio programme about art mysteries. What happened? Choose the correct option (a–c).**

a A forgery was sold to the Louvre Museum in Paris.

b An original work of art was stolen from the Louvre Museum.

c An expert from the Louvre bought a stolen work of art.

5 🔊6.3 **STUDY SKILLS Listen to the story again. Make notes on what these people did. Compare with your partner.**

> Eduardo de Valfierno   Vincenzo Peruggia
> Yves Chaudron

6 **Valfierno was never caught by the police. Why do you think this was? Tell your partner.**

Working with words: noun + preposition

7 **Look at the examples. Then find these nouns in the text:** *damage, area, idea, work.* **Which prepositions follow these nouns?**

What could be the cause of such unusual patterns? Other observers had a different reaction to the circles.

See Working with words: Page 105

Grammar: second conditional

8 **Complete these sentences from the text.**

Condition	Result
If wind was the cause,	the circles (**1**) .... be so complex.
If I had one,	I (**2**) .... earn money from the tourists.
If we made something like that,	people (**3**) .... think a flying saucer had landed.

> We use *could* when the result is a possibility, but not a certainty.
> We use *if* in the part of the sentence with the past simple verb. When the sentence starts with *if*, we use a comma at the end of the *if*-clause.

See Grammar Explorer: Page 124

9 **Choose the correct option.**

We use the second conditional to talk about **the past / the present and the future**.

10 **Match the sentence beginnings (1–5) with the endings (a–e). Then write the verbs in the correct forms.**

1 If our village .... (**have**) a crop circle,
2 If the forger .... (**be not**) such a good artist,
3 If you .... (**paint**) my portrait,
4 If a museum .... (**exhibit**) a fake,
5 If you .... (**say**) this was by da Vinci,

a I .... (**put**) it on my wall.
b nobody .... (**believe**) you.
c people .... (**come**) to see it.
d it .... (**be**) very embarrassing.
e he .... (**not fool**) people.

Speaking

11 **Work in pairs. In how many ways can you complete the sentences?**

1 If aliens landed in the school yard, …
2 If I found a valuable painting, …
3 If I wanted to be a famous artist, …
4 If we appeared on TV, …
5 If I discovered a crop circle, …
6 If I sold one of my paintings for a lot of money, …

> ## Study skills
>
> ### Answering questions
>
> When you listen to a text, you won't understand every word. Don't worry!
> 1 Focus on the questions you need to answer.
> 2 Listen for the answers and ignore the other information.
> 3 Don't be put off by unfamiliar words.

Apollinaire, and the painter Pablo Picasso! The real criminal was a man called Eduardo de Valfierno.

He'd organised a plan to steal and copy the painting. Valfierno had paid a man called Vicenzo Perugia to steal the original painting. He'd paid a forger called Yves Chaudron to make not one, but six copies of the Mona Lisa, which Valfierno then sold to private collectors.

Valfierno knew that the collectors could not ask an art expert to check the paintings, because this would show that they were guilty of buying a stolen work of art.

Presenter: So Valfierno made millions of dollars – but what happened to the original painting?

Nigel: Well, Perugia, the thief, tried to sell it to an Italian museum. He ended up in prison and the Mona Lisa was eventually returned to the Louvre.

Presenter: Good. And that's where you can see it now.

5 Listening for detail

 6.4 CD 2 track 14

This is a note-taking exercise. Play the recording through two or three times, and perhaps also pause at the end of each paragraph. Make sure students do not write complete sentences, but just the key words and phrases.

6 Speaking: speculation about Valfierno

Ask students to use phrases from 6A (e.g. *could have, might have*) to talk about Valfierno's situation.

Grammar and skills

7 Working with words: noun + preposition

Read the two examples with the class, and ask them to find them in the text and circle them. For further practice, see *Working with words*, page 105.

8 Grammar presentation: second conditional

Ask students to find the sentences in the text and complete the table with the appropriate modal and verb. Then present the grammar note underneath. See also *Grammar Explorer*, page 124.

9 Grammar explanation

Students choose the correct option to complete the sentence.

10 Grammar: sentence completion and matching

Explain to **weaker students** that clauses 1–5 are all 'if' clauses, so the verb will be in the past simple, and a–e are the result clauses, so the verb will use *would* or *could*. Students may prefer to complete the clauses before matching.

11 Speaking practice

Encourage students to produce as many interesting sentences as they can. Elicit suggestions from the whole class.

Ask **weaker students** to write down one sentence for each of the six prompts.

Study skills: answering questions

Present the suggestions in the box and discuss them with the whole class.

85

6C Requests

Spread aims

Vocabulary: art

Functions: making and responding to requests

Skills: reading and listening for detail

Pronunciation: words containing *au*

Writing an apology

---

1 Reading and listening for detail

 6.5 CD 2 track 15

Students read the dialogue and identify the correct sign.

Stronger students can cover the text and just listen.

Weaker students can listen and follow the text.

2 Reading for detail

Students read the text to find the answers.

Extension: students form groups of three to read the dialogue. They can do it three times, changing roles each time. Encourage them to play their roles with expression.

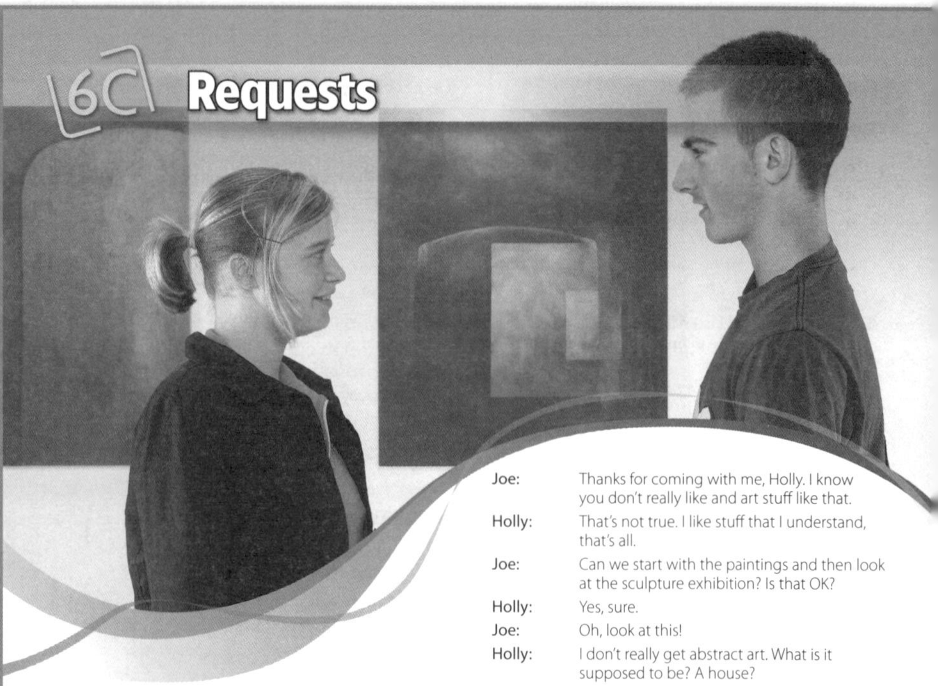

3 Speaking: matching expressions and functions

Establish the difference between *asking someone to do something* (you ask another person to perform an action) and *making a request* (you ask another person if you can do something) before students start this exercise.

4 Useful expressions: intonation

 6.6 CD 2 track 16

Play the recording through a couple of times while students just listen and follow. Then play it and pause after each expression for them to repeat chorally and individually.

They can then do further practice in pairs, helping each other with their intonation.

5 Reading for detail

Students match the signs with the places.

Tell **weaker students** that 3 is not used.

6 Speaking: responding to requests

Students work in pairs to role play the situations; one student makes the request and the other responds appropriately. They should take it in turns initiating the dialogue.

7 Pronunciation: words containing *au*

Students look at the words in the box in pairs and decide how they are pronounced. Elicit suggestions from the whole class.

8 Pronunciation check

 6.7 CD 2 track 17

Play the recording through a couple of times while students just listen and check their pronunciation. Then pause after each word for them to repeat chorally and individually. Take care with words where the stress is not on the first syllable: au**di**tion, Au**stra**lia, autobi**og**raphy, be**cause**.

6C Requests

Reading and listening

1 *6.5* **Read and listen to the dialogue. Which sign was in the entrance to the gallery?**

A ADMISSION FREE
(EXCEPT FOR SPECIAL EXHIBITIONS)

B NO PHOTOGRAPHY OR VIDEO FILMING *EXCEPT BY PERMISSION.*

C *Please* DO NOT TAKE FOOD OR DRINK INTO THE EXHIBITION ROOMS.

2 **Read the dialogue again. Answer the questions.**
1 What kind of art does Holly like?
2 What does Joe want to do?
3 What would Joe like to borrow?

Joe:	Thanks for coming with me, Holly. I know you don't really like and art stuff like that.
Holly:	That's not true. I like stuff that I understand, that's all.
Joe:	Can we start with the paintings and then look at the sculpture exhibition? Is that OK?
Holly:	Yes, sure.
Joe:	Oh, look at this!
Holly:	I don't really get abstract art. What is it supposed to be? A house?
Joe:	Maybe. Or it might be a human mind.
Holly:	If it was a human mind, it wouldn't have windows.
Joe:	Perhaps they're not windows!
Holly:	They look like windows to me.
Joe:	Well, I like it. It would be nice to get a photo of it. Do you mind holding my camera bag for a minute?
Holly:	No, not at all, but are you sure you can do that? Maybe you should ask the attendant.
Joe:	OK ... Excuse me, would it be all right if I took a photo of this picture?
Attendant:	I'm sorry, photography isn't allowed. There's a sign in the entrance.
Joe:	Oh, I didn't see it.
Attendant:	Would you like to buy a print? There are posters and postcards in the gallery shop.
Joe:	Right, thanks. So, Holly, is it all right if we go to the shop on the way out?
Holly:	Yes, that's fine.
An hour later	
Joe:	Could you tell us the price of these posters, please?
Assistant:	Yes, of course. The cheapest ones start at £15.
Joe:	Oh! Holly, can you lend me some money? I'd really like to get a poster.
Holly:	Sorry, I've only got enough for my bus fare.
Joe:	OK, never mind. Could I have this postcard, please?
Assistant:	That's 95 pence. Thank you.

68

3 Find the *Useful expressions* in the dialogue. Write the functions (1–3) in the gaps (a–c).

1 asking someone to do something
2 responding to a request
3 making a request

USEFUL EXPRESSIONS

a ....
Can we **start** with the paintings?
Would it be all right if **I took** a photo?
Is it all right if we go to the shop?
Could I **have** this postcard, please?
b ....
Do you mind **holding** my camera bag?
Could you **tell** us the price of these posters, please?
Can you **lend** me some money?
c ....
Yes, sure.
No, not at all.
I'm sorry.
Yes, of course.

4 🔊6.6 Listen and repeat the *Useful expressions*. Focus on your intonation.

Writing: an apology

1 Read the note and the email. Find the following information.

1 what happened
2 why it happened
3 the consequences

2 Holly uses *due to* and *as a result* to explain the situation. Find these expressions in her message. Which expression introduces a cause? Which expression introduces a result?

3 Complete the sentences using *due to* or *as a result*.

1 .... the terrible weather, the football match was cancelled.
2 The school bus broke down. .... , the day trip was cancelled.
3 .... the illness of the main singer, the school concert was postponed.
4 There was a fire in the school kitchen this morning. .... , there is no hot food today.

4 Write an apology for one of the situations in Exercise 3. Give an explanation of the problem. Use Holly's message to help you.

5 Where would you see these signs? Match the signs (A–C) with three of the places (1–4).

Poetry, Biography and Art History downstairs. **A**

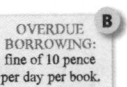
OVERDUE BORROWING: fine of 10 pence per day per book. **B**

PLEASE DO NOT TOUCH THE WORKS OF ART ON DISPLAY. **C**

1 an art gallery   3 a gift shop
2 a bookshop   4 a public library

6 Work in pairs. For each situation, make a request, and respond. Take turns.

1 You want to know if you can listen to your MP3 in the library.
2 You want a passer-by to take your photo.
3 You want to know if there is a café in the museum.
4 You want to borrow your friend's favourite book.

Pronunciation: words containing *au*

7 How do you pronounce these words? Compare with your partner.

astronaut   audience   audition   aunt
Australia   author   autobiography
autograph   because   caught   cause
daughter   saucer   sausage

8 🔊6.7 Listen and repeat the words in Exercise 7.

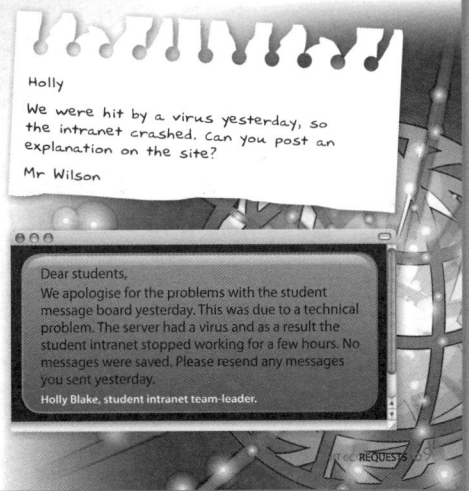

Holly
We were hit by a virus yesterday, so the intranet crashed. Can you post an explanation on the site?
Mr Wilson

Dear students,
We apologise for the problems with the student message board yesterday. This was due to a technical problem. The server had a virus and as a result the student intranet stopped working for a few hours. No messages were saved. Please resend any messages you sent yesterday.
Holly Blake, student intranet team-leader.

Communicate

Students can later practise the words in pairs, helping each other with their stress and pronunciation.

Writing: an apology

1 Reading for detail

Students read the note and email and find the information.

2 Using *due to* and *as a result*

Students should find and underline the expressions, then work with a partner to decide how each one is used.

3 Writing: using *due to* and *as a result*

Students complete the sentences with the two expressions, following the rule in Exercise 2.

4 Writing a short apology

Students should write a formal apology and exchange it with another student for peer checking of language used.

6D British best-sellers

Spread aims

Vocabulary: books

Skills: reading and listening for detail

Culture: British best-sellers

CLIL: Art and English: Leonardo da Vinci

KEY

2 1 *The Strange Case of Dr Jekyll and Mr Hyde*
2 *The Hobbit*
3 *Frankenstein*

3 1, 3 Gothic horror
2, 4 fantasy literature

4 book: novel / story
genre: kind / style
best-seller: hit / success

5 1 so successful   2 was made
3 Due to

6 J K Rowling, Acton Bell, George Eliot

---

1 Warm-up

Students work through the sentences deciding if they agree with them or not. Elicit some answers from the whole class.

2 Reading and listening for detail

 *6.8 CD 2 track 18*

Students find the name of the book in the text to complete each sentence.

Stronger students can cover the text and just listen.

3 Reading for detail

Students read and decide which sentences in Exercise 1 apply to Gothic horror, and which to fantasy literature.

4 Vocabulary: books

Students find two similar words in the text for each of the three words in the box.

5 Writing: paraphrasing sentences

Students complete the second sentence to mean the same as the first.

6D British best-sellers

Reading

1 **Work in pairs. Do you agree with any of the sentences?**

1 I like books that scare me.

2 I like to escape into a different world when I read.

3 I like stories that keep me awake at night.

4 I like to read about characters that have magic adventures.

2 *6.8* **Read about some books by British authors and write the name of the books.**

1 .... is about a struggle between good and evil.

2 .... was originally written as a children's story.

3 .... is about a frightening experiment.

3 **Read the text again. Which sentences (1–4) in Exercise 1 are about Gothic horror and which are about fantasy literature?**

4 **Find two more words or expressions in the text with similar meanings to each of these words.**

> book   genre   best-seller

5 **Read the first sentence. Complete the second sentence so that it gives the same information.**

1 a It was such a successful novel that other writers copied it.

b The novel was .... that other writers copied it.

2 a A studio made the book into a film.

b The book .... into a film.

3 a Wizards became popular as a result of *Harry Potter's* success.

b .... *Harry Potter's* success, wizards became popular.

Culture

'Best-sellers' are not simply a modern-day publishing phenomenon. There have always been books that were instantly popular.

Occasionally, a novel is so successful that it starts a new kind of writing. *Frankenstein*, published in 1818 by Mary Shelley, is a good example. The scary story of Victor Frankenstein, a scientist who manages to create a human life, was an immediate success with the public. It was the first real Gothic horror novel. The book was quickly adapted for the theatre and as a result became even more well-known. Nowadays, we are all familiar with Hollywood versions of a 'mad scientist' who is forced to destroy his evil creation.

An evil force is also at the centre of *The Strange Case of Dr Jekyll and Mr Hyde* (1886) by Robert Louis Stevenson. The story of a 'good' man who regularly turns into an evil version of himself appealed to many readers. The book was a best-seller within months. It was the origin of 20th-century characters like the Hulk and 'superheroes' who lead a double life.

Gothic horror was, in fact, one of the key literary genres of 19th-century Britain. Perhaps the best-selling genre of the 20th century was fantasy, characterised by parallel worlds inhabited by magic creatures. J.R.R.Tolkien is often called the 'father of modern fantasy' literature. Although he didn't originate the style, it became very popular due to the success of *The Hobbit* and *The Lord of the Rings* series. Tolkien had written *The Hobbit* for children and he was surprised when it was a hit with adults too. Another best-selling fantasy series, the *Harry Potter* books, by J.K. Rowling, also appeals to both children and adults. How many people do you know who have read these books?

70

Help **weaker students** by writing the phrases they will need on the board (*so successful, was made, due to*).

6 Listening for detail

 6.9 CD 2 track 19

Students listen and find out which of the authors were women.

Give **weaker students** the tapescript to follow on the second or third listening.

Tapescript

Are names important? Do you think it matters if a book is written by a man or a woman? When you see the names J.K. Rowling, George Eliot and Acton Bell, you may not immediately think they are women, but they are women writers. One of the first women

writers to realise the importance of a name was Mary Shelley, the author of Frankenstein. Mary Shelley was only 20 when the book was published, and her father was a well-known writer. She decided to publish Frankenstein anonymously. Many reviewers liked the book, and thought it was impressive. Some reviewers found out the identity of the author and said that since it was by a woman, they wouldn't comment on it. When Frankenstein became a huge success, Mary Shelley decided that she could put her name on the book.

A few years later, three talented sisters, the Bronte sisters, were trying to publish their poetry. At first, they used the names of Acton, Currer and Ellis Bell – which could be men's or women's names. Later they were successful under their own names of Anne, Charlotte and Emily

Listening

6 🔊6.9 **Which of these writers are women? Listen to a radio programme and check.**

> J.K. Rowling   C.S. Lewis   J.R.R.Tolkien
> George Eliot   Acton Bell

7 🔊6.9 **Listen again and choose the correct option (a–c).**

1 What happened when some journalists found out that Mary Shelley was the author of *Frankenstein*?
   a They refused to review the book.
   b They refused to believe she'd written it.
   c They gave it a bad review.

2 Why did Mary Ann Evans use a man's name?
   a So that she could earn more money.
   b So that she would be considered as a serious author.
   c So that she could write more than one style of novel.

3 Why did J.K. Rowling's publisher want her to use her initials?
   a Because they thought boys might not read books by a woman.
   b Because her first names are very complicated.
   c Because they didn't know whether she was a woman or a man.

Art and English
Leonardo da Vinci

1 **Write down three things you know about Leonardo da Vinci.**
Read the text and see if these things are mentioned.

Leonardo da Vinci was born in Florence, Italy, in 1452. At that time, Europe was at the start of a long period of artistic and intellectual development called the Renaissance. Da Vinci was a perfect example of a 'Renaissance man'. He was incredibly talented in many areas of both the arts and the sciences, and today is regarded as one of the greatest painters of all time. He also did thousands of drawings, not only artistic but also technical. As he himself wrote, in 1482: 'I can execute sculpture in bronze, marble or clay. Also, in painting, I can do as much as anyone, whoever he may be.'

Self-portrait, 1515

Da Vinci had many ideas that seem modern even today. He was a vegetarian and in his painting 'The Last Supper' he didn't show any meat on the table. He was obsessed with birds and flight. He used to buy birds in cages and release them into the wild. His writings showed that he understood some laws of physics 200 years before Sir Isaac Newton. Many of his notes and drawings have survived – 13,000 pages of them – ranging from shopping lists to plans for helicopters! Some of his most important scientific writings are now owned by Bill Gates. Da Vinci wrote his notes in code and in right-to-left mirror writing. Perhaps this was because he didn't want people to steal his ideas, or perhaps, since he was left-handed, it was easier. We will probably never know.

2 **Read the text again. Find all other things you find out about da Vinci.**

3 **What do you think is the most interesting thing about da Vinci? Compare with your partner.**

Project
Choose a popular novel from your country. Write a paragraph about it and use illustrations of the story.

UNIT 6D BRITISH BEST-SELLERS 71

Culture

Project: a novel

Students should produce a poster with a mixture of paragraphs of information about the life and work of a popular novelist in their country, and illustrations of their work. Have a 'show-and-tell' session where they can present their poster to others (probably in small groups) and read what others have written.

Art and English: Leonardo da Vinci

1 Warm-up

With books closed, students write what they know about Leonardo da Vinci. Elicit ideas from the whole class, and list them on the board. Do not comment on what students say; accept and note everything. Ask them to read the text and check what they said. Have a discussion about whether each item on the board was confirmed, contradicted or not mentioned.

2 Reading for detail

Students read to find out further interesting information about Leonardo da Vinci. Elicit answers and list them in two columns on the board.

3 Discussion

Students discuss da Vinci and his achievements from a personal point of view. Elicit ideas from the whole class and open a wider discussion.

Bronte. Around the same period of time, a writer called Mary Ann Evans decided to call herself George Eliot. She could see that women were regarded as writers of trivial, romantic fiction, but she was determined to be regarded as a serious writer. She wrote seven successful novels as George Eliot, and at the same time worked as a journalist under her own name.

It seems unusual that at the end of the 20th century the name of the author still had a big impact. But in 1997, the publishers of the first Harry Potter *book* were going to aim the book at children aged nine to eleven. They worried that boys in this age range would not buy books written by a woman, so they asked the author, Joanne Rowling, if they could use her initials. In fact, she hasn't got a middle name, so the 'K' in J.K. Rowling is taken from her grandmother. Perhaps the success of the Harry Potter books will bring some changes in the attitudes of publishers.

7 Listening for detail

💿 *6.9 CD 2 track 19*

Present the questions to help students to focus on the task, then play the recording through twice.

6E Consolidation Units 5 and 6

Spread aims

Listening and **reading:** developing subskills

Consolidating understanding of the key grammar points from Units 5 and 6

KEY

Listening

1 reading / books

2/3 1 b   2 a ✓   3 c

4 a   **5** c

Reading

1 1 watercolour exhibition
2 sculpture

2 A gym   B switch off mobiles / loud   C History / display
D Special offer / titles / mysteries and thrillers

3 A gym / sports hall / centre
B library / hospital   C museum
D bookshop

4 1 C   2 A   3 D   4 –   5 B

Listening

1 & 2 Identifying the main idea

Present and discuss the strategies. Students decide on the topic, then match each option to a group of words in 2.

3 Listening for key words

 *6.10 CD 2 track 20*

Students listen and tick any words in Exercise 2 which they hear the speaker use.

Tapescript

I don't read very much. I'd like to read more actually, but I'm really busy. When I've got some free time, I really enjoy a good, old-fashioned detective story. You know, stories about murder and mystery, and so on. If I haven't got much time, I read a magazine, usually about computers because that's my hobby. There are some really interesting computer magazines and things are always changing, so there's always something new, which I like.

Listening

Identifying the main idea

- Read the task instruction and the options. Identify the overall topic if it is mentioned.
- Look carefully at the meaning of each option – remember the topic words may be similar in each case.
- The first time you listen, choose the correct answer. The second time, check your answers.

1 Look at the three options in a listening task. Which topic have they got in common?

The man talks about
- **a** reading for pleasure.
- **b** the books he reads on holiday.
- **c** his favourite author.

2 Match the groups of words (1–3) with the options (a–c) in Exercise 1.

1. guidebooks   beach   airport bookshop
2. detective stories   interesting magazines   hobby
3. writer   first book   new title

3 *6.10* Now listen and tick the words you hear in Exercise 2.

4 *6.10* Listen again and do the task in Exercise 1.

5 *6.11* You will hear someone talking about her hobby. Listen and choose the correct option (a–c).

- **a** The woman is a sculptor.
- **b** The woman makes presents out of unusual objects.
- **c** The woman does abstract paintings.

Reading

Identifying the situation

- Find the key words in the notices which can help you identify the place or situation.
- Read the first notice again, look at the options and find the one which matches.
- Repeat this for the other notices. Then check them again.

1 Read the notices from an art gallery. Find the words which tell you the notice is from an art gallery.

2 Read these notices and choose the key words.

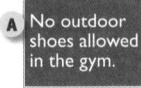
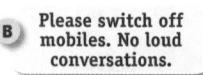
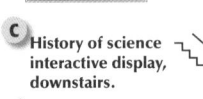

3 Write places where you can see the notices in Exercise 2.

4 Match the signs (a–d) in Exercise 2 with the places (1–5). There is one extra place.

1. in a museum
2. in a school
3. in a bookshop
4. in a cinema
5. in a library

---

4 Listening for the main idea

 *6.10 CD 2 track 20*

Students listen and choose the topic from Exercise 1.

5 Further practice

 6.11 CD 2 track 21

Students listen and decide what the woman's hobby is.

Tapescript

I love painting and I usually spend most of my weekends painting or going to see paintings. I was always good at art at school, and for a while I tried sculpture, but I'm a much better painter than a sculptor! I enjoy looking at abstract paintings and still life. My own style is quite abstract too. I use bright colours and geometric shapes. I've never sold a painting – it's just a hobby – but I like to give people my paintings for their birthday. Usually, people are quite happy to get one.

Reading

1 & 2 Identifying key words

Read and discuss the strategies. Students find the key words in Exercise 1 and 2.

3 Identifying places

Students decide where the signs in Exercise 2 might be.

4 Matching

Students match the signs with the places listed.

a/an or the?

We use *a/an* to talk about one of many things, not a specific thing. We use *the* to refer to a specific thing.

Leonardo da Vinci was a genius. He had an idea for a helicopter.

Have you been to the new Leonardo da Vinci exhibition yet?

1 Complete the sentences with *a*, *an* or *the*.

1 Have you ever seen .... vampire?
2 I'm going to write .... novel.
3 Which was .... first book Agatha Christie wrote?
4 I got .... amazing picture for my birthday.

the for specific things

We use *the* with things we have already mentioned and when the context makes it clear which thing we mean.

I'm wearing a gold ring and a silver ring. The silver ring is new.

I love this painting. The colours are bright and exciting.

2 Complete the sentences with *a*, *an* or *the*.

1 I like my English class. .... teacher is great.
2 We've got .... cat and .... dog. .... cat is called Ginger.
3 We're going to .... cinema. Do you want to come?
4 I do my homework after school. I do it in .... living room.

the only one

We use *the* when there's only one of the thing we're talking about.

3 Choose the correct option.

1 I like looking at **a / the** moon.
2 We live in **a / the** big city.
3 Pollution is bad for **an / the** environment.
4 Are you connected to **a / the** Internet?
5 Which is **a / the** oldest World Wonder?

the with types of things and groups

We use *the* + noun or plural nouns without *the* to talk about types of things.

The kangaroo is an Australian animal. Koalas live in trees.

4 Choose the correct option.

1 **Bats / The bat** is nocturnal.
2 **Helicopters / The helicopter** was first drawn by Leonardo da Vinci.
3 **Violins / The violin** are string instruments.
4 **Kiwis / The kiwi** is found only in New Zealand.
5 **Crocodiles / The crocodile** live in rivers.

We use *the* + adjective to talk about a group of people.

5 Complete the sentences with phrases from the box. There are two extra phrases.

| the homeless | the military | the poor |
| the rich | the sick | the young |

1 Older people don't understand .... these days.
2 It's a luxury hotel especially for ....
3 I'd like to be a doctor and help ....
4 We need to build more houses for ....

Names

We use *the* with the names of seas, oceans, rivers, canals, deserts, groups of islands, mountain ranges, countries ending in *-s* and *Kingdom* or *Republic*

6 Read the sentences. Cross out *the* where it is not needed.

1 We're going on holiday to the United States and the Mexico.
2 I live in the United Kingdom, which is part of the Europe.
3 The Irish Sea is between the Ireland and the England.
4 I'd love to go climbing in the Alps or swimming in the Bahamas.
5 The Sahara and the Nile are in the Africa.

5 the + adjective pairs

Present the grammar box. Students then complete the sentences.

Tell **weaker students** that *the military* and *the poor* are the extra phrases.

Extension: students can write two more sentences for the extra phrases.

6 Names

Present the grammar box. Students then cross out *the* where it is not needed.

Extension: students can write some other sentences with errors and swap them with a partner.

1 a / an or the

Present the grammar box and check understanding before students start to do the exercise. Elicit some examples of the use of *a / an / the* from the class before they do Exercise 1.

2 the for specific things

Present the grammar box and make sure students have a firm grasp of the background to the distinction between definite and indefinite objects before they do this exercise; elicit examples.

3 the only one

Present the grammar box. Ask for other examples where *the* refers to the only one (e.g. the president, the Pope, the Catholic Church, the United Nations).

4 the with types of things and groups

Present the grammar box. Offer some plural sentences (e.g. *Cats are popular pets*) for students to change into singular ones using *the* (e.g. *The cat is a popular pet*). Have students make up others.

Review Units 5 and 6

Spread aim

Reviewing vocabulary, grammar and functions from Units 5 and 6; giving students the opportunity to assess their own progress

KEY

1 1 glass 2 paper 3 leather
4 brick 5 metal

2 1 square 2 triangle
3 circle 4 oval 5 rectangle

3 1 autobiography
2 romance 3 cookery
(book) 4 history (book)
5 humour

4 1 portrait 2 landscape
3 play 4 drawing 5 still life

5 1 to 2 in 3 away 4 of
5 out

6 1 was built 2 is being
restored 3 has been
visited 4 has not been
found 5 is being cleaned

7 1 The statue was not
destroyed by fire.
2 How was the rock moved?
3 Why has the building been
closed?
4 The secret has not been
revealed.
5 When was the city
abandoned?

8 1 will
2 can't
3 can
4 must
5 won't

9 1 must 2 might 3 must
4 can't 5 could

10 1 were / was 2 would you
believe 3 would grow
4 would be, passed 5 could go

Review Units 5 and 6

Vocabulary

1 Write the materials.

1 ....
2 ....
3 ....
4 ....
5 ....

1 mark per item: .../5 marks

2 Write the shapes.

1 ....
2 ....
3 ....
4 ....
5 ....

1 mark per item: .../5 marks

3 Write the type of book.

1 about somebody's own life ....
2 about a love story ....
3 about food and recipes ....
4 about the past ....
5 it makes you laugh ....

1 mark per item: .../5 marks

4 Write the words.

1 a painting of a person ....
2 a painting of the country ....
3 it's performed in a theatre ....
4 a picture done with a pencil ....
5 a painting of objects ....

1 mark per item: .../5 marks

5 Write the prepositions.

1 What's your reaction .... this sculpture?
2 Do you believe .... ghosts?
3 We think our dog has run ....
4 What was the cause .... the accident?
5 My pen has run .... of ink.

1 mark per item: .../5 marks

Grammar

6 Complete the sentences with the correct form of the passive.

1 Petra (**build**) .... 2,000 years ago.
2 This statue (**restore**) .... now.
3 The tomb (**visit**) .... by many people since its discovery.
4 The ship disappeared in the Atlantic. It (**not / find**) ....
5 You can't visit the church while it (**clean**) ....

1 mark per item: .../5 marks

7 Rewrite each active sentence in the passive.

1 Fire did not destroy the statue.
2 How did they move the rock?
3 Why have they closed the building?
4 Nobody has revealed the secret.
5 When did they abandon the city?

1 mark per item: .../5 marks

8 Choose the correct option.

1 The museum **can / will** be opened by the Queen.
2 Most stars **can't / will** be seen without a telescope.
3 Many objects **can / must** be made from gold.
4 Phones **must / won't** be switched off at all times.
5 The work **mustn't / won't** be finished in time.

1 mark per item: .../5 marks

9 Choose the correct option.

The door was locked, so the thief (**1**) **can / must** have used a key. He (**2**) **can't / might** have gone into the house when the owners left. They could smell cigarettes, so the thief (**3**) **must / mustn't** smoke. He (**4**) **can / can't** be very clever because he didn't steal valuable objects. Or he (**5**) **could / mustn't** have been interrupted when the owners returned.

1 mark per item: .../5 marks

10 Complete the second conditional sentences.

1 I'd collect art if I (**be**) .... rich.
2 If you saw a UFO, (**you / believe**) .... it?
3 If I had a garden, I (**grow**) .... vegetables.
4 I (**be**) .... happy if I (**pass**) .... the exam.
5 If the shop was open, we (**can / go**) .... in.

1 mark per item: .../5 marks

74

92

Communicate

11 Match the sentence beginnings (1–5) with the endings (a–e).

1 Could you
2 Yes,
3 Would it be all right if we
4 No,
5 Do you mind

a not at all.
b showing me this picture, please?
c of course.
d sat here?
e tell me the time, please?

2 marks per item: …/10 marks

12 Complete the dialogue with the expressions.

because   so that   what for   why
to get my hair cut

Kate: Can you give me ten pounds, please?
Dad: (1) …………? That's a lot of money.
Kate: I want (2) ………….
Dad: (3) ………… do you want to do that? It looks lovely the way it is.
Kate: (4) ………… it's too long, Dad.
Dad: OK then, here you are.
Kate: Thanks. The hairdresser's is on Percy Street.
Dad: Why are you telling me that?
Kate: (5) ………… you can come and get me later!

2 marks per item: …/10 marks

13 Does the 'o' in these words sound like the *o* in *gold* /əʊ/ or *some* /ʌ/? Write G or S.

1 above   …………
2 chose   …………
3 come   …………
4 done   …………
5 money   …………
6 old   …………
7 oval   …………
8 so   …………
9 stone   …………
10 won   …………

1 mark per item: …/10 marks

14 Complete the sentences with these words.

as   as a result   due to   so that   to

1 The road was closed ………… the snow.
2 ………… the weather was so bad, we stayed at home.
3 I used my mobile ………… call for help.
4 It snowed all night. …………, there was no electricity.
5 We lit some candles ………… we could see.

2 marks per item: …/10 marks

15 Complete the letter with these words.

a   all   any   at   for   if   of   some
the   to

Dear Parents,

We apologise (1) ………… the changes to our parent–teacher meetings this term. This is because (2) ………… the building work in (3) ………… school. As you know, we are having (4) ………… fire alarm system installed, following the damage (5) ………… the gym last month. Since this work will affect (6) ………… the classrooms, there are changes to (7) ………… meeting dates and places. Please look (8) ………… the new programme and contact Mr Banks (9) ………… you have (10) ………… questions.

Mrs Smith
Head teacher

1 mark per item: …/10 marks

Total: …/100

I can...
I can talk about purpose and reason.
I can make and respond to requests.

Project: A great artist

Page aim

Reading for detail; writing about a famous artist

Warm-up

Ask students to think and talk about paintings, and name some artists and paintings that they like. You could bring a few pictures of famous paintings (e.g. da Vinci's *Mona Lisa*, van Gogh's *Sunflowers*) and ask students what they know and like/dislike about them.

1 Discussion

Ask students to look at the Turner painting and talk to a partner about it. Then elicit some ideas from the whole class. Indicate the phrases they can use to talk about it. Don't reveal the title (see below) until the end of the discussion, to allow students' creativity and imagination to work on the picture.

Background information

This oil painting is called *Snow Storm – Steam-Boat off a Harbour's Mouth* and it was first exhibited in 1842. The boat is in the centre of a vortex made of the snow storm and the waves, all of which seem to spiral around it. For further information on Turner and images of his work, see:

http://en.wikipedia.org/wiki/
  J._M._W._Turner
http://j-m-w-turner.co.uk/
http://tate.org.uk/britain/turner/

2 Reading for detail

Ask students to read the article and answer the questions individually, then check with a partner. Elicit the answers from the whole class.

A great artist

1 Look at the picture and say what you think about it. Use some of the following phrases:

> It could/must/can't be … It could/must/can't have …
> The painter could/must/can't have …
> The weather could/must/can't have …

2 Read the article and answer the questions.

Joseph Mallord William Turner was born in London in 1775. He studied art from a very young age and at 13 he was selling his own drawings from his father's shop window. When he was just 15, one of his paintings was put in an exhibition at the Royal Academy. Slowly, he became well known and he became a member of the Royal Academy. Although he was better known for his oil paintings, he also made prints and he was recognised as a master of watercolours too.

Turner travelled throughout Europe and he particularly loved Venice. He was interested in light and he was passionate about the weather and the changes he noted on the sea and in the sky. As time went on, the objects in his paintings became less clear and the paintings became a romantic expression of his own feelings. His work was admired by many other painters such as Claude Monet, who was keen to study his style.

Turner spent a great deal of his adult life alone. He even travelled alone, and he never let anyone see him while he was working. No one knows the cause of his unsociable behaviour. He might have been worried that people would copy his technique, but it is more likely that he had become so involved in his work that he found it difficult to be with people.

Turner died in 1851. He had wanted all of his paintings to stay in one building for the people of Britain but this didn't happen until many years after his death. In more recent years, a new wing of the Tate Gallery in London was opened to display Turner's paintings. The Turner Prize, which has been a famous art prize in Britain since 1984, was named after him.

1 Which statement is true about the young Turner?
  a He made money from his art.
  b He worked for his father.
  c He started studying art at the age of 13.
2 Turner …
  a preferred watercolours to printmaking.
  b was much better at oil painting.
  c was very good at more than one type of painting.

3 The weather was important to Turner because
  a it often stopped him from painting.
  b he liked the effect that it had on the light.
  c he disliked the English weather so he travelled in Europe.
4 As time passed, Turner
  a painted less detail in his work.
  b studied the styles of others.
  c was less sure of what to paint.

5 The writer says that Turner
  a was worried about people stealing his paintings.
  b sometimes worked with other painters.
  c did not like to be with other people.

6 We can understand from the article that Turner must have …
  a found a building for all of his paintings.
  b expressed a wish for his paintings to stay together.
  c been quickly forgotten after his death.

Project

Write an article about a famous artist from your country.
- Say what kind of art he/she is famous for
- Give brief biographical information.
- Mention why he/she is different to other artists
- Include any interesting facts you can find about the artist's life or work
- Remember to use modal verbs for speculation
- Find pictures to show the artist's work

76

Original works by Turner have a very high value. In 2010, his painting *Modern Rome – Campo Vaccino* was sold for a record-breaking price of nearly 30 million pounds.

Students could complete the activity paragraph by paragraph, or as a complete single task.

Project

Present the Project box and discuss the instructions with the class. You may wish to suggest that students can write about any artist they like rather than just someone from 'your country'. Ask them to write 150–200 words about the artist, and find pictures to illustrate their writing. They could produce this as a poster, with the writing and pictures stuck on it, or as an illustrated article.

Presentation

When they have finished, arrange a 'show-and-tell' session, where they can look at each other's work and discuss it.

NATIONAL GEOGRAPHIC

Moments in history

> Grammar
Learn about the third conditional, *could/should have done* and *wish* and *if only*.

> Vocabulary
Learn words for science and technology, and words connected with politics. Work with prefixes, and suffixes.

> Skills
Read about mathematical and scientific codes, Nelson Mandela, and South African life.

Listen to comments about four famous people, and a tour of Cape Town.

Write a story.

> Communicate
Talk about regrets and make criticisms.

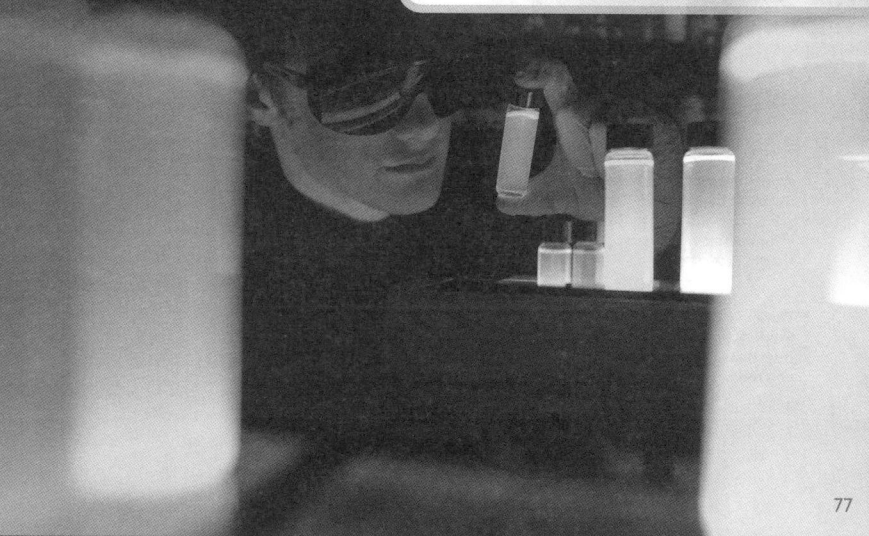

1 Look at the photo and choose the best options to complete the description.

This scientist is doing an (**1**) **experiment** / **innovation** in a (**2**) **data** / **laboratory**. He's probably testing a (**3**) **theory** / **knowledge** as part of his (**4**) **research** / **discovery**. The (**5**) **results** / **machine** could lead to a new medical application.

2 Work in pairs. What are these scientists famous for?

Marie Curie	Charles Darwin
Alexander Fleming	Guglielmo Marconi
Isaac Newton	Louis Pasteur

3 ○ 7.1 Listen to the conversation and check your answers to Exercise 2.

4 Work in pairs. Who was the greatest scientist of all time? Explain your reasons to your partner. Use the words in the vocabulary box to help you.

application	innovation	research
data	knowledge	result
discovery	laboratory	test
experiment	machine	theory

77

Moments in history

Unit aims

Grammar: third conditional; *could / should have done, I wish* and *if only*

Vocabulary: science and technology; politics; prefixes and suffixes

Functions: talking about regrets and making criticisms

Reading about: mathematical and scientific codes; Nelson Mandela; South African life

Listening to: comments about famous people; a tour of Cape Town

Writing a story

KEY

1 1 experiment 2 laboratory 3 theory 4 research 5 results

2 Marie Curie – discovered radioactivity Charles Darwin – explained how life on earth evolved Alexander Fleming – discovered penicillin Guglielmo Marconi – developed radios Issac Newton – first to understand gravity Louis Pasteur – created the rabies vaccine

---

1 Vocabulary: science

Students complete the description by choosing the best option in each case.

Extension: have students repeat the words in the box in Exercise 4. Note the syllable stress: appli**ca**tion, dis**co**very, ex**pe**riment, inno**va**tion, la**bo**ratory, ma**chine**, re**search**, re**sult**.

2 Speaking: famous scientists

In pairs, students discuss what the scientists are famous for.

3 Listening for detail

 7.1 CD 2 track 22

Students listen and check their answers.

Tapescript

Holly: Have you seen that new programme on TV, The greatest scientists of all time? They talk about a different scientist every week and then you can vote for the one you think was the most important.

Dan: So who are you going to vote for?

Holly: I'm not sure yet. Maybe Isaac Newton. I mean, he was the first person to understand gravity, wasn't he? And that's quite important. Or Guglielmo Marconi – we wouldn't have radios and TVs without Marconi.

Dan: I don't know … there were a few people experimenting with similar things at the same time as Marconi. Anyway, isn't that more about

technology, not science? What about someone like Alexander Fleming?

Holly: Did he discover penicillin? Yes, that's quite a major discovery. And medical applications have really saved lots of lives. Like Louis Pasteur. He created the vaccine against rabies.

Dan: I didn't know that! Oh, I know who I would vote for – Marie Curie. Without her research, we wouldn't understand radioactivity. And that's important for all sorts of things, including treating cancer …

Holly: And what about Charles Darwin? Darwin's theories explain how life on Earth evolved. What could be more important than that?

4 Discussion

Students discuss the topic in pairs.

7A Cracking the code

Spread aims

Grammar: third conditional
Vocabulary: prefixes
Functions: talking about conditions
Reading articles about Enigma and DNA

KEY

1 chromosome / DNA / gene; cryptology / cipher / message

2 Enigma: 1 A German military code 2 Marian Rejewski / Poland 3 France, Britain 4 They understood German war plans

DNA: 1 the structure of DNA 2 Rosalind Franklin 3 Crick and Watson 4 They published their theory and won the Nobel Prize

4 decipher, decode

5 1 would have been 2 hadn't shown 3 Would ... have shared

6 1 shared 2 shared 3 was not

7 1 If Rejewski hadn't worked ... 2 ... if they had known ... 3 ... if her father ... 4 If Franklin had gone ...

---

1 Vocabulary: connecting words

Students use their knowledge and their dictionaries to link the words in the box together.

Tell **weaker students** to put the words into two groups of three.

2 Reading for detail

Students, in pairs, read their respective texts and answer the questions individually, then share the information.

3 Reading for detail

Stronger students cover the texts and just listen.

Weaker students listen and follow the text.

Students listen for any differences in what they read / hear and what their

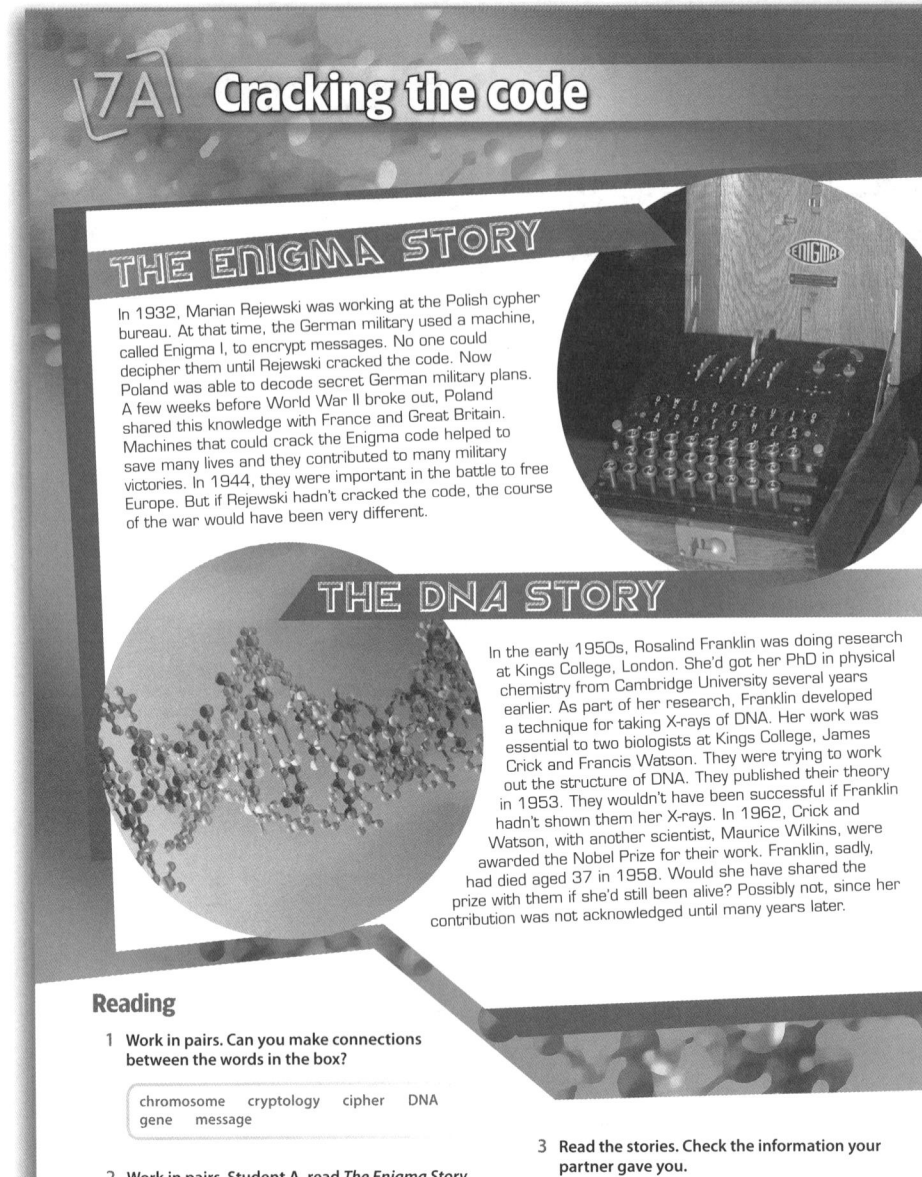

7A Cracking the code

THE ENIGMA STORY

In 1932, Marian Rejewski was working at the Polish cypher bureau. At that time, the German military used a machine, called Enigma I, to encrypt messages. No one could decipher them until Rejewski cracked the code. Now Poland was able to decode secret German military plans. A few weeks before World War II broke out, Poland shared this knowledge with France and Great Britain. Machines that could crack the Enigma code helped to save many lives and they contributed to many military victories. In 1944, they were important in the battle to free Europe. But if Rejewski hadn't cracked the code, the course of the war would have been very different.

THE DNA STORY

In the early 1950s, Rosalind Franklin was doing research at Kings College, London. She'd got her PhD in physical chemistry from Cambridge University several years earlier. As part of her research, Franklin developed a technique for taking X-rays of DNA. Her work was essential to two biologists at Kings College, James Crick and Francis Watson. They were trying to work out the structure of DNA. They published their theory in 1953. They wouldn't have been successful if Franklin hadn't shown them her X-rays. In 1962, Crick and Watson, with another scientist, Maurice Wilkins, were awarded the Nobel Prize for their work. Franklin, sadly, had died aged 37 in 1958. Would she have shared the prize with them if she'd still been alive? Possibly not, since her contribution was not acknowledged until many years later.

Reading

1 Work in pairs. Can you make connections between the words in the box?

> chromosome   cryptology   cipher   DNA
> gene   message

2 Work in pairs. Student A, read *The Enigma Story*. Student B, read *The DNA Story*. Answer the questions. Then tell your partner about the story you read.
  1 What was the 'code'?
  2 Who shared information?
  3 Who did they share it with?
  4 What were the consequences?

3 Read the stories. Check the information your partner gave you.

Working with words: prefixes

4 Look at the examples. Which two of these three words have the same meaning?

encrypt   decipher   decode

See Working with words: Page 106

78

partner said, and then discuss it with them, using the texts in the book to make their points.

4 Working with words: prefixes

Students use dictionaries to find out which two of the three words have similar meaning to each other.

See *Working with words*, page 106, for further practice.

5 Grammar presentation: third conditional

Students complete the sentences from the two texts.

6 Grammar: third conditional

Students complete the sentences about what actually happened, based on the conditional sentences in Exercise 5. Make sure students understand the connection between the sentences here and those in Exercise 5. Present the grammar note, and if necessary, present *Grammar Explorer*, pages 124–125, to check students' understanding of this tense.

7 Identifying *if*-clauses

Students indicate where *if* can go in the sentences.

Grammar: third conditional

5 Complete these sentences from the text.

1 If Rejewski hadn't cracked the code, the course of the war .... very different.

2 They wouldn't have been successful if Franklin .... them her X-rays.

3 .... she .... the prize with them if she'd still been alive?

See Grammar Explorer: Page 124

6 Read the sentences in Exercise 5 again and choose the correct option.

1 Poland **shared** / **did not share** information.

2 Franklin **shared** / **did not share** her data.

3 Franklin **was** / **was not** alive when the Nobel prize was awarded.

> We use the third conditional to talk about imagined results of events in the past.

7 Mark the correct position of *if* in each sentence.

e.g. The course of the war would have been different ..if.. Poland hadn't shared the Enigma information.

1 Rejewski hadn't worked at the Polish cypher bureau, he wouldn't have deciphered the code.

2 Would Germany have used the Enigma machines they had known the Polish could decode their messages?

3 Franklin wouldn't have studied chemistry her father hadn't allowed it.

4 Franklin had gone to a different university, Watson and Crick wouldn't have met her.

8 Complete the sentences with the correct form of the verbs.

1 If Roentgen .... (**not discover**) X-rays, Franklin .... (**not be able**) to do her research.

2 .... Newton .... (**write**) the laws of motion if he .... (**not study**) physics?

3 If Leonardo da Vinci .... (**be**) right-handed, ... he .... (**write**) in code?

4 If Einstein .... (**obey**) his father, he .... (**become**) an electrical engineer.

5 Marconi .... (**not develop**) the radio so quickly if he .... (**stay**) in Italy.

9 Read about the discovery of penicillin. Then write four sentences in the third conditional. Use the two underlined verbs in each sentence. Use *not* where necessary.

Alexander Fleming (**1**) went on holiday and (**1**) left some dishes in his laboratory. He hadn't (**2**) cleaned the dishes, so bacteria (**2**) grew on them. When he got back from holiday, he didn't (**3**) throw the dishes away, and he (**3**) noticed one unusual dish where the bacteria hadn't grown.

Fleming saw a mould on the dish, and realised that this mould was killing the bacteria. He (**4**) investigated the mould and (**4**) discovered penicillin.

10 Imagine you are the person in each situation. What would you say? Write four sentences using the third conditional.

1 study / understand

2 not explode / listen to the teacher

3 not get lost / bring a map

4 follow the recipe / not be a disaster

Speaking

11 Work in pairs. Tell your partner about a time something went wrong for you or your family. Use the ideas in the box or your own ideas.

> family pets   on holiday   cooking   going out   domestic disasters   family parties

A: *Once, our dog ran away. If the door had been closed, he wouldn't have got out.*

B: *Did you find him?*

Fast finishers

Look at this sentence beginning. How many endings can you think of? If I'd worked harder, …

Tell **weaker students** that *If* starts sentences 1 and 5 and ask them to mark where it goes in sentences 2, 3, 4.

8 Third conditional gap-fill

Students fill the gaps with the correct forms of the verbs.

Remind **weaker students** that the verb that follows *if* is always going to be *had* + past participle, while the verb in the other clause will always be *would have* + past participle.

9 Writing third conditional sentences

Students use the information in the text to write third conditional sentences.

Give **weaker students** the first clause for each sentence and ask them to complete them.

10 Further writing practice

Students have to write complete sentences of their own based on what they see in the pictures and the prompts given underneath.

Give **weaker students** the first clause for each sentence.

11 Speaking: talking about past problems

Students use the third conditional to talk about the topics in the box related to their own real experiences.

Grammar

KEY

8 1 hadn't discovered, wouldn't have been able   2 Would … have written, hadn't studied   3 had been, would … have written   4 had obeyed, would have become   5 wouldn't have developed, had stayed

9 (possible answers) 1 If Fleming hadn't gone on holiday, he wouldn't have left the dishes in his laboratory.   2 Bacteria wouldn't have grown on the dishes if he had cleaned them.   3 If he had thrown the dishes away, he wouldn't have noticed the unusual dish where the bacteria hadn't grown.   4 If he hadn't investigated the mould, he wouldn't have discovered penicillin.

10 (possible answers) 1 If I had studied harder, I would have understood the formula.   2 It wouldn't have exploded if I had listened to the teacher.   3 We wouldn't have got lost if we had brought a map.   4 If I had followed the recipe, it wouldn't have been a disaster.

Fast finishers

Students complete the sentence in as many ways as possible – it doesn't have to be true or related to them. Encourage them to make up amusing or strange endings.

97

7B Rebels

Spread aims

Grammar: *could / should have done*
Vocabulary: politics; suffixes
Functions: talking about possibilities
Reading about Nelson Mandela
Listening to comments about famous rebels

KEY

2 campaign (N/V), democracy (N), election (N), freedom (N), government (N), law (N), leader (N), policy (N), politics (N), protest (N/V), right (N/V), vote (N/V)

3 policy, campaign, protest, government, freedom, election

4 1 T 2 F 3 F 4 NI

5 1 b 2 a

6 1 b 2 d 3 a

---

1 Warm-up

Students look at the five photos and discuss what they know about the people. Elicit ideas from the whole class (they will find the answers later in the section).

2 Vocabulary: politics

Students classify the words, using a dictionary if you wish. Some words can be both noun and verb. They then decide on the correct translations. Elicit answers from the whole class.

3 Reading: scanning for detail

Students scan the text looking for the words.

4 Reading and listening for detail

 7.2 CD 2 track 23

Present the sentences to help students to focus on the information they need.

5 Grammar: *could / should have done*

Students match the sentences and the meanings. See also *Grammar Explorer*, page 125.

7B Rebels

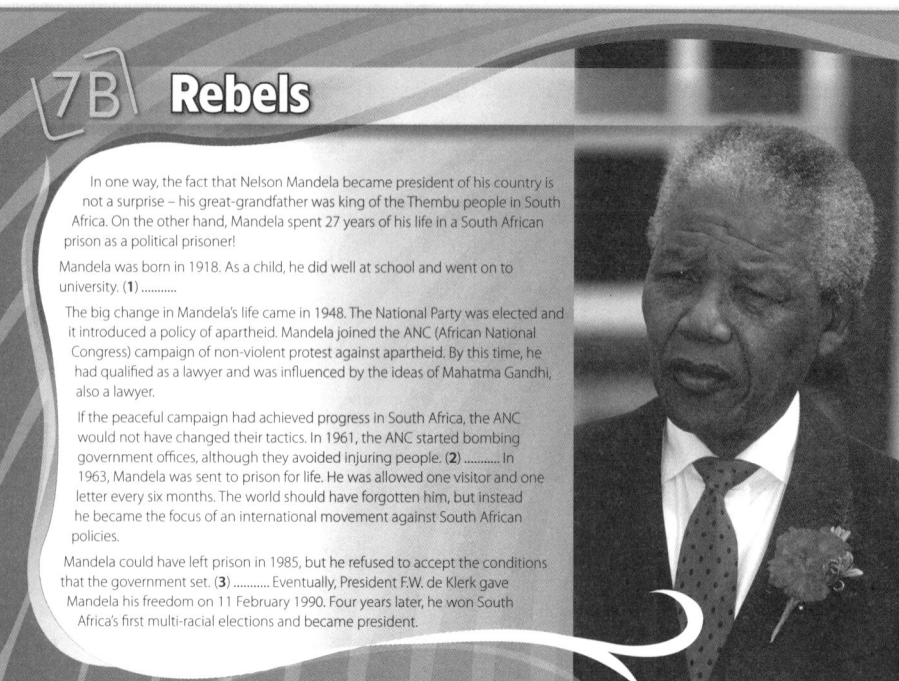

In one way, the fact that Nelson Mandela became president of his country is not a surprise – his great-grandfather was king of the Thembu people in South Africa. On the other hand, Mandela spent 27 years of his life in a South African prison as a political prisoner!

Mandela was born in 1918. As a child, he did well at school and went on to university. (**1**) ....

The big change in Mandela's life came in 1948. The National Party was elected and it introduced a policy of apartheid. Mandela joined the ANC (African National Congress) campaign of non-violent protest against apartheid. By this time, he had qualified as a lawyer and was influenced by the ideas of Mahatma Gandhi, also a lawyer.

If the peaceful campaign had achieved progress in South Africa, the ANC would not have changed their tactics. In 1961, the ANC started bombing government offices, although they avoided injuring people. (**2**) .... In 1963, Mandela was sent to prison for life. He was allowed one visitor and one letter every six months. The world should have forgotten him, but instead he became the focus of an international movement against South African policies.

Mandela could have left prison in 1985, but he refused to accept the conditions that the government set. (**3**) .... Eventually, President F.W. de Klerk gave Mandela his freedom on 11 February 1990. Four years later, he won South Africa's first multi-racial elections and became president.

Nelson Mandela

Speaking

1 Look at the photos. What do you know about these people? Tell your partner.

Reading and listening

2 Work in pairs. How do you say these words in your language? For each word, write N (noun) or V (verb). Some words are both.

> campaign democracy election freedom
> government law leader policy
> politics protest right vote

3 **STUDY SKILLS** Read quickly through the text about Nelson Mandela. How many words from the vocabulary box can you find?

4  7.2 **Read and listen to the text. Are the sentences true or false – or is there not enough information to decide?**

1 Mandela's family was important in South African society.
2 Mandela was the leader of the National Party.
3 Nobody outside South Africa knew about Mandela until 1990.
4 F.W. de Klerk was against apartheid.

80

Grammar: *could/should have done*

5 Look at the examples (1–2). Match them with the meanings (a–b).

1 The world should have forgotten him.
2 Mandela could have left prison in 1985.

a It was possible, but it did not happen.
b It was logical, but it did not happen.

See Grammar Explorer: Page 125

6 Read the text again and complete the gaps (1–3) with the sentences (a–d). There is one extra sentence.

a He could have spent his whole life in prison, but a new president was elected.
b He should have graduated, but he had to leave after protesting against the university policies.
c He could have met Mahatma Gandhi when he was in prison.
d However, many people thought the ANC shouldn't have taken this action.

---

6 Reading and matching

Students match three of the sentences to the gaps in the text.

Tell **weaker students** that sentence c is not included.

7 Sentence completion: *could / should*

Students complete the sentences as instructed.

8 Listening for detail

 7.3 CD 2 track 24

Students could match the speakers to the people in the photos on first listening, then match to the sentences a–e.

Give **weaker students** the script to follow on the second listening.

Extension: ask who sentence d applies to (Martin Luther King).

Tapescript

1 In my opinion, Mahatma Gandhi was one of the most important people of the 20th century. His ideas about non-violent, peaceful protest influenced so many civil rights movements all around the world. He first developed his ideas when he lived in South Africa. And he could have stayed there, but he went back to India to lead the Indian independence protest against the British. I know that there was a lot of violence associated with Indian independence, so imagine what it would have been like without

| Emmeline Pankhurst | Mahatma Gandhi | Che Guevara | Aung San Suu Kyi |

7 Read the first sentence. Complete the second sentence with *could*, *couldn't*, *should* or *shouldn't*.

e.g. I didn't know you were looking for a dictionary. I *could have* lent you mine.

1 I worked hard for that exam. I .... have got a better mark.
2 I think you were the best in the competition. You .... have won.
3 Why didn't you tell me you were in hospital? I .... have visited you.
4 You did your best. You .... have done any more.
5 I made a mistake. I voted for Shaw, but I .... have voted for Rogers.
6 The result of the election was a surprise. Nobody .... have predicted it.

Listening

8 🔊 7.3 Listen to four people talking about the people in the photos on this page. Match the speakers (1–4) with the statements (a–e). There is one extra statement.

a Without this person's actions, British women wouldn't have won the right to vote. ....
b This person's political party should have been in government after the election. ....
c This person could have had a comfortable life as a doctor. ....
d The American civil rights movement couldn't have existed without this person. ....
e Without this person's influence, many more people could have died in India. ....

9 🔊 7.3 Listen again and complete the sentences.

1 Mahatma Gandhi lived in .... and India.
2 Aung San Suu Kyi was a .... in her own home.
3 Emmeline Pankhurst and her .... went to prison several times.
4 Che Guevara worked as a .... with the poor and the sick.

Working with words: suffixes

10 Look at the examples. Find other words in Exercise 2 which can have different forms.

politics: He was a political prisoner.
election: The National Party was elected.

See Working with words: Page 106

Speaking

11 Work in groups and discuss these questions.

1 Who or what did the people on this page rebel against?
2 What would you have done in these situations?
3 Can you name any more rebels?

Study skills

Dictionary skills

1 Your dictionary sometimes gives more than one meaning for a word. Look carefully at the context to make sure you choose the right meaning.
2 How many meanings can you find for these words: *right* and *course*?
3 What's the difference between these words: *politics*, *policy* and *police*?

UNIT 7B REBELS 81

Grammar and skills

KEY	
7	1 should 2 should 3 could 4 couldn't 5 should 6 could
8	1 e 2 b 3 a 4 c
9	1 South Africa 2 prisoner 3 daughters 4 volunteer
10	democracy – democrat, democratic; freedom – free; government – govern, governor; law – lawyer; leader – lead; protest – protestor; vote – voter

a really good athlete. His father said he had 'rebel blood' in his veins! Later, when Guevara was training to be a doctor, he travelled through South America and worked as a volunteer with the poor and the sick. He was shocked at the conditions he saw. That's when he decided to leave behind the comfortable life that he could have had, and give up medicine for politics.

9 Listening for detail

🔊 **7.3 CD 2 track 24**

Students listen and read again and complete the sentences.

10 Working with words: suffixes

Present the examples and ask students to find other examples in the box in Exercise 2. See also *Working with words*, page 106.

11 Speaking: famous rebels

Students discuss the questions in groups of four. Elicit ideas from the class and start a wider discussion.

Study skills: dictionary skills

Present the advice in the box and discuss the ideas with the class.

Gandhi! If he hadn't been there, it could have been much more violent.

2 I admire Aung San Suu Kyi. She's the leader of a political party in Burma, called the National League for Democracy. Her party won the election in 1990 and so they should have been the new government. But the military government – that's the army – refused to give up power. Aung San Suu Kyi could have run away to another country, but she didn't.

She stayed in Burma and she's been a prisoner in her own home. If she had left, the people who voted for her would have been disappointed. She's a democratically elected leader!

3 Did you know that New Zealand was the first country to give women the right to vote in elections, in 1893? In Britain,

women couldn't vote until twenty five years later, in 1918! And that was only women over the age of 30! Lots of women went to prison, many times, in the campaign to get the vote, including Emmeline Pankhurst and her three daughters. They had a terrible time in prison. I think the Pankhursts were amazing. They never gave up. Eventually, in 1928, there was a new law, and women had the same rights as men. That's what they should have had in 1918!

4 Che Guevara inspires me. He was born in Argentina. He wasn't poor – his father was an engineer – but he always cared about the poor. When he was young he had quite bad asthma, so I suppose he could've stayed at home reading books, but in fact he became

7C Regrets and criticisms

Spread aims

Vocabulary: school work

Functions: talking about regrets and making criticism

Skills: reading and listening for detail

Pronunciation: silent letters

Writing a story

KEY

1 1 Joe 2 Mrs Evans 3 Mr Lee

2 a) He didn't have enough time. Dan says: *You should've asked Mrs Evans for more time.*
b) The topic he chose was difficult. Dan says: *If you'd told us earlier, we could've helped you with it.*

3 Regret: I wish I was more organised. I wish I'd spoken to her last week! I wish we could help you. I shouldn't have chosen this topic. Criticism: You should have asked Mrs Evans for more time.

---

1 Reading and listening for detail

 *7.4 CD 2 track 25*

Present the three questions to help students to focus on the information they need.

Stronger students cover the text and just listen.

Weaker students listen and follow the text.

2 Reading for detail

Students should note the problems and comments; check the answers with the whole class.

3 Reading: deciding on functions

Ask students to underline the expressions in the dialogue and decide what the feeling of the speaker is for each one. Present the *Grammar Explorer*, page 125, if students are not clear about the structures.

Tell **weaker students** that sentence 1 in the box expresses regret and that

---

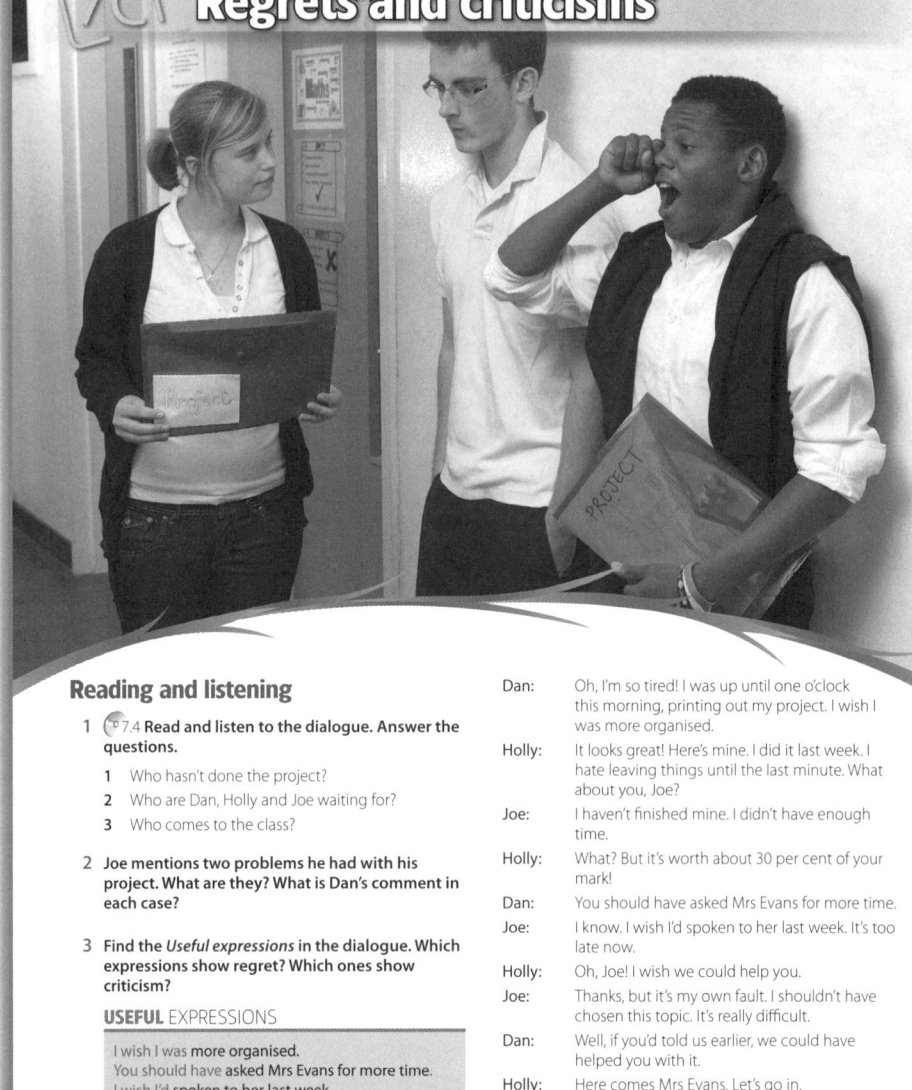

Regrets and criticisms

Reading and listening

1 7.4 **Read and listen to the dialogue. Answer the questions.**

  1 Who hasn't done the project?
  2 Who are Dan, Holly and Joe waiting for?
  3 Who comes to the class?

2 **Joe mentions two problems he had with his project. What are they? What is Dan's comment in each case?**

3 **Find the *Useful expressions* in the dialogue. Which expressions show regret? Which ones show criticism?**

USEFUL EXPRESSIONS

I wish I was **more organised**.
You should have **asked Mrs Evans for more time**.
I wish I'd **spoken to her last week**.
I wish we could **help you**.
I shouldn't have **chosen this topic**.

See Grammar Explorer: Page 125

Dan:	Oh, I'm so tired! I was up until one o'clock this morning, printing out my project. I wish I was more organised.
Holly:	It looks great! Here's mine. I did it last week. I hate leaving things until the last minute. What about you, Joe?
Joe:	I haven't finished mine. I didn't have enough time.
Holly:	What? But it's worth about 30 per cent of your mark!
Dan:	You should have asked Mrs Evans for more time.
Joe:	I know. I wish I'd spoken to her last week. It's too late now.
Holly:	Oh, Joe! I wish we could help you.
Joe:	Thanks, but it's my own fault. I shouldn't have chosen this topic. It's really difficult.
Dan:	Well, if you'd told us earlier, we could have helped you with it.
Holly:	Here comes Mrs Evans. Let's go in.
Dan:	No, it isn't Mrs Evans – it's Mr Lee! That's weird.
Mr Lee:	Good morning, everyone. Now, Mrs Evans is ill, but she'll be back next Monday. She says you should carry on with your projects and you can hand them in next week.
Dan:	Joe Todd, you are so lucky!

82

---

there are two more similar sentences; sentence 2 expresses a criticism and there is one more like that.

4 Useful expressions: intonation

 7.5 CD 2 track 26

Play the recording through a couple of times while students listen and follow. Then pause after each sentence for them to repeat chorally and individually. They can then do further practice in pairs.

Extension: put students into groups of three to practise the dialogue. The student with the role of Joe can also be Mr Lee. They should do it three times, changing roles each time.

5 Listening for detail

7.6 CD 2 track 27

Present the responses and ask students to think about possible statements for each response before they listen. Play each statement twice.

Tapescript

1 *I'm really tired today.*

2 *You're going to be late for school.*

3 *Oh, no! I've deleted all my photos from my camera!*

4 *I've decided I don't want to go on the camping trip.*

Reproduced student page

4 ● 7.5 **Listen and repeat the** *Useful expressions.* **Focus on your intonation.**

5 ● 7.6 **Listen to each statement and choose the best response (a–c).**

1 a You shouldn't have gone to bed so late.
  b You should have stayed up.
  c I wish I hadn't gone to bed early.

2 a You shouldn't have set your alarm clock.
  b I should have been at school.
  c I wish I'd set my alarm clock.

3 a I wish I'd taken your photo.
  b You should have read the instructions.
  c You shouldn't have used my camera.

4 a I should have told you yesterday.
  b I wish we'd gone camping.
  c I wish you'd told me earlier.

Speaking

6 **Work in pairs. For each situation, make one comment of regret and one of criticism. Take turns.**

A: *I wish I hadn't eaten all of that!*
B: *You should have shared it with me!*

Writing: a story

1 **Read Fay's story and answer the questions.**

1 When did the events in the story happen?
2 Who and what was involved?
3 What two things did Fay do to solve the problem?
4 How did the story end?

2 **Look at the words in red. What kind of words are they? What follows them?**

3 **Rewrite the pairs of sentences as one sentence. Use the preposition given.**

1 I switched on my computer. Then I checked my emails. (**after**)
2 I wrote down my password. Then I logged off the site. (**before**)
3 I solved the problem. I didn't phone the helpline. (**without**)
4 I changed my password. I made my account more secure. (**by**)

4 **Think about a time you had a problem. Write a paragraph about what happened and how you solved the problem. Use Fay's story to help you.**

1 eat / share

2 study / help

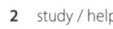

3 practise / bring

4 wear / borrow

Pronunciation: silent letters

7 ● 7.7 **Listen to these words and look at the spelling. Find the silent letters in each word. Then listen, check and repeat.**

campaign castle doubt foreign
half island knowledge psychologist
scientist would

My IT disaster story

Last week I had an IT disaster! I forgot my email password! I should have written it down somewhere when I set up the account, but I didn't. After trying about six different versions of my password, my email account locked me out. I had no idea how to unlock it and I was desperate to read my emails. There was a telephone helpline number, but they are usually really expensive. I decided to ask my friend Dan before phoning the helpline. But after spending about half an hour on it, he gave up! So I rang the helpline and the first thing the girl said was 'Press the CAPS LOCK key.' It worked!

Teacher notes

6 Speaking: expressing regret and criticism

Students use the pictures and prompts to make short dialogues, with one person expressing regret and the other criticism.

7 Pronunciation: silent letters

 7.7 CD 2 track 28

Students read the words in the box and underline the silent letters. Ask them to say the words, then play the recording and let them listen and check. Play the recording again, pausing after each word for them to repeat chorally and individually.

Extension: students make a list of other words they know with silent letters in them.

Writing: a story

1 Reading for detail

Students read Fay's story and answer the questions.

2 *after / before + ing* form

Students answer the question in a whole-class setting.

3 Grammar: writing practice

Students rewrite the two sentences as one using the word in brackets,

Communicate

KEY

5   1 a 2 c 3 b 4 c

6   2 I wish I'd studied more. You should've asked me for help. 3 I wish I'd practised my French. You should have brought a phrase book. 4 I wish I'd worn a raincoat. You should have borrowed mine.

7   campaign, cas̲tle, doub̲t, foreign, hal̲f, is̲land, k̲nowledge, p̲sychologist, sc̲ientist, woul̲d

Writing

1   1 last week 2 Fay and her computer; Dan; a helpline 3 She called the helpline, she pressed the CAPS LOCK key. 4 happily – she unlocked her email account

2   Adverbs; a gerund (-*ing* form)

3   1 After switching on my computer, I checked my emails. 2 I wrote down my password before logging off the site. 3 I solved the problem without phoning the helpline. 4 By changing my password I made my account more secure.

remembering to change the verb that follows into the -*ing* form.

4 Writing a story

Students write about a true personal event. They should use Fay's story as a model. Ask students to write down the structure of the story as a set of notes before they write it out fully (e.g. for Fay's story: *forgot email password – didn't write it down – tried 6 times – email account locked – desperate to read emails – helplines expensive – phoned Dan – he tried but gave up – phoned helpline – girl said press CAPS LOCK – it worked*).

7D South African life

Spread aims

Vocabulary: adverbs

Skills: Reading and listening for detail

Culture: life in South Africa

CLIL: History and English: the human journey

KEY

2 languages: 11 official languages, including English, Afrikaans, IsiZulu
animals: blue whales, antelopes, zebras, humpback whales; rhinoceros, leopards, elephants, springbok

---

1 Warm-up

Students in pairs exchange ideas about what they imagine South Africa to be like. They should note down ideas. Elicit ideas from the whole class and discuss what people say. List any languages and animals they think of.

2 Reading: scanning for detail

Students scan the text and check their answers, then find out any additional information about languages and animals.

3 Reading and listening for detail

 *7.8 CD 2 track 29*

Present the questions before students listen and read, to help them to focus on the information they need.

Stronger students cover the text and just listen.

Weaker students listen and follow the text.

4 Vocabulary: adverbs and adjectives

Students find the adverbs from the box and note the adjective they relate to and what it is they describe.

Follow-up: students can make up some adverb-adjective-noun combinations of their own.

Reading

1 Work in pairs. Imagine you went on holiday to South Africa. What languages would you hear around you? What animals would you see?

2 Read the text quickly and check your answers to Exercise 1.

84

Culture

South Africa

Rainbow Nation

In the northern part of South Africa, archaeologists have discovered some particularly interesting human fossils. They are more than two million years old – the earliest ever found. The region is known as the 'Cradle of Humankind'. Today, South Africans come from places as different as India and the Netherlands as well as southern Africa itself. Each group has its own history and language. There are eleven official languages, including English, Afrikaans and IsiZulu, and many more unofficial ones. This exceptionally colourful mix of cultures gives South Africa its unofficial name, Rainbow Nation.

Sea life

On South Africa's east coast, the warm Indian Ocean comes down from the tropics. To the west, the cold Atlantic currents arrive from the Antarctic. It's a recipe for a rich diversity of sea life and about 2,000 species visit these waters at different times of the year. It's one of the best places in the world to see whales close up. The blue whale is incredibly large. At 30 metres long and 170 tons, it's the biggest animal in the world. The humpback is slightly smaller but gives spectacular displays, throwing its body out of the water. Humpbacks often come surprisingly close to boats to have a look at the human species!

On safari

South Africa covers one per cent of the land surface of Earth, yet it has amazingly varied habitats. Ten per cent of the planet's bird, fish and plant species, and six per cent of mammal and reptile species, live here. From antelopes to zebras, the country is bursting with wildlife. The Kruger National Park is home to rhinoceros, leopards, elephants and the symbolic springbok, whose name is given to the national rugby team. Both local people and foreign tourists enjoy thrilling safari holidays here.

---

5 Listening for detail

 7.9 CD 2 track 30

Read through the sentences with the class to focus them.

Give **weaker students** a copy of the tapescript to follow as they listen.

Tapescript

Welcome to our walking tour of Cape Town. Please look at your map and press 'play' for each of the numbered places.

1 *We begin our tour at the National Assembly building. This is the home of the South African government. Cape Town is one of the three capital cities in South Africa. The other two are Pretoria and Bloemfontein. Cape Town is also the oldest city in South Africa. It was the very first European town, established in 1652.*

2 *Here we are at the Table Mountain Cableway. The cable car takes you 302 metres up to the top of the mountain, from where you get fantastic views over Cape Town to the north, and the Atlantic Ocean to the west and the south.*

3 *There is lots to see here in the harbour. It's one of the city's most popular tourist sites. There are hundreds of shops and a fantastic aquarium. This is also the departure point for the ferry to Robben Island. The island, which was used as a prison from the 17th to the 20th centuries, is now a museum.*

Embedded student book page

3 🔊 7.8 **Read the text again and answer the questions.**

1 Why is South Africa also called the Rainbow Nation?
2 Why are there so many marine species around South Africa?
3 What's special about the wildlife in South Africa?

4 Find the adverbs in the text. What adjective does each one describe? What noun does each adverb–adjective combination describe?

particularly exceptionally
incredibly slightly
surprisingly amazingly

Listening

5 🔊 7.9 **Listen to the first part of a Cape Town walking tour. Are the sentences true or false?**

1 Cape Town is the oldest city in South Africa.
2 You can get to Table Mountain by cable car.
3 The harbour is an industrial area of Cape Town.
4 Robben Island was used a prison for three centuries.

6 🔊 7.10 **Listen to the second part of the tour. Complete the information.**

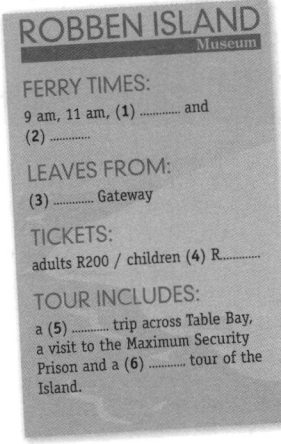

ROBBEN ISLAND Museum

FERRY TIMES:
9 am, 11 am, (1) .... and (2) ....

LEAVES FROM:
(3) .... Gateway

TICKETS:
adults R200 / children (4) R............

TOUR INCLUDES:
a (5) .... trip across Table Bay, a visit to the Maximum Security Prison and a (6) .... tour of the Island.

History and English
The human journey

1 Look at the map. Find the part of the world where you live. When did humans first arrive there?

2 Read the text and find two ways that scientists work out where humans came from originally.

Every individual has a unique 'genome' – the information coded in our DNA. Our genome holds information about our history. By comparing genomes from different people around the world, biologists can see where our ancestors came from.

Now, as part of research into this subject, South African Archbishop Desmond Tutu has had his genome deciphered. In the same study, four tribal leaders from southern Africa have also had their genomes sequenced. One of the things the study revealed is that the tribesmen have a gene that makes a high-fat diet more likely to cause them health problems. The information has been added to a database, GenBank. This is an open, public database that scientists can consult for their research.

In the past, the ideas we had about our origins came from fossils and other archaeological studies. Scientists believed that humans inhabited Africa first and then spread out to the other continents. Now, by comparing the DNA in the chromosomes of people from different areas of the world and fossil DNA, genetic evidence proves that this theory is correct.

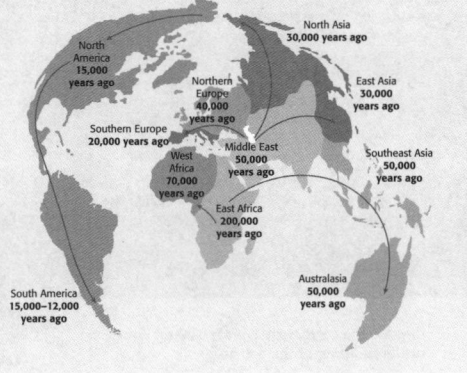

North Asia 30,000 years ago
North America 15,000 years ago
Northern Europe 40,000 years ago
East Asia 30,000 years ago
Southern Europe 20,000 years ago
West Africa 70,000 years ago
Middle East 50,000 years ago
Southeast Asia 50,000 years ago
East Africa 200,000 years ago
South America 15,000–12,000 years ago
Australasia 50,000 years ago

3 What other useful information can our genome give us?

 Project

Choose a famous person from the field of science or politics in your country. Ask six people what they think about the person. Prepare a presentation about the person's achievements and how they are viewed today.

UNIT 7D **SOUTH AFRICAN LIFE** 85

Culture

3 1 Because people from a whole range of cultures live there. 2 Because the warm Indian Ocean meets the cold Atlantic currents from Antarctica. 3 It is very varied: ten percent of the world's bird, fish and plant species live there, and six percent of mammal and reptile species.

4 particularly interesting, human fossils; exceptionally colourful, mix of cultures; amazingly varied, habitats; incredibly large, blue whale; slightly smaller, humpback whale; surprisingly close, humpback whale / to the boats

5 1 T 2 T 3 F 4 T

6 1 1 o'clock   2 3 o'clock
3 Nelson Mandela   4 100
5 return   6 bus

History and English

2 from fossils and archaeological study, or from genetic evidence

3 Information about possible health problems.

Presentation Day, when they give their presentation in groups of five or six.

History and English: the human journey

1 **Pre-reading**

Present the task and elicit the answer from the class.

2 & 3 **Reading for detail**

Students read the text and find the answers.

---

6 **Listening for detail**

 7.10 CD 2 track 31

Ask students to read through the gapped text and think about the information they need to listen for (e.g. times, a place, a price).

Tapescript

The ferry has four departures every day. They are at 9 o'clock, 11 o'clock, 1 o'clock and 3 o'clock. They leave from the Nelson Mandela Gateway, which takes its name from Robben Island's most famous prisoner, who spent much of his 27 years in prison there. Tickets for the ferry and tour cost 200 Rand for adults and 100 Rand for children. Included in this ticket price is the return trip to and from the island, a visit to the maximum security prison, and also a bus tour of the island. The museum itself was opened in 1997 and became a World Heritage Site in 1999. There are regular exhibitions of photography, painting etc. in the museum.

Project: presentation about a famous person

Ask students to choose a person to research – it would be more interesting if you got a spread of people through the class. The students research attitudes to their chosen person during class time, and then research their life outside class. They should prepare a presentation about the person. Arrange a

True story: John Glenn

Page aim

Reading for interest on the topic of the unit

Warm-up

With books closed, ask students what they know about the history of space exploration. Try to elicit some key events, names and dates. (e.g. Oct 1951: Sputnik 1 (Russia) first satellite; Nov 1957: Sputnik 2 (Russia) – Laika (dog) – first living creature in space; April 1961: Vostok 1 – Yuri Gagarin – first Russian in space; Feb 1962: Mercury – Atlas 6 – John Glenn – first American in space; June 1963: Vostok 6 – Valentina Tereshkova – first Russian woman in space; 1965: Aleksei Leonov – first Russian space walk; 1966: Luna 9 – first safe landing of an object on the moon; July 1969: Apollo 11 (USA) – Neil Armstrong/Buzz Aldrin walk on the moon; April 1981: first Space Shuttle (USA); 1986-2001: Russian Mir space station operated; 2000 – continuing: International Space Station operates; April 2001: Dennis Tito – first space tourist)

1 Reading for detail

Ask students to read the article about John Glenn and complete the time line about his life individually, then check with a partner. Elicit answers from the whole class.

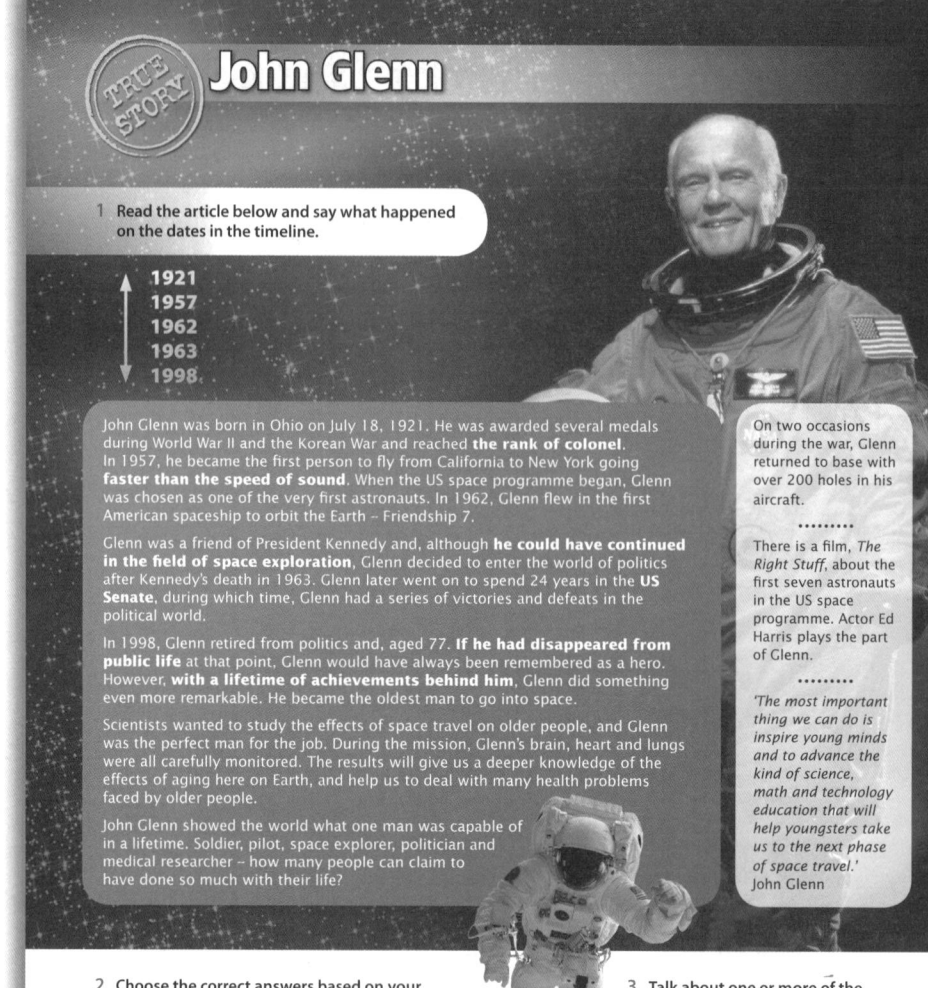

2 Vocabulary

Students read the extracts from the text and decide which of the two words or phrases have the meaning implied in the text. They should do this individually, then check with a partner. Elicit the answers from the whole class.

3 Discussion

Ask students to form groups of three or four and discuss one of the five topics listed in great depth, or several of them more briefly. They should appoint a secretary who keeps notes of the points raised by the group, and represents their ideas in the whole class discussion which follows.

Extension

Students take one of the five topics and write about it in depth. Later they can get together with others who have written about the same topic and read each other's writing and discuss their ideas.

Shopping

> **Grammar**
Learn about reported statements and questions.

> **Vocabulary**
Learn words for shops and services, and words connected with money.
Work with reporting verbs, and word combinations with *money*.

> **Skills**
Read about a surprising scientific discovery, spending, and shopping online.
Listen to someone doing a shopping questionnaire, and to a telephone conversation following an online purchase.
Write a formal letter.

> **Communicate**
Return things to shops.

1 Look at the photo. Complete the sentence in as many ways as you can.

The girl has been …

2 Work in pairs. You have two minutes. Write things you can buy in the places in the vocabulary box. Now compare your list with a new partner.

baker's	butcher's	greengrocer's	newsagent's	post office
bank	chemist's	hairdresser's	shoe shop	travel agency
bookshop	florist's	library	supermarket	

3 8.1 Write questions for a survey about shopping habits. Then listen and check your questions.

1 what / favourite shops?   3 who / usually go with?
2 where / like going?   4 you / always know what you want?

4 8.1 Listen again and tick the answer the person gives.

1	a	clothes	b	sports gear	c	music
2	a	small shops	b	big shops	c	shopping malls
3	a	your parents	b	your friends	c	by yourself
4	a	yes	b	no	c	it depends

5 Work in pairs. Ask and answer the questions from the survey.

UNIT EIGHT 8

Shopping

Unit aims

Grammar: reported statements and questions

Vocabulary: shops, services; reporting verbs; word combinations with *money*

Functions: returning things to shops

Reading about: a surprising scientific discovery; spending; shopping online

Listening to: a shopping questionnaire; a conversation after an online purchase

Writing a formal letter

KEY

3 1 What are your favourite (kinds of) shops?   2 Where do you like going (shopping)?   3 Who do you usually go with?   4 Do you always know what you want?

4 1 a   2 c   3 b   4 a

D: Oh, I wouldn't like to go shopping by myself! And going with my parents would be even worse! I usually go with my friends, although some of the shops don't really like it if there's a big group of us. But it's more fun going with friends.

I: OK. And my last question is, do you always know what you want to buy or do you like just looking around?

D: I usually go with a specific idea. Like, if I want a T-shirt, I know which one I want before I go to the shop because I've seen it in a magazine or something. I don't like just wandering around looking at stuff. The shop assistants keep asking you if they can help you, and that annoys me a bit.

I: OK. Thanks very much for answering my questions.

4 Listening for detail

 8.1 CD 2 track 32

Students listen and choose the answer which Dan gives to each question.

5 Speaking: doing a survey

Students ask a partner the questions and note the answers.

---

1 Warm-up

Students look at the photo and think of different ways to complete the sentence.

2 Vocabulary: shops and services

Students have to write as many things as they can think of for each place. They then change partners, and ask them 'What can you buy at a baker's?' etc. Check the answers with the whole class.

3 Survey questions

 8.1 CD 2 track 32

Students use the prompts to write questions for a shopping survey.

Tapescript

I = interviewer, D = Dan

I: Hi – can I ask you some questions about shopping?

D: Yes, sure.

I: OK. First, what are your favourite kinds of shops?

D: Clothes shops! Definitely.

I: And where do you like going shopping – to big shops, in shopping malls, or small shops?

D: Well, I usually go to the Metro Mall – you know, the big shopping centre? They've got all kinds of shops there, and it's easy to get there by bus from where I live.

I: Right. And who do you usually go with? Do you go shopping by yourself or with other people?

8A Advertising

Spread aims

Grammar: reported statements

Vocabulary: advertising; reporting verbs

Functions: reporting what people said

Reading about a problem with an advert

KEY

1 products: coffee, chocolate
brand: Starbucks

3 1 a blackcurrant drink
2 the students who did the
experiment   3 Glaxo-
SmithKline, the manufacturers
of Ribena   4 a TV programme

4 1 T   2 T   3 F

5 claimed, were told (passive),
suggested, reported, stated,
confirm

1 Warm-up

Students look at the adverts and find
out what products they are advertising,
then identify a brand (if necessary,
elicit or explain what this is).

2 Speaking: adverts

Present the five statements and
ensure students understand them.
Ask students to read the two adverts
and note down their ideas. Elicit
ideas and initiate a whole-class
discussion.

Background information: The
World Fairtrade Organization aims
to ensure fair prices for producers
(particularly in less developed
countries) and helps producers
to develop knowledge, skills and
resources to improve their lives.
The movement also aims to
raise awareness amongst western
consumers. The International
Fairtrade Certification Mark can be
found on products (e.g. chocolate,
sugar, tea, coffee, tropical fruit) that
meet Fairtrade standards.

3 Reading and listening
for detail

🔊 *8.2 CD 2 track 33*

Present the questions to help
students to focus on the information
they need.

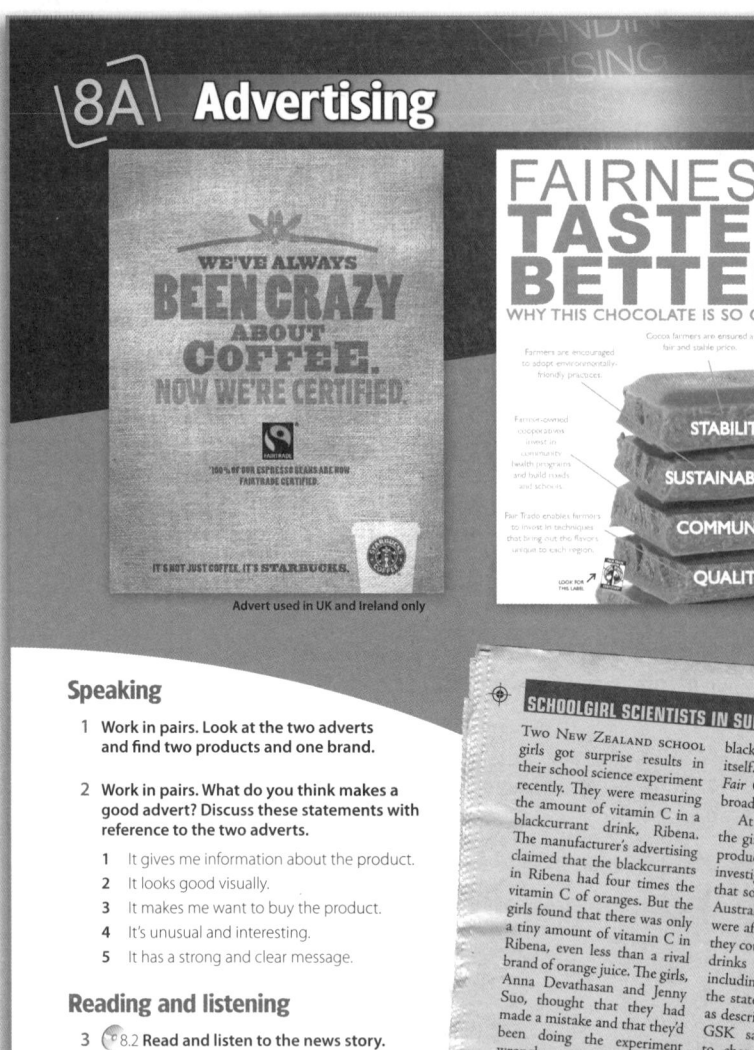

4 Reading for detail

Students read the text and decide
whether the statements are true or false.

5 Working with words:
reporting verbs

Present the example sentence and
make sure students understand that
a *reporting verb* is the verb which
introduces what people say. See also
Working with words, page 107, for
further practice.

6 Grammar presentation:
reported statements

Do this as a whole-class activity.
Students decide what the advert's
actual words were.

7 Grammar: reported
statements

Ask the whole class to answer this
question. Refer also to *Grammar
Explorer*, pages 125–126.

8 Grammar: finding reported
statements

Students find the reported versions
in the text and underline them.
Present the grammar note about
pronoun changes and make sure
students understand what changes
are required.

Weaker students identify key words
in the sentences to help them find
the reported speech in the text.

Grammar: reported statements

6 Look at the example from the text. Then choose the actual word in the adverts.

The manufacturer's advertising claimed that the blackcurrants in Ribena had four times the vitamin C of oranges.

'The blackcurrants in Ribena *have / had* four times the vitamin C of oranges.'

7 How does the verb change when the words are reported?

See Grammar Explorer: Page 125

8 Read the actual words that were spoken. Then find the sentences in the text that report the words.

1 'We've made a mistake.'
2 'We've been doing the experiment wrongly.'
3 'The information in the advert refers to blackcurrants.'
4 'We will broadcast the story.'
5 'Only some of our products in Australia and New Zealand are affected.'
6 'We can confirm that Ribena drinks in all other markets contain the stated levels of vitamin C.'
7 'We are going to change the labels on the Australian and New Zealand products.'

> We also change pronouns when we report people's words. 'We've made a mistake.' → They thought they'd made a mistake.

9 Complete the table with the words in the box.

> could   did   had   had been   were
> would

Direct speech	Reported speech
has	had
have	(1) ....
do	did
does	(2) ....
will	(3) ....
is	was
are	(4) ....
can	(5) ....
was	(6) ....

10 Read these comments. What did the people actually say? Write their words.

1 A government spokesman said that shoppers were showing more interest in Fairtrade values.
2 The Fairtrade director said that people could enjoy Fairtrade values with Starbucks coffee.
3 The Starbucks director said they had had a partnership with Fairtrade for over a decade.
4 A spokesman for a farmers' cooperative said they would benefit from guaranteed prices.

11 Read what an advertising executive, Marisa, says about her work. Report her words.

e.g. 'I've worked in advertising for ten years.'
Marisa said she'd worked in advertising for ten years.

1 'A good advert is easy to understand.'
2 'My best advert was very simple.'
3 'I've always used humour in my adverts.'
4 'An advert can't use misleading information.'

12 Write a sentence for each picture beginning 'The advert said ...'

1 'Megasmile will make your teeth white!'
2 '4eva glasses have a life-long guarantee.'

3 'NatureTan has been extensively tested.'
4 'Each designer shirt is totally unique.'

Speaking

13 Work in pairs. Choose four people you both know. Work alone and write something each person said yesterday. Now report the words to your partner. Can they guess the person?

A: *This person said we could go home early today.*
B: *Mrs Wilson?*

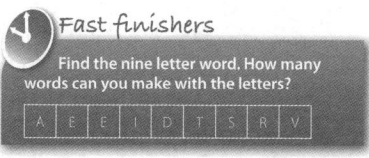
Fast finishers
Find the nine letter word. How many words can you make with the letters?

A E E I D T S R V

Grammar

6 have

7 It changes to a tense further in the past

8 1 The girls ... thought that they had made a mistake ...   2 ... and that they'd been doing the experiment wrongly.   3 They were told that the information in the advert referred to blackcurrants ...   4 ... *Fair Go* said that they would broadcast the story.   5 ... GSK reported that some of their products in Australia and New Zealand were affected.   6 They stated that they could confirm that Ribena drinks in all other markets ... contained the stated levels of vitamin C. 7 GSK said they were going to change the labels ...

9 1 had   2 did   3 would   4 were   5 could   6 had been

10 1 'Shoppers are showing more interest in Fairtrade values.'   2 'People can enjoy Fairtrade values with Starbucks coffee.'   3 'We have had a partnership with Fairtrade for over a decade.'   4 'We will benefit from guaranteed prices.'

11 1 Marisa said (that) a good advert was easy to understand. 2 She said (that) her best advert had been very simple.   3 She said (that) she'd / she had always used humour in her adverts.   4 She said (that) an advert couldn't use misleading information.

12 1 The advert said (that) Megasmile would make my / your teeth white. 2 The advert said (that) 4eva glasses had a life-long guarantee.   3 The advert said (that) NatureTan had been extensively tested.   4 The advert said (that) each designer shirt was totally unique.

Fast finishers

Students find the nine-letter word (*advertise*) and then make as many words as possible with the letters.

---

9 Verb change table

Students complete the table with the words in the box.

10 Writing direct speech

Students read the reported speech and write down what the people actually said.

11 Reporting what people said

Students turn the direct speech into reported speech.

Encourage **stronger students** to use the reporting verbs they listed in Exercise 5.

12 Reporting what adverts said

Students turn the advert slogans into reported speech.

13 Personalised speaking practice

Read through the instructions with the class and make sure they understand how the 'guessing game' works.

Give **weaker students** a list of people (e.g. their mother, a teacher, a classmate, a grandparent). The students write one thing each of these people said to them, and their partner has to guess which of the four said it.

8B Spending money

Spread aims

Grammar: reported questions
Vocabulary: money
Reading about spending habits
Listening to a shopping questionnaire

KEY

1 1 pocket money / cash
2 bank account / credit card /
debit card / savings   3 cash
machine / credit card / debit
card   4 coins / notes / credit
cards / debit cards

2 1 b   2 a   3 c

3 1 Emma   2 Diane   3 Emma
4 Rachel   5 Rachel   6 Diane

---

1 Vocabulary: money

Present the words in the box and
make sure students understand the
difference between a *credit card* and
a *debit card*. Students complete the
questions and then practise with a
partner.

2 Reading for gist

Students use clues in the speech
bubbles to match the people to the
photos.

3 Reading and listening
for detail

 8.3 CD 2 track 34

Present the sentences before the
students read and listen, and elicit
what the interviewer's actual words
were. Explain that students must
deduce which question matches each
speech bubble.

4 Working with words:
combinations with *money*

Read the examples and ask students
to think of other combinations with
money. See also *Working with words*,
page 107.

5 Writing direct speech

Students write the original direct
questions for the reported questions.
Present the grammar note about
changing possessive adjectives.

8B Spending money

Speaking

1 Complete the questions (1–4) with words from
the vocabulary box. More than one question is
possible. Then work in pairs, and ask and answer
the questions. Take turns.

1 How much .... do you get every week?
2 Have you got your own .... ?
3 Have you ever used a .... ?
4 Are there any .... or .... in your pocket?

> bank account   budget   cash
> cash machine   coin   credit card
> debit card   note   pocket money
> savings   wages

Reading and listening

2 An interviewer asked three people about money.
Read quickly what they said. Then look at the
photos, and match the people (1–3) with the
photos (a–c).

3 8.3 Read and listen to what the people said
again. Complete the interviewer's questions with
the people's names.

1 The interviewer asked .... if she knew how to
budget.
2 .... was asked if she'd saved a lot when she was
younger.
3 The interviewer asked .... if she had any credit
cards.
4 .... was asked if she'd ever bought anything
online.
5 The interviewer asked how much .... would
spend this weekend.
6 The interviewer asked .... what she was going
to spend her savings on.

Yes, I do, actually. My mum's shown me
how to do it. I'm going to a summer camp
in France this year and I'll need to make
my money last for a month. So she's been
helping me to work out how much I'll
need for travel, for entertainment and things
like that.

No, I haven't got any credit cards – I'm
not old enough. When I go to France
I'm going to take an emergency
supply of twenty-euro notes!

1 Emma

No, I haven't. I prefer to pay for things with cash
and you can't do that on the Internet! My wages
are paid directly into my bank account and I get
money out of the cash machine once a week.

I'll probably spend quite a lot of money
at the weekend. It's my daughter's
birthday and I want to take her to
London for the day.

2 Rachel

No! I used to be terrible with money! I used to waste all my
pocket money on sweets and rubbish every week. Once, I
wanted to buy an expensive book. It was about the artwork
in *Lord of the Rings*. My dad said I could have all the coins that
were lying around the house. I managed to find £23.60!

These days I put all my loose change
in a big jar. That's my savings. I'm
waiting until the jar is full. Then I'm
going to buy something amazing
with what I've saved.

3 Diane

---

6 Writing reported questions

Present the example and ensure that
students understand what to do.

7 Personalised practice

Students write their own questions
from Exercise 1 as reported questions.

8 Listening for gist

 8.4 CD 2 track 35

Present the definitions and ask
students which they think is the best
definition and why. Students then
listen and check.

Tapescript

A: *This is an interesting questionnaire.*
You should do it.

B: *What's it about?*

A: *It's called 'Are you a shopaholic?'*

B: *Well, I'm not a shopaholic! I just like*
going shopping, that's all.

A: *Prove it to me. Answer the*
questionnaire.

B: *Oh, OK. Go on.*

A: *Will you give honest answers?*

B: *Of course I will. What's the first*
question?

A: *OK. Do you go shopping more than*
three times a week?

B: *Three times a week … yes, I do.*

A: *The last time you went shopping, did*
you spend more than your budget?

B: *Budget? I don't usually have a*
budget. I spend what I want to.

A: *And have you ever bought more than*
you needed?

Working with words: word combinations with *money*

4 Look at the examples. How many more combinations with *money* do you know?

I'll probably spend quite a lot of money this weekend.
I used to be terrible with money!

See Working with words: Page 107

Grammar: reported questions

5 Look at the example. Then write the direct questions for the reported questions.

The interviewer asked Emma if she had a bank account.
The interviewer asked, 'Have you got a bank account?'

1 The interviewer asked Emma if she needed to buy euros.
2 The interviewer asked Rachel what they would do in London.
3 Rachel was asked if she'd ever used a cash machine.
4 Diane was asked how much money she'd saved.
5 The interviewer asked Diane what she was going to buy with her savings.

See Grammar Explorer: Page 127

> We also change possessive adjectives when we report people's words, e.g. *your* → *her/ his*.

6 Report the interviewer's questions.

e.g. 'Are you good with money?'
    The interviewer asked me if I was good with money...

1 'Are you saving any money at the moment?'
2 'Where do you keep your savings?'
3 'What will you buy with your savings?'
4 'Have you ever won any money?'
5 'Did you spend a lot yesterday?'

7 Write the questions you asked your partner in Exercise 1 as reported questions and write the replies.

e.g. *I asked Kate how much pocket money she got every week.*
    She said she got 50 pounds a month.

Listening

8 (8.4 **STUDY SKILLS**) Work in pairs. Which is the best definition of a shopaholic (a–c)? Listen to someone doing a shopping questionnaire and check your answer.

a Shopaholics go shopping more often than necessary and often buy unnecessary things.
b Shopaholics feel in control of their shopping habits and usually don't spend more than budget they set themselves.
c Shopaholics feel stressed when they are in a shop and only buy things that they've seen advertised.

9 (8.4) Listen again. Tick the questions that you heard.

Wayne asked Charlie …

1 if he went shopping more than three times a week.
2 what his favourite shops were.
3 if he had spent more than his budget on his last shopping trip.
4 if he had ever bought more than he needed.
5 how he felt when he was shopping.
6 if he was influenced by advertising or by his friends.

Speaking

10 Write the direct questions for the reported questions in Exercise 9.

e.g. *Do you go shopping more than three times a week?*

11 Work in pairs. Ask your partner the questions from the shopping questionnaire. Take turns.

A: *Do you go shopping more than three times a week?*
B: *No, I don't. I usually go shopping about once a week.*

12 Work with a new partner. Report your conversation.

Study skills

Listening and checking

Before you listen to an exam text, read the information or the exam questions.

1 Find the key words to listen for.
2 When you listen, check for this information.
3 Don't forget that the same ideas can be expressed in different ways.

B: *Well, yes. Sometimes.*
A: *And how do you feel when you're shopping? Relaxed, excited or stressed?*
B: *Oh, ermm, let me think. I feel relaxed, I suppose.*
A: *Right, next question. Are you influenced by advertising? Or by your friends?*
B: *No, I don't think I'm influenced by either advertising or my friends. I just buy what I like.*
A: *OK well, according to this, you're probably a shopaholic. Listen: 'People who are addicted to shopping go shopping three or more times a week and don't stick to a budget. They often buy more than they really need and the act of shopping makes them feel relaxed. Usually they feel in control*

of their shopping habits; for example, they don't accept that their behaviour can be influenced by adverts.' That's you!
B: *Oh, come on!*
A: *Look, here's another questionnaire. 'Are you addicted to the Internet?' Do you want to do it?*
B: *No, thanks. I'm going out – to the shops.*

9 Listening for detail

 **8.4 CD 2 track 35**

Present the question before students listen.

Give **weaker students** the tapescript to follow on the second or third listening.

Grammar and skills

KEY

4 Possible answers: earn money, get money, waste money, save money

5 1 'Do you need to buy euros?'
2 'What will you do in London?' 3 'Have you ever used a cash machine?'
4 'How much money have you saved?' 5 'What are you going to buy with your savings?'

6 The interviewer asked me:
1 if I was saving any money at the moment.
2 where I kept my savings.
3 what I would buy with my savings.
4 if I had ever won any money.
5 if I had spent a lot yesterday.

8 a

9 1 ✓ 3 ✓ 4 ✓ 5 ✓ 6 ✓

10 2 What are your favourite shops?
3 Did you spend more than your budget on your last shopping trip?
4 Have you ever bought more than you needed?
5 How do you feel when you're shopping?
6 Are you influenced by advertising or your friends?

10 Writing direct questions

Students write direct questions for the questions in Exercise 9.

11 Speaking: the 'shopaholic' questionnaire

Students in pairs ask each other the questions and note the answers.

12 Reporting a converstaion

Students tell a new partner what their previous partner said about their shopping habits.

Study skills: listening and checking

Present the suggestions and discuss the ideas given.

8C Returning things

Spread aims

Vocabulary: shopping

Functions: returning things to shops

Skills: reading and listening for gist and detail

Pronunciation: syllable stress

Writing a formal letter

KEY

2 1 Dan had already got it.
  2 She asks for her money back.
  3 They decide to get a credit note.

3 Can I help you? A
  Have you got the receipt? A
  I'd like to return this game. C
  I'm afraid we don't usually give refunds. A
  Is there something wrong with it? A
  Would it be possible to get my money back? C
  Would you like a credit note? A

---

1 Reading and listening for gist

 *8.5 CD 2 track 36*

Students should answer the question without looking at the dialogue, then read and listen to check.

2 Reading for detail

Students read the dialogue again and answer the questions.

3 Useful expressions

Students decide who says each sentence in the box.

4 Useful expressions: intonation

 *8.6 CD 2 track 37*

Play the recording a couple of times while students follow and listen. Then play it again for them to repeat.

5 Listening for gist

 *8.7 CD 2 track 38*

Ask students to identify the places in the pictures before they listen.

Give **weaker students** the transcript to follow on the second or third listening.

8C Returning things please pay here

Reading and listening

1 *8.5* **Look at the photo. What are Dan and Holly doing? Read and listen to the dialogue and check your answer.**

2 **Read the dialogue again. Answer the questions.**
  1 What is the problem with the video game?
  2 What does Holly ask for?
  3 What do Holly and Dan decide to do?

3 **Look at the *Useful expressions*. Write C for customer or A for assistant next to each expression.**

USEFUL EXPRESSIONS

Can I help you?
Have you got the receipt?
I'd like to return this **game**.
I'm afraid **we don't usually give refunds**.
Is there something wrong with it?
Would it be possible to **get my money back**?
Would you like **a credit note**?

4 *8.6* **Listen and repeat the *Useful expressions*. Focus on your intonation.**

92

Assistant:	Can I help you?
Dan:	Yes, please. I'd like to return this game.
Assistant:	I see. Is there something wrong with it?
Dan:	No, no. My friend bought it for me for my birthday, but I've already got it.
Holly:	I should have asked him which games he had before buying it, I suppose!
Assistant:	Yes, but it's nice to try and surprise people, isn't it? Have you got the receipt?
Holly:	Yes, I have. Here you are.
Assistant:	Would you like a credit note, or do you want to exchange it for another game?
Holly:	Would it be possible to get my money back?
Assistant:	Well, I'm afraid we don't usually give refunds unless the goods are faulty.
Holly:	Oh, I see.
Assistant:	But a credit note is valid for six months and we have a huge range of games, CDs and DVDs. You can use it to buy anything in the shop. And you can use it online too.
Holly:	What do you think, Dan?
Dan:	Let's get a credit note. I'm sure I can find something I like!

Tapescript

1

Assistant: Good morning, sir. Can I help you?

Man: Yes, I'd like to return this jumper.

Assistant: I see. Is there a problem?

Man: Well, it's the wrong size. It's too big for me. It says 'medium', so I thought it would fit. I didn't try it on when I bought it.

Assistant: Do you have the receipt?

Man: Oh, yes. I only bought it yesterday.

Assistant: So, would you like to exchange it for a bigger size?

Man: Yes, please.

Assistant: No problem.

2

Woman: Excuse me.

Assistant: Yes? Can I help you?

Woman: Yes, look at these yogurts. They're past their sell-by date.

Assistant: Are you sure?

Woman: Well, it's the first of June today, and this label says the 10th of April.

Assistant: I'm sorry about that. Thanks for telling me.

Woman: No problem. Do you have any other yogurts?

Assistant: Yes – just one moment, please. Here you are.

Student page (reproduced)

5 ⊙8.7 **Listen and match the conversations (1–3) with the places (a–d). There is one extra place.**

Speaking

6 **Match the items with the problems. More than one match is possible.**

a CD	the wrong size
a pair of earrings	the wrong format
a T-shirt	faulty
a DVD	broken
a webcam	past its sell-by date
some cheese	you already have one

7 **Work in pairs. You are a shop assistant and a customer. Write dialogues about the things in Exercise 6. Use the *Useful expressions* to help you. Then take a role each and practise your dialogues.**

Pronunciation: syllable stress

8 ⊙8.8 **Listen to the words. Which syllables are stressed? Listen again and repeat the pairs of words.**

1 a refund   to refund
2 advertise   advertisement
3 advertise   advertising
4 democracy   democratic
5 investigate   investigation
6 politics   politician
7 qualified   qualification

4 **Write a letter of complaint. Use an example from your own experience, or invent a product and a problem. Use Fay's letter to help you.**

Writing: a formal letter

1 **Read the letter and choose the correct option (a–c).**

a Fay is asking for information.
b Fay is making a complaint.
c Fay is making a suggestion.

2 **Read again and put this information in the correct sequence.**

1 an explanation of another problem
2 an explanation of the problem
3 Fay's response to the first problem
4 the reason for writing the letter
5 what action Fay requests

3 **Look at the expressions in red in the letter. Then choose the correct option.**

1 **In spite of / Because of** the terrible service, I don't buy anything from that website.
2 The shoes were really expensive. **In spite of that, / Because of that,** I bought them.
3 The website sold cheap DVDs. **Despite the price, / Because of the price,** the quality was good.
4 The film got an Oscar. **Despite this, / Because of this,** I didn't think it was very good.

Dear Sir / Madam,

I am writing to complain about the service from your website.

Two months ago, I ordered three DVDs from you. The information on the website said they were for Europe (Region 2). Despite this, when they arrived, they were for Region 1. I returned the DVDs to you with a note explaining what had happened and asking for a refund.

In spite of my letter, you have sent me the wrong items again, this time the Blu-ray versions of the titles.

Please could you refund my PayPal account or send me the correct (Region 2) format DVDs. I enclose the receipt.

Yours faithfully,

Fay Johnson

UNIT 8C RETURNING THINGS 93

Communicate

for them to check, and again for them to listen and repeat.

Writing: a formal letter

1 Reading for gist

Present the options before students read the letter.

2 Sequencing

Students read the letter and match each part with the correct summary.

3 *Despite, in spite of, because of*

Present the examples in red in the text and elicit the meaning. Students select the best option for each sentence.

4 Writing a formal letter

Students write a letter of their own.

Weaker students use Fay's letter as a model. They first circle the details that need changing, then replace with their own details.

3

Assistant: Good afternoon, madam. Can I help you?

Woman: Yes, I'd like to return these tins of paint.

Assistant: Is there something wrong with them?

Woman: Yes. It's the wrong colour!

Assistant: I'm sorry? What do you mean?

Woman: It says 'white' on the tins. But inside, the paint is yellow.

Assistant: I'm really sorry. That's never happened before. Would you like to exchange them for white? Or I can give you a refund.

Woman: I'll take the white paint, please. Can you check each one, please?

Assistant: No problem.

6 Vocabulary: matching items and problems

Students work in pairs to decide which problem could match each item. Elicit answers from the class and discuss the possibilities.

7 Writing a dialogue

Students in pairs write and practise a dialogue using one of the situations in Exercise 6.

8 Pronunciation; syllable stress

 *8.8 CD 2 track 39*

Ask students to read the words and mark in pencil where they think the stress falls. Then play the recording

8D Shopping online in the UK

Spread aims

Vocabulary: linking phrases; online shopping

Skills: reading and listening for detail

Culture: online shopping

CLIL: Maths and English: statistics

KEY

4 apart from = except for
as well as = in addition to

5 1 I download albums as well as / in addition to singles.
2 I buy books online instead of going to a bookshop.
3 I don't buy much online except for / apart from music.
4 I use Paypal as well as / in addition to credit cards to buy things online. 5 I don't like many shops, apart from / except for clothes shops.

---

1 Warm-up

Students discuss the photos with a partner, then in a whole-class setting. If they can't identify all the items, they will find the answers in the text when they do Exercise 3.

2 Speaking: online shopping

Students discuss the three questions together. Elicit some responses from the whole class.

3 Reading and listening for detail

 *8.9 CD 2 track 40*

Students read and listen to the text and compare their answers to Exercises 1 and 2.

Stronger students cover the text and just listen.

Weaker students listen and follow the text.

4 Vocabulary: linking phrases

Students find the expressions in the text and underline them. They then decide which ones mean the same thing.

5 Using linking phrases

Students use the expressions from Exercise 4 in the sentences.

6 Listening for detail

 8.10 CD 2 track 41

Present the task and category headings to help students to focus on the details they need. Check that they understand all the categories (e.g. *item*) and suggest that they predict possible answers for each category.

Give **weaker students** the tapescript to follow on the second or third listening.

8D Shopping online in the UK
Culture
Britain

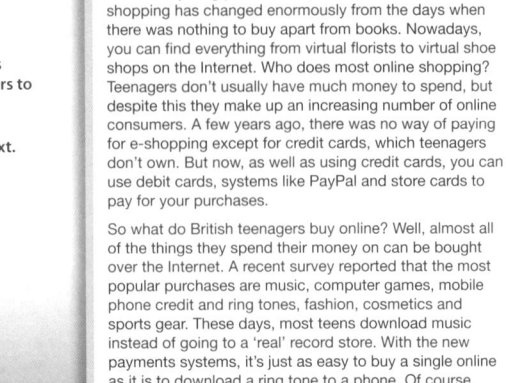

Reading

1 Look at the photos. What do you think they show?

2 Work in pairs and discuss these questions.
1 Do you buy things online? Why? / Why not?
2 Do you have your own money? Where or who does it come from?
3 What do you spend most money on?

3 8.9 Read the text. Check your answers to Exercise 1. Then compare your answers to Exercise 2 with what it says in the text.

4 Find the following expressions in the text. Which ones mean the same thing?

apart from   as well as   except for
in addition to   instead of

What kind of shop would you go to if you wanted to buy an Apollo 17 spacesuit? Or a swimming pool? Or a UFO detector? Can you even buy such things? Just go online and do a search. You can order them all on the Internet.

Is there anything you can't buy online these days? Internet shopping has changed enormously from the days when there was nothing to buy apart from books. Nowadays, you can find everything from virtual florists to virtual shoe shops on the Internet. Who does most online shopping? Teenagers don't usually have much money to spend, but despite this they make up an increasing number of online consumers. A few years ago, there was no way of paying for e-shopping except for credit cards, which teenagers don't own. But now, as well as using credit cards, you can use debit cards, systems like PayPal and store cards to pay for your purchases.

So what do British teenagers buy online? Well, almost all of the things they spend their money on can be bought over the Internet. A recent survey reported that the most popular purchases are music, computer games, mobile phone credit and ring tones, fashion, cosmetics and sports gear. These days, most teens download music instead of going to a 'real' record store. With the new payments systems, it's just as easy to buy a single online as it is to download a ring tone to a phone. Of course, teenagers rely mostly on their parents for their income, (apart from some aged 15 and over who earn money from a part-time job). In addition to this, most teenagers prefer money instead of a gift for a birthday or Christmas. In general, young people in the UK today have a lot more cash than their parents did when they were young, and there are many more things to spend it on.

94

Tapescript

Assistant: Good morning – Shoebox online. Can I help you?

Customer: Yes, I'm phoning about a pair of trainers that I bought from your website.

Assistant: Yes – what's the problem?

Customer: Well, you've sent the wrong size. I ordered size 39 – it's written here on the receipt – but the trainers you've sent are size 37. So they're far too small.

Assistant: OK – could you give me the reference number of the trainers? You'll find it on the receipt.

Customer: It's PQ2975.

5 Rewrite the sentences using expressions from Exercise 4.

1 I download albums and singles online.
2 I buy books online. I don't go to a bookshop.
3 I don't buy much online, only music.
4 I use PayPal and credit cards to buy things online.
5 I don't like many shops. I like clothes shops.

Listening

6 🔊 8.10 **Listen to the telephone conversation following an online purchase. Complete the missing information.**

1 item ....
2 problem ....
3 reference number ....
4 payment method ....
5 price ....

Project

Design a survey to find out what your classmates spend their money on. Ask the questions and present the results as a chart or diagram. Write a short text to accompany the diagram.

Maths and English
Statistics

1 **Work in pairs. Do you know what a 'pie chart' is? Look at the text and check your answer.**

2 **Read the text and do the activities. Compare your answers with your partner.**

Statistics is the part of maths which deals with using information that is expressed in numbers. This information is often called 'data'. Data can be shown in the form of tables, graphs, charts and other diagrams. This is a useful way of making the key information clear. However, charts and diagrams usually present a summary of the main information – they don't explain the details of the information.

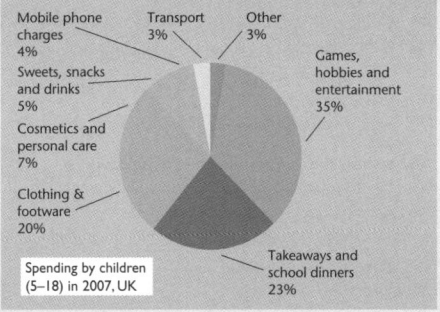

Mobile phone charges 4%
Transport 3%
Other 3%
Sweets, snacks and drinks 5%
Cosmetics and personal care 7%
Clothing & footware 20%
Games, hobbies and entertainment 35%
Takeaways and school dinners 23%

Spending by children (5–18) in 2007, UK

Activity 1 What do the percentages in the pie chart add up to? Why?

Activity 2 Look at the pie chart carefully. Then read the information below. Which data is also shown in the pie chart?

1 In 2007, children aged five to 18 spent most on games, hobbies and entertainment.
2 This category includes spending on music, computer games and DVDs.
3 On average, children spent about £13 a week, although 13 to 15-year-olds spent over £20 a week compared to much less for younger children.
4 Children spent 23 per cent of their total spending on meals and a much smaller amount on sweets and snacks.
5 About 4 per cent of total spending was on mobile phone charges, but this was accounted for only by children over 11.
6 About 20 per cent of spending was on clothes and footwear.
7 Girls spent about double the amount that boys did on clothes. Young teenage boys, on the other hand, spent about five times as much as girls on games and hobbies.

3 **Does any of the information in the pie chart surprise you? Explain why.**

Culture

Maths and English

1 It looks like a pie. It's a circle divided into different sections to show how different groups make up the whole.

2 1 100%, because 100% is always the whole of something.   2 The chart shows items 1, 4 and 6, and part of 5 (About 4 per cent of total spending was on mobile phone charges).

2 Reading for detail

Students read the article and examine the pie chart before completing Activities 1 and 2.

3 Speaking about the findings

Students discuss what they have discovered about the habits of UK teenagers, and in particular, information that they found surprising. Elicit comments from the class and open up a discussion.

Assistant: *Just a moment ... yes, that's Converse baseball trainers?*

Customer: *Yes, that's right.*

Assistant: *And you paid by Paypal, is that correct?*

Customer: *Yes, £37.50.*

Assistant: *OK. If you return them to us in the same packaging, please, we'll send you a new pair, size 39. You won't need to pay for the postage if you use the address I'm going to give now.*

Project: money survey

Students should use ideas from this unit to writ questions about money and spending habits. They should have about ten questions. They then ask each of their classmates and record the answers. The results should then be presented graphically – as charts, diagrams and tables. Organise a feedback session, with students in groups of five or six presenting their findings to the rest of the group.

Maths and English: Statistics

1 Pre-reading

Students discuss what they think a 'pie chart' is in pairs, then check their understanding in the text. Make sure students understand what a *pie* is and how it relates to a pie chart (i.e. meat, vegetables or fruit baked in a pastry case which is usually circular, e.g. *apple pie, steak pie*. It is divided into sections for eating, like a pie chart).

8E Consolidation Units 7 and 8

Spread aims

Reading and **grammar** practice

Consolidating understanding of the key grammar points from Units 7 and 8

KEY

Reading

1 1 c 2 a 3 b

2 (possible answers)
1 Would you like to …?
2 Could you tell me … please? / Do you know …?
3 I think … / I don't think … / In my opinion …
4 I'm sorry. / I apologise.
5 I'd rather … / I prefer …
6 What should I … ?/ Do you think I should …?
7 I'm afraid …
8 You should …
9 I wish … / I shouldn't have …

3 I'm really sorry (apologising for something)   I shouldn't have (expressing a regret)   Can we talk about it later? (inviting somebody to do something)   Please accept my apologies (apologising for something)

4 a

5 a 6 b 4 c 1 d 9 e 2 f 3

6 1 c 2 a 3 c

Reading

Identifying the writer's purpose
• Read the text and the options quickly.
• Think about typical expressions that express the functions described in the options. Look for these in the text.
• **Important!** You don't need to understand every word in the text to be able to do the task.

1 Match the sentences (1–3) with the functions (a–c).

1 I went out to do some shopping.
2 You didn't go out, did you?
3 You shouldn't have gone out.

a checking information
b making a criticism
c giving a reason

2 Write at least one expression for each function.

1 inviting somebody to do something
2 asking for information
3 expressing an opinion
4 apologising for something
5 expressing a preference
6 asking for advice
7 making a complaint
8 making a recommendation
9 expressing regret

3 Read the note and choose the expressions that match functions in Exercise 2.

> Hi Jen,
> How are you today? I'm really sorry about last night. I was in a bad mood, but I know that's no excuse for my behaviour. I shouldn't have shouted. Please accept my apologies. Can we talk about it? I'll call you later.
> Anna

4 Choose the correct option (a–c).

Read Anna's note. Why has she written to Jen?
a to apologise
b to ask for help
c to give advice

5 Match these expressions (a–f) with six of the functions (1–9) in Exercise 2 in the left-hand column.

a What do you think I should do?
b I'm really sorry about that.
c Would you like to go for a burger?
d I wish I hadn't told you.
e Could you tell me where the bookshop is?
f The film seemed a bit boring to me.

6 Read each statement and choose the best option (a–c).

1 You are in a shop. You want to know the price of a camera. What do you say?
a I'd like to return this camera.
b Can I help you?
c Could you tell me how much this is, please?
2 You lent your friend a DVD. He says he didn't enjoy it. How do you respond?
a Why do you say that?
b What did you think of it?
c Because I liked it.
3 You answer a phone call for your sister. She's not at home. What do you say?
a Can you take a message?
b Can I leave a message?
c Can I take a message?

Reading

1 Identifying functions

Present the bullet points and discuss the strategies suggested for identifying the writer's purpose. Students read the sentences and match them with the functions.

2 Predicting expressions for functions

Students write an example expression for each of the functions given. They can do this in pairs.

Follow-up: students can write several expressions for each function.

3 Matching expressions to functions

Students find expressions for some of the functions listed in Exercise 2.

4 Reading for gist

Students decide what the overall function of the note from Anna is.

5 Identifying functions

Students match the six sentences with the nine functions in reading Exercise 2.

Tell **weaker students** that functions 5, 7, and 8 are not exemplified.

6 Further practice

Students choose the correct option for each situation.

wish + past simple

wish + past simple refers to situations in the present.

I wish they had this shirt in yellow.

1 Look at the picture above. Which sentence (a or b) is true?

a The shop hasn't got the colour he wants.

b The shop has got the shirt in yellow.

2 Complete the sentences with the correct form of the verb.

1 I wish it .... (**be**) cheaper.

2 I wish I .... (**like**) green.

3 I wish it .... (**not have**) a round neck.

wish + past perfect

wish + past perfect refers to situations in the past.

I wish I'd tried this on in the shop.

3 Look at the picture above. Which sentence (a or b) is true?

a He tried the jacket on before he bought it.

b He bought the jacket without trying it on first.

4 Complete the sentences with the correct form of the verb.

1 I wish I .... (**buy**) a smaller size.

2 I wish I .... (**not be**) in a hurry.

3 I wish you .... (**come**) with me.

5 Complete the table with the verbs.

isn't had been was wasn't

situation in the present	I wish the shirt (**1**) .... cheaper, but it (**2**) ....
situation in the past	I wish the shirt (**3**) .... cheaper, but it (**4**) ....

6 Read each sentence or each pair of sentences. Say if *I wish* refers to the past (PA) or the present (PR).

1 I wish I'd seen the advert. Then I would have known about the offer. ....

2 I wish my local shop sold Fairtrade products. ....

3 I wish you'd bought Fairtrade chocolate. It tastes great and the farmers get more money. ....

4 I wish I didn't have to go shopping. There's a great match on TV. ....

5 I wish the sales were on. I'm short of money. ....

6 I wish you'd asked me – I would have lent you some money. ....

7 Read the first sentence and complete the second sentence.

1 These Nike trainers are too expensive for me. (**wish / cheaper**)

2 When I went to the bank yesterday, it was shut. (**wish / know**)

3 They only sell that version of the film online. (**wish / have a PayPal account**)

4 I didn't know the Top Shop sale finished yesterday! (**wish / you tell me**)

5 I don't get much pocket money. (**wish / get more**)

6 I'd love to buy this DVD. (**wish / more money**)

8 Look at the picture. Write sentences with *I wish* and the ideas from the box or ideas of your own. Write three sentences you would say during the match and three sentences you would say after the match.

be a Chelsea supporter
be in the crowd
play better
score more goals
Porto win
Porto have a better goalkeeper

HALF-TIME SCORE:
CHELSEA 2. PORTO 0

CONSOLIDATION **UNITS 7 AND 8** 97

---

7 Writing conditional sentences with *wish*

Students write the correct second sentence based on the information in the first sentence.

8 Writing practice

Students look at the picture and write their own sentences with *I wish*, using ideas from the box or their own ideas.

Grammar

1 *Wish* + past simple

Students read the grammar note and look at the picture, then decide which of the statements is true.

2 Completing sentences

Students complete the sentences with the correct form of the verb.

3 *Wish* + past perfect

Students read the grammar note and look at the picture, then decide which statement is true.

4 Completing sentences

Students complete the sentences with the correct form of the verb.

5 *Wish* + past simple or past perfect

Students complete the table with the correct verbs, following the information in the grammar notes.

6 Identifying past and present situations

Students decide what period of time the sentences refer to.

Review Units 7 and 8

Spread aims

Reviewing vocabulary, grammar and functions from Units 7 and 8; giving students the opportunity to assess their own progress

KEY

1
1 laboratory 2 research
3 theory 4 discovery
5 machine

2
1 democracy 2 elections
3 government 4 vote
5 right

3
1 butcher's 2 baker's
3 newsagent's 4 post office
5 greengrocer's

4
1 cash machine 2 pocket
money 3 wages 4 coins
5 credit card

5
1 disconnect 2 unlock
3 disagree 4 unpack
5 decode

6
1 would have eaten
2 wouldn't have been
3 would / could have walked
4 wouldn't have missed
5 wouldn't have had to

7
1 had followed 2 hadn't used
3 had listened 4 hadn't been
5 had helped

8
1 should 2 could
3 shouldn't 4 should
5 couldn't

9
1 She said that it was an
excellent product.
2 She said that she had seen
the advert on TV.
3 She said that she had been
to that shop a few times.
4 She said that they would be
home at 8 p.m.
5 She said that John couldn't
come to dinner.

10
1 He asked where I was going.
2 He asked if I read many
magazines. 3 He asked if I
would be at home on Sunday.
4 He asked if I had finished
work. 5 He asked where I
had gone the day before / the
previous day.

Review \ Units 7 and 8

Vocabulary

1 Write the words. They are all nouns.

1 a place where scientists work l............
2 investigating something r............
3 a scientific idea t............
4 finding something new d............
5 a piece of equipment m............

1 mark per item: .../5 marks

2 Complete the paragraph with words about politics.

In a country that is a (**1**) d............ , there are (**2**) e............ to choose a new (**3**) g............ . At this time, people can (**4**) v............ for the politician they prefer. In most countries, everyone over the age of 18 has the (**5**) r............ to participate.

1 mark per item: .../5 marks

3 Write the places where you can buy the things.

1 ....
2 ....
3 ....
4 ....
5 ....

1 mark per item: .../5 marks

4 Complete the sentences.

1 When the bank is closed, we use the c............ m............ .
2 My mum gives me £5 p............ m............ every Friday.
3 I need a job that pays better w............ .
4 I save all my 20-pence c............ in a jar.
5 You can't have a c............ c............ until you are 18 years old.

1 mark per item: .../5 marks

5 Write verbs that have the opposite meanings.

1 connect ....
2 lock ....
3 agree ....
4 pack ....
5 encode ....

1 mark per item: .../5 marks

Grammar

6 Complete the endings of the third conditional sentence.

If I had got up earlier this morning, …

1 I............ (**eat**) breakfast.
2 I............ (**not / be**) late for school.
3 we............ (**walk**) to school together.
4 I............ (**not / miss**) the French exam.
5 I............ (**not have to**) see the head teacher.

1 mark per item: .../5 marks

7 Complete the endings of the third conditional sentence.

The experiment would have worked if …

1 we............ (**follow**) the instructions.
2 you............ (**not / use**) the wrong chemical.
3 I............ (**listen**) to the teacher.
4 we............ (**not / be**) in a hurry.
5 the teacher............ (**help**) us.

1 mark per item: .../5 marks

8 Complete the sentences with *could, couldn't, should* or *shouldn't*.

1 I'm sorry I'm late. I............ have phoned.
2 If I'd known you were going shopping, we............ have gone together.
3 You............ have said that. It wasn't nice.
4 You............ have asked me before you borrowed my phone!
5 Don't worry! You............ have helped – we needed an expert.

1 mark per item: .../5 marks

9 Report the words. Begin with *She said … .*

1 'It's an excellent product.'
2 'I saw the advert on TV.'
3 'I've been to that shop a few times.'
4 'We'll be home at 8 p.m.'
5 'John can't come to dinner.'

1 mark per item: .../5 marks

10 Report the questions. Begin with *He asked … .*

1 'Where are you going?'
2 'Do you read many magazines?'
3 'Will you be at home on Sunday?'
4 'Have you finished work?'
5 'Where did you go at the weekend?'

1 mark per item: .../5 marks

98

Communicate

11 **Match the statements (1–5) with the follow-up comments (a–e).**

1 I can't do this homework.
2 I forgot my mum's birthday.
3 It's too late to go shopping now.
4 My friend is upset with me.
5 There are no tickets left!

a I shouldn't have argued with her.
b I wish I'd asked the teacher for help.
c I wish we'd got here earlier.
d I wish I'd looked at the time earlier.
e I should have written it on the calendar.

2 marks per item: …/10 marks

12 **Complete the dialogue with the expressions.**

> can I help you   have you got the receipt
> I'm afraid   we'd like to return
> would you like

Assistant: Good morning, (1) …………… ?
Lee: Yes, (2) …………… this DVD.
Assistant: OK, it hasn't been opened. That's fine. (3) …………… ?
Lee: Yes, we have. Here you are.
Assistant: OK, is there another DVD you want?
Lee: We haven't looked, actually.
Assistant: (4) …………… a credit note, instead?
Lee: Would it be possible to get my money back?
Assistant: Well, (5) …………… we don't usually give refunds.
Lee: Oh well, I suppose we can choose something. Let's have a look.

2 marks per item: …/10 marks

13 **Which letter is silent in each word?**

1	bomb	…………	6	foreign	…………
2	castle	…………	7	half	…………
3	could	…………	8	island	…………
4	design	…………	9	know	…………
5	doubt	…………	10	scientific	…………

1 mark per item: …/10 marks

14 **Complete the sentences with these words.**

> before   despite that   except for
> in spite of   without

1 We solved the problem ………… asking for help.
2 ………… deciding to buy the GPS, we looked at the price.
3 ………… the bad weather, lots of people came to our picnic.
4 I don't like any fruit ………… bananas.
5 My camera was cheap, but ………… it takes great photos.

2 marks per item: …/10 marks

15 **Complete the letter with these words.**

> about   after   as   because   for   if   in
> to   us   when

Dear Sir / Madam,
I am writing to complain (**1**) ………… the service in your shop. We went there last Saturday (**2**) ………… my son wanted (**3**) ………… buy a games console. (**4**) ………… waiting for at least ten minutes, an assistant served us. My son asked him several questions about the console he was interested (**5**) ………… , but the assistant didn't know anything. (**6**) ………… well as this, he was quite impolite.

He told (**7**) ………… to read the information leaflet (**8**) ………… we wanted to know about the consoles. (**9**) ………… I asked to speak to the manager, the assistant disappeared and did not return. We then left the shop.

We have been customers at your shop (**10**) ………… many years, but I'm afraid we will not return in the future.
Yours,
Mr D. Harris

2 marks per item: …/20 marks

Total: …/100

I can...
I can talk about regrets.
I can make criticisms.
I can return things to shops

KEY

11 1 b   2 e   3 d   4 a   5 c

12 1 Can I help you   2 we'd like to return   3 Have you got the receipt   4 Would you like   5 I'm afraid

13 1 final b   2 t   3 l   4 g   5 b   6 g   7 l   8 s   9 k   10 first c

14 1 without   2 Before   3 In spite of   4 except for   5 despite that

15 1 about   2 because   3 to   4 After   5 in   6 As   7 us   8 if   9 When   10 for

Unit 1

Page aim

Additional exercises for practice of
verb + preposition *at* and *to* and
noun + noun combinations

KEY

Verb + preposition *at, to*

1 listen to, look at, speak to, write to

2 1 at   2 to   3 at   4 to

3 1 listening / to listen to
2 write to   3 laugh at
4 explain … to

5 1 at   2 to   3 to   4 at

6 Students' own answers

Noun + noun

1 phone line, security guard, soap opera, talent show

2 celebrity guest, fan club, headline, music/TV/film review, website

3 1 summer clothes
2 horseshoe
3 rubbish tip
4 security guard

4 Students' own answers

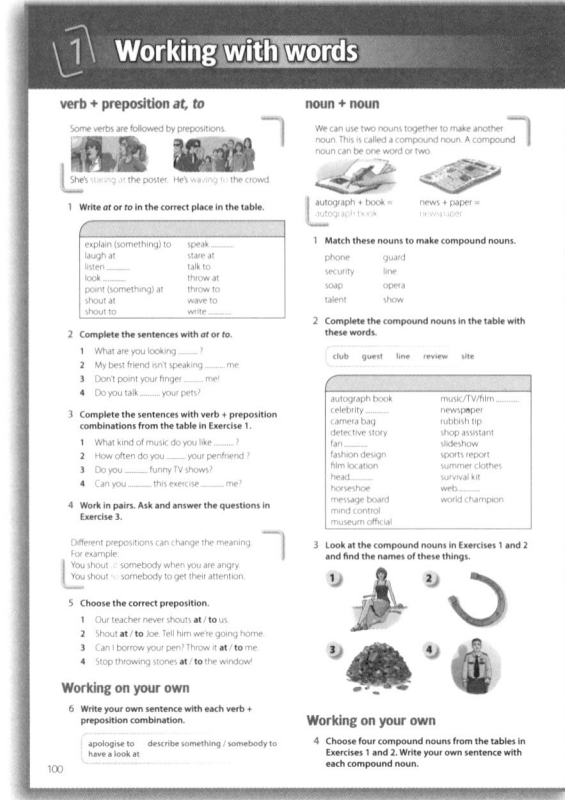

Unit 2

Page aim

Additional exercises for practice of
abstract nouns and **verb + *-ing***

KEY

Abstract nouns

1 Uncountable: advice, information, luck
Countable: feeling, idea

2 1 memory   2 intelligence
3 imagination   4 behaviour

3 1 fear   2 happiness   3 anger
4 love   5 sadness

4 Students' own answers

Verb + *-ing*

1 dancing, making notes, rescuing, swimming

2 suggested answers:
1 swinging (something)
2 making notes, practising, repeating (something).
3 public speaking, flying
4 fishing, painting, drawing, riding
5 hunting, pulling (something)
6 fixing (something), singing, telling jokes

3 Students' own answers

4 Students' own answers

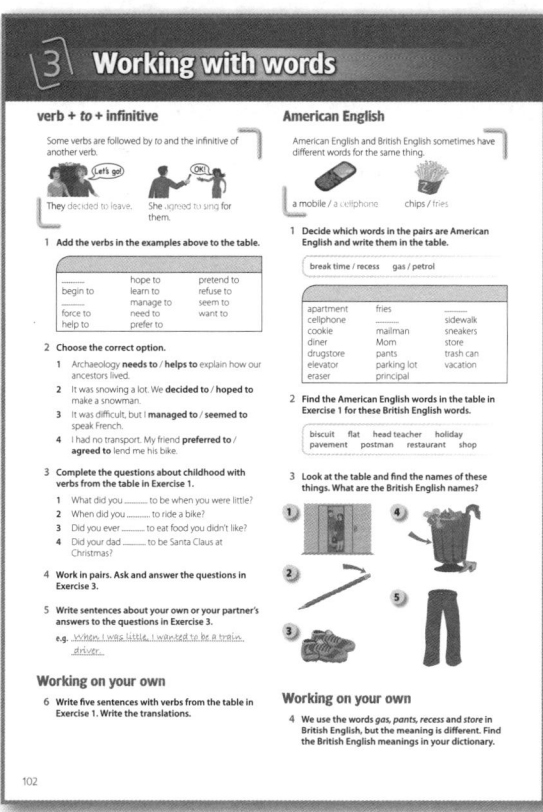

Unit 3

Page aim

Additional exercises for practice of **verb + to + infinitive** and **American English**

KEY

Verb + *to* + infinitive

1 agree to, decide to

2 1 helps to   2 decided to   3 managed to   4 agreed to

3 1 want   2 learn   3 refuse   4 pretend

5 Students' own answers

6 Students' own answers

American English

1 gas, recess

2 1 cookie (biscuit)   2 apartment (flat)   3 principal (head teacher)   4 vacation (holiday)   5 sidewalk (pavement)   6 mailman (postman)   7 diner (restaurant)   8 store (shop)

3 1 elevator (lift)   2 eraser (rubber)   3 sneakers (trainers)   4 trash can (rubbish bin / waste bin)   5 pants (trousers)

4 gas – a transparent substance like oxygen
pants – men's underwear for the lower body
recess – an area set back in a wall, e.g with shelves or a cupboard
store – a place where you keep things you will need later (e.g. *store room, store cupboard*)

Unit 4

Page aim

Additional exercises for practice of **adjective + to + infinitive** and **verb + noun** combinations

KEY

Adjective + *to* + infinitive

1 difficult / hard to, lovely / nice / exciting / surprising to

2 1 d   2 b   3 c   4 a

3 1 happy   2 dangerous   3 sad   4 unusual

4 Students' own answers

5 Students' own answers

6 Students' own answers

Verb + noun

1 get a job, have an idea, make a mistake, win a race

2 drive a vehicle, get help, have a career, make a decision, spend hours

3 1 Have   2 get   3 get   4 have

4 1 makes   2 spend   3 win   4 scores   5 make

5 Students' own answers

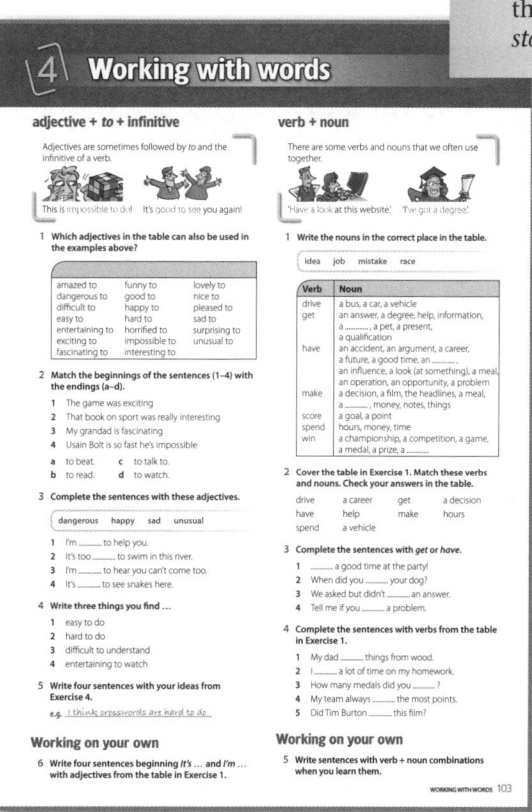

Unit 5

Page aim

Additional exercises for practice of **adjective order** and **verb + preposition**

KEY

Adjective order

1 1 size   2 age   3 colour
4 origin   5 material

2 1 correct   2 incorrect
(blue plastic)   3 correct   4
incorrect (ancient Egyptian)

3 1 a square-shaped, plastic box
2 an oval, metal mirror
3 a tall, round building
4 a triangular, concrete
   sculpture

4 Students' own answers

Verb + preposition

1 pay for, think about, value as

2 1 from   2 into   3 for   4 in

3 1 vote   2 wait   3 ask   4 look

4 1 for   2 as   3 into   4 in

5 Students' own answers

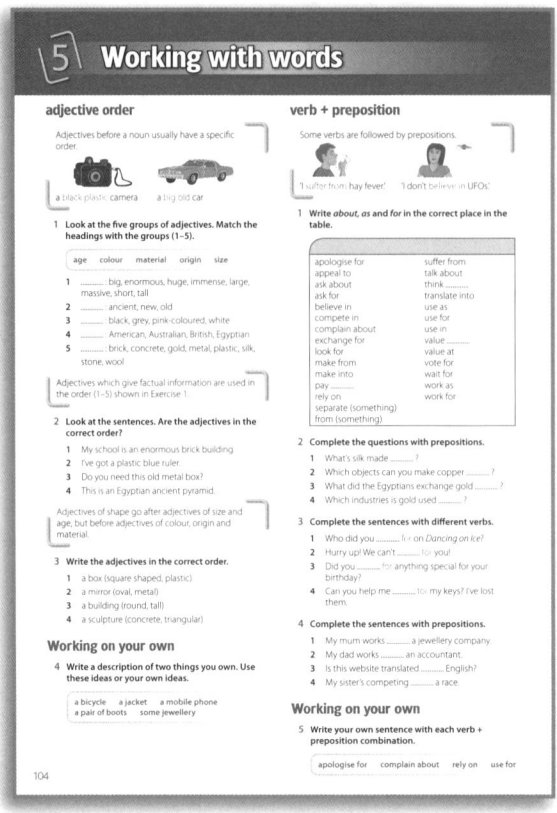

Unit 6

Page aim

Additional exercises for practice of **phrasal verbs** and **noun + preposition** combinations

KEY

Phrasal verbs

1 give up, run away

2 1 calculate   2 come   3 used
4 go to a different place

3 1 back   2 in   3 work / find
4 set

4 1 turn into   2 take off
3 carry on   4 throw away

5 Students' own answers

Noun + preposition

1 answer to, explanation for,
map of

2 1 to   2 with   3 to   4 of

3 1 to   2 about   3 with   4 of

4 1 recipe   2 cure   3 reason

5 Students' own answers

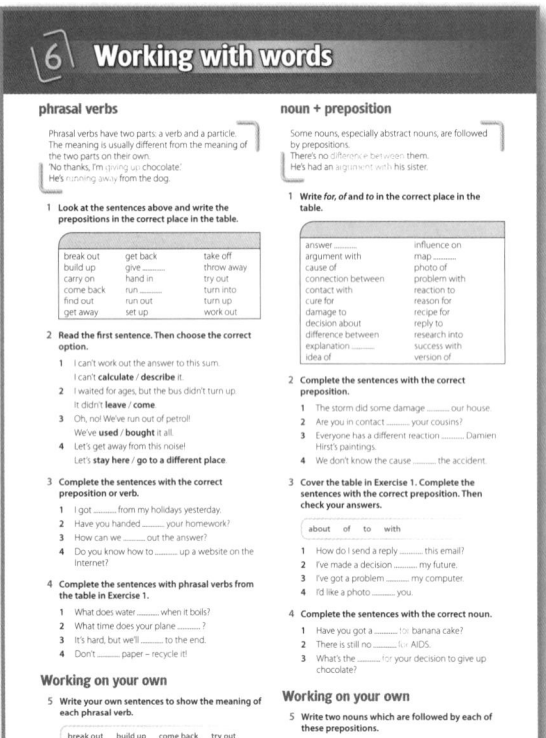

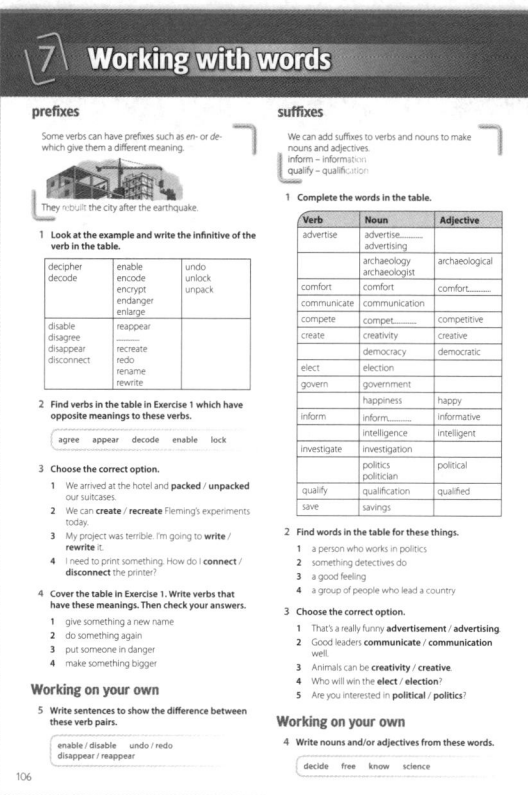

Unit 7

Page aim

Additional exercises for practice of **prefixes** and **suffixes**

KEY

Prefixes

1 rebuild

2 agree – disagree, appear – disappear, decode – encode, enable – disable, lock – unlock

3 1 unpacked   2 recreate
3 rewrite   4 connect

4 1 rename   2 redo
3 endanger   4 enlarge

5 Students' own answers

Suffixes

1 advertisement, competition, information, comfortable

2 1 politician   2 investigation
3 happiness / comfort
4 government

3 1 advertisement
2 communicate   3 creative
4 election   5 politics

4 Students' own answers

Unit 8

Page aim

Additional exercises for practice of **reporting verbs** and **word combinations with** *money*

KEY

Reporting verbs

1 ask

2 1 claimed   2 asked   3 told
4 suggested

3 1 e   2 c   3 a   4 b   5 d

4 Students' own answers

Word combinations with *money*

1 1 borrow   2 gave   3 spent
4 lend

2 1 c   2 a   3 e   4 d   5 b

3 1 b   2 a   3 e   4 c   5 d

4 Students' own answers

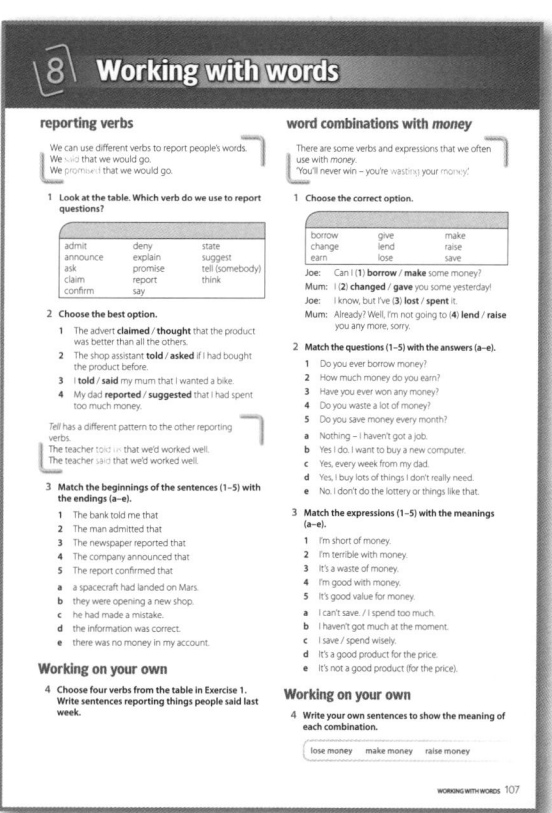

Video Worksheet U1
The adventure capital of the world

Warm-up

Write the words *bungee jumping, skydiving, ice climbing* on the board. Ask students to say what you do in these sports, and to add more adventure sports to the list. Find out if any students have done exciting or adventurous sports, and ask them what they felt like doing these sports. Finally, ask students where people can do sports like these. Show the location of Queenstown, New Zealand on a map.

1 Before you watch

Direct students' attention to the picture and and ask them how they think it might relate to the title of the video. Read the introduction with the students and elicit or explain any unfamiliar vocabulary. For question number three, elicit a range of adjectives from students and write these on the board.

2 While you watch

Before playing the video, give students time to read the questions and the multiple-choice answers. Play the video up to *we worked it out that if you did one of every type of activity you'd be here for 60 days!* Then ask students to complete the exercise.

3

Give students a little time to read the sentences and predict the answers, before playing the first half of the video again to check all answers.

4

Before playing the second half of the video, allow students a few moments to read the questions and the multiple-choice answers. Play the rest of the video.

5

Give students a little time to read the sentences and predict the answers, before playing the second half of the video again to check all answers.

6 After you watch

Explain that this is a fun memory test. It is unlikely that any student will remember all the facts correctly. Get students to complete the exercise individually, or to challenge their partner. Play the whole film again so they can check their answers.

---

1 The adventure capital of the world

New Zealand is a land of many beautiful and quiet natural places. Queenstown, on South Island, is beautiful, but it isn't quiet. People go to Queenstown looking for thrills and excitement. It is the adventure sports capital of the world. Bungee jumping actually began in Queenstown.

Before you watch

1 **Read the introduction and discuss the questions.**

 1 Why do people visit Queenstown?
 2 Which adventure sport is Queenstown particularly famous for?
 3 What would you feel like if you did a bungee jump?

While you watch

PART ONE: Activities around Queenstown

2 **Watch the first part of the film and choose the correct answer (a, b or c).**

 1 The bungee jump is about:
  a 34 metres. b 134 metres. c 440 metres.
 2 Jet boats were especially designed for New Zealand's:
  a rivers. b lakes. c seas.
 3 How do people in Queenstown feel about being 'the adventure capital of the world'?
  a Important. b Excited. c Proud.

3 **Complete the sentences (1–3) below.**

 1 Visitors to New Zealand can experience the New Zealand l............ .
 2 The jet boats can work in s............ water.
 3 Jet boats are also good at giving customers a t............ .

Watch again and check your answers.

PART TWO: In the mountains

4 **Watch the second part of the film and choose the correct answer (a, b or c) for each question.**

 1 How do hikers get down from the mountain?
  a They walk. b They fly. c They ski.
 2 What do adventure sports in New Zealand help?
  a Helicopter companies.
  b Local culture.
  c The tourism industry.
 3 According to Van Asch, who has the best bungee jumping experience?
  a People who have jumped many times.
  b People who aren't frightened.
  c People who have to try hard to jump.

5 **Complete the sentences (1–3) below.**

 1 From the mountain, it's a five-minute f............ by helicopter back to the city.
 2 The b............ of adventure tourism in New Zealand is the Kawarau Bridge.
 3 The Kawarau Bridge was the world's first commercial bungee-jumping s............ .

Watch again and check your answers.

After you watch

6 **Test your memory. How many of these options can you remember? Test your partner then watch the whole film.**

 1 The first bungee jumper feels **excited / ready**.
 2 The jet boat driver makes the boat **jump over a rock / spin around**.
 3 The tour guide says the hikers stay at the top of the mountain for **five hours / ten minutes**.
 4 Marlene, the bungee jumper, **wants to jump again immediately / never wants to jump again**.

Tapescript

[Narrator]: New Zealand is a land of many beautiful and quiet natural places. Queenstown isn't one of them.

[Bungee Instructor]: Diving out that way, here we go: five, four, three, two, one, push it out!

[Narrator]: People come from around the world to do adventure sports in Queenstown – especially bungee jumping.

[Henry Van Asch, Bungee Jump Worker]: The gap there from the underside of that little silver jump pod out there is 134 metres, which is about 440 feet.

[Narrator]: That's a long way down! But the sport must be fun. There are many people waiting for a chance to do it. What do they feel like before a jump?

[Bungee Jumper 1]: I'm so ready! Bring it on!

[Bungee Jumper 2]: I'm getting excited actually, yeah.

[Bungee Instructor]: Five, four, three, two, one . . .

[Narrator]: If you like exciting adventure sports, New Zealand is the place to do them.

[Van Asch]: New Zealand people have a very immediate lifestyle a lot of the time, and that's what people can experience when they come here.

[Brendan Quill, Jet boat Driver]: Ha! Nothing like it!

[Narrator]: Riding in a jet boat is a special experience. It's yet another New Zealand adventure invention. There's no propeller, so the boats can work in shallow water.

[Quill]: These machines . . . you can spin 'em on a dime!

[Narrator]: Jet boats were especially designed to get around New Zealand's shallow rivers, but they're also really good at giving customers a thrill.

[Quill]: Ha ha ha! Yee hee hee! This is one of the number-one pastimes of people coming to New Zealand . . . more importantly probably Queenstown.

[Narrator]: In New Zealand, it seems that nearly every day someone creates another adventure sport.

[David Kennedy, Destination Queenstown]: You know we quite proudly call ourselves 'The Adventure Capital of the World'. There are so many adventure activities to do here. In fact, we worked it out that if you did one of every type of activity you'd be here for 60 days!

[Narrator]: One of the newest adventures involves a five-hour hike up a mountain. The best part is, at the end of the hike, the hikers don't have to walk all the way down again.

[Buxtom]: We'll stay here for ten minutes or so . . . fifteen minutes. And then we'll jump in the helicopter and fly back to Queenstown.

[Narrator]: The helicopter turns the five-hour hike into a five-minute flight back to the city. These different adventure sports really help the tourism industry in New Zealand. They're also part of an adventurous culture that goes back to the birthplace of adventure tourism in New Zealand – the Kawarau Bridge. The bridge was the world's first commercial bungee jumping site.

[Bungee Watcher]: I think it's great – if somebody else is doing it!

[Narrator]: High wire bungee and bridge bungee are both thrilling and slightly frightening sports.

[Bungee Instructor]: Here we go Marlene, leaning forward: five, four, three, two, one!

[Van Asch]: The people who have to really try hard to jump are the ones that get the most out of it.

[Narrator]: At least that's what some people think.

[Bungee Instructor]: How was that?

[Marlene]: I'm never bungee jumping again!

[Narrator]: Maybe for some people, jumping once is enough.

[Bungee Jumper 1]: Cheers!

[Bungee Jumper 2]: Ah, we deserve that.

[Bungee Jumper 3]: That was a good one!

[Narrator]: Most jumpers are happy that they did it. Here in the land of adventure, the only question may be: what will they think of doing next? Whatever it is, someone here in The Adventure Capital of the World will be ready to give it a try!

Video Worksheet U2
Orangutan language

Warm-up

Ask students what they know about how animals communicate with each other (e.g. bird song, dogs barking, whale 'song' and dolphin 'squeaks', bees 'dancing'). Discuss whether there are animals that communicate with humans, and if so, how they do it. For example dogs wag their tails – what do students think this means?

1 Before you watch

Direct students' attention to the picture and and ask them how they think it might relate to the title of the video. Read the introduction with the students and elicit or explain any unfamiliar vocabulary.

Students discuss the questions in pairs. For question number three, write some prompt questions on the board (e.g. *habitat? food? activities? numbers? threats?*). Students may know the answers, or they can speculate about them.

2 While you watch

Before playing the video, give students time to read the questions and the multiple-choice answers. Play the video up to *Basically, she can use the symbols to get her point across, which is the essential purpose of language.* Then ask students to complete the exercise.

3

Give students a little time to read the sentences and predict the answers, before playing the first half of the video again to check all answers.

4

Before playing the second half of the video, allow students a few moments to read the questions and the multiple-choice answers. Play the rest of the video.

5

Give students a little time to read the sentences and predict the answers, before playing the second half of the video again to check all the answers.

Orangutan language

Orangutans are primates that come from Indonesia and Malaysia. They are highly intelligent animals, and in Malay their name actually means 'person of the forest' because they are so like humans. Orangutans can even communicate through language. At the National Zoo in Washington, D.C., two orangutans named Inda and Azie are part of a project with researcher Rob Shumaker.

Before you watch

1 **Read the introduction and discuss the questions.**

　1　What does 'orangutan' mean in Malay?
　2　Who are Inda and Azie?
　3　What do you know about orangutans?

While you watch

PART ONE: The orangutan language project

2 **Watch the first part of the film and choose the correct answer (a, b or c) for each question.**

　1　What is the aim of the project?
　　a　To teach the orangutans English.
　　b　To understand how orangutans behave in captivity.
　　c　To understand more about orangutan mental ability.
　2　What is Inda learning?
　　a　How to use a computer.
　　b　A vocabulary of different symbols.
　　c　To communicate with visitors.
　3　What can Inda do?
　　a　She can make sentences with symbols.
　　b　She can draw symbols of food.
　　c　She can find objects.

3 **Complete the sentences (1–3) below.**

　1　Orangutans are highly developed p............s.
　2　Apes in captivity need a s............ physical and mental environment.
　3　The language programme is a v............ activity for the orangutans.
Watch again and check your answers.

PART TWO: Think tank

4 **Watch the second part of the film and choose the correct answer (a, b or c).**

　1　Azie ... Inda.
　　a　is the same as
　　b　isn't as intelligent as
　　c　isn't as social as
　2　The Think Tank exhibit at the zoo:
　　a　educates the public.
　　b　rescues wild orangutans.
　　c　is a behind-the-scenes activity.
　3　According to Shumaker, why has the language project been successful?
　　a　Because he developed the symbols.
　　b　Because Inda and Azie enjoy it.
　　c　Because it's important.

5 **Complete the sentences (1–3) below.**

　1　Each orangutan is an i............ .
　2　Orangutans could become e............ in the wild in the next ten to twelve years.
　3　Shumaker says the language project is a t............ e............ .
Watch again and check your answers.

After you watch

6 **Watch the whole film. Are the sentences true (T) or false (F)?**

　1　At the National Zoo, the orangutans have lots of freedom to move around.　T / F
　2　Inda is sometimes quicker than the computer.　T / F
　3　All the orangutans in the language project show the same progress.　T / F
　4　Inda and Azie are sister and brother.　T / F

6 After you watch

Get students to complete the exercise individually, then check their answers in pairs. Play the whole film again so they can check their answers to the true / false questions. Elicit corrections for the statements which are false.

Tapescript

[Narrator]: Orang-utans. These highly developed primates come from Indonesia and Malaysia. They are so much like humans that their name actually means 'person of the forest' in Malay. They can even communicate through language. And at the National Zoo in Washington, D.C., two orang-utans named Inda and Azie are showing the world just how well they can do it. Rob Shumaker is the coordinator of the Orang-utan Language Project.

[Rob Shumaker, Orang-utan Language Project]: We are really adding to what we understand about orang-utan mental ability. I also think that we're doing something very, very good for these individual orang-utans.

[Narrator]: Shumaker believes that orang-utans and other apes in captivity need a stimulating physical and mental environment. The zoo allows its orang-utans to move around freely and gives them choices on where to go. Even Shumaker's language programme is voluntary for them.

[Shumaker]: It gives the orang-utans some choice and some agency about what they do day to day. And I think that's incredibly important for a species that has this much going on mentally. She's just naming the object.

[Narrator]: Shumaker works daily with the orang-utans in the programme to develop their language skills. Today he's working with Inda, a 20-year-old female orang-utan. Inda is learning a vocabulary of symbols that she connects with objects, such as bananas, apples and cups. Every day, visitors watch as Shumaker and Inda perform certain exercises on the computer to test what language she knows. But even apes have to wait for slow computers!

[Shumaker]: Oh, hold on. The computer's not responding quickly enough, but she's doing it correctly. Try again.

[Narrator]: Inda can identify food and objects using symbols, as well as put symbols together to form simple sentences with a verb and an object. Basically, she can use the symbols to get her point across, which is the essential purpose of language.

[Shumaker]: Each one learns their own way. Each one has their own types of questions that they are better or worse at. And the big emphasis is they are individuals, and their progress is not the same as the other orang-utans just because it's orang-utan.

[Narrator]: For example, Inda's brother Azie is not as social as his sister. At first, Shumaker thought that Azie was not as intelligent, but that's not true at all. In fact, Azie is very intelligent; he just isn't always as interested in communicating as his sister is. The Orang-utan Language Project is part of an exhibit at the National Zoo called 'Think Tank'. The exhibit explores the process of thinking, and actually involves visitors to the zoo in the programme.

[Lisa Stevens, Think Tank Curator]: What's really nice about Think Tank is that it brings a lot of the behind-the-scenes activities and research that involve animals right up front where it should be, where people are going to see it.

[Narrator]: Zoo officials hope that exhibits like Think Tank will educate the public and increase conservation efforts. Orang-utans could become extinct in the wild in the next ten to twelve years.

[Shumaker]: Give people a chance to know more about what's going on mentally for orang-utans. I know that that increases their regard for them.

[Narrator]: Shumaker personally developed the symbols for the orang-utans' vocabulary, but he says that the project has really been successful because of Inda and Azie.

[Shumaker]: I think of this language project as really a team effort between me, and Inda, and Azie. And we all work together on this. This is not my project; it's our project. And I want them to voluntarily participate.

When they do that, I know that they're doing it because they enjoy it, and they like it, and they want to be involved with it. And that's important.

[Narrator]: It's easy to see that Shumaker has been successful. The orang-utan language team of Inda, Azie, and Shumaker certainly enjoy their work!

KEY

1
1 'Person of the forest' (because they are so much like humans).
2 Two orang-utans at the National Zoo in Washington, D.C.
3 (possible answers) habitat – rainforests, away from people; food – fruit, leaves; activities – they live in trees, use tools to find food, make leaves into useful objects; numbers – endangered species, numbers falling dramatically due to human activity; threats – deforestation, hunting by people

2
1 c 2 b 3 a

3
1 primates
2 stimulating
3 voluntary

4
1 c 2 a 3 b

5
1 individual 2 extinct
3 team effort

6
1 T 2 T 3 F 4 T

Video Worksheet U3
Dinosaur search

Warm-up

If possible, find some pictures of a variety of fossils, including some dinosaur bones or eggs, and ask students to try and identify them. Build up a mind map on the board with the word *fossils* at the centre, and elicit as much information as possible from the students: how they are made, where they are found, how old they are, which are the most common types, etc.

1 Before you watch

Direct students' attention to the picture and and ask them how they think it might relate to the title of the video. Read the introduction with the students and elicit or explain any unfamiliar vocabulary.

Students discuss the questions in pairs. For question number three, the warm-up activity will have provided possible answers.

2 While you watch

Before playing the video, give students time to read the questions and the multiple-choice answers. Play the video up to *We're just hoping for the water truck to get here in time.* Then ask students to complete the exercise.

3

Give students a little time to read the sentences and predict the answers, before playing the first half of the video again to check all answers.

4

Before playing the second half of the video, allow students a few moments to read the questions and the multiple-choice answers. Play the rest of the video.

5

Give students a little time to read the sentences and predict the answers, before playing the second half of the video again to check all answers.

3 | Dinosaur search

In the Sahara Desert there are so many dinosaur fossils buried under the sand that you could call it Africa's dinosaur graveyard. Palaeontologist Dr Paul Sereno and his team are looking for clues to find these dinosaur bones. Some of the bones have been hidden there for hundreds of millions of years. The team goes to Niger and makes an amazing discovery.

Before you watch

1 Read the introduction and discuss the questions.

1 Why is the Sahara desert 'Africa's dinosaur graveyard'?
2 How long have the bones been in the Sahara?
3 Do you know any other kinds of animals that have left fossils?

While you watch

PART ONE: Working in the Sahara desert

2 Watch the first part of the film and choose the correct answer (a, b or c) for each question.

1 Dr Sereno hasn't been back to the Sahara since 1997. Why not?
   a Because he didn't find any fossils in 1997.
   b Because it isn't easy to plan this kind of trip.
   c Because he was working on other fossils.
2 What happens when the team gets to Niger?
   a They find bones everywhere.
   b They don't find any bones.
   c The bones take a long time to find.
3 What problem does the team have?
   a They haven't got much water.
   b Their water truck doesn't arrive.
   c They spend a day and a half without water.

3 Complete the sentences (1–3) below.

1 The Sahara desert is a dinosaur **g**............ .
2 The **s**............ for dinosaur bones is led by Dr Sereno.
3 Dinosaurs were **p**............ animals.

Watch again and check your answers.

PART TWO: The discovery

4 Watch the second part of the film and choose the correct answer (a, b or c) for each question.

1 What is the team's biggest discovery?
   a A prehistoric crocodile leg.
   b A prehistoric crocodile pelvis.
   c A prehistoric crocodile jaw.
2 How was the 'super croc' different from today's crocodiles?
   a It was much bigger.
   b It was far smaller.
   c It was much older.
3 What do the experts know about the 'super croc'?
   a They know what it ate and how it hunted.
   b They don't know very much about it yet.
   c They know it lived in the desert.

5 Complete the sentences (1–3) below.

1 The team doesn't have to **w**............ about finding fossils.
2 The team carefully documents each **f**............ they make.
3 The team will find more information about the 'super croc' in the **s**............ .

Watch again and check your answers.

After you watch

6 Watch the whole film. Put the events (a–f) in the order in which they happened.

a Brady Barr visited the team.
b The palaeontology team found bones from lots of animals.
c The team almost ran out of water.
d Dr Sereno first found fossils in the Sahara.
e The team discovered part of a prehistoric crocodile.
f Dr Sereno took a team back to Niger.

110

---

6 After you watch

Tell students to write the numbers 1–6 next to the sentences a–f. Give students time to put the events in order and compare with a partner before playing the entire video again to check answers and feed back.

Tapescript

[Narrator]: This is the Sahara Desert . . . Africa's dinosaur graveyard. It's a place of many secrets.

Some have been hidden under the sand for hundreds of millions of years. Now, a team of scientists is searching for these secrets. Palaeontologist Dr Paul Sereno and his team are looking for clues. They hope that these clues will lead them to dinosaur bones.

[Dr Paul Sereno, Palaeontologist]: We're on the trail of a number of dinosaurs – and we begin to paint a much better picture of this time each time we come.

[Team member]: Hey! Back there!

[Narrator]: Dr. Sereno first discovered fossils in the Sahara when he was travelling there in 1997. Since then, he's been carefully planning more visits. But planning this kind of travel isn't easy. Weather, methods of travel, the team's safety, and timing are all important issues. After a lot of hard work, Dr. Sereno and his team have made it back to Niger. They've returned to the dinosaur graveyard that he visited years before. Now, the dinosaur search can begin. There are bones everywhere and it doesn't take long to find them.

[Team member 1] It's part of a shoulder girdle.

[Team member 2] It's a distal end of a limb bone right there.

[Team member 3] We've got what looks like a leg.

[Team member 4] Hey look at this! It's a pelvis! Wait, you're stepping on it!

[Narrator]: The team finds bones from several prehistoric animals and they're very happy about it. Unfortunately, life isn't so good in other ways.

[Sereno]: After today, we'll have a day and a half's worth of water. We're just hoping for the water truck to get here in time.

[Narrator]: Luckily, it does. There's one more thing they don't have to worry about and that's finding enough fossils! The team makes one important discovery after another. They carefully document each find. Then, one day, they have their biggest discovery yet: the jaw of the prehistoric crocodile sometimes called 'super croc'! This discovery is big – very big. In fact, it's so big that the team soon gets a visit from National Geographic crocodile expert, Brady Barr. This ancient animal was very, very large. It was far bigger than the crocodiles that live today. The questions that scientists have about super croc are big too. What did it look like? What did it eat? How did it hunt? Brady Barr and Dr Sereno can't answer these questions yet. However, they realise that they probably won't find the answers in the desert sand. They'll probably find them in the swamp. Studying the crocodiles of today may tell these experts even more about the 110-million-year-old bones. The palaeontology team has made a great discovery. Now a new search – one for more information – must begin.

KEY

1
1 Because there are so many dinosaur fossils buried there.
2 'Hundreds of millions' of years. (Dinosaurs lived from about 230 million to 65 million years ago.)
3 (possible answers) birds, fish, snails, crocodiles etc.

2 1 b   2 a   3 a

3
1 graveyard
2 search
3 prehistoric

4 1 c   2 a   3 b

5 1 worry   2 find   3 swamp

6 1 d   2 f   3 b   4 c   5 e   6 a

Video Worksheet U4
The Olympians

Warm-up

On the board, write the names of three or four Olympic athletes that your students will recognise. Add the events that the athletes compete in and get students to match them. Ask which sporting event links the athletes, then ask students which country they associate with the Olympic Games and why. Note that the video is only about the summer Olympics. The winter Olympics began in 1901.

1 Before you watch

Direct students' attention to the picture and and ask them how they think it might relate to the title of the video.

Students should read the questions first, followed by the introduction. Only the first two questions refer to the introduction. Encourage them to discuss the questions in pairs in their own language. For question number three, their answers will probably depend on how close you are to an Olympic year!

2 While you watch

Before playing the video, give students time to read the questions and the multiple-choice answers. Play the video up to *This gave the throwers more power, accuracy, and distance*. Then ask students to complete the exercise.

3

Give students a little time to read the sentences and predict the answers, before playing the first half of the video again to check all answers.

4

Before playing the second half of the video, allow students a few moments to read the questions and the multiple-choice answers. Play the rest of the video.

5

Give students a little time to read the sentences and predict the answers, before playing the second half of the video again to check all answers.

VIDEO WORKSHEET
The Olympians

The modern Olympic Games are held every four years in a different country. The world's top athletes test their skills and determination in their sports. The Olympic Games began in ancient Greece as part of a festival which was dedicated to the Greek god Zeus. The event was a mix of athletic skill and religion. There was a long period when the games were not held. The modern games were brought back to life in Athens in 1896.

Before you watch

1 Read the introduction and discuss the questions.

1 What are the origins of the Olympic Games?
2 Why do we call today's games 'the modern Olympic Games'?
3 How many Olympic cities and Olympic events can you name?

While you watch

PART ONE: The athletes

2 Watch the first part of the film and choose the correct answer (a, b or c) for each question.

1 Where did the athletes in the ancient games come from?
  a Greece.   b Olympia.
  c The ancient Greek world.
2 What were the rules for athletes in the ancient games?
  a Athletes had to be under 30 years old.
  b Athletes had to train for ten months.
  c Athletes had to enter five different events.
3 Which event tested animal-hunting skills?
  a The discus.   b The long jump.
  c The javelin.

3 Complete the sentences (1–3) below.

1 The Olympic Games represented the highest form of physical **a**............ .
2 Runners ran in front of a **c**............ of up to 40,000 people.
3 Long jumpers at the time used to hold **w**............**s** in their hands.

Watch again and check your answers.

PART TWO: The events

4 Watch the second part of the film and choose the correct answer (a, b or c) for each question.

1 Which sports took place in the Palaestra?
  a Wrestling and boxing.
  b Chariot racing and horse riding.
  c Discus and long jump.
2 What were the categories in wrestling and boxing?
  a Men and women.   b Men and boys.
  c Size and weight.
3 Why did Theodosius I stop the Olympics?
  a Because he started new Roman games.
  b Because he stopped all Greek festivals.
  c Because they were related to ancient religious figures.

5 Complete the sentences (1–3) below.

1 Some Olympic events tested strength, others tested **s**............ .
2 Boxing matches in the ancient games had no **t**............ **l**............**s**.
3 The Olympic olive wreath was a sign of **d**............ .

Watch again and check your answers.

After you watch

6 Test your memory. How many of these questions can you answer? Test your partner then watch the whole film.

1 According to legend, who was Coroebus?
2 What were the five pentathlon sports?
3 Which events took place in the Hippodrome?
4 What did Olympic winners used to win?
5 There was a long period without the Olympics. How many years was this?

6 After you watch

Explain that this is a fun memory test. It is unlikely that any student will remember all the facts correctly. Get students to complete the exercise individually, or to challenge their partner. Play the whole film again so they can check their answers.

Tapescript

[Narrator]: Today, the Olympic Games are held every four years in a different country. It's an opportunity for the world's top athletes to test their skills and determination in individual or team sports. They compete for the Olympic gold medals, which only winners can receive. To understand the modern Olympics better, we must return to the origin of the Games: Greece.

For the ancient Greeks, the Olympic Games represented the highest form of physical achievement. The games were a mix of athletic skill and religion. They were celebrated in a festival dedicated to the Greek god Zeus. The Olympics were also a time of political calm. During the Olympic Games, there was peace across the land. Athletes travelled from all over the ancient Greek world to compete in beautiful green Olympia.

According to legend, a runner named Coroebus was the first Olympic champion in 776 B.C. He was a cook who defeated all other competitors in a foot race. Foot races were central events in the ancient games at the time. Men competed with no shoes or clothes. They were covered only in olive oil as they ran down a straight path in front of a crowd of up to 40,000 people.

Over the centuries, the competitions became more serious. Olympic rules required athletes to train for at least ten months before the big event. They then had to train with expert judges for the 30 days before they competed. Being able to run fast continued to be important, but the games also began to include the five pentathlon sports: discus throwing, javelin throwing, running, the long jump, and wrestling. Most of these are still part of today's decathlon.

Discus throwers competed in much the same way as now, but their discus was made of stone. This material was later replaced by metals such as bronze. Long jumpers at the time used to hold weights in their hands to give them more momentum. The extra weight helped to push the athletes through the air when they jumped. The javelin probably came directly from the skills used to hunt animals. Like today's javelin, the ancient javelin was a pointed wooden stick about the same height as a man. However, they used to have a special leather finger holder. This gave the throwers more power, accuracy, and distance.

While some ancient Olympic events required determination and strength, others focused on one thing: speed. This was the case for the equestrian events of chariot racing and horse riding, which happened in the riding ring of the Hippodrome.

The Palaestra was the ancient Greek wrestling and boxing training area. In wrestling, the winner was the first man to throw his opponent to the ground three times. Boxing matches in the ancient games had no time limits. Boxers wrapped pieces of leather around their wrists for support and fought as long as they could. This was usually until one man said that he was defeated or one was hit so hard that he could no longer fight. Surprisingly, in wrestling and boxing, size and weight were not important. Competitors were placed in just two categories: one for men and the other for boys.

Athletes now receive gold, silver, and bronze medals for finishing in first, second, or third place. In ancient times, though, there was only one winner for each event. The prize for winning was an olive wreath. At the time, an Olympic olive wreath was a sign of distinction or social position. Winners could return to their village as highly respected individuals and be treated as demigods.

In AD 393, nearly 12 centuries after they first started, the Olympic Games were stopped by Roman Emperor Theodosius I. He decided that there would be no more festivals that were related to ancient religious figures. It was 1,500 years before the Olympic Games were brought back to life in Athens in 1896. Although they have changed over the years, one thing has always remained the same: the Olympic Games still celebrate sports in the exciting Olympian way!

KEY

1
1 The Olympic Games began in ancient Greece as part of a festival which was dedicated to the Greek god Zeus.
2 After the ancient games, there was a long period, until 1896, when the games were not held. So we call this period of the games 'modern' to distinguish it from the games in ancient Greece.
3 (possible answers) Summer Olympics: 2000 Sydney, 2004 Athens, 2008 Beijing, 2012 London, 2016 Rio de Janeiro. Wikipedia provides an up-to-date list of the different sports disciplines.

2 1 c 2 b 3 c

3
1 achievement
2 crowd
3 weights

4 1 a 2 b 3 c

5 1 speed 2 time limits
3 distinction

6
1 He was the runner who was the first Olympic champion in 776 BC.
2 discus throwing, javelin throwing, running, the long jump, and wrestling
3 chariot racing and horse riding
4 an olive wreath
5 1,500 years

Video Worksheet U5
Silk weavers of Vietnam

Warm-up

Ask students to tell you what they know about Vietnam. Which part of the world is it in? Are there lots of big industrial cities or lots of farms and villages? Show the location of Vietnam on a world map. Ask students what they know about the 'Silk Route'. Show the general path of the route on a world map and ask students what goods they think were traded between east and west in the past. (See also the 'Gold fever' text in Unit 5B.)

1 Before you watch

Direct students' attention to the picture and and ask them how they think it might relate to the title of the video.

Students should read the questions first, followed by the introduction. Encourage them to discuss the questions in pairs. For questions 1 and 2 ask students to justify their answers with information from the introduction. For question 3, draw the cycle on the board and ask the class to supply the words. (The fourth stage, when the adult moth lays eggs, is not mentioned in the video.)

2 While you watch

Before playing the video, give students time to read the questions and the multiple-choice answers. Play the video up to *The cocoons must be brought to the spinning house before the cycle is complete.* Then ask students to complete the exercise.

3

Give students a little time to read the sentences and predict the answers, before playing the first half of the video again to check all answers.

4

Before playing the second half of the video, allow students a few moments to read the questions and the multiple-choice answers. Play the rest of the video.

5

Give students a little time to read the sentences and predict the answers, before playing the second half of the video again to check all answers.

6 After you watch

Explain the re-ordering of the questions, perhaps doing the first one on the board as an example. Write the answers to the questions (see key) on the board if your students need this support. Give students time to complete the questions and compare with a partner before playing the entire video again to check answers and feed back.

In China, the technique of making silk fabric from the cocoons of moths was kept secret for over 2,500 years. Then other countries learned how to produce silk. In the Vietnamese town of Vong Nguyet, village people keep and feed the moths and collect the cocoons. The silk fibres from the cocoons are made into thread. Then silk cloth is made by weaving the threads.

Before you watch

1 **Read the introduction and discuss the questions.**

  1 Which country did silk come from originally?
  2 Is silk a natural or an artificial fabric?
  3 What are three stages in the life cycle of a silkworm moth?

While you watch

PART ONE: The silkworms

2 **Watch the first part of the film and choose the correct answer (a, b or c).**

  1 Chinese royal families used to think that silk was worth more than:
    a gold. b diamonds.
    c water.
  2 How long do the silkworm caterpillars live for?
    a Three days. b Three weeks.
    c Three months.
  3 How long does it take a caterpillar to complete a cocoon?
    a Three hours. b Three days.
    c Three weeks.

3 **Complete the sentences (1–3) below.**

  1 The caterpillars eat only **m**............. **l**............. .
  2 A silk **f**............. comes out of the caterpillar's head.
  3 The farmers don't allow the caterpillar to become an **a**............. moth.

Watch again and check your answers.

PART TWO: Making the silk

4 **Watch the second part of the film and choose the correct answer (a, b or c) for each question.**

  1 What is the first step in making the silk?
    a Find a single thread. b Heat the cocoons.
    c Break the cocoons.
  2 What are the modern spinning machines like?
    a They give higher quality thread, but are slower.
    b They give lower quality thread, but are faster.
    c They give higher quality thread and are faster.
  3 How much silk material can be made in two and a half hours?
    a One metre. b Two metres. c Ten metres.

5 **Complete the sentences (1–3) below.**

  1 When the cocoons are heated, the silk becomes **l**............. .
  2 Silk cloth is made on machines called **l**.............**s**.
  3 The process of **w**............. the silk cloth is very slow.

Watch again and check your answers.

After you watch

6 **Watch the whole film. Put the words and phrases in the correct order to make questions. Then answer the questions.**

  1 secret / by / taken away / was / which / a Chinese princess?
  2 the caterpillars / placed / when / are / on tree trunks?
  3 found / must / by / what / be / hand?
  4 be / the silk thread / will / where / sent?
  5 all of / must / what / watched / be / the time?

112

Tapescript

[Narrator]: The cocoons of moths have been used to create high quality fabric for over 4,000 years.

A Chinese tradition says that it was discovered by Empress Hsi Ling-Shih. When a cocoon fell into her teacup, the Empress discovered a long, thin fibre of silk.

The royal families of China loved silk and thought it was worth more than gold. The secret of its production was kept by China for 2,500 years. It is said that eventually the secret was taken away by a Chinese princess. One day the princess left to get married in India. In her hair she hid some silkworm caterpillars and mulberry seeds for their food.

In the Vietnamese town of Vong Nguyet, silk-making has been an important business for over 1,200 years. Many of the village people keep silkworms in their living rooms. Each basket contains hundreds of silkworm caterpillars.

This is the young, or larval, stage of a moth called *Bombyx mori*. Taking care of these caterpillars is hard work. The caterpillars have to eat every two hours during the day and every three hours throughout the night. They eat only mulberry leaves. The caterpillars live only three weeks, and spend all their time eating.

After three weeks, the caterpillars are placed on tree branches. Here, they begin to spin their cocoon. They create this cocoon to protect themselves as they turn into adult moths. First the caterpillar creates a loose pattern of fibres. Eventually, it becomes closed off from the world.

The silk fibres come from a part of the caterpillar's mouth called the salivary glands. The insect spins its head around and an unbroken silk fibre comes out. This fibre ranges from 400 to 600 metres long. To complete the cocoon the caterpillar doesn't stop working for three days.

The silk farmers cannot allow the caterpillar to become an adult moth. If it did, it would eat its way out, and the silk would be broken. The cocoons must be brought to the spinning house before the cycle is complete.

Throughout the village of Vong Nguyet, people turn the cocoons into silk thread. The first step is to heat the cocoons so that the silk becomes loose. The end of each cocoon must be found by hand and spun together. Usually a single thread needs ten or more cocoons.

Vu Thi has been making silk for many years, and is continuing a long tradition.

[Vu Thi, Silk Maker]: *Making silk is good work because it is the work of the ancestors. The silk being spun here is done in the old way, as it has been for many years. This machine over here makes it in the new way.*

[Narrator]: The old spinning machines haven't changed much for over a thousand years. The modern machine next to them has been designed for a finer, higher quality silk thread. It is much faster, but the ends of the silk fibres still have to be found by hand. Once the silk thread is made, it will leave Vong Nguyet and be sent to the weaving town of Van Phuc. Here the silk is made ready for the weaving machines, called looms. Small buildings here have machines from the 1940s.

The process of weaving silk is very slow and the machines must be watched all the time. It takes around two and a half hours to make one metre of silk material. After a lot of work on the part of man and moth, the silk cloth is finally completed. Despite the invention of cheaper materials, natural silk is still loved for its beauty and comfort. This amazing product of man and moth continues to be extremely popular around the world.

KEY

1
1 China – they kept the technique secret for 2,500 years.
2 Natural – it's made from silk fibres produced by a caterpillar. Artificial fabrics are things like nylon, made from chemicals.
3 caterpillar (=larva) >> cocoon >> adult moth >> lays eggs

2
1 a   2 b   3 b

3
1 mulberry leaves
2 fibre
3 adult

4
1 b   2 c   3 a

5
1 loose   2 looms   3 weaving

6
1 Which secret was taken away by a Chinese princess?
The secret of silk production.
2 When are the caterpillars placed on tree trunks?
When they are three weeks old.
3 What must be found by hand?
The end of each cocoon.
4 Where will the silk thread be sent?
To the weaving town of Van Phuc.
5 What must be watched all the time?
The looms.

Video Worksheet U6
Sleepy Hollow

Warm-up

Brainstorm words about New York on the board. Emphasise ideas like *big, modern, noisy, busy* etc. Then explain that New York is the largest city in an American state, also called New York, which is about the size of England and Wales together. If possible, show this on a map of the USA. Ask students to add contrasting words for what they think New York state could be like. Try to build up a city / countryside contrast.

1 Before you watch

Students should read the questions first, followed by the introduction. As a follow up to question 1, ask students to speculate what life in a town with the name of 'Sleepy Hollow' might be like. Students have to infer the answer to question 2 as the introduction does not directly state the town itself is famous.

2 While you watch

Before playing the video, give students time to read the questions and the multiple-choice answers. Play the video up to *as he took off and headed down to get to that churchyard bridge*. Then ask students to complete the exercise.

3

Give students a little time to read the sentences and predict the answers, before playing the first half of the video again to check all answers.

4

Before playing the second half of the video, allow students a few moments to read the questions and the multiple-choice answers. Play the rest of the video.

5

Give students a little time to read the sentences and predict the answers, before playing the second half of the video again to check all answers.

Sleepy Hollow

American author Washington Irving wrote a well-known story about a town called Sleepy Hollow. The town is near New York City, in the Hudson River Valley. It was a quiet town of farmers when Irving visited it 200 years ago. Although the town has changed into a busy place, the people who live there still love and celebrate Irving's scary story, 'The Legend of Sleepy Hollow.'

Before you watch

1 **Read the introduction and discuss the questions.**

  1 Where is Sleepy Hollow?

  2 Why is it famous?

  3 What do Sleepy Hollow residents think of the legend?

While you watch

PART ONE: The story

2 **Watch the first part of the film and choose the correct answer (a, b or c) for each question.**

  1 Who was Ichabod Crane?

    a A horseman with no head.

    b An American writer.

    c A teacher in the story.

  2 Who were the old storytellers in the town of Sleepy Hollow?

    a Farmers.   **b** Grandpas.

    c Schoolmasters.

  3 What happens in the story of Sleepy Hollow?

    a The headless horseman hides in the church.

    b The headless horseman falls off the bridge.

    c The teacher races away from the headless horseman.

3 **Complete the sentences (1–3) below.**

  1 **D**............ people came to live and farm in Sleepy Hollow in the 1600s.

  2 Washington Irving visited the town when he was a **y**............ .

  3 Katrina Van Tassel is a **c**............ in the story.

Watch again and check your answers.

PART TWO: The town

4 **Watch the second part of the film and choose the correct answer (a, b or c) for each question.**

  1 How do the town's residents celebrate the story every year?

    a They eat in 'The Horseman' restaurant.

    b They light jack-o-lanterns in the dark.

    c It's part of the Halloween festival.

  2 When did Washington Irving live in the town?

    a When he was writing the story.

    b When he was a child.

    c When he was an adult.

  3 What happened when the trains came?

    a A car factory was built.

    b Washington Irving left.

    c A factory closed.

5 **Complete the sentences (1–3) below.**

  1 Carmen Cruz asks herself if the story is **r**............ or a legend.

  2 A jack-o-lantern with a **c**............ in it can weigh 20 pounds.

  3 There's a **c**............ of books written by Irving in his old house by the river.

Watch again and check your answers.

After you watch

6 **Watch the whole film. Are the sentences true (T) or false (F) – or is there not enough information (N) to decide?**

  1 Sleepy Hollow is a real town.   **T / F / N**

  2 The headless horseman rode a horse called Gunpowder.   **T / F / N**

  3 Irving's house is open to visitors.   **T / F / N**

---

6 After you watch

Get students to complete the exercise individually, then check their answers in pairs. Play the whole film again so they can check their answers to the true / false / not enough information questions. Elicit corrections for the statements which are false.

Tapescript

[Narrator]: In the hills of New York's Hudson River Valley lies Sleepy Hollow – a town known primarily for a very scary legend. . .

The Dutch came to Sleepy Hollow in the 1600s, and started to farm the land. At this old house, you can still see what life was like in the 17th and 18th centuries. You can see farm carts and horses, and learn how to cut wood. Although it's a fun place to visit, the town is most famous today for the story of a tall, thin teacher and a horseman with no head. Storyteller Jonathon Kruk explains the legend:

[Jonathon Kruk, Storyteller]: Now dwelling in these parts, in a tenant house, was a certain schoolmaster by the name of Ichabod Crane.

[Narrator]: American author Washington Irving visited this area as a youth. Later he wrote *The Legend of Sleepy Hollow* about the people and the places in this town. Bill Lent looks after the Old Dutch Church in Sleepy Hollow. He explains how the story started.

[Bill Lent, Sexton, Old Dutch Church]: Grandpas were the entertainment centre around the fireplace in the evening.

[Narrator]: Bill says the old storytellers created the shocking legend to help keep the kids under control. Bill knows everything about the story, and shows tourists where famous characters are buried.

[Bill Lent]: And when he was writing the book, he remembered the name on the stone: Katrina Van Tassel – lead female character in *The Legend of Sleepy Hollow*.

[Narrator]: In the story, the teacher, Ichabod Crane, rode his horse towards this bridge by the Old Dutch Church, racing from the headless horseman.

[Jonathon Kruk]: Ichabod urged his horse, Gunpowder, on 'come, come,' but the horse needed no further urging as he took off and headed down to get to that churchyard bridge.

[Narrator]: At *The Horseman* restaurant, the locals say they love hearing the legend.

[Carmen Cruz, Sleepy Hollow Resident]: So many times I ask myself, 'is it real or just a legend'?

[Narrator]: Every year Sal Tarantino plays the headless horseman in the town's Halloween festival.

[Sal Tarantino, Headless Horseman]: The hardest problem is a real jack-o-lantern. We've tried that several times. A good-sized jack-o-lantern with the right candle in it weighs about 20 pounds. And to hold that out on your arm and try to control the horse at 40 miles an hour in the dark doesn't work too well.

[Narrator]: Irving did not actually write the legend here in Sleepy Hollow. But he was deeply affected by the town, and as an adult returned to live here in this large house by the Hudson River. In the house is a complete collection of books written by Irving, including his famous short stories. Today you can come to visit Irving's house by train. The manager here says that Irving wasn't pleased when the train first arrived, because of the pollution and the noise. When the trains came, things began to change immediately. In 1899 the country's first car factory was built in Sleepy Hollow. The factory recently closed down. But the town is still busy.

Nearly two centuries after Irving wrote *The Legend of Sleepy Hollow*, people still find this place magical. And the legend lives on even today. The storyteller says that, if you listen, you may still recognise the sound of the headless horseman of Sleepy Hollow.

KEY

1 1 Near New York city, in the Hudson River Valley.
2 Washington Irving wrote about it. His story is well-known, and is called *The Legend of Sleepy Hollow*.
3 They love and celebrate the story.

2 1 c   2 b   3 c

3 1 Dutch
2 youth
3 character

4 1 c   2 c   3 a

5 1 real   2 candle   3 collection

6 1 T   2 F   3 T

Video Worksheet U7
Wild animal town

Warm-up

Ask the students which part of Africa Zimbabwe is in, and show its location on a map. With the class, brainstorm animals that they think live there. Then ask them for adjectives to describe some of the animals, and to say how they would feel if they came face-to-face with these animals. Where would people normally see these animals? On safari, in a zoo or in the street?

1 Before you watch

Direct students' attention to the picture and and ask them how they think it might relate to the title of the video.

Students should read the questions first, followed by the introduction. For question three, students have to provide their own answers.

2 While you watch

Before playing the video, give students time to read the questions and the multiple-choice answers. Play the video up to *At night time, it's the animals' time.* Then ask students to complete the exercise.

3

Give students a little time to read the sentences and predict the answers, before playing the first half of the video again to check all answers.

4

Before playing the second half of the video, allow students a few moments to read the questions and the multiple-choice answers. Play the rest of the video.

5

Give students a little time to read the sentences and predict the answers, before playing the second half of the video again to check all answers.

6 After you watch

Get students to attempt the exercise individually, then check in pairs before watching the film again and having class feedback.

7 Wild animal town

Kariba is a town of 30,000 people in Zimbabwe. The town was built in a wildlife area, so elephants and other wild animals lived in the area first. While the town developed and grew, the people and animals got used to each other. Now they live side by side. Glenn Tatham lives in Kariba and he has worked with animals his whole life. He says that Kariba is unlike anywhere else on Earth.

Before you watch

1 **Read the introduction and discuss the questions.**

  1 Where is Kariba?
  2 What is unusual about Kariba?
  3 What problems could there be in a town where both people and animals live?

While you watch

PART ONE: Kariba by day

2 **Watch the first part of the film and choose the correct answer (a, b or c).**

  1 Buffaloes:
    a are the most dangerous animals in Africa.
    b are not at all dangerous.
    c can be frightening at times.
  2 The hippos in Kariba:
    a are wild.   **b** are tame.
    c have been captured.
  3 Why was Kariba built originally?
    a Because people wanted to live near animals.
    b Because the river Zambezi was a good place to live.
    c Because people working on the dam needed somewhere to live.

3 **Complete the sentences (1–3) below.**

  1 Glenn Tatham used to be a **w**............ .
  2 The town of Kariba was built **i**............ **t**............ **b**............ .
  3 There is **t**............ between the people and the animals in Kariba.

Watch again and check your answers.

PART TWO: Kariba by night

4 **Watch the second part of the film and choose the correct answer (a, b or c) for each question.**

  1 What happens at night in the town?
    a The animals cause a lot of problems.
    b The animals are attacked by dogs.
    c The animals do what they want.
  2 What happens in game corridors?
    a Animals can move freely.
    b People can drive freely.
    c New developments are allowed.
  3 According to Tatham, who has the right to stay in the town?
    a The animals.
    b The people.
    c Both the animals and the people.

5 **Complete the sentences (1–3) below.**

  1 There have been very few human **i**............ .
  2 Tatham goes down to the lake after each day's **r**............ **h**............ .
  3 In Kariba, there is a **b**............ between animals and people.

Watch again and check your answers.

After you watch

6 **Watch the whole film and answer the questions.**

  1 Which animals can you see on the streets of Kariba?
  2 Where was a dam built in the 1950s?
  3 What are the 'rules' about life in Kariba?
  4 What problems might affect the wild animals in the future?

114

Tapescript

[Narrator]: It's rush hour in Kariba, Zimbabwe. As people hurry though this town of 30,000 people, they must remember one thing: elephants have the right of way! The town of Kariba was built in a wildlife area. While the town developed and grew, the people and animals simply got used to each other. Glenn Tatham used to be a warden in a national park, and he's lived and worked with animals his whole life. Tatham grew up in Kariba, and says that it's unlike anywhere else on Earth.

[Glenn Tatham, Kariba, Zimbabwe]: Kariba has lions, elephants, buffaloes, leopards, all the antelope species that occur, right up against the town, and in the town. The fact that elephants are meandering through the towns, past the schools, past the supermarkets – that's unheard of!

[Narrator]: Wild animals walk around freely in Kariba. A herd of buffaloes hides in the trees that are near the town's streets. They may not look dangerous, but when they're bothered, they're some of Africa's most frightening animals. Just a few metres behind these children, hippopotamuses, or hippos, swim in a pond.

[Tatham]: They're totally wild, absolutely wild. These are not in any way or form tame or trained or captured. They are completely wild hippos!

[Narrator]: Kariba was established in the late 1950s. At the time, a dam was being built across the Zambezi River to produce hydroelectric power. Kariba was built out in the bush because the people who were working on the project needed a place to live. When the dam was completed, the town remained and a kind of tolerance developed between the people and the animals. It's a living situation that works pretty well, but it does have rules.

[Tatham]: The animals know that the daytime – apart from the baboons and the odd elephant – but in the daytime, you don't meander amongst the people. At night time, it's the animals' time.

[Narrator]: As night comes, people anxiously return home, and elephants walk into the town centre. By midnight, with most of the town asleep, the animals are free to do whatever they want to do. The animals sometimes destroy lawns and pick up trees. Wild animals seem like they own the town as they walk around it. They don't appear to be troubled by barking dogs, or by any people who dare to walk among them. On dark nights, many humans have run into dangerous situations. Sometimes they've surprised elephants or other wild creatures, such as these buffaloes which are hidden in the bushes just a few metres from the street. Although the animals come out every night, there have been very few human injuries or deaths. One of the reasons for this may be the game corridors that have been established in the town. These are special areas where the animals can move freely and city development is not allowed. Despite these measures, there will likely be more problems. Kariba is growing, and it's unclear how long these game corridors will remain protected.

[Tatham]: When I look at some of these elephants, who are not so young now – born in the mid-'40s as I was – then I can identify with them because they've grown up here, and I've grown up here. So it's their home.

[Narrator]: Tatham feels that the animals have a right to stay in their home, just like the people of the town do. At the end of each day, when 'rush hour' is over, Tatham often goes down to the lake with his wife to watch the wildlife. Tatham knows that Kariba has established a slightly uncomfortable balance. However, he also knows that the world is becoming more and more developed every day. Natural lands are being taken away from animals as towns grow. Fortunately, it looks like the wild animal town of Kariba may have found a balance that works.

Video Worksheet U8
Madagascar perfume

Warm-up

Write the following words on the board and ask students which ones they think apply to Madagascar: *hot, tropical, cold, snow, sunny, rainforest, desert, mountains, industrial areas.* Which part of the world is it in? Show the location of Madagascar on a world map. Explain that because Madagascar is an island, there are many species of plants and animals there that do not exist anywhere else in the world (endemic species).

1 Before you watch

Direct students' attention to the picture and and ask them how they think it might relate to the title of the video.

Students should read the questions first, followed by the introduction. Ask students to suggest other products, in addition to perfumes and fruit juices, that might use essences to improve their scent or flavour.

2 While you watch

Before playing the video, give students time to read the questions and the multiple-choice answers. Play the video up to *everything from bath products to fruit juices.* Then ask students to complete the exercise.

3

Give students a little time to read the sentences and predict the answers, before playing the first half of the video again to check all answers.

4

Before playing the second half of the video, allow students a few moments to read the questions and the multiple-choice answers. Play the rest of the video.

5

Give students a little time to read the sentences and predict the answers, before playing the second half of the video again to check all answers.

6 After you watch

Explain the re-ordering of the sentences, perhaps doing the one on the board as an example. Give students time to complete the sentences and decide if they are true or false before playing the entire video again to check answers and feed back.

---

8 Madagascar perfume

The island of Madagascar is renowned for its distinctive wildlife, but some scientists visit the island for other reasons. A group of Swiss scientists is in Madagascar to investigate the island's smells and tastes. They are looking for new essences in plants and flowers.

Before you watch

1 **Read the introduction and discuss the questions.**

1 What is Madagascar famous for?

2 Where are essences found?

3 How are essences used?

While you watch

PART ONE: Looking for the essences

2 **Watch the first part of the film and choose the correct answer (a, b or c) for each question.**

1 Where exactly do the scientists go to look for new flowers?
 a To the river.   b Along a forest path.
 c Into the tops of the trees.

2 What happens in the laboratory?
 a The scientists recreate the scents.
 b The scientists store the flowers.
 c The scientists analyse the essences.

3 Why is Professor Kaiser happy?
 a Because he found a new flower on the Tampolo River.
 b Because he's had a great experience in Madagascar.
 c Because he has recreated a very similar scent to the one he found.

3 **Complete the sentences (1–3) below.**

1 Vanilla and jasmine are two flower **s**............s.

2 The scientists get to the treetops by **b**............ .

3 The scents are used in a **v**............ of products.

Watch again and check your answers.

PART TWO: Using the essences

4 **Watch the second part of the film and choose the correct answer (a, b or c).**

1 The scientists have found some fruit:
 a whose taste is special.
 b whose taste is unknown.
 c whose smell is unusual.

2 What are the scientists' discoveries like?
 a Sometimes they're fantastic.
 b Sometimes they aren't new.
 c Sometimes they aren't very special.

3 What proportion of the new scents and flavours will be used in products?
 a Almost all of them.   b Only a few of them.
 c About half of them.

5 **Complete the sentences (1–3) below.**

1 The scientists can use new fruit essences to make new **f**............**s**.

2 Willi Grab says the fruit tastes **j**............ and acidic.

3 The next time you **p**............ perfume, you could be smelling a scent from Madagascar.

Watch again and check your answers.

After you watch

6 **Watch the whole film. Put the words and phrases in the correct order to make sentences. Then decide if the sentences are true (T) or false (F).**

1 a flower. / discovered / claimed / a scientist / he
 .... **T / F**

2 reported that / technology / used / the narrator / the scientists / to recreate scents.
 .... **T / F**

3 he / on the Tampolo River. / had experienced / said that / the scent / Professor Kaiser
 .... **T / F**

Tapescript

[Narrator]: The island of Madagascar is renowned for its distinctive wildlife. But these Swiss scientists are interested more in the island's smells and tastes – and the chance to find essences for entirely new perfumes and flavours.

This scientist says he discovered a flower yesterday. The bud has just opened, and he expects the flower's scent to be very appealing, perhaps primarily a mix of vanilla and jasmine. The Swiss team goes by river, deep into the forest, then by balloon up into the treetops, hoping to obtain new flowers and fruits. The scientists bring the essences back to the laboratory, where they use technology to recreate the scents.

[Professor Roman Kaiser, Chemist]: I'm quite happy, it's already very close to this beautiful stephanotis scent as I experienced it on the Tampolo River.

[Narrator]: The scents and flavours will be used in a variety of products for purchase in stores all over the world – everything from bath products to fruit juices.

This scientist says they have found two or three types of fruit whose taste is still unknown. They may be able to use these new essences to change existing flavours, and perhaps derive entirely new flavours. But not all the discoveries are special.

[Willi Grab, Chemist]: Juicy? Acidic? A little bit earthy? Watery? Nothing fantastic. Nothing special!

[Narrator]: Only a few of these scents and flavours will be exported to markets and eventually displayed in stores. But the next time you're purchasing perfume, you could be smelling 'the secrets of Madagascar.'

KEY

1
1 Its distinctive wildlife.
2 In plants and flowers.
3 In products such as perfumes and fruit juices. (possible additional products: cosmetics, shampoos, soaps, air fresheners, household cleaning products, yoghurts, sweets etc.)

2 1 c   2 a   3 c

3 1 scents   2 balloon   3 variety

4 1 b   2 c   3 b

5
1 flavours
2 juicy
3 purchase

6
1 A scientist claimed he discovered a flower. T
2 The narrator reported that the scientists used technology to recreate scents. T
3 Professor Kaiser said that he had experienced the scent on the Tampolo River. T

Grammar Explorer

Unit 1

present simple, continuous and perfect

present simple

We use **present simple** to talk about:
- a regular activity, habit, activity often repeated
  I watch The X Factor every week.
- a permanent state
  My sister works in a department store.

We also use **present simple** to talk about:
- facts, general truths, laws of nature
  Pollution causes global warming.
- feelings and thoughts (see below: *verbs without a continuous form*)
  I hate TV soap operas.

Affirmative		
I/You/We/You/They He/She/It	make ... / watch ... / etc makes ... / watches ... / etc	
Negative		
I/You/We/You/They He/She/It	don't (do not) doesn't (does not)	make ... / watch ... / etc
Questions		
Do Does	I/you/we/you/they he/she/it	make ... / watch ... / etc?
Short answers					

	I/you/ we/you/they	do.		I/you/ we/you/they	don't.
Yes,			No,		
	he/she/it	does.		he/she/it	doesn't.

present continuous

We use the **present continuous** to talk about:

- an activity in progress – that is, which is happening now, at the time when we are talking
  Please be quiet – I'm watching my favourite TV show, and you're making so much noise I can't hear the singers!

- a temporary situation, around the time when we are talking
  He applied to be a contestant on a talent show, and he's waiting to hear if he's been accepted.

Affirmative		
I'm You're/We're/ You're/They're He's/She's/It's	(I am) (You/We/You/They are) (He/She/It is)	watching TV.
Negative		
I'm not You/We/You/They aren't He/She/It isn't	(I am not) (are not) (is not)	watching TV.
Questions		
Am Are Is	I you/we/you/they he/she/it	watching TV?
Short answers				

	I am.			I'm not.
Yes,	you/we/you/they are.		No,	you/we/you/they aren't.
	he/she/it is.			he/she/it isn't.

Notice the contrast between the present simple and the present continuous:

Present simple	
regular activity	permanent state
Present continuous	
activity in progress	temporary situation

verbs without a continuous form

Some verbs are called 'stative' or 'state' verbs, because they describe a state, feeling or thought rather than an action. We don't normally use present continuous with these verbs. They include:

> *believe, hate, know, like, love, need, prefer, seem, sound, think, understand, want*

I love reality TV shows. (Not: I ~~am loving~~ ...)
That celebrity seems quite arrogant. (Not: That celebrity ~~is seeming~~ ...
I think this show is a bit boring. (Not: I ~~am thinking~~ ...)
Many teenagers want to become famous through reality TV. (Not: Many teenagers ~~are wanting~~ ...)

present perfect

We use the **present perfect** to talk about:
- an action that happened during a period of time that started in the past and goes up to the present. (Exactly when the action happened is not known or not important.)
  I've watched this programme before.
  (an hour ago? a week ago? a year ago?)

- a state that began in the past, but continues up to the present.
  She has been a successful singer since she was a teenager.
  (She is still a successful singer now.)

- an action that has been completed a very short time ago.
  (This is almost always used with *just*.)
  They have just announced the winners of the competition.
  (They announced this a few seconds/minutes/etc ago.)

- an action that happened in the recent past, but which has a result in the present.
  (Notice that although we understand that the action happened in the past, we do not mention exactly when it happened.)
  He isn't on the show tonight because he's broken his leg.
  (Perhaps he broke it a few days ago, but we emphasise the result that this has tonight.)

Affirmative		
I/You/We/You/They He/She/It	've (have) 's (has)	been ... / done ... / etc
Negative		
I/You/We/You/They He/She/It	haven't (have not) hasn't (has not)	been ... / done ... / etc

Question		
Have	I/you/ we/they	(ever) been ... / done ... / etc?
Has	he/she/it	

Short answers					
Yes,	I/you/we/they have.	No,	I/you/we/they	haven't.
	he/she/it has.		he/she/it	hasn't.

present perfect and past simple

We have seen that we use the **present perfect** to talk about something happening in the past, as long as the action or time period has some connection with the present.

However, we do not use the present perfect to talk about completed action at a finished time in the past – we use the **past simple** instead.

We use this when:
- we say or understand when the action happened
  My favourite contestant left the show last week.
- we know that the period of time in which it happened is completely in the past and does not continue up to the present
  Charles Dickens wrote more than a dozen famous novels.
  (He died in 1870.)

present perfect with ever and never

We can use the words **ever** and **never** with the present perfect to refer to **experiences** – that is, something which someone has/hasn't done, at any time in their whole life up to the present.

We use **ever** in present perfect questions.
Ever always goes before the main verb.
Have you ever been on TV?

We use **never** in negative sentences with the present perfect.
Never always goes before the main verb.
I've never met a rock star.

present perfect with It's the first time ...

We can also use **It's the first/second/etc time ...** with the present perfect to talk about experiences.
This expression is mainly used in affirmative sentences.
We begin the sentence with *It's the first time*, followed by subject + verb in the present perfect.
In informal spoken English, we often add the word *ever* for emphasis. **It's the first time I've (ever) spoken to a TV celebrity.**

present perfect with for and since

We use the word **for** with the present perfect to talk about *duration* – that is, how long it has been from the start of a state or situation until now.
For is followed by a phrase that describes a period of time.
She has been a singer for three years.

We use the word **since** with the present perfect, for a state or situation which has continued up to the present, to talk about when it started.
Since is followed by a time/day/year/etc, or a phrase that describes a particular time.
She has been a singer since 2007.
I have loved cartoons since I was a young child.

yet, still, already and *just*

yet

We use the word **yet** with the **present perfect** in questions and negative sentences.
Yet with the present perfect always goes at the end of the sentence or clause.
We use *yet* to suggest that if something has not already happened, we expect it will happen soon.
Have you seen the new reality show yet?
No, I haven't seen it yet. I'll watch it this evening, though.

Grammar Explorer

We can also use **yet** with the **present simple** in questions and negative sentences.
As with the present perfect, *yet* with the present simple always goes at the end of the sentence or clause.
Is it time for the show to start yet?
No, it isn't time yet. It starts after the news.

still

We use the word **still** with the **present perfect** in negative sentences.
Still with the present perfect always goes immediately before *haven't/hasn't*.
We use *still* to show that something has not happened/changed yet; it often suggests that someone would expect the action/situation/etc to have happened/changed by now.
I still haven't decided who to vote for on The X Factor.

We can also use **still** with the **present simple** and **present continuous** in questions and affirmative sentences.
Still with the present simple goes before the main verb, but after the verb *be*.
I'm a teenager now, but I still like watching some children's TV shows.
He didn't sing very well on last night's show, but he's still my favourite contestant.
Still with the present continuous goes between the auxiliary *be* and the main verb in *-ing*.
I'm going to be a bit late, I'm afraid – I'm still trying to decide what to wear.

We can also use **still** with the **present simple** and **present continuous** in negative sentences, but this is not very common.
I've listened to this song several times, but I still don't understand what it's about.

already

We use the word **already** with the **present perfect** in affirmative sentences.
Already with the present perfect usually goes between *have/has* and the main verb.
We often use *already* to suggest that something has happened sooner than we expected.
She's only 19, but she has already starred in a popular comedy series on TV.

We can also use **already** with the **present simple** in affirmative sentences.
Already with the present simple usually goes before the main verb, but after the verb *be*.
The show only started a week ago, but I already know which contestant I like best.
The new show is already very popular.

just

We usually use the word **just** with the **present perfect** in affirmative sentences.
Just with the present perfect always goes between *have/has* and the main verb.
We use *just* to show that something has happened a (very) short time ago.
A new soap opera has just started on this channel. I watched the first episode last night.

because and because of

Because and **because of** are both used to introduce the reason for the action, state, opinion, etc which is mentioned in the main part of the sentence.
Because (of), followed by the reason, comes after the main part of the sentence.

Because is followed by a clause – that is, subject + full verb.
This soap opera is popular because it deals with real-life situations.
She's my favourite singer because she's got such an unusual voice.

Because of is followed by a noun or noun phrase.
Filming the outdoor scenes for the series was delayed because of rain.
This show isn't suitable for children, because of all the violence and bad language.

Notice that in written English, *because* and *because of* join the state, opinion, etc and the reason into one sentence.
In informal spoken English, the state, opinion, etc may be mentioned in the speaker's previous sentence, and the reason may be given in a separate (grammatically incomplete) sentence.
A: I really like this comedy series.
B: Do you? Why?
A: Because it's so funny!

Unit 2
present perfect continuous

We use the **present perfect continuous** to talk about a continuous activity which began in the past and has continued up to the present.

A 'continuous activity' is a single activity, rather than a series of actions, which was in progress all the time.
'Has continued up to the present' means that the activity is still in progress now (or has just finished).

present perfect simple				
have /has	+	past participle		
present continuous				
		be	+	present participle
present perfect continuous				
have / has	+	been	+	-ing

We form the present perfect continuous with **have been** or **has been**, followed by the **present participle** of the main verb.
We form the negative with **haven't been** or **hasn't been**, followed by the present participle of the main verb.
We make present perfect continuous questions by putting **Have/Has** before the subject, and then **been**, followed by the present participle of the main verb.
In short answers we use **have/has** or **haven't/hasn't**. We DON'T use **been** or the main verb.

Affirmative			
I/You/We/You/They He/She/It	've (have) 's (has)	been	studying / etc
Negative			
I/You/We/You/They He/She/It	haven't (have not) hasn't (has not)	been	studying / etc
Question			
Have Has	I/you/ we/they he/she/it	been	studying / etc?
Short answers					
---	---	---	---	---	---
Yes,	I/you/ we/they he/she/it	have. has.	No,	he/she/it I/you/ we/they	haven't. hasn't.

present perfect continuous with for and since

We use the word **for** with the present perfect continuous to talk about *duration* – that is, how long it has been from the start of a continuous activity until now.
For is followed by a phrase that describes a period of time.
I've been studying English *for four years*.

We use the word **since** with the present perfect continuous, for an activity which has continued up to the present, to talk about when it started.
Since is followed by a time/day/year/etc, or a phrase that describes a particular time.

I've been studying English	since	*2007*.
	since	*the age of twelve.*

present perfect continuous and present perfect simple

We have seen that we use the **present perfect continuous** to talk about a continuous activity beginning in the past and continuing up to the present.
I've been sending *emails all morning*.
(We see this as one activity.)

However, we use the **present perfect simple** – not the present perfect continuous – to talk about:
- a series of completed actions beginning in the past and continuing up to the present
  I've sent *fifteen emails so far this morning*.
  (By emphasising the number, we present this as fifteen separate actions.)

- a single decision, conclusion, etc which is the result of the continuous activity
  I've *already received several replies*.
- a state, thought or feeling, beginning in the past and continuing up to the present; see Unit 1: *verbs without a continuous form*
  I've been reading *this book for over an hour, but I haven't understood* (not 'haven't been understanding') *what it's about*.

relative clauses

We can join two short sentences together by making the second sentence into a **relative clause**; the first sentence contains the main information, and the relative clause gives further information about this.

The relative clause contains a pronoun or adverb which relates to a noun in the first sentence.
A bonobo *is a very intelligent animal*. (main information)
It *is a type of chimpanzee*. (further information)
(The pronoun 'it' relates to the noun 'bonobo'.)

We join the two parts of the sentence by changing the pronoun into a **relative pronoun** (e.g. *which*) and putting it next to the noun it relates to, followed by the rest of the relative clause.
(Notice that the relative pronoun REPLACES the subject pronoun – we DON'T use both pronouns together.)
A bonobo*, which is a type of chimpanzee*, is a very intelligent animal. (Not: which i̶t̶ is a type ...)

defining and non-defining relative clauses

The meaning of the first sentence is sometimes incomplete without the further information given in the relative clause. The relative clause defines the noun in the first sentence, and so it is a **defining relative clause**.
People *are afraid of heights*. (Which people? All people? Some people? The meaning of the sentence is not complete.)
They *have acrophobia*. (This defines which people we mean.)
People *who have acrophobia* are afraid of heights.

The animals *are chimpanzees*. (Which animals? The meaning of the sentence is not complete.)
They *are closest to humans*. (This defines which animals we mean.)
The animals *which are closest to humans* are chimpanzees.

If the meaning of the first sentence is complete on its own, the relative clause doesn't define the noun in the first sentence – it simply gives extra information – and so it is a **non-defining relative clause**.
Crows *can make their own tools*. (The meaning of the sentence is complete.)
They *are the most intelligent birds*. (This gives extra information.)
Crows*, which are the most intelligent birds*, can make their own tools.

Notice that a **defining relative clause** becomes part of the meaning of the main sentence, and so we DON'T use commas to separate the relative clause and the rest of the sentence.
People <u>who have acrophobia</u> are afraid of heights.
The animals <u>which are closest to humans</u> are chimpanzees.

With a **non-defining relative clause**, we DO use commas, before and after the relative clause, to separate the extra information from the main part of the sentence.
A bonobo, <u>which is a type of chimpanzee</u>, is a very intelligent animal.
Crows, <u>which are the most intelligent birds</u>, can make their own tools.

relative pronouns and relative adverbs

We have seen forming a relative clause involves replacing a pronoun or adverb with a relative pronoun or relative adverb. The **relative pronouns** we use are *who*, *which* and *whose*. The **relative adverbs** we use are *when* and *where*.

For **people**, we use the relative pronoun *who* to replace the pronouns *he, she, they, etc*.
People are afraid of heights. They have acrophobia.
People who have acrophobia are afraid of heights.

For **animals/things**, we use the relative pronoun *which* to replace the pronouns *it, they, etc*.
A bonobo is a very intelligent animal. It is a type of chimpanzee.
A bonobo, which is a type of chimpanzee, is a very intelligent animal.

For **people** <u>and</u> **animals/things**, we use the relative pronoun *whose* to replace the pronouns *his, her, their, its, etc*.
Derren Brown is a famous hypnotist. His TV show is very popular.
Derren Brown, whose TV show is very popular, is a famous hypnotist.

The bird couldn't fly. Its wing was broken.
The bird whose wing was broken couldn't fly.

For **times**, we use the relative adverb *when* to replace the adverb *then*.
At eight o'clock there is a lot of traffic. Most people are going to work then.
At eight o'clock, when most people are going to work, there is a lot of traffic. (Notice that 'then' goes next to 'eight o'clock', followed by the rest of the relative clause)

For **places**, we use the relative adverb *where* to replace the adverb *there*.
The place is a laboratory. Scientists do experiments there.
The place where scientists do experiments is a laboratory.
(Notice that 'where' goes next to 'place', followed by the rest of the relative clause)

In **defining** relative clauses – but not in non-defining relative clauses – we can use *that* instead of *who* or *which*.

People who have acrophobia are afraid of heights.
People that have acrophobia are afraid of heights.

The animals which are closest to humans are chimpanzees.
The animals that are closest to humans are chimpanzees.

question tags

Question tags are short questions added to the end of a statement. We use them mainly in spoken English. Question tags show that:
- the speaker expects/invites the listener(s) to say that they agree with the statement.
  My dog is lovely, (statement) *isn't he?* (question tag)
  – the speaker expects the answer 'Yes, he is.'
  You don't mind, (statement) *do you?* (question tag)
  – the speaker expects the answer 'No, I don't.'
- the speaker is not completely sure that the statement is correct, and wants to check.
  You're joking, (statement) *aren't you?* (question tag)
  – the speaker is not completely sure and wants to check.

We form a question tag with the same modal, auxiliary or form of *be* which is used in the statement, followed by the appropriate subject pronoun.
We do not use a name or a noun phrase in the question tag.
Joe will do the introduction, won't he? (Not: 'won't ~~Joe~~')
That dog is really smart, isn't it? (Not: 'isn't ~~that dog~~')

The question tag is the opposite of the statement – that is, if the statement is affirmative, the question tag is negative, and if the statement is negative, the question tag is affirmative.
Holly is (affirmative) *very organised, isn't* (negative) *she?*
Joe hasn't (negative) *got a good memory, has* (affirmative) *he?*

If there is no modal, auxiliary or form of *be* in the statement, we use *don't/doesn't*.
You know what to do, don't you?
Joe keeps forgetting things, doesn't he?

Unit 3
past perfect

We have seen that we use the present perfect to talk about an action/event that happened at some time before the present.

In the same way, we use past perfect to talk about an action/event that happened at some time before another action, event or time in the past. Exactly when the earlier action/event happened is usually not known or is not important.
When I arrived at the station, the train had already left.
(It left at some time – 1 minute? 5 minutes? – before I arrived.)
By six o'clock the sun had set.
(It set at some time – 5.30? 5.45? 5.59? – before six o'clock.)

We don't have to present the two actions/events in the same order in which they happened, but we must use the past perfect for the one which happened first.
Dinosaurs had been extinct for millions of years by the time the first humans evolved.

By the time the first humans evolved, dinosaurs had been extinct for millions of years.

We form the past perfect with **had/hadn't + past participle** of the main verb. It has the same form for all subjects (*I, he, we, etc*).

We form questions in the past perfect by putting **Had** before the subject, followed by the **past participle** of the main verb.

Affirmative		
I/You/He/She/It/We/You/They	had	been ... / made ... / etc
Negative		
I/You/He/She/It/We/You/They	hadn't (had not)	been ... / made ... / etc
Questions		
Had	I/you/he/she/it/we/you/they	been ... / made ... / etc ?
Short answers		
Yes, No,	I/you/he/she/it/we/you/they	had. hadn't.

used to

We can use **used to** for:
- past habits, states, etc. that are now finished
  I used to play with toy cars when I was a little boy. (I don't now)
  People used to believe the Moon was made of cheese. (now we know it isn't)
- things that existed or often happened in the past but do not exist/happen now.
  There used to be a farm here. (now there's a shopping mall)

The form is **used to + bare infinitive** of the main verb. It has the same form for all subjects (*I, you, he, etc*).

We form the negative with **didn't + use to + bare infinitive** of the main verb. Again, the form is the same for all subjects (*I, you, he, etc*).
People didn't use to have electricity in their homes. (now they do)

We form questions with **Did + subject + use to + bare infinitive** of the main verb.
Did you use to live in Manchester? (you live London now)

result clauses

Result clauses are used in sentences which first describe a situation and then say what happened/happens/will happen/etc as a result of this situation.
The result clause joins the situation and the result in a single sentence.

Situation	Result
The food was very salty.	*I couldn't eat it.*

The food was so salty that I couldn't eat it.

We form result clauses with **so + adjective + that ...** or **such (a/an) + adjective + noun + that ...** . (Remember that with uncountable nouns we don't use *a/an*.)
The food was very salty. (adjective)
The food was so salty that I couldn't eat it.

It was a very salty meal. (adjective + countable noun)
It was such a salty meal that I couldn't eat it.
It was very salty food. (adjective + uncountable noun)
It was such salty food that I couldn't eat it.

We can also form result clauses with **so many + plural noun** or **so much + uncountable noun**.
There *were so many people (plural)* **at the restaurant** *that we couldn't get a table.*
I *ate so much food (uncountable) that* **afterwards I felt ill.**

Unit 4
tenses used for the future

The basic tense we use to talk about the future is the **future simple** – but this is not the only tense we use. We use a variety of tenses to talk about:
- **future plans and arrangements**
- **predictions**
- **promises, offers, etc**

future plans and arrangements

Will is only ONE of the tenses we use to talk about the future. When we talk about future plans and arrangements, we can use **will**, **going to**, **present continuous** and **present simple**. Each of these shows something slightly different about the plans/arrangements.

- **will** is used to talk about **'on-the-spot' decisions** – that is, decisions we make at the moment of speaking, usually about the near future. It is just a general decision – we have not yet made any plans or arrangements.
  I'm hungry – I think I'll make myself a sandwich.

- **going to** is used to talk about **plans** for the near future, but **without definite arrangements** (or without mentioning these); after thinking about it, we know what we want to do and we will arrange the details later.
  I'm going to do all my homework on Friday evening so I'll have the rest of the weekend free.

As well as for informal plans about the near future, we use **going to** for our **ambitions** in the more distant future.
I'm going to go to art college next year. I'm going to study graphic design.

- the **present continuous** is used to talk about **definite arrangements** for the near future; we know (and usually mention) final details such as day/date, time and place.
  I'm flying to Prague tomorrow on the ten o'clock flight from Heathrow.

- **present simple** is used to talk about **'timetable'** arrangements which someone else makes, such as timetables for buses and trains, airline flight schedules, cinema times, the starting time of football matches, etc.
  The film starts at eight o'clock, so I'll meet you outside the cinema at half past seven.

predictions

- We can use **will**, **may** and **might** for predictions about the future, based on what we think, believe or hope.
  One day we will probably send astronauts to Mars.

- We can use **going to** for predictions about the future, based on what we see or know – that is, based on some evidence in the present.
  Look at those big black clouds! It's going to rain.

- We can also use **future continuous** for predictions – see *future continuous*, below.

Will, **may** and **might** have the same form for all subjects (*I, you, he*, etc). The main verb after these modals is in the **bare infinitive**.
The negative of **will** is **won't** (*will not*) and it is the same for all subjects. The negative of **may** and **might** is **may not** and **might not**, and these are also the same for all subjects.

Using **may** instead of **will** often suggests we are not so sure about our prediction, and **might** usually suggests we are even less sure. We often use these modals after *I think*, *I'm sure*, etc, and/or with words such as *probably*, *perhaps*, *certainly*, etc, to show more clearly how sure we are about our prediction.
I'm sure I will find a career in design when I leave school.
I think I may work as a graphic designer.
Perhaps I might even become a fashion designer.

other uses of will

In addition to future plans and arrangements and predictions, *will* is used for:

- **offers**
  I'll help you with your homework if you like

- **promises**
  Can I borrow this CD? I promise I won't lose it.

- **warnings**
  If you do that again I'll be angry.

- **requests**
  Will you water my plants while I'm on holiday, please?

- **statements of fact about the future**
  It's my Mum's birthday next week. She'll be 45.

future continuous

The **future continuous** is used for actions that (we expect or predict) will be in progress at a specific time in the future.
At this time tomorrow, I'll be lying on the beach.

I can't meet you at six o'clock, because I'll be doing my homework.
People will be using much more solar power in twenty years' time.

We form the future continuous with **will/won't + be + -ing**. It has the same form for all subjects (*I, he, we, etc*).
We form questions in the future continuous by putting **Will** before the subject, and then **be**, followed by the **-ing** form of the main verb.

Affirmative			
I/You/He/She/It/We/You/They	'll (will)	be	doing ... / going ... / etc
Negative			
I/You/He/She/It/We/You/They	won't (will not)	be	doing ... / going ... / etc
Questions			
Will	I/you/he/she/it/we/you/they	be	doing ... / going ... / etc ?
Short answers			
Yes, No,	I/you/he/she/it/we/you/they	will. won't.	

time expressions used for the future

Time expressions such as **after**, **as soon as**, **before**, **by the time**, **when**, **while** and **until** can be used to talk about the future, but they are not followed by *will* – instead, they are followed by a present tense (usually the present simple).

- **after, before** – used to show a sequence of actions/events
  I'll get dressed after I have a shower.
  (Not: *after I ~~will~~ have*)
  Finish your homework before you watch TV.
  (Not: *before you ~~will~~ watch*)

- **as soon as** – emphasises 'immediately after this'
  I'll go to bed as soon as I get home.
  (Not: *as soon as I ~~will~~ get*)

- **by the time** – means 'at some time before this'
  It'll be midnight by the time we finish.
  (Not: *by the time we ~~will~~ finish*)

- **when** – means 'at this time'
  Send me an email when you know what your plans are.
  (Not: *when you ~~will~~ know*)

- **while** – used for two things happening at the same time; mainly used with continuous tenses
  I'll be sitting at home while my friends are having a great time at the party. (Not: *while my friends ~~will be~~ having*)

- **until** – shows that something will change/happen after this, but not before
  Please remain seated until the exam is over.
  (Not: *until the exam ~~will be~~*)

Unit 5

the passive: present simple, past simple, present continuous, past continuous, present perfect

In active voice, the subject of the sentence is the person/thing/etc that does the action. When we use the **passive**, the subject is the person/thing/etc that the action happens to.

In other words, the object of a sentence in active voice becomes the subject of the sentence in the passive. If we want to say who/what does the action (the 'agent') in the passive, we use *by*.

SUBJECT	VERB	OBJECT	
The Ancient Greeks	*built*	*the Parthenon.*	(Active)

The Parthenon	*was built*	*by the Ancient Greeks.*	(Passive)
SUBJECT	VERB	AGENT	

We use the passive when we want to emphasise the subject and/or the action itself. If it is not important or not clear who/what the agent is (e.g. *someone*, *they*, *people*, etc), then we don't include it.

*They **have discovered** the remains of a Roman settlement.*
= The remains of a Roman settlement have been discovered ~~by them~~.

tenses in the passive

We form the passive with ***be*** + the **past participle** of the verb which is used in the active sentence; the tense of *be* is the same as the tense of the verb in the active sentence.

Simple tenses			
present	*is / are*		+ past participle
past	*was / were*		
Continuous tenses			
present	*is / are*	*being*	+ past participle
past	*was / were*		
Present perfect			
	has / have	*been*	+ past participle

*Thousands of tourists **visit** the city every day. (present simple)*
= The city is visited by thousands of tourists every day.

*Volcanic ash **covered** Pompeii. (past simple)*
= Pompeii was covered by volcanic ash.

*Tourism **is destroying** the local culture. (present continuous)*
= The local culture is being destroyed by tourism.

*They **were taking** the treasure to Spain. (past continuous)*
= The treasure was being taken to Spain ~~by them~~.

*They **have restored** many of the old buildings. (present perfect)*
= Many of the old buildings have been restored ~~by them~~.

the negative form of the passive

We form the negative by adding *n't* to the first modal/auxiliary in the sentence – that is, ***isn't/aren't*** in the present simple/continuous, ***wasn't/weren't*** in the past simple/continuous, and ***hasn't/haven't*** in the present perfect.
Damage to the monument isn't caused by the weather, but by tourists.
The building wasn't being used until they turned it into a museum.
A solution to the problem hasn't been found yet.

questions in the passive

We form questions in the passive by putting the first modal/auxiliary in the sentence – ***Is/Are***, ***Was/Were*** or ***Has/Have*** – before the subject.
Were famous places always protected by special laws?
Is the statue being displayed to the public?
Has anything been discovered about the people who lived here?

We can also begin questions with **question words** such as ***What***, ***Why***, ***Where***, ***How*** etc to ask for extra information rather than a simple 'Yes' or 'No' answer.
What is the statue made of?
Why has the ancient city been closed to tourists?
How were the Pyramids built?

the passive with modal verbs

We have seen that we form the passive with ***be*** **+ past participle**, and that the tense/form of *be* is the same as the tense/form of the verb in the active sentence.

If a sentence in active voice contains a modal such as ***can/can't***, ***must/mustn't*** or ***will/won't***, the modal is followed by the **bare infinitive**.
In the same way, if a sentence in the passive contains one of these modals, the modal is followed by the bare infinitive of ***be***, and then the past participle of the main verb.

They can make beautiful jewellery from gold.
Beautiful jewellery can be made from gold.

People must do something about the problem.
Something must be done about the problem.

causative form

We use the **causative form** to talk about an action which the subject does not do themselves.
That is, someone else does the action for them (for example, cuts their hair, fixes their computer, etc), but the subject has the result of the action (a new haircut, a computer that works properly, etc).

The causative form is **have + object + past participle** of the main verb.
Have is used as a normal verb in any tense.
I have my teeth checked every six months. (the dentist checks them)
Sandra had her car repaired yesterday. (a mechanic repaired it)
They're going to have the house painted. (painters are going to paint it)
Len has had his hair dyed blonde. (the hairdresser has dyed it)

As with the passive, we don't mention the agent (that is, the person who actually does the action) if it is obvious, not important or not clear.
She's having her hair cut this afternoon ~~by the hairdresser~~.

We can also use **get + object + past participle**, especially with tenses for the future, to emphasise that we will make arrangements for someone else to do something for us, or tell someone else to do it.

Unit 6
modal verbs for speculation

Speculation is guessing – that is, trying to decide, based on incomplete evidence, whether a suggested explanation, theory, etc is possible, impossible or probable.

We use the modal verbs **may**, **might**, **could**, **can't**, **couldn't** and **must** to speculate about an event or situation.
May, **might** and **could** all show that we think the explanation is possible; **can't** and **couldn't** show that we think this is impossible; and **must** shows that we think this is probable or perhaps almost certain.
Notice that we do not normally use **can** to speculate, and we NEVER use **mustn't**; we normally use **couldn't** only for speculation about the past.

When we speculate about the present, the modals are followed by a normal **bare infinitive**.

(Situation: I don't know where my keys are)
They may / might / could be in my school bag, I suppose. (it's possible)
They can't be in my purse – I've looked there. (it's impossible)
They must be in the pocket of my other jeans – I think that's where I left them. (it's probable)

When we speculate about the past, the modals are followed by a bare **perfect infinitive** – that is, **have + past participle** of the main verb.

(Situation: I don't know why my friend didn't call me last night)
She may / might / could have fallen asleep, I suppose. (it's possible)
She can't / couldn't have forgotten – she always calls me. (it's impossible)
She must have lost her mobile again. (it's probable)

second conditional

We use the **second conditional** to talk about an imaginary action, situation or result which depends on an imaginary condition – *not* a real condition – in the present and/or future.

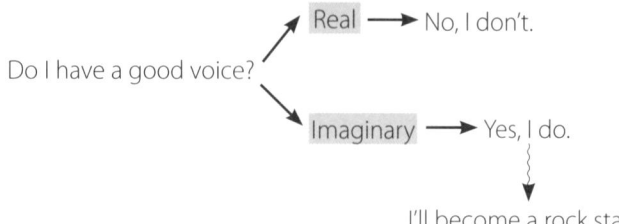

If I had a good voice, I'd become a rock star.

We form the second conditional with **If + past simple** for the condition, followed by **would /wouldn't * + bare infinitive** for the resulting action or situation. We do not use **would** for the condition.

* We can also use could/couldn't or might/mightn't, but this is the most common pattern.

We can put the two parts of the sentence in any order – but notice that when the sentence begins with the condition, we must put a comma between the condition and the result.
If I knew the answer (condition), I'd tell you (result).
I would live in a big house (result) if I had lots of money (condition).

> Notice that the use of past simple in the condition does not show completed action – it shows 'not real'.
> **If + past simple** = imaginary ('unreal'), in the present/future.

Unit 7
third conditional

We use the **third conditional** to talk about an imaginary action, event or situation in the past, which depends on an imaginary past condition.
The imaginary condition and the resulting action or situation are the opposite of what really happened.

> **What really happened:** *He didn't take a map, so he got lost.*
> **Imaginary situation:** *He took a map, so he didn't get lost.*
> *If he had taken a map, he wouldn't have got lost.*

We form the third conditional with **If + past perfect** for the condition, followed by **would/wouldn't * + have + past participle** for the resulting action or situation.

* We can also use could/couldn't or might/mightn't, but this is the most common pattern.

We can put the two parts of the sentence in any order – but notice that when the sentence begins with the condition, we must put a comma between the condition and the result.
If we had been more careful (condition)*, the accident wouldn't have happened* (result)**.**
I wouldn't have missed my train (result) *if I had got up early* (condition)**.**

could/should have done

We use **could(n't) have / should(n't) have + past participle** to talk about events, actions and situations in the past; we usually imagine something which is in contrast to what really happened.

could(n't) have

We use **could(n't) have + past participle** to talk about:
- **possibility**
  Why did you do that? You could have had an accident! (*This was a possibility – but it didn't happen.*)
- **ability / opportunity**
  Why didn't you tell me about your problem? I could have helped you. (*I had the ability to help you – but I didn't know, so I didn't help.*)
  Che Guevara could have become rich. (*He had the ability and/or opportunity to do this – but he decided not to.*)
  Don't feel bad - you couldn't have prevented what happened. (*Even if you had tried harder / in a different way, it wouldn't have worked.*)

should(n't) have

We use **should(n't) have + past participle** to talk about right and wrong. This includes:
- **results**
  Our team should have won the match – we were much better than them. (*This would have been the 'right' result – but it didn't happen.*)
- **regrets / criticism**
  I should have studied harder for the exam. (*This would have been the right thing to do – but I didn't do it.*)
  You shouldn't have shouted at her. (*You did shout at her – but it was the wrong thing to do.*)

regrets and criticism

Regrets are the feelings we have when we realise that we have made a bad decision in the past – that is, we did something that was wrong, or didn't do the right thing.

Criticism is when we tell someone else that they did something that was wrong, or didn't do the right thing.

I wish and *If only ... !*

We use *I wish* and *If only ... !* to make statements about imaginary situations which are the opposite of what really happened; they show that we regret what really happened.

When we talk about the past, *I wish* and *If only* are followed by the past perfect.

I stayed up late last night. (what really happened)
I wish / If only I hadn't stayed up late last night!

I didn't do my homework yesterday. (what really happened)
I wish / If only I'd done my homework yesterday!

We can use *I wish ... !* in the same way to criticise what someone else did or didn't do.

You told everyone my secret. (what really happened)
I wish you hadn't told everyone my secret!

You weren't honest about this. (what really happened)
I wish you'd been honest about this!

should(n't) have

We can also use **should(n't) have + past participle** to express our regrets or to criticise someone else's actions in the past.

I didn't think about it carefully. (what really happened)
I should have thought about it carefully.

I left it until the last minute. (what really happened)
I shouldn't have left it until the last minute.

You didn't listen to me. (what really happened)
You should have listened to me.

Unit 8
reported statements
direct and reported speech

Direct speech gives the exact words someone said and uses quotation marks ('...') to show this.
Reported speech gives the meaning of what somebody said, but doesn't use all their exact words and doesn't use quotation marks. For example, we use reported speech when we tell somebody else what another person said.
'I'll meet you here tomorrow,' John said to Susan. (*Direct speech*)
John said he would meet Susan there the next day. (*Reported speech*)

backshift

When we report what a person said, the time of speaking is not the same as the time of reporting. For example, what was the present at the time of speaking has usually already become the past at the time of reporting.

Grammar Explorer

For this reason, we often use 'backshift' in reported speech – that is, the tense of a verb used in direct speech moves one step back into the past.

Direct Speech	Reported Speech
Present Simple *'We are very happy with the product.'*	Past Simple *He said they were very happy with the product.*
Present Continuous *'We are trying to make the product even better.'*	Past Continuous *He said they were trying to make the product even better.*
Present Perfect *'We have made several changes this year.'*	Past Perfect* *He said they had made several changes that year.*
Past Simple *'We made several changes last year, too.'*	Past Perfect* *He said they had made several changes the year before, too.*
Present Perfect Continuous *'We have been making the product for 10 years.'*	Past Perfect Continuous* *He said they had been making the product for 10 years.*
Past Continuous *'We were making the product 10 years ago.'*	Past Perfect Continuous* *He said they had been making the product 10 years before.*
will *'Customers will notice a big difference.'*	*would* *He said customers would notice a big difference.*
can *'Customers can order products online.'*	*could* *He said customers could order products online.*
must / have to *'We must keep our customers satisfied.'*	*had to* *He said they had to keep their customers satisfied.*

* Notice that present perfect and past simple both 'backshift' to the same tense – past perfect. Present perfect continuous and past continuous both 'backshift' to past perfect continuous.

other changes in reported speech

When we report what a person says, the place, listener(s), etc at the time of speaking are often different to the place, listener(s), etc at the time of reporting.

For example, imagine that on Monday John speaks to Susan in the park: - *'I'll meet you here tomorrow,' John said.*
On Friday, Susan is in the cafeteria, telling a friend about the conversation; what was 'tomorrow' when John spoke is now several days ago, what was 'here' is now far away, and so on. What Susan reports is: - *John said he would meet me there the next day.*

Direct Speech	Reported Speech
I – we	he/she – they
me – us	him/her – them
my – your – our	his/her – their
here	there
this – these	that – those
now	then / at that time
last night/week/etc	the night/week/etc before / the previous night/week/etc
this morning/afternoon/etc	that morning/afternoon/etc
next week/July/etc	the next week/July/etc / the following week/July/etc
yesterday	the day before / the previous day
today	that day / the same day
tomorrow	the next/following day

reporting verbs

In direct speech, the exact words someone uses can show us if they are speaking (e.g.) politely, angrily, etc; in reported speech, where we don't use their exact words, we can use different **reporting verbs** to show this sort of information.

Direct speech	Reported speech
'Sit down – now!' he shouted.	*He ordered me to sit down.*
'Sit down,' he said.	*He told me to sit down.*
'Sit down, please,' he said.	*He asked me to sit down.*
'Would you like to sit down?' he said.	*He invited me to sit down.*
'I'd sit down if I was you,' he said.	*He advised me to sit down.*

Reporting verbs we use in this way include:
> advise   ask   invite   order
> remind   tell   warn

The normal pattern is **verb + object (+ not) + full infinitive**
The teacher told her students (not) to open their books.
But: we usually don't *invite* or *remind* someone not to do something
we usually <u>only</u> *warn* someone <u>not</u> to do something

There are other reporting verbs which don't follow the pattern of **verb + sb* + full infinitive**. *(In the patterns shown below, sb means 'somebody' and sth means 'something'.)* These verbs include:
accuse sb* of + -ing
'You stole her bag,' the policeman said to him.
→ *The policeman accused <u>him of stealing</u> her bag.*

admit + -ing
'Yes, I stole her bag,' he said.
→ He **admitted** <u>stealing</u> her bag.

apologise for + -ing
'I'm sorry I stole your bag,' he said to her.
→ He **apologised** <u>for stealing</u> her bag.

deny + -ing
'No, I didn't steal her bag,' he said.
→ He **denied** <u>stealing</u> her bag.

describe sth* (to sb*)
'My bag was big and brown,' she said to the policeman.
→ She **described** <u>her bag</u> (to the policeman).

offer ~~sb~~ + full infinitive
'I'll carry your bag for you,' he said to her.
→ He **offered** <u>to carry</u> her bag.

refuse ~~sb~~ + full infinitive
'No, I won't give your bag back,' he said to her.
→ He **refused** <u>to give</u> her bag back.

reported questions

We make a statement into a **direct question** by putting
a modal, auxiliary or form of *be* before the subject. If the
statement does not have a modal, auxiliary or form of *be*, we
add *do/does/did* before the subject.
I like shopping. *(Statement)*
Do you like shopping? *(Direct question)*

We can also make a statement into a direct question
beginning with a **question word** such as ***What***, ***When***, ***How***,
etc. Again, we put a modal, auxiliary or *be* before the subject,
and if the statement does not have a modal, auxiliary or *be*,
we add *do/does/did* before the subject.
I like buying clothes. *(Statement)*
What do you like buying? *(Direct question)*

A **reported question** begins with a phrase such as *She asked
me ...* , and the rest of the reported question goes back to
the word order of statements – that is, **subject + modal/
auxiliary** (if there is one) **+ verb**. Notice also that we use
backshift, as in reported statements.
She asked me what I liked buying. *(Reported question)*

If the direct question does not begin with a question word,
we use the word ***if*** in the reported question. Again, the word
order goes back to the word order of statements.
Do you save money regularly? *(Direct question)*
She asked me if I saved money regularly. *(Reported question)*

Unit 1 Worksheet

STUDENT A

Choose your favourite celebrity (e.g. actor, actress, singer, musician, sportsperson or TV personality) and make notes about him or her on each of the topics listed. Write your notes in the 'You' column. Answer your partner's questions about this person but do not give his/her name. Then ask your partner questions about his/her celebrity and write notes in the 'Your partner' column. Can you guess who it is?

	You	Your partner
Age		
Nationality		
Profession		
Team / group / film		
Physical description		
Main achievements		
Why I like him/her		
What I don't like		
Other information		
Who am I?		

✂ -

STUDENT B

Choose your favourite celebrity (e.g. actor, actress, singer, musician, sportsperson or TV personality) and make notes about him or her on each of the topics listed. Write your notes in the 'You' column. Ask your partner questions about his/her celebrity and write notes in the 'Your partner' column. Can you guess who it is? Then answer your partner's questions about your celebrity.

	You	Your partner
Age		
Nationality		
Profession		
Team / group / film		
Physical description		
Main achievements		
Why I like him/her		
What I don't like		
Other information		
Who am I?		

Unit 2 Worksheet

STUDENT A

Choose eight family members or people you know well and in the 'My family' columns write who they are (e.g. *cousin, sister* etc.) and adjectives to describe their personality (e.g. *nosy, bossy, superstitious, practical, moody, funny, entertaining, happy, sad, quiet, noisy*). Take turns to ask questions (e.g. *Who is number 1? What is she like?*) and answer your partner's questions about each person (e.g. *Number 1 is my sister. She's very quiet and practical, and she's good at making things.*). Note the answers in the 'My partner's family' column.

My family		My partner's family	
1		1	
2		2	
3		3	
4		4	
5		5	
6		6	
7		7	
8		8	

STUDENT B

Choose eight family members or people you know well and in the 'My family' columns write who they are (e.g. *cousin, sister* etc.) and adjectives to describe their personality (e.g. *nosy, bossy, superstitious, practical, moody, funny, entertaining, happy, sad, quiet, noisy*). Take turns to ask questions (e.g. *Who is number 1? What is she like?*) and answer your partner's questions about each person (e.g. *Number 1 is my sister. She's very quiet and practical, and she's good at making things.*). Note the answers in the 'My partner's family' column.

My family		My partner's family	
1		1	
2		2	
3		3	
4		4	
5		5	
6		6	
7		7	
8		8	

Unit 3 Worksheet

STUDENT A

Think about when you were younger. What did you use to do that you don't do now? What didn't you use to do that you do now? What did your family use to do that they have stopped doing? Make some notes in the 'My past' column for each of the categories. If you want to add some other categories, use the 'Other' rows at the bottom of the table. Answer your partner's questions, and then ask him/her about his/her past (e.g. *What did you use to eat?*) and write down sentences about what they tell you in the 'My partner's past' column.

	My past	My partner's past
Food / drink		
Sports / games		
Pets		
Likes / dislikes		
Interests / hobbies		
Places visited / holidays		
People known / visited		
TV programmes / music		
Other: _____		
Other: _____		

✂ -

STUDENT B

Think about when you were younger. What did you use to do that you don't do now? What didn't you use to do that you do now? What did your family use to do that they have stopped doing? Make some notes in the 'My past' column for each of the categories. If you want to add some other categories, use the 'Other' rows at the bottom of the table. Answer your partner's questions, and then ask him/her about his/her past (e.g. *What did you use to eat?*) and write down sentences about what they tell you in the 'My partner's past' column.

	My past	My partner's past
Food / drink		
Sports / games		
Pets		
Likes / dislikes		
Interests / hobbies		
Places visited / holidays		
People known / visited		
TV programmes / music		
Other: _____		
Other: _____		

Unit 4 Worksheet

STUDENT A

In the table below you have some of the information about the jobs of six people, and three things they have to do in their jobs; your partner has the missing information. Ask your partner questions to complete the table (e.g. *What job does Julie do? What's the first / second / third thing that Clare does in her job?*).

	Paul	Sarah	Barry	Julie	Steve	Clare
	Football manager		Chef		Postal worker	
1		Chooses photos and pictures	Selects meat and vegetables at the market	Visits companies		Learns how to shoot guns
2	Organises the team	Designs adverts and books			Delivers letters	
3				Does calculations		Wears a uniform

STUDENT B

In the table below you have some of the information about the jobs of six people, and three things they have to do in their jobs; your partner has the missing information. Ask your partner questions to complete the table (e.g. *What job does Barry do? What's the first / second / third thing that Paul does in his job?*).

	Paul	Sarah	Barry	Julie	Steve	Clare
		Graphic Designer		Accountant		Soldier
1	Discusses tactics with the players				Wears a uniform	
2			Invents new dishes	Looks at income and spending		Gives people orders
3	Supervises the training of the players	Chooses colours	Puts food onto the plates attractively		Collects mail from post boxes	

Unit 5 Worksheet

STUDENT A

Write at least two things which can be made of each of the materials in the list below. Then take it in turns to guess one of your partner's objects by asking questions (e.g. *What colour is the object made of rubber? Is it in the house / the classroom? Can you wear it? How big is it?*). You have 2 minutes for each object. Write the objects you guess correctly in the table below.

	My object 1	My object 2	My partner's object 1	My partner's object 2
Rubber				
Plastic				
Leather				
Stone				
Wood				
Wool				
Metal				
Glass				

✂ -

STUDENT B

Write at least two things which can be made of each of the materials in the list below. Then take it in turns to guess one of your partner's objects by asking questions (e.g. *What colour is the object made of rubber? Is it in the house / the classroom? Can you wear it? How big is it?*). You have 2 minutes for each object. Write the objects you guess correctly in the table below.

	My object 1	My object 2	My partner's object 1	My partner's object 2
Rubber				
Plastic				
Leather				
Stone				
Wood				
Wool				
Metal				
Glass				

Unit 6 Worksheet

STUDENT A

You and your partner are detectives who are trying to solve a murder mystery.
You have some information about the crime, and your partner has some different
information. Find out and make notes on what your partner knows. Discuss the
evidence together, decide what you know and speculate on who committed the crime,
e.g. *Mr Carr must have died at … The murderer could / may / might have been X because …*
It can't be Y because … It must be …. Write five sentences.

- Robert Carr was the Managing Director of Carr Electronics, a company that makes computer parts. The company was having serious problems, and Robert wanted to make some changes to the company to save money.
- Mr Robert Carr's body was found by his secretary, Mrs Janet Gibbs. She immediately called the police. Mr Carr had been hit on the head with a heavy glass vase from his desk. He had been dead for about four hours.
- Jonathan Carr admitted that he and his father had had an argument because he didn't agree with the changes his father wanted to make to the company. He was worried that he was going to lose his job as Deputy Director.
- Alice Carr had had an argument with Robert Carr, because he hadn't made his divorce payments to her.
- The police found evidence that the back door of Robert Carr's house had been forced open.

Notes

Robert Carr (victim) _____

Mr Janet Gibbs (secretary) _____

Jonathan Carr (son) _____

Alice Carr (ex-wife) _____

Other evidence _____

- -

STUDENT B

You and your partner are detectives who are trying to solve a murder mystery.
You have some information about the crime, and your partner has some different
information. Find out and make notes on what your partner knows. Discuss the
evidence together, decide what you know and speculate on who committed the crime,
e.g. *Mr Carr must have died at … The murderer could / may / might have been X because …*
It can't be Y because … It must be …. Write five sentences.

- At 11 a.m. on Thursday 9th June the dead body of Mr Robert Carr was found in his study at his home.
- Robert Carr's son, Jonathan Carr, had visited him in the evening of Wednesday 8th June. They had eaten dinner together and discussed the problems with the company. Jonathan left at ten o'clock and drove back to his flat in London.
- Robert Carr's divorced wife, Alice, had spoken to him on the phone at 22.30 on the evening of Wednesday 8th June. She was in her flat at the other end of the village where they both live, five minutes walk away.
- Mrs Janet Gibbs admitted that she was very angry with Robert Carr because he hadn't paid her wages for the past two months.
- When the contents of Robert Carr's house were checked by the police a number of valuable items were missing – some Chinese vases, two French paintings and some English silver knives.

Notes

Robert Carr (victim) _____

Mr Janet Gibbs (secretary) _____

Jonathan Carr (son) _____

Alice Carr (ex-wife) _____

Other evidence _____

Unit 7 Worksheet

STUDENT A

Below are some notes on all the problems you had last week. Your partner will ask you about them (e.g. *What happened (to you) on Monday? Did you have any problems on Tuesday?*), and you will tell him/her what happened. Use full sentences and add any extra information you can think of (e.g. *I got up really late on Monday, because I went to bed late the night before. So when I woke up it was already 7.45. I got dressed quickly and I didn't have any breakfast, but I had missed the bus ...*). Your partner will then make suggestions about what you *could / should have done* to avoid the problems. Take it in turns to ask your partner about his/her problems and make suggestions.

Day	Problem
Monday	got up late / missed the bus / late for school
Tuesday	walked 2km to main post office to collect a parcel / post office shut
Wednesday	went to buy new shoes / at the cash desk no wallet / left it at home
Thursday	arranged to cycle to the country with friends after school / went home to get bike / brother had taken it
Friday	had a bad headache / went to a party with friends as planned / had to leave early / headache worse

STUDENT B

Below are some notes on all the problems you had last week. Your partner will ask you about them (e.g. *What happened (to you) on Monday? Did you have any problems on Tuesday?*), and you will tell him/her what happened. Use full sentences and add any extra information you can think of (e.g. *On Monday I got home from school as usual at 4 o'clock, but the door was locked and there was nobody at home. I looked in my bag, but I didn't have my key. Then it started to rain really hard ...*). Your partner will then make suggestions about what you *could / should have done* to avoid the problems. Take it in turns to ask your partner about his/her problems and make suggestions.

Day	Problem
Monday	got home from school at 16.00 / hadn't got a house key / nobody was at home / it started to rain / no umbrella / mother home at 18.00
Tuesday	got up / went to school by 08.00 as usual / school closed for National Holiday
Wednesday	fell over on the way home from school / cut leg / went to volleyball training at 18.00 / couldn't play because leg hurt too much
Thursday	mum gave you a shopping list / lost it / bought wrong things at the shop / mum angry
Friday	went to meet friend in town at 18.30 / friend didn't come / mobile phone had no credit

Unit 8 Worksheet

STUDENT A

Situation 1: You are a customer. Your grandmother bought you a portable DVD player and screen for your birthday last Saturday. It cost 150 euros. You need it for your film studies course at school. Take it back to the shop. Tell the shop assistant (your partner) that it has several problems, and you want them to replace it or give you the money back. Explain what is wrong with it:

- The screen doesn't close properly so it's difficult to carry.
- It takes a long time to read a DVD before it plays it.
- It won't play Blue-ray DVDs although it says on the box that it will.

Depending on what the sales assistant tells you, decide what to do.

Situation 2: You are a shop assistant. A customer comes in with a digital camera. It cost 120 euros.

- Ask what the problem is with the camera.
- Apologise for the problems. Say that you think the camera has been damaged, as it is normally a very good camera.
- Ask if they have a receipt.
- Tell them that they can exchange it for another camera of the same model, or they can have a credit note for 120 euros.

Useful phrases

Sales assistant:
Hello, can I help you?
Is there something wrong with it?
What is the problem exactly?
Have you got the receipt?
I'm afraid we can't ... but we can ...
Would you like a credit note?

Customer:
I'd like to return this ...
I'm not at all happy with it.
It doesn't seem to be working.
I think it's faulty / broken.
Would it be possible to get my
   money back?

STUDENT B

Situation 1: You are a shop assistant. A customer comes in with a portable DVD player and screen. It cost 150 euros.

- Ask what the problem is with it.
- Tell them no other customers have ever had problems with this model.
- Explain that they have to switch on the Blue-ray function to play Blu-ray DVDs.
- Say that you can't replace it – you don't have another one of the same model.
- Say that you can't give them a refund, but they can have a credit note, or exchange it for another model.

Situation 2: You are a customer. You bought a digital camera with money you were given for your birthday. It cost 120 euros. Take it back to the shop with the receipt. Tell the shop assistant (your partner) that you'd like them to replace it or give you the money back. Explain what is wrong with it:

- The case was broken when you took it out of the box.
- The photos you have taken are not very good quality and you think it is faulty.
- It says on the box that you can take up to 300 photos, but you have only taken 10 and there is no more memory.

Depending on what the sales assistant tells you, decide what to do.

Useful phrases

Sales assistant:
Hello, can I help you?
Is there something wrong with it?
What is the problem exactly?
Have you got the receipt?
I'm afraid we can't ... but we can ...
Would you like a credit note?

Customer:
I'd like to return this ...
I'm not at all happy with it.
It doesn't seem to be working.
I think it's faulty / broken.
Would it be possible to get my
   money back?

Vocabulary

1 Complete the sentences with these words.

audience	programme	journalist
channel	listener	article

1 There was a large ___audience___ at the theatre last night.

2 'Which _____ is the film on? BBC or ITV?'

3 There was an interesting _____ about snakes on TV last night.

4 Did you see that _____ about reality TV in *The Times*?

5 Paul is a sports _____ for the local paper.

6 A(n) _____ complained about yesterday's radio play.

2 marks for each correct answer. Total _____ / 10

2 Complete the sentences with words about the mind.

1 You need to t *h i* n *k* carefully about your future.

2 Do you r _ _ _ m _ _ r what I said yesterday?

3 I don't u _ d _ _ s _ _ _ d what this word means.

4 Sarah is a very c _ e _ _ _ v _ girl.

5 My grandfather's m _ m _ _ y isn't very good now.

6 Can you i _ _ g _ _ e what life will be like in 20 years?

2 marks for each correct answer. Total _____ / 10

Grammar

3 Complete the sentences with the present simple or present continuous form of the verbs.

Peter (1) ___lives___ (live) in Manchester. He (2) _____ (like) football very much, and today he (3) _____ (watch) a very important match: Manchester United (4) _____ (play) Manchester City! Peter (5) _____ (sit) with some friends in his usual seat. He always (6) _____ (go) to Manchester United's home matches, and he often (7) _____ (travel) to see them play in different places. It's half-time now, and Peter and his friends (8) _____ (drink) some tea – it's cold this afternoon. Peter (9) _____ (think) that Manchester United will win, but his friends (10) _____ (be) not so sure. Manchester City (11) _____ (win) 1-0 at the moment, and the second half will be difficult.

1 mark for each correct answer. Total _____ / 10

4 Complete the sentences with *yet, still, already* or *just*.

1 Mike has ___just___ finished his homework.

2 I've ———— seen this James Bond film.

3 He's in England, but he hasn't visited London ————.

4 Lucy ———— hasn't cleaned her room!

5 Have you washed your hair ———— ?

6 I've ———— heard a great new song!

1 mark for each correct answer. Total _____ / 5

5 Complete the sentences with the present perfect continuous form of these verbs.

work	study	live	take	sit	go

1 Dan ___has been working___ in the USA for two years.

2 Grandma looks ill. She (not) _____ her tablets every day.

3 _____ you _____ to ballet classes for a long time?

4 Mike _____ Bulgarian since he moved to Sofia.

5 How long _____ they _____ in the sun?

6 We _____ in this street for thirty years.

1 mark for each correct answer. Total _____ / 5

6 Write each pair of sentences as one sentence, using *when, where, which, who* or *whose*.

1 John is a gardener. He works for Mrs Brown.
John, who works for Mrs Brown, is a gardener.

2 Ann lives next door. Her garden is lovely.
_____

3 Margate is nice. We go there on holiday.
_____

4 In June it is usually sunny. We go to Margate.
_____

5 Ramsgate is also a seaside town. It is smaller than Margate.
_____

6 Mr Jones is Scottish. He teaches us history.
_____

1 mark for each correct answer. Total _____ / 5

7 Complete the sentences with the correct tag.

1 You live here, ___don't you___ ?

2 They haven't got a computer, _____ ?

3 Your mother works in a bank, _____ ?

4 It's his birthday tomorrow, _____ ?

5 You're not tired, _____ ?

6 He isn't here today, _____ ?

1 marks for each correct answer. Total _____ / 5

Communicate

8 Complete the dialogue with these phrases.

I think	That's true	In my opinion
Do you think so	That's because	I don't think so

Anna: I saw *AlphaBeta* on TV last night. (1) *I think* they're great.

Paul: (2) _____ ? I don't like them. Their songs sound old-fashioned!

Anna: (3) _____ . They're very different. I really like them.

Paul: (4) _____ they're good-looking boys!

Anna: (5) _____ it doesn't matter what they look like. What matters is the music.

Paul: (6) _____ ! But I'm not sure that *AlphaBeta* really sing quality songs …

2 marks for each correct answer. Total _____ / 10

9 Complete the dialogue with suitable words or phrases.

Tom: What (1) *have you been* doing? I haven't seen you (2) _____ ages!

Jo: I (3) _____ working in my dad's shop this week.

Tom: He's got a bookshop, (4) _____ ?

Jo: Yes, I've (5) _____ worked there a few times, but this time I was in the children's section because the girl (6) _____ usually works there was ill.

2 marks for each correct answer. Total _____ / 10

Reading

10 Read the text. Are the sentences true (T) or false (F)?

Many young people – actors, musicians, sports stars – are not ready for the way their life changes when they become famous. Performing in public is only a small part of the job. Once they are stars, then newspaper journalists, television reporters and photographers follow them everywhere. Everything they say or do becomes a headline on the front page of the world's newspapers. They find that it is impossible to have a normal relationship with their boyfriend or girlfriend, because the media try to find out everything about them and their families, too. And, of course, if they refuse to speak to reporters, then the newspapers say they are arrogant or unfriendly. If they are lucky, young stars get a good manager who helps to protect them from this kind of attention. Surprisingly, money can also cause problems when young people suddenly become very rich. They don't always know what to do with it, and if they are not careful, they can spend too much buying unnecessary luxuries to show how rich they are. It is important for them to save their money for the future, because no footballer knows how long they will stay healthy and fit, and no pop star can be sure that their next hit will not be their last one.

1 ___T___ Many famous young people have problems with their fame.

2 _____ Performing to an audience is the most difficult thing for stars.

3 _____ The attention of the media is the only problem for famous people.

4 _____ Journalists don't like it if stars don't speak to them.

5 _____ It is easy for young stars to find a helpful manager.

6 _____ Fame does not always last a long time.

1 mark for each correct answer. Total _____ / 5

11 Read the text again and answer these questions with full sentences.

1 Why do stars find media attention difficult?
Because everything they do is in the papers.

2 What happens when they have a relationship?
_____

3 What happens if they try to keep their lives private? _____

4 Why is a good manager important for them?
_____

5 What happens if they don't know what to do with their money? _____

6 Why do they need to plan for their future?
_____

1 mark for each correct answer. Total _____ / 5

Listening

CD 2 track 42

12 Listen to two people talking about a film. Are the sentences true (T) or false (F)?

1 ___T___ Mike and Jill have just seen a new Jane Fond film.

2 _____ Mike thought the film was very good.

3 _____ Jill liked the new Jane Fond actor.

4 _____ Jill thought Brady made the film too funny.

5 _____ Mike says that Fond films have always had funny parts in them.

6 _____ Paul likes the new film too.

2 marks for each correct answer. Total _____ / 10

Writing

13 Write five sentences about a film, a book or a band. Say what you like and don't like.

2 marks for each correct sentence. Total _____ / 10

Total _____ / 100

Vocabulary

1 Complete the sentences with the correct words.

1 There are sixty __seconds__ in a minute.
2 There are sixty minutes in one _____.
3 There are twenty-four hours in one _____.
4 There are seven days in one _____.
5 There are fourteen days in one _____.
6 There are four weeks in one _____.
7 There are twelve months in a _____.
8 There are ten years in a _____.
9 There are one hundred years in a _____.
10 There are one thousand years in a _____.
11 All of the first ten sentences are about _____.

1 mark for each correct answer. Total _____ / 10

2 Complete the sentences with these jobs.

| actor | accountant | mechanic |
| architect | paramedic | engineer |

1 A(n) __actor__ works in films and theatres.
2 A(n) _____ works with machines and buildings.
3 A(n) _____ looks after your money and business.
4 A(n) _____ helps people in an accident or an emergency.
5 A(n) _____ designs houses and other buildings.
6 A(n) _____ fixes your car when it won't go.

2 marks for each correct answer. Total _____ / 10

Grammar

3 Complete the sentences with the correct form of the past perfect.

1 John __had practised__ (practise) a lot before the competition.
2 Jane _____ (eat) her dinner before I got home.
3 _____ Pete _____ (see) the pictures before the meeting?
4 Mike _____ (not visit) Rome until last summer.
5 The boys _____ (win) several prizes before they left school.
6 Lizzie _____ (not buy) anything when I met her.

1 mark for each correct answer. Total _____ / 5

4 Complete the sentences with the correct form of *used to*.

1 Billy __used to__ be very good at maths when he was at school.
2 Jane _____ ride a horse when she was a girl.
3 _____ you _____ play tennis?
4 Alan _____ like baked beans, but now he does.
5 Where _____ they _____ go on holiday?
6 Sam _____ be very pretty as a girl.

1 mark for each correct answer. Total _____ / 5

5 Match each sentence (1–10) to a function (a–c).

a stating a plan or intention
b talking about an arrangement at a specific time
c making a prediction

1 __a__ Paul is going to travel round France next summer.
2 _____ I think Brazil will win the next World Cup.
3 _____ My dad's going to work in the garden tomorrow.
4 _____ They're having a party on Sunday 16th May.
5 _____ He says he'll win the 100 metres race.
6 _____ They're picking her up at 4 p.m.

2 marks for each correct answer. Total _____ / 10

6 Complete the sentences with the future continuous.

1 When I am eighteen I __I'll be living__ (live) in another country.
2 In two years she _____ (study) at university.
3 Next week I _____ (start) my new job.
4 In June Julie _____ (travel) in Italy.
5 They _____ (play) five teams in the competition.
6 _____ you _____ (stay) with your aunt in New York?

1 mark for each correct answer. Total _____ / 5

7 Underline the best option.

1 I *'m meeting* / *will meet* James later to discuss our project.
2 We *will meet* / *are meeting* Ann at 11 p.m.
3 She *will* / *is* probably *be* / *going to be* late, as usual.
4 Take an umbrella, I think it *will* / *'s going to* rain.
5 Look at the time! You *'re going to miss* / *are missing* the train!
6 They *will win* / *are winning* the match if they play like this.

1 mark for each correct answer. Total _____ / 5

Communicate

8 Complete the conversation with the correct form of these verbs.

~~peel~~	boil	grill	bake	slice	heat up

Matt: OK, Gill. Let's start the lunch.

Gill: Great! What do you want me to do?

Matt: Can you start by (1) ___*peeling*___ and (2) _____ the carrots? I'm going to (3) _____ the fish, and (4) _____ the oven so that it's hot enough to (5) _____ the apple pie.

Gill: OK. I'll heat some water to (6) _____ the carrots in when they're ready.

2 marks for each correct answer. Total _____ / 10

9 Complete the conversation with *want, rather, like* or *prefer*. Use one word only.

Mum: What would you (1) ____*like*____ to do this afternoon?

Jon: I (2) _____ to go to the museum.

Mum: What about you Sue?

Sue: I'd (3) _____ read my book.

Pat: I'd (4) _____ to go to the park.

Mum: OK. Well, I'd (5) _____ to get the shopping done, and I (6) _____ shopping on my own. Why don't you go to the park and I'll meet you later?

2 marks for each correct answer. Total _____ / 10

Reading

10 Read and answer the questions. Use full sentences.

Last week workers digging the new metro tunnel under the eastern part of the city found some Roman remains. This new find seems like the most exciting discovery in the area so far. The archaeologists from the town museum say that it's probably going to be bigger than Alpana – the small Roman town in the hills 15 km to the north. So the metro builders have stopped digging for a month, and the archaeologists have invited people from all over Europe to come and help them in this race against time. They will be working day and night before work has to start on the metro again. From their first studies, it looks as though this new discovery is a small city, probably dating from the 1st century A.D. It seems to have many of the buildings we associate with Roman cities – baths, large public buildings and a theatre – as well as stone roads, shops and houses. They have already put the first artefacts on display in the museum – some gold coins, old pots and tools. The director of the museum is asking permission to extend the area they are digging next week into the park and car parks on either side of the metro works to see what other buildings and objects they can find.

1 What are they building in the town?

   They're building a new metro tunnel.

2 What did they find while they were digging?

   _____

3 What and where is Alpana?

   _____

4 Who came to study the remains first?

   _____

5 Why are they in a 'race against time'?

   _____

6 What two things are happening to make the work faster? _____

1 mark for each correct answer. Total _____ / 5

11 Read the text again and answer the questions with short answers.

1 Are they building a new underground car park in the city? ___*No, they aren't*___

2 Have they discovered big buildings as well as shops and houses? _____

3 Does the city date from the 1st century B.C.? _____

4 Does the museum director want to dig in other parts of the city? _____

5 Can you see some of the finds in the museum? _____

6 Are the archaeologists only working at weekends? _____

1 mark for each correct answer. Total _____ / 5

Listening

 *CD 2 track 43*

12 Listen and circle the correct answers.

1 The dish they are cooking is called
(a) hot-roasted chicken ⟨(b) pot-roasted chicken⟩
(c) fat-roasted chicken

2 How much butter do you need?
(a) 5g   (b) 15g   (c) 50g

3 Which cooking methods are mentioned?
(a) roasting and heating up   (b) frying and roasting   (c) frying and boiling

4 When cooking the chicken you should turn it
(a) 3-4 times   (b) 34 times (c) 43 times

5 You should cook it for
(a) 60 minutes   (b) 90 minutes
(c) 30 minutes

6 You should cook the chicken at
(a) 80°C   (b) 108°C   (c) 180°C

2 marks for each correct answer. Total _____ / 10

Writing

13 Write ten sentences about a special food.

- Describe the dish.
- List the ingredients.
- Explain the cooking methods.
- Say what you like about it and when you eat it.

1 mark for each correct sentence. Total _____ / 10

Total _____ / 100

Vocabulary

1 Complete the sentences with these words.

~~brick~~ glass leather wood plastic rubber

1 Houses are often built out of ____brick____.

2 A lot of furniture is made out of _____.

3 We use _____ to make bicycle tyres.

4 Bottles are often made out of _____.

5 We get _____ from the skins of cows.

6 _____ can be used to make many different things.

2 marks for each correct answer. Total _____ / 10

2 Underline the correct word.

1 *Still life / Landscape* painting shows views of the country.

2 You use a pencil to do a *drawing / painting*.

3 *Fiction / Poetry* tells an imaginary story.

4 A *play / portrait* is performed in a theatre.

5 A *novel / sculpture* is made out of metal or stone.

6 *Oil / Abstract* is a type of paint which artists use.

2 marks for each correct answer. Total _____ / 10

Grammar

3 Rewrite each active sentence in the passive.

1 They made these shoes in Italy.
These shoes were made in Italy.

2 They are using the old church as a concert hall.
_____

3 They always give gifts to children in hospital.
_____

4 They were painting the bridge all month.
_____

5 The workers have restored the old house.
_____

6 They brought the vases from Greece.
_____

1 mark for each correct answer. Total _____ / 5

4 Rewrite each active sentence in the passive using a modal verb.

1 They can make sandals out of old rubber tyres.
Sandals can be made out of old rubber tyres.

2 You must use butter to make the best cakes.
_____

3 They will turn the old papers into cardboard.
_____

4 You can find diamonds in this part of Africa.
_____

5 She will make two dresses from this material.
_____

6 You must practise these songs carefully.
_____

1 mark for each correct answer. Total _____ / 5

5 Match each sentence (1–10) to one of the meanings (a–c).

a It's possible

b It's impossible

c It's almost certain

1 __a__ He could be one of the men who robbed the bank.

2 _____ She couldn't be a murderer – she's too nice.

3 _____ They must have done it – look at their faces!

4 _____ Paul could have taken the money.

5 _____ Dan must have known about the plan.

6 _____ Lenny couldn't have done it – he was in France.

1 mark for each correct answer. Total _____ / 5

6 Complete the second conditional sentences with the correct verb forms.

1 If I ____went____ (go) to the party, Lucy ____would come____ (come) with me.

2 We _____ (not visit) the zoo if it _____ (rain).

3 If you _____ (see) that film, you _____ (not like) it.

4 If she _____ (want) that dress, her mum _____ (buy) it for her.

5 They _____ (play) football all day if you _____ (allow) them to.

6 Your sister _____ (bring) her guitar if Steve _____ (ask) her to.

1 mark for each correct verb. Total _____ / 10

7 Complete the sentences with *a* or *the*.

1 Have you ever been in __a__ boat on the sea?

2 We're going to _____ theatre on Saturday night.

3 Have you ever seen _____ pyramids in Egypt?

4 _____ piano is a beautiful instrument.

5 We collected money to help _____ poor.

6 I'm going to buy _____ new bike on Saturday.

1 mark for each correct answer. Total _____ / 5

Communicate

8 Complete the dialogue with these expressions.

~~why~~	what for	because	to win	so that	for

John: (1) _____Why_____ are you waiting here in the street, Andy?

Andy: (2) _____ I'm meeting my dad.

John: (3) _____?

Andy: He's taking me to the sports club (4) _____ I can start training.

John: Training for what?

Andy: (5) _____ the athletics championships next year. I want (6) _____ the 100 metres!

2 marks for each correct answer. Total _____ / 10

9 Complete the dialogue with these expressions.

~~can I~~	is it all right	of course
yes, sure	could you	do you mind

Marie: (1) _____Can I_____ have some money, please, Mum?

Mum: (2) Yes, _____. How much do you want?

Marie: (3) _____ giving me £50?

Mum: £50? That's a lot of money! (4) _____ tell me what it's for?

Marie: (5) _____. It's for the trip to London.

Mum: Well, (6) _____ if we pay next week? I'll need to get some cash.

2 marks for each correct answer. Total _____ / 10

Reading

10 Read the text and answer the questions. Use full sentences.

I had been out walking in the hills all day last Saturday, and I didn't get home until about seven o'clock. As I came to the garden gate, I found that it was open. This didn't surprise me – the postman could have left it open. But as I walked down the garden path I saw that the front door was also open. I started to feel frightened. Surely I couldn't have left the door open? Could someone have broken into my house to steal things? Might there be a thief in my house now? I wondered if I should call the police, but just then I heard footsteps coming along the hall to the door. Perhaps I should have picked up something to use as a weapon … but before I could move, a woman came out and saw me: 'Oh, Mr Roberts!' she said. 'You frightened me!' 'You frightened me too.' I replied. 'I thought you were a thief!' 'I'm so sorry,' said the woman. 'But I left my bag here when I came to do the cleaning this morning, and I just came back to get it now.'

1 What is the name of the writer of this story?

His name is Mr Roberts.

2 Why was Mr Roberts coming home late?

_____

3 What two strange things did he find?

_____

4 What did Mr Roberts think might have happened?

_____

5 Why didn't he call the police?

_____

6 Who was in his house and why?

_____

1 mark for each correct answer. Total _____ / 5

11 Read the text again. Are the sentences true (T) or false (F)?

1 __F__ The writer had been cycling all day.

2 _____ He was surprised to find his garden gate open.

3 _____ He was scared when he also found his front door open.

4 _____ He heard someone inside his house.

5 _____ He picked up a stone to hit the thief with.

6 _____ Both Mr Roberts and the woman were frightened.

1 mark for each correct answer. Total _____ / 5

Listening

🔘 *CD 2 track 44*

12 Listen to the text. Are the sentences true (T) or false (F)?

1 __F__ The writer had been here before.

2 _____ The art books are on the fourth floor.

3 _____ The writer found a lot of books on abstract painting.

4 _____ The tables are made of metal.

5 _____ He used an electronic card to take out the books.

6 _____ He took four books out of the library.

2 marks for each correct answer. Total _____ / 10

Writing

13 Write an email to a friend. Write 10 sentences.

- Apologise because you didn't meet him / her at the time you agreed.

- Explain what happened and why.

- Describe any other consequences.

- Suggest new times and places when you can meet.

1 mark for each correct sentence. Total _____ / 10

Total _____ / 100

Test Units 7 and 8   Part A

Vocabulary

1 Complete these sentences about science.

1 An i _n n o_ v _a_ t _i o n_ is something very new in the world of science.
2 Scientists do a lot of r _ s _ _ r _ _.
3 An _ x p _ _ _ m _ _ t is when scientists try out an idea.
4 Scientists often work in a l _ b _ _ _ t _ _ y.
5 A _ _ s c _ v _ _ y is when scientists find something new.
6 A scientist can have a t _ _ _ r y in his head about why something happens.

2 marks for each correct answer. Total _____ / 10

2 Match the things bought (1–6) with these shops.

| baker's | butcher's | chemist's |
| florist's | greengrocer's | newsagent's |

1 bread and cakes   _baker's_
2 flowers and plants   _____
3 pills and medicine   _____
4 chicken and sausages   _____
5 magazines and comics   _____
6 potatoes and pears   _____

2 marks for each correct answer. Total _____ / 10

Grammar

3 Complete the third conditional sentences.

1 If I _had run_ (run), I _would have caught_ (catch) the bus.
2 If she _____ (work) harder, she _____ (pass) her exams.
3 He _____ (win) the race if he _____ (not fall) over.
4 They _____ (not enjoy) the journey if they _____ (come).
5 If I _____ (go) to the party, I _____ (meet) her sooner.
6 She _____ (arrive) sooner if the train _____ (not be) late.

1 mark for each correct verb. Total _____ / 10

4 Complete the sentences.

1 Paul _should have gone_ to school yesterday. (should / go)
2 Linda _____ the film last night. (could / watch)
3 _____ Mike _____ him the answer yesterday? (should / tell)
4 Lizzie _____ her grandmother last week. (could not / visit)

5 Our team _____ that match – we played badly. (should not / win)
6 _____ Pattie _____ us if we'd asked? (could / help)

1 mark for each correct answer. Total _____ / 5

5 Report the words. Begin with _She said…_

1 'I really like tennis.'
She said that she really liked tennis.
2 'It's raining hard.'
_____
3 'I don't feel very well.'
_____
4 'I will go there immediately.'
_____
5 'I can come at eight o'clock.'
_____
6 'I was there in 2006.'
_____

1 mark for each correct answer. Total _____ / 5

6 Report the questions. Begin with _He asked …_

1 'Is there a match tomorrow, Bill?'
He asked Bill if there was a match the next day.
2 'Can I borrow your bike, Cathy?'
_____
3 'Will you go with me, Joan?'
_____
4 'Did you watch the match, George?'
_____
5 'What is in the box, Mike?'
_____
6 'Have you got an umbrella, Dick?'
_____

1 mark for each correct answer. Total _____ / 5

7 What did the people say? Write their words.

1 Paul said he had gone there the day before.
'I went there yesterday.'
2 Louise said that she wouldn't buy a new dress.
_____
3 He asked if she was working at the weekend.
_____
4 Sally said she couldn't meet me for lunch.
_____
5 Bill asked June if she had got a bike.
_____
6 Ron said that they didn't like the film.
_____

1 mark for each correct answer. Total _____ / 5

Communicate

8 Complete the conversation with these expressions.

| I should have | You should have | I wish I'd |
| wouldn't have | I shouldn't have | You could have |

Alison: (1) _I should have_ stayed at home on Saturday. The party was awful.

May: You didn't have to stay. (2) _____ gone home.

Alison: (3) _____ listened to you, then I wouldn't have gone at all!

May: (4) _____ phoned me. I would have come and taken you home early.

Alison: I know. (5) _____ stayed so long. I'm really tired and I haven't studied for the test.

May: But if you hadn't gone to the party, you (6) _____ seen Dan.

2 marks for each correct answer. Total ____ / 10

9 Complete the conversation. Use one word in each gap. Contractions (I'd) count as one word.

Assistant: Good morning. (1) _Can I help you_?

Bobby: Yes. (2) _____ _____ _____ return this camera.

Assistant: I see. Is there (3) _____ _____?

Bobby: Well, it doesn't work. I'd like my money (4) _____, please.

Assistant: Have you got (5) _____ _____?

Bobby: Yes, here it is.

Assistant: As the camera is faulty we can give you (6) _____ _____.

Bobby: Thank you very much.

2 marks for each correct answer. Total ____ / 10

Reading

10 Read the text. Are the sentences true (T) or false (F)?

Charles Darwin was born in 1809, and after attending school in rural England he went to the University of Edinburgh Medical School to become a doctor like his father. However, he found the lectures boring and the surgery unpleasant, and so he spent much of his time studying natural history. In 1828 his father sent him to do an arts degree at Christ's College, Cambridge so that he could become a priest. Once again, Darwin spent most of his time studying natural history, and from December 1831 until October 1836 he travelled round the world on the *HMS Beagle*. His main research task was to look at the geology of South America, and he collected many fossils, as well as different forms of life. His studies eventually lead to him publishing *On the Origin of Species* in 1859. Many people did not like his theories but they eventually changed the way people looked at evolution.

1 _T_ Darwin's father was a doctor.

2 _____ Darwin became a doctor too.

3 _____ He went to Cambridge to study geology.

4 _____ He spent five years on *HMS Beagle*.

5 _____ While he was on *HMS Beagle* he published *On the Origin of Species*.

6 _____ Everybody accepted his ideas on evolution.

1 mark for each correct answer. Total ____ / 5

11 Read the text again and answer the questions.

1 Why did Darwin's father want him to become a doctor?

Because he was a doctor, too.

2 Why didn't Darwin enjoy studying medicine?

_____

3 What did he actually study in Edinburgh?

_____

4 Why did his father send him to Cambridge?

_____

5 What was his main area of research on *The Beagle*?

_____

6 What else did he collect in South America?

_____

1 mark for each correct answer. Total ____ / 5

Listening

🔊 *CD 2 track 45*

12 Listen and decide if the sentences are true (T) or false (F).

1 _T_ This is an advertisement for a holiday in South Africa.

2 _____ The special prices start at the end of June.

3 _____ The special prices last for one month.

4 _____ The tour cannot be changed.

5 _____ Swaziland is the best place for a safari.

6 _____ Cape Town has great beaches to relax on.

2 marks for each correct answer. Total ____ / 10

Writing

13 Write ten sentences about the life of a famous person. Think about these things:

- their early life
- why they became famous
- what they achieved
- what they could / should have done

1 mark for each correct sentence. Total ____ / 10

Total ____ / 100

Vocabulary

1 Complete the sentences with the newspaper words in the box.

~~front page~~	podcast	headline
readers	reporter	website

1 Did you see that picture on the
_____*front page*_____ of *The Times* yesterday?

2 Several _____ telephoned the paper to complain about it.

3 The _____ for the main article said *No more war!*

4 I looked at newspaper's _____ on my computer.

5 Did you listen to the _____ on your MP3 player?

6 The _____ from *The Sun* was the first at the scene of the crime.

2 marks for each correct answer. Total ____ / 10

2 Complete the words about a TV show.

1 The p _r e s e n_ t _e r_ of this show is a famous actor.

2 The stars had to au _ _ t _ _ n for a place in the show.

3 There was a long r _ h _ _ r _ _ l every day.

4 The first _ p _ s _ d _ of the new series is on TV tonight.

5 I don't want to watch this. It's a r _ p _ a _ of an old show.

6 I like seeing all the famous people on c _ l _ b _ _ _ y shows.

2 marks for each correct answer. Total ____ / 10

Grammar

3 Put the verbs in brackets into the present simple or present continuous.

Jane (1) _____*is*_____ (be) a student at Queen Anne's School in Birmingham. She (2) _____ (like) sports very much and (3) _____ (play) in the school hockey and tennis teams. At the moment she (4) _____ (try) to do her homework in her bedroom, but she (5) _____ (think) about the woman she (6) _____ (train) with every afternoon – Mrs Smith. Together they (7) _____ (work) on Jane's fitness at the moment, and it (8) _____ (be) very hard. Now Jane's mother (9) _____ (call) her. 'Your sisters (10) _____ (be) ready to go out,' she says. '(11) _____ you _____ (go) with them?'

1 mark for each correct answer. Total ____ / 10

4 Mark the place in the sentence where the word in brackets should go.

1 Peter has _X_ finished his dinner . (just)

2 I have read those books . (already)

3 Have you seen that comedy film ? (yet)

4 Lucy hasn't written her history essay . (still)

5 The girls have won their first tennis match . (just)

6 The teacher hasn't marked my work . (yet)

1 mark for each correct answer. Total ____ / 5

5 Complete the sentences with the present perfect continuous or past perfect.

1 I _*hadn't been*_ (not be) to Africa before my father took me.

2 I _____ (know) about it for a week before I told her.

3 Paul _____ (study) hard for his exam tomorrow.

4 How long _____ you _____ (play) the piano for?

5 George _____ (want) to meet Chris, and yesterday he did.

6 That man _____ (stand) there for about two hours.

1 mark for each correct answer. Total ____ / 5

6 Write questions in the future continuous.

1 where / you / live / in five years / ?
Where will you be living in five years?

2 where / they / stay / on holiday / ?
_____

3 how / we / travel / to work / next year?
_____

4 what / she / study / at university / ?
_____

5 who / he / visit / in London / ?
_____

6 Why / they / stay / there / for three weeks?
_____

1 mark for each correct answer. Total ____ / 5

7 Complete the sentences with a question tag.

1 He works in a shop, _____*doesn't he*_____ ?

2 They don't like swimming, _____ ?

3 Paul's got a bike, _____ ?

4 You're not very happy, _____ ?

5 It's a school holiday tomorrow, _____ ?

6 We're leaving soon, _____ ?

1 mark for each correct answer. Total ____ / 5

Communicate

8 Complete the radio interview with different verbs in the present perfect and question words.

Jon: So, where (1) _have_ you _been_ so far?

Marie: I (2) _____ just _____ some time in northern India.

Jon: (3) _____ _____ were you there for?

Marie: Five days.

Jon: And (4) _____ _____ have you travelled since you started your journey?

Marie: About 3,000 kilometres.

Jon: And what interesting sights (5) _____ you _____?

Marie: I (6) _____ _____ some beautiful temples.

2 marks for each correct answer. Total ____ / 10

9 Write suitable questions in this interview.

> do you want to see   you like it   have you seen
> do you think so   did you think of it   do you like her

Mick: I'm talking to some of the people watching the flim stars arrive. John, who (1) _do you want to see_?

John: I'd like to see Peter Castle. (2) _____ his new film?

Mick: *Death Point?* Yes. What (3) _____ ?

John: I thought it was really exciting.

Mick: And Patsy, did (4) _____, too ?

Patsy: Well, not really. I want see Shirelle.

Mick: Why (5) _____ ?

Patsy: Because she's a great singer and actress.

Mick: (6) _____?

Patsy: Oh, yes, I love her songs.

2 marks for each correct answer. Total ____ / 10

Reading

10 Read the text and answer the questions.

I have never seen an animal which is as intelligent as my Uncle Peter's dog, Bobby. Bobby does all the usual things which dogs do, such as sitting or fetching a stick when told to. He can also follow more complicated instructions such as 'Put the ball on the table', and knows how to do this with any ball and any table, even ones he hasn't seen before. If my uncle says 'Bark twice', Bobby barks twice. He can do this for all the numbers up to ten. Bobby also seems to have a good memory. My uncle hides something – for example, he puts a green ball into the cupboard where Bobby can see it – and says 'Here's the green ball'; he leaves it there for a week or more, and then asks 'Where's the green ball?' and Bobby goes and puts his paw on the correct cupboard door. It's quite an amazing thing to see him do this. And Bobby likes all the normal things which dogs like, too, such as going for a walk, and swimming in the local river, and he's a very friendly dog too.

1 Does the author think Bobby is intelligent?
_____ Yes, he does. _____

2 Can Bobby follow difficult instructions?
_____

3 Does Bobby only use the same ball and table?
_____

4 Is Bobby able to count up to twenty?
_____

5 Can Bobby remember where things are?
_____

6 Is Bobby a normal, active dog? _____

1 mark for each correct answer. Total ____ / 5

11 Read the text again. Answer the questions with full sentences.

1 What are the usual things which all dogs can do?
They can sit and fetch a stick when told to.

2 What can Bobby do with unknown balls and tables? _____

3 What does Bobby do when Uncle Peter says a number? _____

4 How do we know that Bobby has a good memory? _____

5 What tells you that the author is surprised at what Bobby can do? _____

6 Apart from these special things, what is Bobby like? _____

1 mark for each correct answer. Total ____ / 5

Listening

CD 2 track 46

12 Listen and answer the questions.

1 How long has the speaker been at school?
She's been at school for thirteen years.

2 What is her problem?
_____

3 What does her father want her to be?
_____

4 What two subjects does she like best?
_____

5 What does her teacher think she should be? Why? _____

6 When is she going to decide what to do?
_____

2 marks for each correct answer. Total ____ / 10

Writing

13 Write ten sentences about what jobs you would and would not like to do and why.

1 mark for each correct sentence ____ / 10

Total ____ / 100

Vocabulary

1 Complete the sentences with the materials.

1 Many buildings are built out of c _o_ n _c_ _r_ _e_ t _e_.
2 Most engines are made out of m _ _ _ l.
3 _ a _ _ r is used for books.
4 _ t _ n _ is an important natural building material.
5 We get w _ _ _ from sheep.
6 F _ b _ _ _ c can be made of cotton or silk.

2 marks for each correct answer. Total ____ / 10

2 Complete the sentences with these words.

> cut painted pierced dyed shaved tested

1 Paul has had his hair ___cut___ – it's really short.
2 Julie's having her ears _____.
3 I had my eyes _____ and got glasses.
4 Joe had his face _____ at the party.
5 Mandy has had her hair _____ red.
6 Mick has had his head _____. He looks funny!

2 marks for each correct answer. Total ____ / 10

Grammar

3 Write second conditional sentences.

1 If / Suzie / work hard / pass / exam
   ___If Suzie worked hard she would pass the exam___
2 If / Ben / sleep / more / feel better / in the morning _____
3 Kenny / enjoy / the concert / if / understand / the words _____
4 If / Janice / cook / dinner / her mother / be / happy _____
5 Don / cycle / to school / if / have / a new bike _____
6 If / Angela / go / to the party / Linda / not like / it _____

1 mark for each correct answer. Total ____ / 5

4 Complete the third conditional sentences.

1 If she ___had seen___ (see) him, she ___would have stopped___ (stop) to talk.
2 If they _____ (know) about it, they _____ (tell) me.
3 She _____ (enjoy) it if she _____ (go) there.
4 We _____ (not understand) it if he _____ (not explain) everything.
5 If Bill _____ (hear) the news he _____ (not be) so happy.

6 Carol _____ (not say) that if she _____ (think) carefully first.

1 mark for each correct verb. Total ____ / 10

5 Report what the people said.

1 'I don't like cooking.'
   He said that he didn't like cooking.
2 'I'm going to the seaside.'
   _____
3 'What did you do in the holidays, Jenny?'
   _____
4 'I'll have my new watch by Friday.'
   _____
5 'Where are my keys, Lily?'
   _____
6 'I can't come until three o'clock.'
   _____

1 mark for each correct answer. Total ____ / 5

6 Rewrite each active sentence in the passive.

1 They bought these souvenirs in Paris.
   These souvenirs were bought in Paris.
2 They always make special cakes at Christmas.
   _____
3 The police have investigated the mystery.
   _____
4 You can grow oranges in this area.
   _____
5 They were washing the car when I arrived.
   _____
6 You must handle these animals gently.
   _____

1 mark for each correct answer. Total ____ / 5

7 Rewrite the sentences using _could have, couldn't have_ or _must have._

1 It is possible that Paul stole my bike.
   Paul could have stolen my bike.
2 It is impossible that Mr Jones killed his wife.
   _____
3 It is almost certain that a gang did the robbery.
   _____
4 I think that perhaps John broke the window.
   _____
5 It is certain that Mike cheated in the test.
   _____
6 It isn't possible that Susan hit your son.
   _____

1 mark for each correct answer. Total ____ / 5

Communicate

8 Complete the conversation. Write one word in each gap.

Jill: Hello, Steve. (1) _Why_ are you so angry?

Steve: (2) _____ I can't get this computer to work again, Jill.

Jill: Really? (3) _____'s the problem?

Steve: (4) _____ I click on the Internet icon, nothing happens.

Jill: Oh dear! What (5) _____ restarting the computer?

Steve: (6) _____ do I do that?

Jill: Just click on *Restart*, here.

2 marks for each correct answer. Total ___ / 10

9 Complete the conversation with suitable words and phrases.

| I'm sure | shouldn't have | could have |
| should have | wish you'd | had to |

Bill: Oh, I'm so tired. (1) _I'm sure_ I'll fall asleep in the exam today.

Jane: You (2) _____ gone to bed early last night.

Bill: But I (3) _____ finish my essay.

Jane: And did you manage to finish it?

Bill: No, I didn't! I (4) _____ left it so late.

Jane: I (5) _____ told me before. I (6) _____ helped you.

2 marks for each correct answer. Total ___ / 10

Reading

10 Read the text and answer the questions.

Machu Picchu, which means *Old Mountain*, is a UNESCO World Heritage Site at 2,430 metres above the Urubamba Valley in Peru. Most archaeologists think it was built around 1450 for the Inca emperor Pachacuti. It is remarkable because it was never discovered and destroyed by the Spanish invaders like many other Inca sites. In fact, it was almost unknown to the outside world until books about it were written by an American called Hiram Bingham in 1911. The site has urban and agricultural areas; the buildings are often built out of huge blocks of carefully cut stone. It is now a major tourist site, visited by almost 500,000 people a year. This has caused problems, and in 2008 it was put on the Watch List of the 100 most endangered sites in the world, because of the environmental damage caused by tourists. In January 2010 heavy rain destroyed roads and railways, and trapped thousands of tourists and local people, so the site was closed until the end of April 2010.

1 What country is Machu Picchu in? _It's in Peru._

2 Who built Machu Picchu? _____

3 When was it built? _____

4 Who rediscovered it? _____

5 What is Machu Picchu made of? _____

6 What problems do tourists cause? _____

1 mark for each correct answer. Total ___ / 5

11 Read the text again. Are the sentences true (T) or false (F)?

1 _T_ Machu Picchu is high up in the mountains.

2 _____ It was built 1,450 years ago.

3 _____ It was built by Hiram Bingham.

4 _____ Half a million tourists go there every year.

5 _____ The buildings at Machu Picchu are very dangerous.

6 _____ It was closed for four months in 2010.

1 mark for each correct answer. Total ___ / 5

Listening

CD 2 track 47

12 Listen to the text. Are the sentences true (T) or false (F)?

1 _F_ Guevara's real name was Che.

2 _____ Guevara was born into a poor illiterate family.

3 _____ Guevara wasn't interested in sport.

4 _____ In 1950 he cycled round Argentina with a friend.

5 _____ In 1953 he cycled round South America.

6 _____ The tour made him understand the effects of capitalism on people.

2 marks for each correct answer. Total ___ / 10

Writing

13 Write about a place you have visited. Write ten sentences. Think about these ideas:

- what you did there
- what you liked
- what you didn't like
- whether you would recommend it

1 mark for each correct sentence. Total ___ / 10

Total _____ / 100

Vocabulary

1 Match the two parts of the compound nouns below.

1 _d_   2 ____   3 ____   4 ____   5 ____
6 ____   7 ____   8 ____   9 ____   10 ____
11 ____

1 shop	**a** tip
2 security	**b** board
3 world	**c** site
4 detective	**d** assistant
5 summer	**e** club
6 message	**f** guard
7 rubbish	**g** design
8 mind	**h** champion
9 fashion	**i** clothes
10 fan	**j** story
11 web	**k** control

1 mark for each correct answer. Total ____ / 10

2 Complete the sentences with the correct preposition.

1 I need to reply __to__ this email today.
2 I think ____ the accident every day.
3 I hope my brother gives ____ smoking.
4 The storm did a lot of damage ____ our house.
5 You should throw ____ those old newspapers.
6 Who will pay ____ the food and drinks?
7 They make the dolls ____ old clothes.
8 He always complains ____ everything.
9 I've had no success ____ growing vegetables.
10 When will Mary come ____ home?
11 You must hand ____ your project on Friday.

1 mark for each correct answer. Total ____ / 10

Grammar

3 Complete the sentences with the correct question tag.

1 You don't like football, _do you_?
2 He's got a new computer, ____?
3 She didn't visit them, ____?
4 You're thirsty, ____?
5 You can swim, ____?
6 She isn't coming, ____?

1 mark for each correct answer. Total ____ / 5

4 Write each pair of sentences as one sentence, using *when, where, which, who* or *whose*.

1 John is our baker. He bakes delicious bread.
   John, who is our baker, bakes delicious bread.

2 Mrs Smith's dog barks all night. She is our neighbour.
   _____

3 Keswick is my favourite town. We spend our holidays there.
   _____

4 Paul is our manager. He is very strict.
   _____

5 In winter it is dark. I get up at six o'clock.
   _____

6 These apples are sweet. I bought them yesterday.
   _____

1 mark for each correct answer. Total ____ / 5

5 Rewrite each active sentence in the passive.

1 People used these caves as homes.
   These caves were used as homes.

2 They are making toys from pieces of wood.
   _____

3 They usually eat special cakes at Easter.
   _____

4 They were preparing everything while we were asleep.
   _____

5 The workers have invented a new machine.
   _____

6 They will finish the research project next week.
   _____

1 mark for each correct answer. Total ____ / 5

6 Complete the second conditional sentences with the correct verb forms.

1 If I __made__ (make) some biscuits, __would__ you __eat__ (eat) them ?
2 If they ____ (buy) me a new bike, I ____ (be) very happy.
3 Peter ____ (help) you do it if you ____ (ask) him.
4 If Jane ____ (win) the competition, she ____ (get) a prize.
5 My dad ____ (enjoy) a holiday there if he ____ (can) afford it.
6 If the match ____ (start) on time, they ____ (finish) it before it rains.

½ mark for each correct verb. Total ____ / 5

Part B

7 **Write third conditional sentences.**

1 If / Jane / win / she / be / very happy

   If Jane had won she would have been very happy.

2 If / the weather / be / better / they / go / camping

   _____

3 Clare / enjoy / the concert / more / if / she / be / by herself

   _____

4 If / David / try / harder / he / make / more progress

   _____

5 The girls / write / more / if / they / have / more time

   _____

6 If / he / not drive / so fast / he / not crash

   _____

1 mark for each correct answer. Total ____ / 5

8 **Report the words. Begin with** *He said… or He asked …*

1 'I don't like drinking coffee.'

   He said that he didn't like drinking coffee.

2 'Paul didn't come to the French lesson.'

   _____

3 'I can bring my guitar.'

   _____

4 'What time will you arrive, Liz?'

   _____

5 'John's new book isn't very funny.'

   _____

6 'Are you flying to France, Jim?'

   _____

1 mark for each correct answer. Total ____ / 5

Part B

Communicate

9 **Complete the dialogue with one word in each gap.**

Paul: Are you coming (1) _with us_ to the swimming pool, Steve?

Steve: I (2) _____ to come, but I have to finish something at home first.

Paul: (3) _____ _____ will you finish? We're leaving at two o'clock.

Steve: I think I (4) _____ _____ ready by then.

Paul: Good. (5) _____ us at the bus station at half-past two.

Steve: OK. (6) _____ _____ are you coming on?

Paul: The number 27. See you!

Steve: Bye.

2 marks for each correct answer. Total ____ / 10

10 **Complete the dialogue with suitable words and phrases.**

| ~~online~~ | PayPal | clothes |
| download | credit card | pocket money |

Interviewer: Do you do any shopping (1) _online_?

Girl: Yes, I (2) _____ music and I sometimes buy books online.

Interviewer: How do you pay for them?

Girl: I don't have a (3) _____, I use (4) _____.

Interviewer: How much (5) _____ do you get?

Girl: £20 a month, but I get £20 for (6) _____ too.

2 marks for each correct answer. Total ____ / 10

Reading

11 **Read the text. Are the sentences true (T) or false (F)?**

Mark Twain is one of the most famous American writers in the world, and is still very popular over one hundred years after his death. His real name was Samuel Clemens, and he was born in Florida, Missouri in 1835, but the Clemens family soon moved to the important Mississippi port of Hannibal, where his father was a judge until his death in 1846. The following year, Twain was apprenticed to a printer, and for the next few years he worked in the printing industry; in this period he wrote a number of short, funny articles for his brother Orion's newspaper *The Hannibal Journal*. He spent four years when he was aged 18–22 travelling around the USA, working in printing and journalism, and educating himself after work by reading in public libraries. He then returned to Missouri and trained as a pilot to guide the steamboats down the dangerous Mississippi river, getting his licence in 1859. He did this job for two years until the start of the Civil War in 1861. Then he travelled west with his brother, working unsuccessfully as a silver miner, then later as a journalist in Nevada and California.

In 1865 he had his first national success when his story *The Celebrated Jumping Frog of Calaveras County* was published in *The Saturday Press*. The following year he travelled to Hawaii, and in 1867 he went to Europe and the Middle East. During these travels he wrote articles for US newspapers. He married Olivia Langdon in 1870, and they stayed married until her death in 1904, having four children together. After his marriage, the family moved to Hartford Connecticut where many of his most successful stories – all of which have a humorous element in them – were written: *The Adventures of Tom Sawyer* (1876) became his most famous story, drawing on his experiences on the Mississippi river. This was followed by *The Prince and the Pauper* (1881), a historical novel about a prince changing places with a poor boy, *The Adventures of Huckleberry Finn* (1884), a sequel to *Tom Sawyer*, and *A Connecticut Yankee in King Arthur's Court* (1889), a time travel story about an American who goes back to the Middle Ages.

Unfortunately, despite making a lot of money through his writing, he wasted most of it backing new inventions and in his publishing company. He lost the modern equivalent of $7.5 million between 1880 and 1894. He prevented disaster by writing more newspaper articles and books, and between 1894 and 1900 went on a lecturing tour round the world, and was able to pay back the money he owed. He was also depressed in later life by the death of three of his children and his wife, but continued writing up until his death from a heart attack in 1910.

1 __T__ Mark Twain was not the writer's real name.

2 _____ He travelled a lot during his life.

3 _____ He spent most of his life working as a riverboat pilot.

4 _____ All of Twain's children died before he did.

5 _____ He didn't make much money from his writing.

6 _____ He was not a successful businessman.

1 mark for each correct answer. Total ____ / 5

12 Read the text again and answer the questions. Use full sentences.

1 What job did Mark Twain do through most of his life.

He was a newspaper journalist.

2 What was the common characteristic of most of Twain's articles and novels?

_____

3 How did Mark Twain educate himself?

_____

4 Where did Mark Twain travel to outside the USA?

_____

5 Why did he travel around the world after 1894?

_____

6 Why was Twain unhappy in later life?

_____

1 mark for each correct answer. Total ____ / 5

Listening

CD 2 track 48

13 Listen to the interview. Are these sentences true (T) or false (F)?

1 __F__ John spent a week studying at the Museum.

2 _____ The museum shows how London developed.

3 _____ John says that the museum is better than a guide book.

4 _____ The museum has actors dressed in the clothes of the times.

5 _____ There are no objects in the museum, only paintings and photos.

6 _____ John enjoyed comparing pictures of London at different times.

1 mark for each correct answer. Total ____ / 5

CD 2 track 49

14 Listen to the girl and answer the questions with short answers.

1 What did she buy at the baker's? _6 bread rolls_

2 What kind of book did she buy? _____

3 What weight of sausages did she buy?

_____

4 What did she do in the newsagent's?

_____

5 What flavour toothpaste did she buy?

_____

6 Did she buy some sandals? _____

1 mark for each correct answer. Total ____ / 5

Writing

15 Write about your shopping habits. Write ten sentences. Think about these questions:

• Where do you like shopping?

• Where are the best shops in your town?

• Who do you go shopping with?

• When do you usually go shopping?

• What things do you like shopping for best?

• Is there anything about shopping you don't like?

1 mark for each correct sentence. Total ____ / 10

Total _____ / 100

Vocabulary

1 Match the two parts of the compound nouns below.

1 _d_ 2 ____ 3 ____ 4 ____ 5 ____
6 ____ 7 ____ 8 ____ 9 ____ 10 ____
11 ____

1 soap	**a** kit		
2 autograph	**b** bag		
3 survival	**c** event		
4 film	**d** opera		
5 sports	**e** stop		
6 talent	**f** guest		
7 phone	**g** resort		
8 camera	**h** review		
9 celebrity	**i** line		
10 ski	**j** book		
11 bus	**k** show		

1 mark for each correct answer. Total ____ / 10

2 Write the correct preposition in these sentences.

1 I'm going to the police station to ask ____about____ my bag.
2 They're going to translate the book _____ French.
3 My boss has a big problem _____ computers.
4 Did you find _____ who took the money?
5 I'm hoping to get _____ from work early on Friday.
6 What was the reason _____ his decision?
7 Are you going to compete _____ the next race?
8 Here's a nice recipe _____ chicken soup.
9 Paul's doing research _____ bird song.
10 I'm afraid we've run _____ of milk and bread.
11 My mother suffers _____ bad headaches.

1 mark for each correct answer. Total ____ / 10

Grammar

3 Complete the sentences with the correct question tag.

1 You like tennis, _don't you_?
2 She hasn't got a bike, _____?
3 You saw the film, _____?
4 They aren't hungry, _____?
5 You mustn't do that, _____?
6 He's arriving soon, _____?

1 mark for each correct answer. Total ____ / 5

4 Write each pair of sentences as one sentence, using *when, where, which, who* or *whose*.

1 Jane is a dressmaker. She made this dress.
   Jane, who is a dressmaker, made this dress.

2 The Browns are very friendly. Their shop is next door.
   _____

3 The Lake District is a beautiful area. We often camp there.
   _____

4 Dr Jones is my doctor. He works very hard.
   _____

5 Saturday is my favourite day. I go shopping.
   _____

6 These presents look expensive. I got them for my birthday.
   _____

1 mark for each correct answer. Total ____ / 5

5 Rewrite each active sentence in the passive.

1 They painted pictures on the walls.
   Pictures were painted on the walls.

2 They are designing clothes for next summer.
   _____

3 They often wear traditional clothes for parties.
   _____

4 They were playing music while we cooked.
   _____

5 The builders have discovered some old ruins.
   _____

6 They will study our island next spring.
   _____

1 mark for each correct answer. Total ____ / 5

6 Complete the second conditional sentences with the correct form of the verbs.

1 If you ___saw___ (see) a horror film, ___would___ you ___close___ (close) your eyes?
2 If they _____ (know) him, they _____ (not tell) me.
3 The girls _____ (come) with us if you _____ (invite) them.
4 If Steve _____ (pass) his driving test, he _____ (take) me to London.
5 Your mum _____ (let) us use it if we _____ (need) to.
6 If they _____ (write) their own songs, I _____ (not listen) to them.

½ mark for each correct answer. Total ____ / 5

7 Use the cues to write sentences in the third conditional.

1 If / Justin / make / dinner / his mother / be / very pleased

If Justin had made dinner, his mother would
have been very pleased.

2 If / not stand / here / they / not see / me / they

3 My sister / reach / the top / if / she / not hurt / her foot

4 If / we / not eat / that fish / we / not feel / so bad.

5 Our dog / walk / home / if / it / get / lost

6 If / Jake / think / more carefully / he / not do / it

1 mark for each correct answer. Total ____ / 5

8 Report the words. Begin with *She said...* or *She asked.*

1 'I like baking cakes.'

She said that she liked baking cakes.

2 'James didn't play the piano for me.'

3 'I can't come before nine o'clock.'

4 'What will you do in London, Pete?'

5 'I don't want to go there.'

6 'Is it going to work, Kay?'

1 mark for each correct answer. Total ____ / 5

Part B

Communicate

9 Complete the dialogue with a suitable word in each gap.

Anne: Are you going (1) ___to___ ___go___ to the concert tomorrow night, Liza?

Liza: Yes, I would (2) _____ to go with you, but I haven't asked my mum yet.

Anne: Oh, Liza! Why (3) _____ you ask her now?

Liza: Because she's not (4) _____ _____ – she's gone shopping.

Anne: Well ask her when she gets back, and then (5) _____ me to let me know.

Liza: OK. (6) _____ _____ does the concert start?

Anne: At eight o'clock.

Liza: Right.

2 marks for each correct answer. Total ____ / 10

10 Complete the dialogue with these words.

spending	waste	note
coins	cash	savings

Interviewer: Could I ask you some questions about your (1) __spending__ habits?

Boy: OK.

Interviewer: How much (2) _____ do you have in your pocket right now?

Boy: I have a £10 (3) _____, and I have a few (4) _____ so about £14.

Interviewer: And do you have any (5) _____ at home?

Boy: Not really, I usually spend all my pocket money quite quickly. And I (6) _____ a lot of it actually on sweets and drinks.

2 marks for each correct answer. Total ____ / 10

11 Read the text and answer the questions.

Plastic is the name given to a wide range of similar materials which are easy and cheap to manufacture, waterproof, and can be pressed into any shape. Think of some of the things you own: toothbrush, computer keyboard, CD box, food bags ... the list is endless. Plastics have replaced many more traditional materials such as glass, wood, leather and metal.

The first plastic was invented in 1855 by an English man called Alexander Parkes, who lived in Birmingham. Named *Parkesite*, it was made using cellulose – a natural material found in plants. The first plastic which was truly synthetic (not made from natural material) was Bakelite. It was discovered in 1907 by Leo Hendrik Baekeland, a Belgian chemist living in New York. It was made public in 1912, and was soon used in the cases for equipment such as clocks, phones and radios. From 1918 onwards many different types of plastics were invented, with a wide range of uses. One of the most significant was nylon, which was developed in the 1930s. It was a cheap material which could be used instead of more expensive silk, particularly for women's stockings and other clothes. Other plastics include acrylic (used in paints and clothing) and polyester (used in fabric for clothes).

However, there are problems with plastics too. They cannot be used in some situations because they are not strong enough to carry heavy weights. Many plastics cannot stand too much heat or they will melt. A more recent concern comes from environmental pollution. Many plastics cannot be destroyed naturally as a material such as wood can. This means that the beaches and countryside of the world are now littered with used plastic bottles and bags. However, the plastics industry has responded to this issue, and many drinks bottles are labelled PET and can be recycled or broken down biologically in the ground.

1 What makes plastic such a useful material?

It can be used in many different situations in

many different forms.

2 How was Parkesite different from Bakelite?

_____

3 What happened with plastics after 1918?

_____

4 What two problems are mentioned about the use of plastics?

_____

5 How are environmental problems being solved?

_____

6 Give two examples of completely different uses and forms of plastic.

_____

1 mark for each correct answer. Total ____ / 5

12 Read the text. Are the sentences true (T) or false (F)?

1 __T__ The first plastic was invented in Birmingham, England.

2 _____ Bakelite was invented in Belgium.

3 _____ Synthetic plastics are often used instead of natural materials.

4 _____ Nylon is used for paints.

5 _____ All plastics are very strong.

6 _____ Many plastics cannot be broken down by air, water and wind.

1 mark for each correct answer. Total ____ / 5

Listening

🔘 *CD 2 track 50*

13 Listen to two friends talking and circle the correct answers.

1 How did Julie feel?
a) happy   b) excited   (c) upset)

2 What green things don't they do at school?
a) recycle paper   b) eat Fairtrade food
c) turn off the lights

3 Which green product didn't Julie want to buy?
a) Fairtrade clothes   b) recycled paper
c) energy-saving light bulbs

4 Which food did Julie buy?
a) a pumpkin   b) bananas   c) chocolate

5 What clothes did Julie buy?
a) a T-shirt   b) nothing   c) a jacket

6 What does Sally suggest Julie should do?
a) recycle paper   b) buy normal products
c) try some other shops

1 mark for each correct answer. Total ____ / 5

🔘 *CD 2 track 51*

14 Listen to the man talking about illegal copying. Are the sentences true (T) or false (F)?

1 __T__ There are different kinds of criminal copying of things.

2 _____ Copying banknotes is not known as forgery.

3 _____ The forgers have technology like x-rays and lasers to help them.

4 _____ It is more difficult to forge a Picasso.

5 _____ Forgers get richer if they copy old master paintings.

6 _____ Despite the experts, art galleries still get fooled by forgeries.

1 mark for each correct answer. Total ____ / 5

15 Write about a visit to somewhere interesting such as a museum, a gallery or a zoo. Write ten sentences. Think about these questions:

• Where and when did you go to?

• Who did you go with?

• How long did you stay there?

• What did you like / not like about the visit?

10 mark for each correct sentence. Total ____ / 10

Total _____ / 100

Answers

Test Units 1 and 2

1 2 channel   3 programme   4 article   5 journalist   6 listener

2 2 remember   3 understand   4 creative   5 memory   6 imagine

3 2 likes   3 is watching   4 is (are) playing   5 is sitting   6 goes   7 travels   8 are drinking   9 thinks   10 are   11 is winning

4 2 already   3 yet   4 still   5 yet   6 just

5 2 hasn't been taking   3 Have … been going   4 has been studying   5 have … been sitting   6 have been living

6 2 Ann, whose garden is lovely, lives next door.   3 Margate, where we go on holiday, is nice.   4 In June, when we go to Margate, it is usually sunny.   5 Ramsgate, which is smaller than Margate, is also a seaside town.   6 Mr Jones, who teaches us history, is Scottish.

7 2 have they   3 doesn't she   4 isn't it   5 are you   6 is he

8 2 Do you think so?   3 I don't think so   4 That's because   5 In my opinion   6 That's true

9 2 for   3 've been   4 hasn't he   5 already   6 who

10 2 F   3 F   4 T   5 F   6 T

11 (Suggested answers)   2 The media want to know everything about them.   3 The media say that they are arrogant and unfriendly.   4 Because they can protect them from media attention.   5 They spend too much money instead of saving for the future.   6 Because they may not be famous for long.

12 2 T   3 F   4 T   5 T   6 F

 CD 2 track 42 Tapescript

Jill: So what did you think of Death Journey, Mike?

Mike: I thought it was great. It was exciting and it has an interesting story.

Jill: In my opinion it was terrible.

Mike: Did you think so? I really like the way they filmed it, and the actors were great.

Jill: I don't think Annette Brady makes a very good Jane Fond – Diana Cragg was much better.

Mike: I don't agree. Why do you say that?

Jill: She seems to make a joke of everything.

Mike: Well, there have always been lots of jokes in Jane Fond films. They're very funny sometimes.

Jill: Yes, but this was too much.

Mike: Well, I still think it was a good film. I'm going to see it again tomorrow, with Paul. I think he'll enjoy it.

13 Students' own answers.

Test Units 3 and 4

1 2 hour   3 day   4 week   5 fortnight   6 month   7 year   8 decade   9 century   10 millennium   11 time

2 2 engineer   3 accountant   4 paramedic   5 architect   6 mechanic

3 2 had eaten   3 Had … seen   4 hadn't visited   5 had won   6 hadn't bought

4 2 used to   3 Did … use to   4 didn't use to   5 did … use to   6 used to

5 2 c   3 a   4 b   5 c   6 b

6 2 'll be studying   3 'll be starting   4 will be travelling   5 'll be playing   6 Will … be staying

7 2 are meeting   3 will … be   4 's going to   5 're going to miss   6 will win

8 2 slicing   3 grill   4 heat up   5 bake   6 boil

9 2 want   3 rather   4 prefer   5 like   6 prefer

10 2 They found some Roman remains.   3 Alpana is a small Roman town 15 km to the north of the city.   4 Archaeologists from the town museum came.   5 Because they have only stopped work on the metro for one month.   6 People are coming from other countries and they will be working day and night.

11 2 Yes, they have.   3 No, it doesn't.   4 Yes, he does.   5 Yes, you can.   6 No, they aren't.

12 2 c   3 b   4 a   5 b   6 c

 CD 2 track 43 Tapescript

Good morning everyone, and here is this morning's Radio Recipe. Today I'm going to tell you how to make pot-roasted chicken. For this you will need one whole chicken, 50 grams of butter, 1 teaspoon of salt, an onion and some herbs. Heat the oven to 180°C. Then, melt the butter and fry the chicken in the butter until it is brown all over. Put some herbs and an onion inside the chicken, and sprinkle the salt over it. Put it in the oven to roast until the chicken is tender. The chicken should lie on its side, and you should turn it three or four times while you cook it. It will take about one and a half hours. When it is ready, cut the chicken into slices and serve with peas and new potatoes.

13 Students' own answers

Test Units 5 and 6

1 2 wood   3 rubber   4 glass   5 leather   6 plastic

2 2 drawing   3 Fiction   4 play   5 sculpture   6 Oil

3 2 The old church is being used as a concert hall.   3 Gifts are always given to children in hospital.   4 The bridge was being painted all month.   5 The old house has been restored (by the workers).   6 The vases were brought from Greece.

4 2 Butter must be used to make the best cakes.   3 The old papers will be turned into cardboard.   4 Diamonds can be found in this part of Africa.   5 Two dresses will be made from this material.   6 These songs must be practised very carefully.

5 2 b   3 c   4 a   5 c   6 b

6 2 wouldn't visit, rained   3 saw, wouldn't like   4 wanted, would buy   5 would play, allowed   6 would bring, asked

7 2 the   3 the   4 the   5 the   6 a

8 2 Because   3 What for   4 so that   5 For   6 to win

9 2 of course   3 Do you mind   4 Could you   5 Yes, sure   6 Is it all right

10 2 Because he had been out all day walking in the hills.   3 The garden gate and the front door were both open.   4 He thought a thief had broken into his house.   5 Because he heard footsteps coming along the hall.   6 It was the cleaner – she had come to get the bag she had left there.

11 2 F   3 T   4 T   5 F   6 T

12 2 F   3 T   4 F   5 T   6 F

 CD 2 track 44 Tapescript

I visited the new City Library for the first time yesterday. It's an amazing building – made of glass and metal. It's much bigger than the old library, and inside it's very bright. I went to the reception desk to get my new plastic membership card, then I went off to explore the building. I went up in the lift to the fifth floor where they have all the art books. It's very beautiful. There are sofas and armchairs to sit in, and lots of wooden tables to work at. I was looking for a book on modern abstract painting, and I found several, so I took a general introduction to the subject with colour pictures. After that I went down to the third floor and got out two new novels to read. Then at the reception desk I checked the books out with my new electronic card.

13 Students' own answers

Test Units 7 and 8

1 2 research   3 experiment   4 laboratory   5 discovery   6 theory

2 2 florist's   3 chemist's   4 butcher's   5 newsagent's   6 greengrocer's

3 2 had worked, would have passed   3 would have won, hadn't fallen   4 wouldn't have enjoyed, had come   5 had gone, would have met   6 would have arrived, hadn't been

4 2 could have watched   3 Should … have told   4 couldn't have visited   5 shouldn't have won   6 Could … have helped

5 2 She said (that) it was raining hard.   3 She said (that) she didn't feel very well.   4 She said (that) she would go there immediately.   5 She said (that) she could come at eight o'clock.   6 She said (that) she had been there in 2006.

6 2 He asked Cathy if he could borrow her bike.   3 He asked Joan if she would go with him.   4 He asked George if he had watched the match.   5 He asked Mike what was in the box.   6 He asked Dick if he had got an umbrella.

7 2 'I won't buy a new dress.'   3 'Are you working at the weekend?'   4 'I can't meet you for lunch.'   5 'Have you got a bike, June?'   6 'We don't like the film.'

8 2 You could have   3 I wish I'd   4 You should have   5 I shouldn't have   6 wouldn't have

9 2 I'd like to   3 a problem   4 back   5 a receipt   6 a refund

10 2 F   3 F   4 T   5 F   6 F

11 2 Because he found the lectures boring and the surgery unpleasant.   3 He studied natural history.   4 To do an arts degree and become a priest.   5 The geology of South America.   6 He collected different forms of life.

12 2 F   3 T   4 F   5 F   6 F

 **CD 2 track 45 Tapescript**

For the holiday of a lifetime come to South Africa! We're offering special prices from July 30th until August 30th – only 2,500 euros per person for flights, accommodation and travel for ten days. You can decide exactly where you want to go! Here are some of our amazing options. Fly into Johannesburg and spend time in the modern city. Travel to the capital, Pretoria: from there you can go on safari into the Kruger National Park looking at all the exotic wildlife – you'll need three days to see all the beautiful animals and birds there! Travel over the border into another country: Swaziland, where you can see a completely different culture, and buy some of the beautiful beadwork and baskets at the famous markets. Another option is Durban, where everyone enjoys relaxing on the beautiful beach. And of course, you mustn't miss Cape Town, where trips can be arranged to see seals and whales in the Atlantic. We promise you an unforgettable holiday … so come to South Africa! But hurry – these prices only last for one month!

13 Students' own answers

End-of-term Test 1

1 2 readers   3 headline   4 website   5 podcast   6 reporter

2 2 audition   3 rehearsal   4 episode   5 repeat   6 celebrity

3 2 likes   3 plays   4 is trying   5 is thinking   6 trains   7 are working   8 is   9 is calling   10 are   11 Are … going

4 2 … have already read …   3 … film yet?   4 Lucy still hasn't …   5 … have just won …   6 … work yet.

5 2 had known   3 has been studying   4 have … been playing   5 had wanted   6 has been standing

6 2 Where will they be staying on holiday?   3 How will we be travelling to work next year?   4 What will she be studying at university?   5 Who will he be visiting in London?   6 Why will they be staying there for three weeks?

7 2 do they   3 hasn't he   4 are you   5 isn't it   6 aren't we

8 2 have … spent   3 How long   4 how far   5 have … seen   6 have … visited

9 2 have you seen   3 did you think of it   4 you like it   5 do you like her   6 Do you think so

10 2 Yes, he can.   3 No, he doesn't.   4 No, he isn't.   5 Yes, he can.   6 Yes, he is.

11 2 He can put any ball onto any table.   3 He barks the correct number of times.   4 Because he can find a ball in cupboard a week later.   5 He says that it is amazing to see Bobby do these things.   6 He likes doing normal dog activities and is very friendly.

12 2 She doesn't know what to study.   3 He wants her to be a doctor.   4 She likes English literature and biology.   5 She thinks she should be a librarian because she likes reading and collects books.   6 She's going to wait for her exam results.

 **CD 2 track 46 Tapescript**

I am in my last year at school – that means I've spent 13 years here listening to teachers and studying. And do you know, I am still not sure what I want to study at university. My father is a doctor, and he'd really like me to be a doctor too. But I don't want to do that, even though I can see that helping other people is very satisfying. I'm not interested in anything to do with finances either … well, maths isn't exactly my best subject at school! I like English literature and I like biology, but those two subjects don't go together very well. My mother used to be a teacher, but I don't think it's the right job for me. One of my teachers said I should become a librarian because I like reading and collecting books, but I don't think that's a very interesting job – it's just a lot of making lists and organising things in a particular order! So, I think I'll wait and see what my exam results are like and then take a year off school to decide what I want to do.

13 Students' own answers

End-of-term Test 2

1 2 metal   3 paper   4 stone   5 wool   6 fabric

2 2 pierced   3 tested   4 painted   5 dyed   6 shaved

3 2 If Ben slept more he would feel better in the morning.   3 Kenny would enjoy the concert if he understood the words.   4 If Janice cooked dinner her mother would be happy.   5 Don would cycle to school if he had a new bike.   6 If Angela went to the party, Linda wouldn't like it.

4 2 had known, would have told   3 would have enjoyed, had gone   4 wouldn't have understood, hadn't explained   5 had heard, wouldn't have been   6 wouldn't have said, had thought

5 2 He said (that) he was going to the seaside.   3 He asked Jenny what she had done in the holidays.   4 He said (that) he would have his new watch by Friday.   5 He asked Lily where his keys were.   6 He said (that) he couldn't come until three o'clock.

6 2 Special cakes are always made at Christmas.   3 The mystery has been investigated (by the police).   4 Oranges can be grown in this area.   5 The car was being washed when I arrived.   6 These animals must be handled gently.

7 2 Mr Jones couldn't have killed his wife.   3 A gang must have done the robbery.   4 John could have broken the window.   5 Mike must have cheated in the test.   6 Susan couldn't have hit your son.

8 2 Because   3 What   4 When   5 about   6 How

9 2 should have   3 had to   4 shouldn't have   5 wish you'd   6 could have

10 2 The Incas   3 Around 1450   4 Hiram Bingham   5 Huge blocks of stone   6 Environmental damage

11 2 F   3 F   4 T   5 F   6 T

12 2 F   3 F   4 F   5 T   6 T

 **CD 2 track 47 Tapescript**

Ernesto (Che) Guevara was born in Rosario in northern Argentina in 1928. As a young man his interests were reading and sports. There were 3,000 books in his parents' house, and he played rugby for the national university side. In 1948 he went to the capital, Buenos Aires, to study medicine. But in 1950 he went off alone on a 4,500 km bicycle tour of northern Argentina, which first made him aware of the difficult life of the poor in rural Argentina. In 1953, he went on an 8,000 km motorcycle tour of South America with a friend. This made him even more aware of the situation of the rural poor in the whole continent, and how North American capitalism was using the people. These were the starting points of Guevara's revolutionary work, which continued until his death in 1967, and made him a hero everywhere.

13 Students' own answers

End-of-year Test 1

1 2 f   3 h   4 j   5 i   6 b   7 a   8 k   9 g   10 e   11 c

2 2 about   3 up   4 to   5 away   6 for   7 from   8 about   9 with   10 back   11 in

3   2 hasn't he   3 did she   4 aren't you   5 can't you   6 is she

4   2 Mrs Smith, whose dog barks all night, is our neighbour.   3 Keswick, where we spend our holidays, is my favourite town.   4 Paul, who is our manager / very strict, is very strict / our manager.   5 In winter, when it is dark, I get up at six o'clock.   6 These apples, which I bought yesterday, are sweet.

5   2 Toys are being made from pieces of wood.   3 Special cakes are usually eaten at Easter.   4 Everything was being prepared while we were asleep.   5 A new machine has been invented (by the workers).   6 The research project will be finished next week.

6   2 bought, would be   3 would help, asked   4 won, would get   5 would enjoy, could   6 started, would finish

7   2 If the weather had been better, they would have gone camping.   3 Clare would have enjoyed the concert more if she had been by herself.   4 If David had tried harder he would have made more progress.   5 The girls would have written more if they had had more time.   6 If he hadn't driven so fast he wouldn't have crashed.

8   2 He said that Paul hadn't come to the French lesson.   3 He said that he could bring his guitar.   4 He asked Liz what time she would arrive.   5 He said that John's new book wasn't very funny.   6 He asked Jim if he was flying to France.

9   2 want (hope)   3 What time   4 will be   5 Meet   6 Which bus

10   2 download   3 credit card   4 PayPal   5 pocket money   6 clothes

11   2 T   3 F   4 F   5 F   6 T

12   2 They were usually humorous.   3 He studied by reading in public libraries after work.   4 He travelled to Hawaii, Europe, the Middle East and around the world.   5 To give lectures and earn enough money to pay off his debts.   6 Because most of his family died before him.

13   2 T   3 T   4 F   5 F   6 T

CD 2 track 48 Tapescript

Interviewer: So can you tell us about your visit to London, John?

John: Yes, I was there for a week. I went to the Museum of the History of London first, to find out about the city.

Interviewer: And what is that like?

John: It's a great museum, and it gives you a really good idea of how London's changed through the ages. You see how the Roman city developed, then William the Conqueror's Norman city …

Interviewer: That's when the Tower of London was built.

John: That's right – so you can see how all the famous London buildings fit together historically.

Interviewer: And what sort of things do you see, because you could read all this information in a guide book.

John: Yes, you could. But what brings the museum alive is that they have some really interesting artefacts – coins, pots, and so on – and then there are scenes from the different periods, with model figures dressed in the clothes of the time. And there are original paintings, as well as photographs of important people and places, and you can see what places used to look like at different times.

Interviewer: It sounds fascinating. So, what did you do …

14   2 poems   3 half a kilo   4 paid the bill (for the papers)   5 strawberry   6 No, she didn't

CD 2 track 49 Tapescript

I always go into town on Saturday morning to do the shopping for my mum. Today I started off at the baker's where I bought six bread rolls. After that I visited the bookshop in the High Street to collect the book of poems I had ordered two weeks ago for my sister's birthday. Then I went next door to Mr Roberts, the butcher's, to buy half a kilo of sausages for breakfast. He makes his own sausages and they're really good. In the newsagent's on the corner I paid the bill for last week's papers which are delivered to our house every day. In Victoria Road I went into the Chemist's for some toothpaste for my little sister – she refuses to use anything but strawberry flavour! And finally, I went to the shoe shop to try and buy some sandals to wear on holiday, but they didn't have anything I liked so I didn't get any.

15   Students' own answers

End-of-year Test 2

1   2 j   3 a   4 h   5 c   6 k   7 i   8 b   9 f   10 g   11 e

2   2 into   3 with   4 out   5 away   6 for   7 in   8 for   9 into   10 out   11 from

3   2 has she   3 didn't you   4 are they   5 must you   6 isn't he

4   2 The Browns, whose shop is next door, are very friendly.   3 The Lake District, where we often camp, is a beautiful area.   4 Dr Jones, who is my doctor, works very hard.   5 Saturday, when I go shopping, is my favourite day.   6 These presents, which I got for my birthday, look expensive.

5   2 Clothes are being designed for next summer.   3 Traditional clothes are often worn for parties.   4 Music was being played while we cooked.   5 Some old ruins have been discovered by the builders.   6 Our island will be studied next spring.

6   2 knew, wouldn't tell   3 would come, invited   4 passed, would take   5 would let, needed   6 wrote, wouldn't listen

7   2 If they hadn't stood here, they wouldn't have seen me.   3 My sister would have reached the top if she hadn't hurt her foot.   4 If we hadn't eaten that fish, we wouldn't have felt so bad.   5 Our dog would have walked home if it had got lost.   6 If Jake had thought more carefully, he wouldn't have done it.

8   2 She said (that) James hadn't played the piano for her.   3 She said (that) she couldn't come before nine o'clock.   4 She asked Pete what he would do in London.   5 She said (that) she didn't want to go there.   6 She asked Kay if it was going to work.

9   2 like   3 don't   4 at home   5 phone (call / ring)   6 What time

10   2 cash   3 note   4 coins   5 savings   6 waste

11   2 Parkesite was made from natural materials, Bakelite was synthetic.   3 Different types of plastics were invented.   4 They cannot carry heavy weights or stand high temperatures.   5 By making plastics which can be recycled.   6 Nylon for clothes and acrylic for paints.

12   2 F   3 T   4 F   5 F   6 T

13   2 b   3 c   4 b   5 b   6 c

CD 2 track 50 Tapescript

Sally: Hi, Julie. You don't look very happy!

Julie: Hello, Sally. I'm in a bit of a bad mood. I wanted to buy some green products, but I can't find any of the things I wanted. I really wanted to do more to help the environment.

Sally: Well, we do a lot of green things at school already – switching off lights and computers, not wasting water and recycling paper.

Julie: Yes, that's great, but I wanted to do more myself at home. I wanted some recycled paper for my schoolwork. And I wanted some Fairtrade cotton T-shirts too, buying Fairtrade products really helps people. But it's really difficult to find those sorts of things.

Sally: So didn't you buy anything?

Julie: Well, I got some Fairtrade bananas. And I got some nice recycled paper. But I couldn't find any Fairtrade clothes anywhere.

Sally: Well, you'll have to explore some other shops next week.

14   2 T   3 F   4 F   5 F   6 T

CD 2 track 51 Tapescript

There are many kinds of crime which involve copying something of value and trying to sell it. Sometimes people try to copy banknotes and coins, which is known as counterfeiting. But perhaps the most interesting form of copying is forgery. Forging an old painting is very difficult nowadays because of modern technology – x-rays, lasers and carbon dating techniques can easily show that a painting isn't as old as it is supposed to be. A 500-year-old painting by Leonardo da Vinci doesn't just have to <u>look</u> like other paintings by him, but the wood it is painted on and the paint itself has to either be, or seem to be, 500 years old too. It's much easier to forge a modern painting, but unless it is a Picasso or a Van Gogh, it will not make as much money as an old master. Another problem is that the forger cannot paint ten new Leonardo da Vinci works, when there are so few originals, as this would make people very suspicious. He can probably only paint one. Despite the problems, every year a famous art gallery somewhere in the world announces that a painting in its collection is not an original but a forgery.

15   Students' own answers

Workbook Answer Key

Revision unit

Page 3

1 1 play 2 'm wearing 3 watch 4 compete 5 enjoys
6 prefers 7 goes 8 're smiling 9 is winning 10 is

2 1 Where is Adrian standing in the picture? 2 How often do
Adrian's friends watch him play? 3 Does Jay like sport?
4 What does Jay do every day? 5 What is Hannah like?
6 Why is everyone looking happy?

3 1 does 2 are made 3 don't make 4 is making 5 is done
6 are, made

4 1 allowed 2 has to 3 can't / mustn't 4 let 5 can 6 can't /
mustn't

5 1 'm not going out with 2 break up 3 are, falling out
4 take after 5 look after 6 get on with

6 1 Saturday 2 7:30 3 community centre 4 £15 5 food
6 whole

Page 4

1 1 did you enjoy 2 travelled 3 went 4 were you doing
5 were trying 6 was rocking 7 lost 8 did you learn
9 were looking 10 found out

2 1 were 2 wasn't 3 were 4 was 5 many 6 Most of
7 lots 8 much

3 1 who 2 which 3 where 4 when 5 whose 6 that / which

4 1 My aunt gave me a guitar for my birthday. 2 Hirst's
diamond skull was sold for £50 million. 3 I wasn't chosen
to be in the school play. 4 Missy Elliot was discovered by a
New York record producer. 5 Freddy Mercury was sent to
boarding school by his parents. 6 Bob Marley's first songs
were released in Jamaica.

5 1 artistic 2 talented 3 classical 4 successful
5 performance 6 exhibition

Page 5

1 1 I haven't seen the dentist for two years. 2 They've lived in
this neighbourhood for twenty years. 3 You haven't taken
your medicine since this morning. 4 I haven't been ill since
I was a child. 5 Ravi hasn't won a competition since 2009.
6 Max has had a bad cough for two weeks.

2 1 put on 2 've decided 3 haven't eaten 4 've lost
5 joined 6 've been 7 've only been

3 1 I've just taken a painkiller. 2 Mary has already had her
vaccinations. 3 Paul hasn't recovered from the flu yet.
4 Lily's already gone to the leisure centre. 5 There's just been
a car accident here. 6 Haven't you seen the doctor yet?

4 1 ordered 2 reminded me 3 told me to 4 asked me
5 warned me not to eat

5 1 c 2 a 3 g 4 f 5 e 6 b 7 d

Page 6

1 1 will 2 will 3 might not 4 may / might 5 will 6 might
not 7 won't 8 won't

2 1 might go 2 'm going to find 3 are, going to do
4 'm going to visit 5 're going to spend 6 might catch
7 might hire 8 might go

3 1 're going to 2 're going to 3 might 4 will
5 are going to 6 won't

4 1 Can you tell me where I can buy a guidebook? 2 Do
you know if there's a hostel near here? 3 Could somebody
explain how the ticket machine works? 4 Do you know when
the cathedral is open to visitors? 5 Does anybody know what
time our train leaves? 6 Could you tell me how much this
souvenir mug costs, please?

5 1 d 2 g 3 a 4 c 5 b 6 f 7 h 8 e

Page 7

1 1 will happen 2 don't look after 3 aren't 4 'll turn
5 won't survive 6 continue 7 'll destroy 8 will, become
9 carry on 10 will kill 11 won't be

2 1 recycled, would be 2 invented, would be able to 3 would
save, turned off 4 would survive, didn't pour 5 Would,
slow, didn't use 6 ate, would be

3 1 very 2 quite 3 much 4 very 5 really 6 a bit

4 1 about 2 about 3 out 4 to 5 about 6 over 7 up

5 1 b 2 g 3 d 4 f 5 a 6 c 7 e

Unit 1

Page 8

1 Across: 2 articles 6 audience 7 headline
Down: 1 video-sharing 3 channels 4 podcast 5 viewer

2 1 lots of 2 more than 3 many 4 many 5 always
6 How many 7 Which

3 1 station, c 2 programme, d 3 listeners, c 4 readers, b
5 front page, a 6 website, b

4 1 Maggie never goes to the theatre. 2 Jason always takes
the bus to school. 3 Shhh! The students are doing an
exam. 4 Which part are you playing in the musical?
5 Penny is writing an email at the moment. 6 Max knows
lots of famous people.

Page 9

5 1 Do you like Leona Lewis? 2 What are you doing? 3 When
does the concert start? 4 Why are you laughing? 5 What
are you reading? 6 How often do you have singing lessons?

6 1 a 2 c 3 b 4 c 5 b 6 a

7 1 has gone 2 Have, been 3 has, voted 4 have signed
5 has fallen 6 has sung

8 1 I've driven 2 you've auditioned 3 I've been 4 Have
you ever won 5 I usually come 6 I enter 7 are you
feeling 8 I'm 9 watch 10 I haven't performed 11 are you
singing 12 I've chosen

9 1 Why is that boy staring at me? 2 Look! The audience is
throwing flowers to the dancers. 3 The photographer is
pointing his camera at you, but he isn't taking any pictures
at the moment. 4 They write notes to each other in class
every day. 5 Those girls over there are looking at a magazine
and laughing at some funny cartoons.

Page 10

1–2 1 F (Brad Pitt has donated around $5 million.) 2 F (Shakira
has worked for UNICEF.) 3 F (Bono has received an award.)

3 1 T 2 F 3 F 4 T 5 T 6 T 7 F

Page 11

4 1 episode 2 act 3 audition 4 winner 5 judge
6 rehearsal

5 1 slide show 2 museum official 3 mind control 4 film
location 5 crowd scenes 6 newspaper 7 headlines
8 sports reports 9 film reviews 10 summer clothes

6 1 'll just get my coat 2 can already walk 3 have already sold
one million copies 4 've just started working 5 are you still
here 6 still haven't started it / haven't started it yet

7 c

8 1 Coronation Street 2 Coronation Street 3 Eastenders
4 Eastenders 5 Coronation Street 6 Eastenders

Page 12

1 1 She seems a bit unfriendly to me. 2 In my opinion, they're
the best girl group. 3 I know what you mean. 4 Why do
you say that? 5 That's because he's really funny. 6 I don't
think so. 7 Do you think so?

2 1 d 2 b 3 a 4 c 5 e

3 1 a 2 c 3 b 4 a 5 c 6 c

Page 13

4–5 bought: brought caught fought taught thought
coughed: laughed

6 1 a   2 b and c   3 a and b   4 c   5 b and c

7 1 d   2 a   3 e   4 b   5 c

8 1 because   2 because of   3 because   4 because of
5 because   6 because of

9–10 Students' own answers

Page 14

1 1 last   2 finally   3 before

2 1 b   2 c

3 1 c   2 a   3 b

4 1 c   2 b   3 c   4 b

Page 16

1 1 do they go   2 does Joe want   3 Do you believe
4 are you sending   5 do your parents like   6 Am I playing

2 1 I think this is the best reality show I've ever seen.
2 The audience is really enjoying tonight's concert and it's
just started.   3 Paul collects autographs. He's collected more
than a hundred.   4 I'm waiting for Emma I hope she hasn't
forgotten about our date!   5 Sasha sings really well, so she's
joined the school choir.

Page 17

3 1 is still trying   2 Have you just switched on, 've already
missed   3 already speaks, 's learning   4 Do you still want
5 hasn't bought

4 2 d   3 a   4 b   5 e

5 2 We can't have a picnic because it's raining.   3 History's
a boring subject because of all the names and dates.
4 Anika's my best friend because we agree about
everything.   5 There aren't any buses today because of a
public transport strike.

Unit 2

Page 18

1 1 think   2 understand   3 creative   4 memory   5 forget
6 Imagine   7 remember

2 1 a   2 c   3 c   4 b

3 1 angry   2 forget   3 memory   4 imagination   5 creative
6 imagine

4 1 ambition   2 truth   3 behaviour   4 fear   5 Happiness
6 danger   7 friendship   8 success

Page 19

5 1 They've been playing rugby.
2 The scientist has been looking at something under
a microscope.
3 The children have been making a cake.
4 The boys have been fighting again.
5 He hasn't been working very hard.
6 I haven't been sleeping well this week.

6 2 has Tina been collecting   3 has Greg been   4 has Sarah
known   5 have you been waiting   6 has dad been making

7 1 f   2 b   3 e   4 d   5 c   6 a

8 1 since   2 for   3 since   4 for   5 for   6 since

9 1 haven't worked out   2 haven't you asked   3 've been
holding   4 Haven't you noticed   5 've been looking   6 Have
you already finished   7 haven't done   8 've been waiting
9 've been   10 haven't understood

Page 20

1 pathways in the brain, hand-eye co-ordination, fast reactions,
social skills

2 1 T   2 F   3 T   4 F   5 T   6 F   7 T   8 F

3 1 Football is a sport which / that people play all over the world.
2 Sheep are animals which can recognise faces.   3 A comedian
is a person who is good at telling jokes.   4 The weekend
is a time when people relax.   5 A surgery is a place where
doctors work.   6 Damien Hirst is an artist whose work is very
expensive.

4 1 Chess, which is my favourite board game, has been around
for centuries.
2 Mrs Clark, who works at the bank, has just had a new baby.
3 The Christmas holidays, when my cousins come to stay, are
great fun.
4 Bono, whose real name is Paul Hewson, has done a lot of
work for charity.
5 Luigi's restaurant, where my mum works, is famous for its
pasta dishes.

Page 21

5 1 b   2 d   3 a   (c is the extra heading)

6 1 Kelly the dolphin   2 an orang-utan   3 the pigs   4 the apes
5 an elephant   6 the pigs

7 1 b   2 a   3 a   4 c   5 b

Page 22

1 1 Isn't the exam next Friday?   2 They're having a party, aren't
they?   3 He doesn't have a good memory, does he?   4 Aren't
we going to the presentation tomorrow?   5 Have you left
your book at home again?   6 I haven't told you this before,
have I?

2 1 d   2 h   3 g   4 a   5 c   6 b   7 e   8 f

3 1 b   2 a   3 c   4 c   5 a   6 c   7 b

4 1 don't   2 does   3 doesn't   4 can   5 isn't

Page 23

5 Question 5 doesn't have falling intonation.

6 b

7 1 very   2 very   3 where   4 whose   5 who's   6 really
7 when   8 which   9 quite

8 1 which   2 where   3 which   4 whose   5 when

9 Students' own answers

10 1 finding out   2 go out   3 sociable   4 funny   5 good
marks   6 dirty clothes   7 annoyed

11 Students' own answers

Page 24

1 **1** 1 a   2 c
2 1 b   2 c

3 1 b

Page 26

1 1 been waiting, for   2 seen   3 been applying, since   4 been
writing, since   5 believed

2 1 have been sending, haven't had   2 has been doing, has
found   3 have been training, have improved   4 have agreed,
have been practising   5 has been taking, has entered

Page 27

3 1 where   2 who   3 when   4 which   5 whose

4 1 Pelé, whose career ended in 1977, was the world's greatest
footballer.   2 The only person who really understands me is
my mum.   3 I think smoking, which is a dangerous habit,
should be banned.   4 The band members, who grew up
together, are close friends.   5 One thing which makes us
different from other species is intelligence.

5 1 doesn't he?   2 isn't it?   3 can they?   4 won't you?
5 don't they?   6 isn't it?   7 have you?   8 shouldn't she?

Review Units 1 and 2

Page 28

1   1 spends   2 'm becoming   3 're working   4 signs   5 're singing

2   1 has never been   2 've been working   3 's been raining   4 has always had   5 have you been waiting

3   1 are starting / have started   2 think   3 is getting   4 's waving   5 's, holding   6 have never seen   7 looks   8 hasn't been going out   9 isn't   10 don't recognise

4   1 We have just heard about the accident.   2 Have you told the fans about it yet?   3 Yes, we've already stopped tonight's show.   4 Hurry up! The taxi has just arrived.   5 Is she still putting on her make-up?

5   1 Stratford-upon-Avon, where Shakespeare lived, is very popular with tourists. / Stratford-upon-Avon, which is very popular with tourists, is where Shakespeare lived.   2 New York, which is on the east coast of America, is known as the city that never sleeps. / New York, which is known as the city that never sleeps, is on the east coast of America.   3 Buddy Holly, who was a singer, died in a plane crash. / Buddy Holly, who died in a plane crash, was a singer.   4 Springtime, when there is a lot of pollen, is the worst time for allergies. / Springtime, which is the worst time for allergies, is when there is a lot of pollen.   5 Ian McEwan, whose latest book has been made into a film, is my favourite author.

6   1 have they   2 aren't you   3 is she   4 do you   5 has he

Page 29

7   1 viewers   2 repeat   3 channel   4 judge   5 DJ

8   1 remember   2 understand   3 feel   4 think / talk   5 imagine

9   1 fear   2 ambition   3 creativity   4 funny   5 moody   6 introvert   7 imaginative   8 logical   9 sociable   10 memory

10   1 into / at   2 at   3 on   4 down   5 on   6 out   7 of   8 of   9 to   10 at

11   1 c   2 e   3 b   4 a   5 d

12   1 when   2 appear   3 which   4 where   5 for   6 episode   7 had   8 of   9 viewers   10 have

Unit 3

Page 30

1   1 millennium   2 decade   3 fortnight   4 minute   5 year   6 month   7 century   8 hour

2   **1** 1 decades   2 century   3 time   **2** 1 years   2 millennium   3 hours

3   1 pottery   2 fossil   3 treasure   4 ruins   5 site

4   1 artefacts   2 jewellery   3 archaeologists   4 fragment   5 Palaeontologists   6 remains

Page 31

5   1 c   2 e   3 f   4 a   5 g   6 d   7 b

6   1 b   2 a   3 d   4 f   5 c   6 e

7   1 had ever seen   2 thought   3 were   4 had looked   5 went   6 brought / had brought   7 had put   8 had taken   9 had sold   10 had stolen   11 made   12 decided

8   1 prefer   2 tried   3 can't wait   4 like   5 want   6 don't need   7 agree

9   1 decided to leave   2 refused to talk   3 managed to pass   4 learned to swim   5 hopes to study   6 seems to understand   7 didn't learn to cook

Page 32

1   1 c   2 a

2   1 b   2 d   3 a   4 g   5 c   6 e   7 f

3   (suggested answers)   1 for lunch on Sunday. / for Sunday lunch.   2 cook / prepare the Sunday roast.   3 the washing up and listened to the radio.   4 started listening to her new Yazoo cassette.   5 answer the phone. / speak to her friend, Melanie.   6 she'd had an argument with her boyfriend.   7 her favourite programme had nearly finished.

Page 33

4   1 b   2 c   3 a

5   1 c   2 a   3 b

6   1 b   2 b   3 a   4 a   5 b

7   1 Did you use to stay   2 used to go   3 had   4 hated   5 didn't use to go   6 used to visit   7 used to go   8 used to stay   9 decided   10 hired

Page 34

1   1 feel   2 looks   3 tastes   4 smells   5 sounds

2   1 f   2 d   3 e   4 c   5 a   6 b

3   1 b   2 a   3 a   4 a   5 b   6 b

4   1 look   2 How long   3 feels   4 How much   5 sounds   6 How far

Page 35

7   1 colourful   2 artistic   3 cool   4 friendly   5 excellent   6 delicious   7 expensive   8 enjoyable   9 busy

8   1 enjoyable   2 expensive   3 colourful   4 busy   5 delicious   6 excellent

9   1 was such a busy café   2 the wall were so great   3 was such a good waitress   4 was such a tasty burger that   5 chips was so large that

10–11   Students' own answers

Page 36

1   1 before   2 who   3 all

2   1 description   2

3   1 questions   2 predict   3 second

4   **1** 1 c   2 b   3 a   **2** 1 b   2 a   3 c

Page 38

1   1 had been   2 Had the Inca empire already disappeared   3 had moved   4 Had any Europeans travelled

2   1 had already started, got   2 was, had made   3 discovered, had caused   4 returned, had broken into   5 finished, had fallen

3   1 found, had left   2 reached, had sailed   3 had never seen, visited   4 had rushed, had already made

4   1 Did, make   2 didn't use, have   3 used, are   4 didn't, be   5 did, had

Page 39

5   1 India used to be part of the British Empire.   2 Did people use to send emails in those days?   3 Most people didn't use to eat healthily in the 1950s.   4 Did books use to be copied by hand before printing was invented?   5 People didn't use to worry about ecology as much as we do now.

6   1 People didn't use to have mobile phones when my parents were teenagers.   2 I used to eat a lot of sweets, but now I'm on a diet.   3 There used to be a farm where the golf course is now.   4 What sort of clothes did you use to wear when you were young, Dad?

7   1 We were having so much fun that we didn't want to stop.   2 My dad's such a careful driver that he's never had a crash.   3 This food is so delicious that I'd like a second helping, please.   4 There were so many people there that we had to queue for hours.   5 It was such great news that Erica was crying with happiness.

Unit 4

Page 40

1 a 6 b 5 c 7 d 3 e 2 f 4 g 1

2 1 electrician 2 chef 3 accountant 4 manager
5 soldier 6 postal worker

3 1 won 2 scored 3 beat 4 scored 5 missed 6 lost

Page 41

4 **A** 1 coach 2 ring 3 referee 4 physiotherapist
B 1 player 2 sponsors' 3 stadium 4 umpires

5 1 e 2 b 3 d 4 g 5 c 6 a

6 (suggested answers) 1 is going to dive (into the water).
2 is going to win the race. 3 is going to land in the water.
4 is going to crash. 5 is going to change the score.
6 is going to receive a medal.

Page 42

1 a

2 1 b 2 a 3 c 4 a 5 b

3 1 short-sleeved 2 V-neck 3 hooded 4 round-neck
5 long-sleeved

4 1 will be wearing 2 will be competing 3 won't be using
4 will be working 5 A will, be doing B will be starting

5 1 from 2 By / In 3 be 4 time 5 Will 6 will

Page 43

6 1 c 2 d 3 a

7 1 F 2 F 3 T 4 F 5 F 6 F 7 F

8 1 mood 2 whenever you like 3 fabric 4 stain 5 are
waterproof

Page 44

1 1 b 2 d 3 f 4 a 5 e 6 c

2 1 a 2 f 3 c 4 e 5 b

3 1 b 2 b 3 a 4 a 5 b 6 c

Page 45

4 1 rather 2 than 3 prefer 4 to 5 like 6 want

5 /s/ basketball, disappear, dress, fossil, hypnosis, sponsor,
used to
/z/ business, busy, design, museum, pleased, presentation,
thousand, used (past simple)

7 1 They're playing in a badminton tournament. 2 at the
leisure centre. 3 the badminton coach.

8 1 when 2 when 3 until 4 as soon as 5 by the time
6 as soon as

9 (suggested answers) 1 they're playing in the tournament.
2 she gets home. 3 she finds out what time they're playing.
4 arrives later this evening. 5 Daisy gets home 6 she knows
more.

10 Students' own answers

Page 46

1 c

2 b

3 1 a 2 b 3 c 4 b 5 b 6 a

Page 48

1 1 starts 2 'm going 3 'll finish 4 's leaving 5 is going to

2 1 'll open 2 starts 3 is going to go 4 are going to do
5 is/are playing 6 'll make

3 1 Mike is doing his French exam on Thursday morning.
2 My mobile has run out of battery – I'll charge it after
school. 3 The football team is going to start training early
this year. 4 The class is visiting the science museum next
Wednesday. 5 I'm going to paint my bedroom a blue-grey
colour.

Page 49

4 1 will win 2 is going to continue 3 will find
4 will manage 5 is going to be

5 1 'll be waiting 2 won't be living 3 'll be camping
4 'll be earning 5 'll be wearing

6 1 At this time tomorrow evening, I'll be baby-sitting for the
people next door. 2 Will you be travelling around Europe
during your gap year? 3 Two years from now, I'll be driving
my own car. 4 You can borrow my camera for your school
trip – I won't be using it. 5 Will Karen be working part-time
in December?

7 1 until 2 I'll call 3 hand 4 when 5 before 6 I have

Review Units 3 and 4

Page 50

1 1 to meet 2 drying 3 swimming 4 to go 5 learning
6 learning 7 to understand 8 living 9 discovering
10 eating 11 talking 12 to find out 13 to rain
14 walking 15 to have

2 1 left, had started 2 had said, caught 3 had gone, was
4 had to, had forgotten 5 arrived, was

3 1 a, b 2 a, b 3 c 4 a 5 a, b

4 1 was 2 saw 3 had thought 4 had 5 used to 6 developed
7 bought 8 went 9 had used 10 had bought

5 1 you do 2 will be sitting 3 be living 4 lose
5 will be using

Page 51

6 1 archaeologist 2 fossil 3 fragment 4 artefact
5 remains 6 palaeontologist

7 1 roast, beef 2 bakes, bread 3 curry, chopping 4 peeling,
apples 5 Boiling, eggs

8 1 diner 2 fries 3 vacation 4 pants 5 store 6 garden
7 flat 8 mobile phone 9 postman 10 break time

9 1 How far 2 How long 3 How much 4 How long
5 How much 6 How often 7 How many

10 1 What time 2 I'd 3 than 4 do you 5 prefer 6 rather
7 don't want 8 Where 9 like 10 How much

Unit 5

Page 52

1 Across: 2 glass 4 wool 5 paper 8 wood 9 fabric
10 brick 11 leather
Down: 1 metal 3 stone 5 plastic 6 rubber 7 concrete

2 1 for 2 as 3 to 4 as 5 to 6 for

3 1 was written 2 was placed 3 hasn't been included 4 was
being built 5 are being created 6 have been nominated

Page 53

4 1 The Salt Mines have been visited by many famous people.
2 Until recently, the salt sculptures were being eroded by
humidity.
3 Malbork Castle was listed as a World Heritage site by
UNESCO in 1997.
4 In 1945, about half of Malbork Castle was destroyed
by fighting.
5 Parts of the castle are still being restored.
6 The main cathedral hasn't been rebuilt yet.

5 1 oval 2 immense 3 rectangular 4 huge 5 little
6 rectangular

6 1 an expensive, leather 2 a small, white, grey
3 an ancient, Egyptian 4 a broken, wooden 5 a shiny, black
6 a huge, stone

7 1 The Ancient Greeks made beautiful, ceramic pots.   2 We bought a huge, round, wooden table.   3 The actress wore a lovely, long, red dress to the ceremony.   4 I gave my grandmother a new, Chinese, silk scarf for her birthday.   5 Let's stay in a nice, modern, American hotel tonight.   6 There are too many ugly, grey, concrete buildings in my city.

Page 54

1 balls, chocolate, clothing, coffee, fruit, scarves, soap

2 title c

3 1 T   2 F   3 F   4 T   5 F   6 T   7 F

4 1 be bought   2 be agreed   3 be improved   4 be given   5 be shown   6 be opened

Page 55

5 c three

6 1 recognise   2 bananas, lemons   3 packet   4 supermarkets   5 products   6 European   7 green

7 1 have become   2 be eaten   3 have been grown   4 saw   5 took   6 were brought   7 were used   8 put   9 have discovered   10 have already been developed   11 be sold

8 1 for   2 in   3 into   4 in   5 of   6 on   7 for   8 into

Page 56

1 1 d   2 a   3 e   4 f   5 b   6 c

2 1 g   2 e   3 c   4 b   5 a   6 d   7 f

3 1 What   2 To   3 Why   4 So   5 Why   6 To   7 for   8 Because

Page 57

4 1 erode   2 clothes   3 stone   4 phone   5 local   6 oval

5 1 A set of three juggling balls.   2 They were made of soft colourful fabric, small, fitted into a child's hand, and each contained a bell.   3 She learned to juggle and joined a juggling club where she also learned lots of other circus skills.

6 a lot on my own because / since / as I didn't have any brothers or sisters.   2 anyone to do juggling with, so the balls were a great present.   3 As / Since / Because I was becoming quite good at juggling.   4 in my town, so I had to travel to the nearest big city.   5 to the club was worth it because I learned so many things.   6 Because / Since / As I'm really good at juggling now.

7–8 students' own answers

Page 58

1 1 T   2 F   3 F   4 T

2 1 1 Mum   2 tea   3 8 o'clock
     2 1 coach   2 Pauline   3   0292 687355
     3 1 Mr White   2 The book you ordered   3 9.00 a.m.
        4 5.00 p.m.

Page 60

1 1 Some historic buildings (in the old town) have been restored (in the old town).   2 The monument was being repaired when it collapsed.   3 The marble statues are being destroyed by smog and acid rain.   4 New discoveries were made at the site recently.   5 Information about life in the past is provided by ancient tools.   6 Julius Caesar was assassinated by Roman senators.

2 1 A cure for the common cold is being researched.
     2 Dozens of houses were destroyed by the explosion.
     3 Angry protesters have broken windows in the building.
     4 The government announced a new plan yesterday.
     5 Homeless people are given a place to sleep by shelters.

Page 61

3 1 Has evidence been found to support this theory?   2 Records of these events weren't written by people who saw them.   3 The archaeological finds weren't excavated carefully.   4 Are important new discoveries still being made today?

4 1 This medicine must be stored in the fridge.   2 Pure gold can't be separated into different materials.   3 Gold can be

used for so many different things.   4 New uses (for gold) may be found (for gold) in the future.   5 The emergency exit doors mustn't be locked.

5 1 Holly has just had her hair cut.   2 My grandfather never wanted to have his photo taken.   3 I had my eyes tested a month ago.   4 Mum is having her car serviced tomorrow.   5 We're going to have the tree in our garden cut down.

Unit 6

Page 62

1 1 d   2 e   3 a   4 b   5 f   6 c

2 1 cookery   2 classic   3 thriller   4 mystery   5 historical   6 romance   7 biography   8 detective   9 humour

3 1 portraits   2 drawing   3 abstract works of art   4 play   5 Watercolour   6 oil   7 non-fiction

4 1 abstract   2 still life   3 oil   4 painting   5 landscapes   6 portraits

Page 63

5 1 d   2 c   3 a   4 f   5 b   6 e

6 1 b   2 a   3 a   4 d   5 f   6 b   7 c   8 e

7 1 It can't be his wife.   2 It must be Lisa Del Giocondo.   3 It might be a self-portrait.   4 He must have cut it off himself.   5 It might have been his friend, Gauguin, who cut it off.   6 It might have been an accident.

8 1 may / might seem   2 couldn't have written   3 must have had   4 couldn't have known   5 must have been   6 may / might / could take   7 may / might never find out

Page 64

1 1 d   2 b   3 a

2 1 T   2 F   3 T   4 F   5 F   6 F   7 T

Page 65

3 1 D   2 C   3 A

4 1 c   2 b   3 b   4 a   5 b   6 c

5 1 d   2 a   3 c   4 b   5 e

6 1 decided, would buy   2 bought, would hang   3 won, would go   4 helped, wouldn't take   5 wanted, would teach   6 had, would be

Page 66

1 1 Can we go to the Dalí museum today?   2 Do you mind waiting outside for a moment?   3 Would it be all right if we ate our sandwiches here?   4 Is it all right if I sit down?   5 Could you hold my rucksack for me?   6 Could I have a look at those ceramic pots, please?   7 Can you take a photo of me?

2 a 4   b 7   c 2   d 1   e 3   f 5   g 6

3 1 d   2 a   3 f   4 e   5 b   6 c

4 1 Would   2 of course   3 Do you mind   4 not at all   5 could   6 Can you   7 I'm sorry

5 1 f   2 c   3 g   4 b   5 a   6 d   7 e

Page 67

6 1 b   2 c   3 b   4 b   5 c

7 1 same   2 same   3 different   4 different   5 different   6 same   7 different

8 1 b   2 d   3 a

9 1a As a result   1b due to   2a due to   2b As a result, the sponsored run   3a As a result   3b due to the stage

10 Students' own answers

Page 68

1 b

2 b

3 a 4   b 5   c 1   d 2

Page 70

1 1 must 2 may 3 have rained 4 feel 5 couldn't

2 1 a It can't be broken. b It may/might/could have got wet. c The battery must need charging. 2 a They may/might/could be in the washing machine. b They can't have been stolen. c My sister must be wearing them.

3 1 can't have disappeared 2 may/might/could have fallen 3 must have left 4 may/might/could have broken 5 can't be 6 must be

Page 71

4 1 could have made her so angry? 2 could my trainers be? 3 could I have made such a stupid mistake? 4 could be trying to get me into trouble?

5 1 didn't have, wouldn't 2 wouldn't, walked 3 bought, could teach 4 wouldn't be, didn't 5 wanted, would send

6 1 Would you lend someone your new camera if you didn't need it yourself? 2 If you won the lottery, what would you do with the money? 3 Why would anyone buy a car if they didn't know how to drive? 4 If you could travel anywhere in the world, where would you go? 5 If a shop assistant gave you too much change, would you keep the extra money?

Review Units 5 and 6

Page 72

1 1 the 2 a 3 The 4 the 5 an 6 the 7 the 8 The 9 the 10 The, –

2 1 When was the city of Petra built? 2 Atlantis was destroyed by earthquakes thousands of years ago. 3 Those paintings still haven't been restored. 4 The students haven't been given their exam results yet. 5 Where is coffee usually grown?

3 1 will be served 2 can't be taken 3 must be accompanied 4 won't be delivered 5 Can these glasses be washed

4 1 can't be 2 must have put 3 must be 4 can't have gone 5 must have left 6 must have been

5 1 If I won the lottery, I'd give some money to charity. 2 He'd play a lot better if he practised more. 3 If you went to Italy, would you visit Rome? 4 Van Gogh would be very rich if he was alive today. 5 If Lisa did some exercise, she'd feel much healthier.

6 1 was 2 a 3 can't 4 The 5 a 6 be 7 The 8 went 9 would

Page 73

7 1 plastic 2 wood 3 wool 4 leather 5 concrete 6 brick

8 1 an ancient, Egyptian mummy 2 an amazing, huge, steel sculpture 3 a beautiful, red, silk dress 4 an immense, oval football stadium 5 a wonderful, old, black-and-white film

9 1 a 2 c 3 a 4 c 5 b

10 1 run out 2 complain about 3 pay for 4 got away 5 took off 6 have, on 7 do, into 8 thought about 9 found out 10 turns up

11 1 What 2 To 3 Why 4 Because 5 Could 6 I'll 7 right 8 looking 9 Not

Unit 7

Page 74

1 Across: 4 laboratory 5 experiment 6 research
Down: 1 data 2 innovation 3 machine

2 1 theory 2 results 3 applications 4 discovery 5 knowledge 6 test

3 1 disappear 2 unpack 3 disconnect 4 decode 5 unlock 6 disagree

4 1 unpacked 2 decode 3 agreed 4 disconnect 5 unlock 6 disappeared

5 1 enable 2 redo 3 enlarged 4 reappeared 5 rebuilt 6 renamed

Page 75

6 1 If Tania had taken an umbrella, she wouldn't have got wet. 2 If John hadn't fallen asleep, he wouldn't have got sunburnt. 3 The pan wouldn't have caught fire if someone had turned off the gas 4 Anna wouldn't have ordered pasta if she had known the portions were so large. 5 Tim and Max wouldn't have gone to the cinema if they had realised it was a romantic film. 6 If you had driven more carefully, we wouldn't have had an accident.

7 1 c 2 a 3 e 4 b 5 d

8 had intended, would have given

9 1 hadn't invented, wouldn't have been able 2 hadn't discovered, wouldn't have had 3 hadn't travelled, wouldn't have taken 4 hadn't known, would they have learned 5 had listened, they wouldn't have been 6 hadn't invented, would have learned

Page 76

1 1 in northern France 2 God 3 nineteen

2 1 c 2 b 3 a 4 f 5 e 6 d

3 1 history 2 freedom and independence 3 leader 4 refused

Page 77

4 **A** 1 democracy 2 right 3 vote 4 election 5 campaign 6 policies
B 1 government 2 freedom 3 politics 4 law 5 protest

5 1 b 2 c

6 1 F 2 F 3 T 4 F 5 T 6 T 7 F

7 1 should 2 could 3 couldn't 4 couldn't 5 could 6 should

8 1 shouldn't have put 2 should have brought 3 should have bought 4 should have told 5 couldn't have been 6 could have left

Page 78

1 1 regret 2 criticism 3 criticism 4 regret 5 regret 6 criticism

2 a 4 b 6 c 2 d 5 e 3 f 1

3 1 wish 2 shouldn't 3 should 4 have 5 had 6 should

4 1 I wish I hadn't split up with Ben last week. 2 I shouldn't have spent all that time at the party dancing with my friends. 3 He could have just told me he wanted to go home. 4 I wish we hadn't argued. 5 I shouldn't have been so stupid. 6 I wish I'd said sorry when I had the chance!

Page 79

7 1 a barbeque in her garden 2 her friend Sonia 3 She didn't make a shopping list or a guest list.

8 1 After 2 before 3 After 4 by 5 without 6 before

9 1 Before phoning our friends, we sat in the garden chatting. 2 We phoned lots of people without making a guest list first. 3 We went shopping before making a shopping list. 4 After checking our phone messages, we made a list of who was coming. 5 Dad helped us by doing the barbecue. 6 After cooking the meat, he realised we hadn't bought any rolls.

10–12 Students' own answers

Page 80

1   1 a   2 c   3 d   4 e

2   1 a   2 d   3 c

3   1 b   2 d   3 c

Page 82

1   1 wouldn't have misunderstood, had been   2 hadn't forgotten, wouldn't have overslept   3 wouldn't have teased, had realised   4 would have sent, had given   5 would have got, hadn't been

2   1 If Mum hadn't had the flu, she would have gone to work.   2 Craig wouldn't have failed the chemistry test if he had studied.   3 If we had told our parents we'd be late, they wouldn't have been worried.   4 He wouldn't have gone to prison if he hadn't broken the law.   5 If Max hadn't written down the wrong address, he could/would have found our house.

3   2 e   3 a   4 f   5 b   6 d

4   1 If I hadn't started stayed up late, I wouldn't have been tired the next day.   2 If I had had enough time, I would/could have finished my project.   3 If I hadn't spent all my pocket money, I would/could have bought the CD.   4 I would/could have got in if I hadn't lost my keys.   5 If I hadn't got soaked in the rain, I wouldn't have caught a cold.   6 I would/could have gone to the party if I hadn't had a headache.

Page 83

5   1 could have gone   2 shouldn't have started   3 should have taken off   4 couldn't have stopped   5 could have been   6 shouldn't have been

6   1 have borrowed my camera without asking.   2 I hadn't watched a horror movie before going to bed!   3 have followed the instructions.   4 I hadn't left my mobile phone at home!   5 have been more careful.   6 I'd done what you suggested!

Unit 8

Page 84

1   1 b   2 h   3 e   4 c   5 a   6 g   7 d   8 f

2   1 sweets, shoe shop   2 rice, butcher's   3 ham, post office   4 make-up, baker's   5 socks, greengrocer's   6 toothpaste, newsagent's

3   1 newsagent's   2 greengrocer's   3 supermarket   4 chemist's   5 hairdresser's   6 travel agency   7 butcher's

4   1 said   2 announced   3 claimed   4 denied   5 confirmed   6 told

5   1 said   2 told   3 admitted   4 asked   5 suggested

Page 85

6   1 could   2 wouldn't   3 had bought   4 were going   5 was working   6 started

7   1 Each of my dresses is unique.   2 We have run out of suncream.   3 Do you want your hair to be much shorter?   4 There's going to be an election in May.   5 Hundreds of people have been arriving at the refugee camp.   6 Lizards make really good pets.

8   1 Danielle asked (if anyone could tell her) what made a good TV advert.   2 Blogger Boy thought that a good advert had to be funny.   3 Jeremy said that a really catchy tune was essential.   4 Helena said that Ford had made a great advert in 2009 (where they had used car parts as musical instruments).   5 Pixie said that she knew which advert Helena was talking about (and that it was really clever).   6 Jon asked if anyone had ever seen a good advert for cleaning products.   7 Alice said that cleaning was boring, but that she was sure that someone would make a cool advert for cleaning products one day.

9   1 us   2 are/were   3 that   4 were   5 would   6 asked   7 if   8 was   9 was   10 had

Page 86

1   photographs a and b

2   1 b   2 b   3 a   4 c   5 a   6 b   7 c

Page 87

3   boots, CDs, clothes, football, leather jacket, notebooks, pens, shoes

4   1 spend   2 a little   3 fills shelves   4 doesn't use   5 bad at   6 once a week

5   1 bank account   2 CDs   3 term   4 leather jacket   5 had an argument   6 clothes

6   1 What are you going to do with your wages?   2 Do you buy your own clothes?   3 Do you still have to ask your parents for money?   4 Can I have some money each month to buy clothes?   5 When did you first learn to budget?

7   1 Emma asked John how often he worked at the supermarket.   2 Holly asked Kate if she had ever used a credit card.   3 Mike asked Sam where he had got his new trainers from.   4 Kim asked David what he was going to buy with his birthday money.   5 The teacher asked us all what we had done their homework.

8   1 wages   2 coins   3 savings   4 budget   5 debit card   6 credit card   7 pocket money

Page 88

1   1 Can I help you?   2 I'd like to return these jeans.   3 Is there something wrong with them?   4 Have you got the receipt?   5 I'm afraid we don't usually give refunds.   6 Would you like a credit note?   7 Would it be possible to get my money back?

2   1 e   2 f   3 b   4 d   5 a   6 c

3   1 lettuce   2 shirt   3 ice cream   4 DVD   5 book

Page 89

4   1 return   2 wrong   3 exchange   4 it   5 back   6 afraid   7 refunds   8 note   9 receipt

5   1 advertise, advertisement   2 democracies, democratic   3 qualified, qualification   4 politics, politician   5 refund, refund   6 investigation, investigate

6   1 the manager of a supermarket   2 the quality of the fruit and vegetables at the supermarket   3 twice   4 to investigate the problem and reply to his letter

7   1 Despite   2 In spite   3 Because of   4 despite   5 In spite   6 Because of

8   Students' own answers

Page 90

1   1 b   2 c   3 a

2   1 b   2 c

3   1 b   2 a   3 b

Page 92

1   1 'The company has been trying to solve the problem since last summer,' he said.   2 'I wasn't/haven't been informed about your complaints,' the manager told her.   3 'You'll have to wait until next week,' she told him.   4 'Your company must/has to improve its image,' they told him.

2   1 he was leaving for Paris that night, but he'd be back soon.   2 he had bought tickets for the concert that Friday.   3 she didn't think she'd be able to go to school the next/following day.   4 he couldn't lend her his book then/at that time because he needed it.   5 they wouldn't win that day unless they played their best.

3   1 'I've never been here/there before in my life,' she said.   2 she didn't know why they kept losing their things.   3 he hated that kind of music.   4 'You'll have to give me my money back,' he told them.

Page 93

4   1 Katy suggested watching TV.   2 Mike offered to carry Wendy's bag.   3 The doctor advised her to stay in bed.   4 The man asked Marcus to turn his MP3 player down.   5 Terry invited Fay to go out with him the next/following day.

5   1 Ben asked Emma what she was doing for her birthday.   2 Alan asked Fiona if she often went shopping.   3 Holly asked Dan how he had learnt to cook.   4 She asked Marcus if he was interested in fashion.

Review Units 7 and 8

1   1 'd bought   2 hadn't cooked   3 sold   4 'd brought
5 was   6 hadn't taken

2   1 had saved, would have bought   2 had gone, wouldn't
have felt   3 Would he have passed, had studied   4 had left,
wouldn't have missed   5 hadn't had, would have come

3   1 If I'd known it was so cold outside, I would have worn a
coat.   2 If he hadn't forgotten to take his phone, he would
have phoned you.   3 If we hadn't stopped to talk to our
friends, we wouldn't have been late for the meeting.
4 If she'd put suncream on, she wouldn't have got sunburnt.

4   1 shouldn't have told   2 couldn't have afforded   3 could
have won   4 should have brought   5 shouldn't have got up

5   1 My aunt promised that she would phone me later.   2 Lucy
explained that she hadn't been to school because she had
been ill.   3 Paul admitted that he'd eaten all the cake.   4 The
teacher announced that the school was going to close at half
past two.   5 The assistant claimed that this was the best face
cream on the market.   6 The weatherman said that it was
going to be hot and sunny tomorrow.   7 Mum asked if I had
had anything to eat yet.   8 Joe told Sarah that he didn't want
to go out with her any more.

6   1 an election   2 policies   3 right   4 campaign
5 democracies

7   1 theory   2 innovations   3 research   4 laboratory
5 experiment

8   1 e   2 b   3 d   4 c   5 a

9   1 pocket money   2 wages   3 spend   4 account   5 cash
6 card

10   1 disappeared   2 unlock   3 disconnected   4 disagree
5 unpack

11   1 comfortable   2 advertisements   3 informative
4 qualifies   5 investigation

12   1 I'd like to return these trainers.   2 Is there something wrong
with them?   3 Yes, they're too small. Would it be possible to
get my money back?   4 I'm afraid we don't give refunds.
5 Would you like to exchange them for something else?
6 Would you like a credit note? It's valid for six months.
7 Have you got a receipt?

Workbook Tapescript

Revision

Page 3

 *R.1 track 01*

Coach:	Hello?
Jade:	Hi Mr Jenkins. It's Jade. How are you?
Coach:	I'm fine. And you?
Jade:	I'm great, thanks. Actually, I'm phoning to ask you about the swimming club disco on Saturday. What time does it start?
Coach:	It starts at seven thirty, at the community centre.
Jade:	OK. How much do the tickets cost?
Coach:	They're fifteen pounds each, including food.
Jade:	OK. And who's coming?
Coach:	The whole team, I think. A lot of parents are coming, too.
Jade:	Really? Is Robert Smith coming?
Coach:	Yes, he is. I know you don't get on with him, but he's OK really.
Jade:	Maybe. I just think he's immature. Anyway, can you put my name down for a ticket, please?
Coach:	Yes, of course. Can you hold on a moment? I'll get the list … OK. So, are you bringing your mum and dad as well?
Jade:	I don't know. I need to ask them. Can I phone you back?
Coach:	Yes, of course. But don't take too long. I'm afraid there are only a few tickets left.
Jade:	I won't! Thanks, Mr Jenkins.
Coach:	You're welcome.

Unit 1

Page 11

 *1.1 track 02*

Presenter:	Hello again and welcome to this week's programme. In the studio today, we have Doreen Clark from the British Film and TV Academy. She's going to be talking about Britain's soap operas. So Doreen, what can you tell us about the most popular British soaps?
Doreen:	Well, as I'm sure you know, the two most important soaps on British TV are Coronation Street and Eastenders. Both programmes are very popular in Britain and you can also watch them in most other English-speaking countries, including Australia, Canada – and in parts of Asia as well. You can also watch Coronation Street in Belgium, the Netherlands and Sweden.
Presenter:	That's interesting! I didn't know that. So could you tell us a bit more about the programmes and their history.
Doreen:	Yes, of course. Coronation Street follows the lives of people living in the same street in a small town in the north of England. It has been on British television for more than 50 years, but it's still very popular. In fact, 'Corrie', as it's known to most people, regularly attracts around ten million viewers a week! Eastenders also has a huge audience, but not quite as big. It's set in London in the 'East End' – that's the area of the city where all the factories were in the past and where all the working people lived. The stories are dramatic and true-to-life and the acting is excellent. As a result, it's won many awards, including five British Academy Television Awards and 50 British Soap Awards.

However, about one million more people watch an episode of Corrie each week than watch an episode of Eastenders.

Presenter:	Why do you think this is? I mean, if Eastenders has better actors and scriptwriters …
Doreen:	Actually, I believe it may be because most of Coronation Street's fans are older. They aren't so busy and have more time to sit down and watch their favourite programme.
Presenter:	So what is a typical Eastenders fan like?
Doreen	Well, that's an interesting question. You see, although Eastenders fans are generally younger, the programme is popular across a wide range of different ages …

Page 13

 1.2 track 03

bought: brought caught fought taught thought
coughed: laughed

Page 14

 1.3 track 04

1 I think French films are brilliant!

2 Have you seen the film Eclipse?

3 TV is really boring these days.

4 What do you think of their new album?

Unit 2

Page 20

 *2.1 track 05*

Interviewer:	Dr Jarvis, is it true that technology is having an effect on the way we use our brains?
Dr Jarvis:	Well, the honest answer is that nobody knows yet. The human brain is very complicated and the age of technology is really just beginning, so we can't be certain of anything. But what IS true is that nowadays, we get most of our information from a computer screen rather than by reading books – and we process a lot more information, much faster. So we aren't thinking in the same way as we did in the past – we may even be making new pathways in the brain. We could, in fact, be in the process of training our minds to behave more like computers.
Interviewer:	So, if I have a brain that is starting to work more like a computer, is that a bad thing?
Dr Jarvis:	No, in some ways it isn't a bad thing at all. It seems to be true that people who use technology a lot often develop better hand-eye co-ordination and fast reactions. For example, one recent study showed that doctors who regularly play video games make fewer mistakes when they are doing operations.
Interviewer:	But I believe you're particularly interested in the way that using technology affects young people. Is that right?
Dr Jarvis:	Yes, that's right. Many young people now spend as much as eight hours each day using technology, which means that they spend much less time having direct social contact with other people. It's possible that when the brain spends more time on technology-related tasks and less time relating to other people, it could start to lose important social skills, such as reading people's feelings from the expression on their faces during conversation.

| Interview: | So that means that today's teenagers could grow up to become unsociable introverts who can't talk to people. |
| Dr Jarvis: | Well, in theory, yes. But in fact, this doesn't seem to be happening. However, there are interesting new observations which … |

Page 23

 *2.2 track 06*

1 Elephants have got very long memories, haven't they?

2 You haven't already seen this film, have you?

3 Kim's been playing the violin for six years, hasn't she?

4 The iPad is like an iBook, isn't it?

5 Your cousin lives in Bangkok, doesn't he?

6 We haven't got to read this book as well, have we?

Page 24

 *2.3 track 07*

Boy 1:	Your family has got lots of pets, hasn't it?
Boy 2:	Well, we've got lots of animals but they're not all pets. We've got chickens, goats and pigs.
Boy 1:	Oh. Do you eat them?
Boy 2:	Sometimes. We mainly keep them so we can have fresh eggs and goat's milk. Oh, and we've got a duck as well.
Boy 1:	You can eat duck eggs, too, can't you?
Boy 2:	Yes, you can. But she doesn't lay any eggs anymore. She's more like a pet. She's really friendly and I think she's quite clever.
Boy 1:	Why do you say that?
Boy 2:	Well, she understands everything I say and she 'talks' back to me! She's also very good at guarding the house.
Boy 1:	What? Just like a dog?
Boy 2:	Yes. She makes a really loud noise if anyone visits, and she attacks their legs!

Unit 3

Page 33

 *3.1 track 08*

1

Before the nineties, not many people had one. We used to use public phones instead. They would be in most public places – in pubs and restaurants, and on street corners. The first time I ever saw one was at the cinema, in a Hollywood movie. It was about some young, ambitious lawyers in New York and they all had huge, black boxes which they held to the side of their heads as they walked down the street. At the time, they seemed really cool. Nowadays, even though some people might get excited about the latest iPhone or something like that, they've just become normal. You hardly notice them because everyone has one.

2

My friends and I used to carry these huge things around with us whenever we went out – you know, down the park or chilling on the street. We used to play our music really loudly and I'm sure we annoyed everyone around us. They were known as ghetto blasters because the fashion started in America where gangs from poor areas – called ghettos – used to hang around on street corners playing loud music. Most teenagers had one and some people even took them to the beach.

3

Anyone who wanted to be cool had one of these. They were popular with all ages, including businessmen as well as young people. A lot of my friends used to listen to theirs while they were studying, but I didn't – I prefer studying without music. I used to listen to it on the train and on the bus though. The problem was that the earphones weren't very good and the sound annoyed other people. I used to take it with me when I went running, even though it was quite heavy. I used to attach it to my shorts.

Page 34

 3.2 track 09

1 What time does the exam start?

2 When are we leaving?

3 How long did the film last?

4 How much did you spend in that shop?

5 How far is it to the nearest petrol station?

6 How many eggs are there in a box?

Page 35

 3.3 track 10

1 There was a quiz on the cruise ship every night.

2 The neighbours in our building are quite quiet.

3 A guide showed us round the ruins.

4 We stopped for a quick drink in a bar.

5 I have orange juice and biscuits every morning.

6 The doctor told me to drink plenty of liquids and eat more fruit.

Page 36

 3.4 track 11

1

Waitress:	Are you ready to order?
Customer:	Yes, we are. We'd like the noodle soup, please.
Waitress:	And for the main course?
Customer:	We'd like Peking Duck, please.
Waitress:	Would you like anything to drink with your meal?
Customer:	Yes. Some water and a coke, please.

2

Customer:	Excuse me, how much are the strawberries?
Assistant:	They're two pounds fifty a kilo.
Customer:	Hmmm.
Assistant:	They're fresh strawberries from local farmers, madam. You won't find any tastier strawberries than these!
Customer:	OK. I'll take half a kilo.
Assistant:	Here you are. That's one pound seventy-five pence please.

3

Boy:	Let's go and look at all the animals!
Girl:	Er …, no thanks.
Boy:	Why not?
Girl:	I prefer to see real, live animals and not dead ones.
Boy:	But it's really interesting. You can see what their bodies are like inside.
Girl:	Maybe. But I think I'll go and look at the artefacts in the next room.
Boy:	OK. I'll meet you in the café later.

Page 36

 **3.5 track 12**

1

Farmer:	*Excuse me. Can I help you?*
Woman:	*Yes. I saw your sign for fresh eggs. Do you have any?*
Farmer:	*Yes, of course. Just knock on the door of the farmhouse and my wife will sell you some.*
Woman:	*OK. Thanks very much.*
Farmer:	*You're welcome. Oh, and don't forget to shut the gate. We don't want to lose the chickens!*

2

Man:	*Excuse me.*
Assistant:	*Yes. How can I help you?*
Man:	*I'm looking for the fresh eggs. Do you know where I can find them?*
Assistant:	*Yes, of course. They're just over there, next to the cakes and bread.*
Man:	*OK, thanks.*

3

Girl:	*Excuse me. Can you help me?*
Boy:	*Yes, of course.*
Girl:	*Where's the nearest supermarket?*
Boy:	*Er … I think there's one at the end of this street, just past the chemist's.*
Girl:	*Thank you very much.*
Boy:	*My pleasure.*

Unit 4

Page 42

 4.1 track 13

Boy:	*Have you ever heard of the 'Bionic Jacket'?*
Girl:	*No, I haven't. Why? What is it?*
Boy:	*It's brilliant! It's a lightweight jacket that heats up inside. It's really comfortable and keeps you warm even in freezing cold weather.*
Girl:	*It sounds fantastic! How does it work?*
Boy:	*Well, it's made of a special lightweight material which gets thicker in low temperatures.*
Girl:	*You mean it grows?*
Boy:	*Exactly! It's got a micro-computer inside that measures the temperature, and the jacket will get thinner when it's hot.*
Girl:	*Wow! That's really clever!*
Boy:	*That's not all! There are little screen displays all over the jacket which show you how warm your body is inside the jacket– and you can programme the temperature you want the jacket to be.*
Girl:	*So … you mean that some parts of the jacket can be warmer or colder than other parts?*
Boy:	*That's right. You can have the sleeves at 22 degrees, for example, and the body of the jacket at 20 degrees. It's great for skiers and snowboarders because they get cold when they stop moving, especially in bad weather.*
Girl:	*That's amazing! Does it have a hood as well?*
Boy:	*No, I don't think so, but we can look it up on the Internet.*
Girl:	*Good idea! I'd like to buy one for my next skiing trip.*
Boy:	*Hmm. It'll probably be really expensive. Do you think you'll be able to afford one?*
Girl:	*Probably not. But I bet some people will be wearing one on the slopes this year!*

Page 45

 4.2 track 14

basketball   business   busy   design   disappear   dress   fossil   hypnosis   museum   pleased   presentation   sponsor   thousand   used (past simple)   used to

Page 45

 4.3 track 15

1   I'm playing in a sponsored basketball match.

2   I'm giving a business presentation tomorrow.

3   He's designed thousands of dresses.

4   She looks after fossils in the museum.

5   People used to send messages by telegraph.

Unit 5

Page 55

 5.1 track 16

Josh:	*I read your blog the other day. It was really good. The only thing is, I'm not sure what the FAIRTRADE Mark looks like.*
Becky:	*Well, it's quite easy to recognise. It's a black square with 'FAIRTRADE' written on it. There are two shapes inside it that look a bit like leaves. One of them is green and the other is blue.*
Josh:	*How big is it?*
Becky:	*Well, it's not huge, but it's big enough to be clearly visible. Sometimes it's on a sticker which is stuck directly onto fruit like bananas and lemons, so it's easy to see against the yellow skin. Otherwise, for products like coffee, sugar, rice or bars of chocolate you need to look for the FAIRTRADE mark on the packet.*
Josh:	*Right. So, where can I buy products with the FAIRTRADE mark?*
Becky:	*Food with the FAIRTRADE mark is sold in most ordinary supermarkets, but there are also special shops, called World Shops where you can buy lots of different Fair Trade products including clothes made from Fair Trade cotton and jewellery. There are World Shops in most European countries.*
Josh:	*Yeah. I think there's one in the High Street, isn't there? I went in the other day, but I don't remember seeing the label you were talking about.*
Becky:	*Ah, well that's because there are different organisations which promote Fair Trade. The Fairtrade Foundation isn't the only one.*
Josh:	*It's getting a bit confusing now. What are these other organisations? And how will I know if I'm really buying Fair Trade products?*
Becky:	*The biggest ones have their own labels. The other two big ones I know about are the World Fair Trade Organisation and the European Fair Trade Association. The World Fair Trade Organisation has a label with Fair Trade Organisation written on it, and a circle above it with blue and green shapes inside that look like people. The European Fair Trade Association label is really easy to recognise – it just uses the letters EFTA, written in green.*
Josh:	*Right. So that's three labels to look out for then. You know what? I think you should put something about the different labels up on your blog.*

Page 57

 **5.2 track 17**

1   above   erode

2   clothes   other

3	done	stone
4	phone	some
5	wonder	local
6	lovely	oval

Page 58

 *5.3 track 18*

1

Hi, Mum. It's me, Lucy. I'm at Sarah's house and her mum's invited me to stay for tea. Is that OK? You don't need to make me anything to eat at home! Can you come and pick me up at about 8 o'clock, please? I'll ring you again later. Bye!

2

Good afternoon. This is a message for Stacey Jones. I'm phoning from the leisure centre to see if she would be interested in coaching the basketball team this month while John – that's our usual coach – recovers from his operation. Please phone back as soon as possible. The number's 0292 687355. Ask for Pauline. Thanks.

3

Hello. This is a message for Mr White. I'm calling about the book you ordered from our bookshop last month. It finally arrived this morning so you can come and pick it up anytime. We're open from 9.00 a.m. until 5.30 p.m. from Monday to Saturday.

Unit 6

Page 65

 *6.1 track 19*

Presenter:	*Today we have with us in the studio the author and researcher Colin Brown who is going to talk about his book Mysteries of the Atlantic. So Colin, you spend several chapters of your book talking about a mystery that has recently been solved.*
Colin Brown:	*You mean the Titanic? Yes Jim, that's a subject I've always been particularly interested in. As you probably know, the Titanic sank in the Atlantic, before it reached its destination of New York, and for over 70 years, it seemed as if this enormous ship had just disappeared off the face of the Earth. However, the wreck was finally found in 1985 and my book looks at all the new information that scientists have discovered about the disaster and what happened on that terrible night.*
Presenter:	*It sounds fascinating! You also talk about new scientific evidence in connection with another disaster – the legend of the lost city of Atlantis.*
Colin Brown:	*Well, for centuries, people have been fascinated by this idea of Atlantis – an ancient but very advanced technological society that really existed. According to the old stories, the gods wanted to punish the people of Atlantis because they had become selfish and dishonest, so they sent earthquakes and volcanoes which caused the city to sink into the sea. Now some people believe that the story of Atlantis is based on the story of Santorini, a Greek island in the Mediterranean, which was destroyed by a volcano about 3,600 years ago. However, Plato, the ancient Greek philosopher who wrote the story, said that Atlantis was destroyed more than 11,000 years ago. So, as you can see, the dates don't match.*
Presenter:	*I see. So Atlantis can't have been an island in the Mediterranean, then.*
Colin Brown:	*Exactly. I believe that Atlantis, if it exists, probably lies somewhere in the middle of the Atlantic, halfway between the coasts of North Africa and Central America.*

Presenter:	*And the other Atlantic mystery you talk about in the book is the Bermuda Triangle, an area in the Atlantic between Miami and the islands of Puerto Rico and Bermuda, where a large number of planes and ships have disappeared. What are your theories about this?*
Colin Brown:	*Well, in my book, I look at the theories about what causes the planes to disappear, such as aliens from another planet or the idea that the Bermuda Triangle is the door to another world. I also explore some of the scientific explanations – to do with the weather and other natural causes.*
Presenter	*And what's your own opinion?*
Colin Brown:	*The truth is, I just don't know. Nobody really knows. There are just no real clues. That's why it remains such a mystery …*

Page 67

 *6.2 track 20*

1	astronaut	caught
2	audience	autobiography
3	audition	because
4	Australia	cause
5	author	aunt
6	autograph	saucer
7	sausage	daughter

Page 68

 *6.3 track 21*

I think I have one of the best jobs in the world! I get to work with people, which I really enjoy, and I also spend my time surrounded by amazing historical objects. I have to learn about all of the artefacts, so that I can answer people's questions. I'm most interested in ancient Greece and I know quite a lot about it, which is why I give talks to visitors. Sometimes, when I'm not busy, I can sit down and read more about Greek history.

Page 68

 *6.4 track 22*

I'm an art student at the local college. I have classes every morning and two afternoons a week. I want to be a sculptor and I'm working on a huge oil painting for my final project. Unfortunately, I don't have space at home to work on my art, so I spend a lot of time in the art room at college. I also do voluntary work at a charity shop two afternoons a week. I organise the shelves and dress the shop window. I also serve the customers and make the tea.

Unit 7

Page 77

7.1 track 23

Matt:	*So, tell me about Rosa Parks, then, since you say she's your heroine! I think I've heard of her. Wasn't she a member of the Civil Rights Movement?*
Ella:	*That's right. She lived in Alabama during the fifties, when African-American people didn't have the same rights as White Americans. For example, they could only sit at the back of the bus and if the white section was full, they had to give up their seats.*
Matt:	*And Rosa refused! I remember this story now. Rosa should have given up her seat for a white man but she wouldn't.*
Ella:	*Exactly. She knew she was breaking the law but she was tired from working all day, and she was fed up with being a second-class citizen. This was her way of protesting.*

Matt: So, what happened? Was she arrested?

Ella: Yes, she was. She spent a night in prison and was made to pay a fine. But she also became famous all over America and civil rights leaders everywhere supported her. They organised a campaign to persuade African Americans not to use the buses, but to walk or cycle to work instead. This meant they stopped shopping in the city centres.

Matt: Did it make any difference?

Ella: It certainly did. The campaign lasted 381 days. If it had lasted any longer, city businesses could have lost a lot of money. As a result, the law was changed and people could sit where they liked.

Matt: That's a great story. Did Rosa do anything else amazing like that?

Ella: Well, she spent the rest of her life working to promote civil rights. She died in 2005 but, six years before, she was awarded a medal by the American government.

Page 79

 7.2 track 24

1 We took our crazy cat to see an animal psychologist.

2 I doubt it'll rain today – just look at that blue sky!

3 The terrorists put a bomb in the hotel.

4 Half of the students in our class joined the campaign.

5 Would you like to visit the castle?

6 The number of foreign visitors to the island has increased.

7 You need a good knowledge of maths if you want to be a scientist.

Page 80

 7.3 track 25

1

I don't really understand politics that well. However, I believe it's important to vote in an election, especially if you're a woman! Next year, I'll be eighteen so I'll be able to vote as well.

2

I've been the student representative at my school for the last three years. Everyone always votes for me. I'd like to be in the government. I think I'd be a good politician, but I'm not sure which party I would join.

3

The government wanted to build a new road through some woods near my house. This would have destroyed the wildlife, so I started a campaign to stop the road. Lots of people supported me and we eventually won.

Page 80

 7.4 track 26

1

I went on holiday to the USA with my parents last summer. We flew to Miami, then we hired a car and toured round Florida. We visited the Everglades National Park where we saw alligators and other wildlife. We had planned to go to Disney World in Orlando but we ran out of time. It was a fantastic trip though.

2

I went to the States quite a few times when I was a child, to visit my aunt. She lives in Jacksonville, in Florida. There are lots of museums, galleries and theatres and hundreds of massive parks, most of them with lakes. The city is very near the coast, so my aunt usually took us to the beach at the weekends.

3

My grandparents took me to Florida when I was seven years old. We stayed in Miami and then went to Disney World, in Orlando, but I can't remember much about it, except that I was too shy to talk to Mickey Mouse! The other day I saw a TV documentary about all the wild animals in Florida, including turtles and American alligators. It was really interesting. I'd love to go back there one day.

Unit 8

Page 87

 8.1 track 27

John: Hi, Emma. Guess what? I got my first wages today!

Emma: That's great! What are you going to do with the money?

John: I'm not sure yet. I got paid in cash so I'll probably spend most of it.

Emma: Don't you think you should put it in your bank account? My mum says it's really important to have some savings for when you're older.

John: Well, my wages aren't very high. It's only a Saturday job at the supermarket, you know – filling shelves, helping customers, that sort of thing. And I don't get pocket money anymore, so I need money when I go out or to buy CDs and stuff.

Emma: Oh. I didn't realise you didn't get pocket money. Do you have to buy your own clothes, as well?

John: No. My mum gives me money for clothes and school stuff – notebooks and pens and things. She puts the money into my account at the beginning of each term, and I take it out when I need it.

Emma: If my mum did that, I'd spend it all in the first week!

John: That's what I did last year! And I soon learned it was a mistake, though, when I had to play football in boots that were too small. I'd spent all my money on a leather jacket and I didn't have any left for boots! After that, I learned to budget – but it was a painful lesson, I can tell you!

Emma: I can't believe your mum let you play football all term without getting you any new boots.

John: She didn't! After a couple of weeks, I told her what had happened and she bought me some new boots as an early Christmas present. But she said I should be more careful in future. So, what about you? Do you still have to ask your parents for money every time you want to buy something?

Emma: Well, I get pocket money once a week but I have to go shopping with my mum for clothes and shoes. We usually end up having an argument. It must be nice to be able to choose your own clothes.

John: It is. It's great to be more independent. Why don't you ask your mum to give you some money to buy clothes once a month, or something?

Emma: Yeah. Good idea! Maybe I will.

Page 89

 8.2 track 28

1 To advertise the new job, they put an advertisement in the job centre.

2 Most European countries are democracies, so they have a democratic system of government.

3 We wanted a qualified scientist, but his only qualification was a degree in history!

4 Are you interested in politics? Yes, I'd like to be a politician one day.

5 I asked if they would refund my money, but they said they didn't give refunds on sale items.

6 The police want to reopen the investigation. They're going to investigate how the husband of the dead woman got all his money.

National Geographic Learning | Cengage Learning

English Explorer Teacher's Book 4
David A. Hill

Publisher: Jason Mann

Commissioning Editor: Alistair Baxter

Development Editor: Manuela Barros

Senior Marketing Manager: Ruth McAleavey

Senior Content Project Editor: Natalie Griffith

National Geographic Liaison: Leila Hishmeh

Cover Designer: Natasa Arsenidou

Text Designer: PreMediaGlobal

Compositor: PreMediaGlobal

Audio: EFS Television Production Ltd

Acknowledgements

The Publisher would also like to thank the following for their invaluable contribution: Karen Spiller and Clare Shaw.

ISBN: 978-1-111-22374-8

National Geographic Learning
Cheriton House
North Way
Andover
Hampshire
SP10 5BE
United Kingdom

Cengage Learning is a leading provider of customized learning solutions with office locations around the globe, including Singapore, the United Kingdom, Australia, Mexico, Brazil and Japan. Locate your local office at: **international.cengage.com/region**

Cengage Learning products are represented in Canada by Nelson Education, Ltd.

Visit National Geographic Learning online at **ngl.cengage.com**

Visit our corporate website at **www.cengage.com**

Photo credits

The publishers would like to thank the following sources for permission to reproduce their copyright protected photographs:

Cover photo: Stephen Alvarez/National Geographic Image Collection

pp 5 (moodboard/Alamy), 6 (Beretta/Sims/Rex Features), 8 (CBS/Landov), 12 (Shutterstock.com), 13c (Shutterstock.com), 13b (Shutterstock.com), 14tl (Philip Ryalls/Redfearns/Getty Images), 14tr (Shutterstock.com), 15 (Vincent J. Musi/National Geographic Image Collection), 16t (Vincent J. Musi/National Geographic Image Collection), 16c (Vincent J. Musi/National Geographic image Collection), 16b (Vincent J. Musi/National Geographic image Collection), 18t (Sodapix/Corbis), 18cl (Peter Knighton/iStockphoto.com), 18cr (Shutterstock.com), 18b (Mike Parry/Minden Pictures/National Geographic Image Collection), 22 (Shutterstock.com), 24cr (Shutterstock.com), 24bl (Beverly Joubert/National Geographic Image Collection), 24br (aleksandrovaphoto/iStockphoto.com), 29 (Shutterstock.com), 30 (International Mammoth Committee/National Geographic Image Collection), 32mr (William Gottlieb/Corbis), 32br (Acik/Bigstockphoto.com), 33bl (Ian Shaw/Alamy), 33 inset (Hulton Archive/Getty Images), 35 (Alistair Wilson 50/50/PA Archive/Press Association Images), 36 (morganl/iStockphoto.com), 37 (Science Museum of Brussels/wikipedia.com), 38t (Shutterstock.com), 38 inset (Shutterstock.com), 39 (lagereek/iStockphoto.com), 40tr (Clive Rose/Getty Images), 40cr (Fred DuFour/Getty Images), 43tl (LajosRepasi/iStockphoto.com), 43tcl (iconogenic/iStockphoto.com), 43bcl (dsteller/iStockphoto.com), 43bl (123foto/iStockphoto.com), 43c (quix429/iStockphoto.com), 43r (iconogenic/iStockphoto.com), 46mr (Filippo Monteforte/Getty Images), 46bl (Maliketh/iStockphoto.com), 46br (Shutterstock.com), 47 (Richard Heathcote/Staff), 52tr (Shutterstock.com), 52cr (Shutterstock.com), 42br (Shutterstock.com), 53 (Atlantide Phototravel/Corbis), 54t (vodkamax/iStockphoto.com), 54c (Mike Theiss/National Geographic Image Collection), 55 (Shutterstock.com), 56 (Robert Clark/National Geographic Image Collection), 59 (Shutterstock.com), 60c (Peter Essick/National Geographic Image Collection), 60b (Peter Essick/National Geographic Image Collection), 61tl (Shutterstock.com), 61tr (npix/iStockphoto.com), 61bl (Shutterstock.com), 61br (Denis/Fotolia.com), 62bg (Shutterstock.com), 62tr (Shutterstock.com), 62bl (Shutterstock.com), 62br (Shutterstock.com), 63 (Albright-Knox Art Gallery/Corbis), 64 inset (Black Dog & Leventhal), 64bg (Shutterstock.com), 66 (Pojbic/iStockphoto.com), 70–71bg (anneleven/iStockphoto.com), 70bl (Houghton Mifflin Harcourt), 70bc (Theodore Von Holst (1810–1844)/wikipedia.com), 70br (Chicago: National Prtg. & Engr. Co.), 71t (ivan-96/iStockphoto.com), 71b (Alinari Archives/Corbis), 76 (The Art Archive/Tate Gallery London/Eileen Tweedy), 77 (Mark Thiessen/National Geographic Image Collection), 78r (Ian Miles, Flashpoint Pictures/Alamy), 78l (Shutterstock.com), 80 (Tim Rooke/Rex Features), 81l (Topical Press Agency/Stringer/Getty Images), 81cl (Fox Photos/Getty Images), 81cr (Joseph Scherschel/Getty Images), 81r (Laruffa/Rex Features), 84t (Volkmar K. Wentzel/National Geographic Image Collection), 84c (MogensTrolle/iStockphoto.com), 84b (gregul/iStockphoto.com), 86t (Andrew Brusso/Corbis), 86c (Shutterstock.com), 87 (Susan Barr/Getty Images), 88l (© Starbucks), 88r (Fair Trade Resource Network), 90bl (Jeff Greenberg/Alamy), 90bc (77studio/iStockphoto.com), 90br (RubberBall/Alamy), 94l (eddie tor/Fotolia.com), 94–95bl (Bestway Inflatables), 95br (Images Scientific Instruments Inc), 108 (Shutterstock.com), 109 (Shutterstock.com), 110 (Shutterstock.com), 111 (Shutterstock.com), 112 (Shutterstock.com), 113 (Shutterstock.com), 114 (Shutterstock.com), 115 (Shutterstock.com)Illustrations by Celia Hart pp 7, 31, 32, 50, 57, 74, 85, 98, 101, 102, 104; Janos Jantner (Beehive Illustration) pp 26, 65, 97, 100, 106; Norbert Sipos (Beehive Illustration) p 93; Eric Smith pp 17, 41, 49, 73, 79, 83, 89, 103

Please note page references are to Student's Book only.

Printed in Greece by Bakis
2 3 4 5 6 7 8 9 10 – 16 15 14